Performing Citizenship in Postdictatorship Chile

performance works

SERIES EDITORS
Patrick Anderson and Nicholas Ridout

This series publishes books in theater and performance studies, focused in particular on the material conditions in which performance acts are staged, and to which performance itself might contribute. We define "performance" in the broadest sense, including traditional theatrical productions and performance art, but also cultural ritual, political demonstration, social practice, and other forms of interpersonal, social, and political interaction that may fruitfully be understood in terms of performance.

Performing Citizenship in Postdictatorship Chile

Cultural Policy and the Making of Political Dramaturgies

✦

Jennifer Joan Thompson

NORTHWESTERN UNIVERSITY PRESS
EVANSTON, ILLINOIS

Northwestern University Press
www.nupress.northwestern.edu

Printed in the United States of America

10 9 8 7 6 5 4 3 2 1

ISBN 978-0-8101-4849-9 (cloth)
ISBN 978-0-8101-4848-2 (paper)
ISBN 978-0-8101-4850-5 (ebook)

Cataloging-in-Publication Data are available from the Library of Congress.

Que viva el teatro.

CONTENTS

ACKNOWLEDGMENTS

This is a book about infrastructures, community, and collaboration, and I write these words with tremendous gratitude for the ways it has been shaped by them. From this project's earliest stages, Jean Graham-Jones has been an exceptional mentor, interlocutor, and advocate. I am deeply appreciative of her knowledge, editorial insights, and compassion. Peter Eckersall and David Savran have been instrumental in establishing the theoretical foundations of this work, and their writing and kindness continue to inspire me. Cristián Opazo helped me to reframe questions and broadened my understanding of this project's scope. I am grateful to him for his scholarship and generosity as I navigated my time in Santiago. Lynette Gibson's support has been invaluable, and she is greatly missed.

I also wish to thank my community at the CUNY Graduate Center. You have inspired me, challenged my thinking, and provided endless support: Stefano Boselli, Ryan Donovan, Amir Farjoun, Andrew Goldberg, Sarah Lucie, Hansol Oh, Bess Rowen, Curtis Russell, Ugoran Prasad, Dan Venning, Alison Walls, and Janet Werther. Eylül Akinci, Phoebe Rumsey, and Mara Valderrama have been incredible, tireless readers and even more incredible, tireless friends. I am deeply indebted to Fabián Escalona who has offered feedback on drafts, helped with translations, and shared his insights about Santiago as well as Chilean theater and history. I am also immensely grateful to the friends I made in Chile. To Eva Cancino Fuentes, Alejandra Díaz, Sol Robayo Solarte, Javiera Severino, and Isidora Parra: thank you for our conversations about theater and cultural policy and for giving me places to dance and places to live.

This project has been made possible by the research support of the Social Science Research Council, Fulbright Foundation, Committee for Globalization and Social Change at the CUNY Graduate Center, Center for Latin American and Caribbean Studies at CUNY, and the Center for Latin American and Latinx Studies at the University of Pennsylvania. Within these networks, Mark Phillip Bradley, Durba Ghosh, and Alex Boodrookas offered critical feedback and support during the conceptualization of this project. Cathy Bartch enabled me to present aspects of this work at Penn. Baird Campbell has been a wonderful colleague and friend, who expanded my disciplinary perspectives and was a great companion when we lost the trail in the Andes. Tracy Davis's insights through the Publication Development Forum helped me articulate the project more fully. Brenda Werth and Katherine Zien provided extremely generative feedback as I developed chapter 5, as did the ASTR working group led by Leticia Robles-Moreno, Marcela Fuentes, and Marcos Steuernagel. My colleagues and students at Penn and SMU—especially Kevin Chun, Margit Edwards, Marcia Ferguson, Blake Hackler, Cat Johnson, Bobbie Lay, Noah Levine, Rosemary Malague, Cary Mazar, and Gretchen Smith—have made it a joy to do what we do.

Thank you to Patrick Anderson and Nicholas Ridout for including this book in the Performance Works series; I am honored to be part of this conversation. I am tremendously grateful to Faith Wilson Stein, Maia Rigas, Elizabeth Yellen, and the editorial team at NUP for their guidance and work throughout this process. I also wish to thank the anonymous readers whose thoughtful and incisive feedback pushed me to think more deeply and write more clearly. It is a much better book for their generosity. Portions of chapter 1 appeared as "Each/Every: CADA's Radically Democratic Dramaturgy of Dissent" in *Theatre Survey* 61, no 1 (2020): 4–27. An earlier version of chapter 4 appeared as "Horizons of Impossibility: The Political Imperative and the Dramaturgy of Guillermo Calderón" in *Theatre Journal* 73, no 2 (2021): 169–187. I thank the editors for their permission to reuse sections of these articles.

I also want to express my gratitude to the remarkable artists, scholars, culture workers, and archivists in Chile who shared their thoughts, time, and resources with me: Cuti Aste, Patricio Bañados, Guillermo Calderón, Alfredo Castro, Jorge Contesse, Leonel Cornejo, Paula Echenique, Diamela Eltit, Marco Espinoza, Nico Espinoza, Andrés García, María Paz González, Camila González Ortiz, Paula González Seguel, Milena Grass, Ramón Griffero, Eduardo Guerrero, Pía Gutiérrez Díaz, María de la Luz Hurtado, Carmina Infante, Manuela Infante, Antonio Kadima, Soledad Lagos, Marco Layera, Agustín Letelier, Eduardo Luna, Héctor Morales, Arturo Navarro, Daniel Palma, Marco Antonio de la Parra, Juan Andrés Piña, Laura Pizarro, Rosa Ramírez, Patricia Rivadeneira, Vicente Ruiz, Willy Semler, Muriel Solis Verdugo, Miguel Angel Soto Vidal, Sibila Sotomayor, Andrea Ubal, Paulina Urrutia, Natalia Vargas, Juan Carlos Vega Briones, and Juan Villegas. I am also grateful to Alejandra Coz Rosenfeld at the Lotty Rosenfeld Foundation, Verónica Sanchez at the Museo de Memoria y Derechos Humanos, and to Patrizio Javier Gecele Muñoz at the Archivo Teatro Universidad Católica for sharing images and providing research support.

And finally, my deepest thanks to my dear friends and family. To Emily Fink and Kate MacCluggage for their fortifying visits to Chile. To Christina Pumariega, for her endless encouragement. To my parents, Marsha and Les Thompson, for whom words are not enough. And to Tom, Eleanor, and Rosie, for everything.

Introduction

Artists and Citizens

On November 25, 2019, the International Day for the Elimination of Violence against Women, hundreds of women convened in central Santiago wearing party clothes and black blindfolds. As a driving beat thumped on portable speakers, the women began a simple choreography, shifting their weight rhythmically as they chanted:

> The patriarchy is a judge
> That judges us for being born
> And our punishment
> Is the violence that you don't see.
>
> The patriarchy is a judge
> That judges us for being born
> And our punishment
> Is the violence that you do see.[1]

As the chant continued, the women called out various institutions of power: the cops, the judges, the president, and the state itself. They pointed to the government and ecclesiastical buildings surrounding them. They circled their arms to implicate the entire state apparatus. "The rapist was you," they asserted, pointing directly ahead. The women, for so long subjects of the patriarchal state, here inverted that dynamic. With this simple gesture they simultaneously demystified systemic state violence and positioned the state as subject to its feminist citizens. "The rapist is you," they insisted in the present tense.

This performance, conceived by the Valparaíso-based feminist collective LASTESIS and titled *Un violador en tu camino* (*A Rapist in Your Path*), posited a deeply serious claim: the patriarchal state is itself the source of rape culture. Yet the energy of the performance was ludic and liberating. Its lyrics were catchy and its simple choreography was easy to replicate. Videos of the performance circulated widely on social media. Since its initial performances, convened by the collective in Valparaíso on

November 20 and Santiago on November 25, other groups have taken up the piece, staging it across Chile and around the world.[2]

LASTESIS's project is to translate feminist theory into performance, making it accessible to a broader audience. Initially, the group intended the song to be performed within a theatrical framework, as part of a larger piece investigating violence against women. However, when the massive uprising known as the *estallido social* (social explosion) convulsed Chile, the theaters were forced to close. LASTESIS adapted their performance for the streets.

The estallido began in October 2019, when protests erupted in response to a 4 percent metro fare hike imposed by Sebastián Piñera's government. However, it quickly became clear that the unrest was about much more. The slogan, "It's not thirty pesos, it's thirty years," encapsulated longstanding discontentment with the failures of Chile's democratic transition and the neoliberal economic model imposed during the civic-military dictatorship of Augusto Pinochet (1973–1990). As millions around the country poured into the streets, activists demanded a radical reorientation of Chilean society. The government responded with extreme repression: demonstrators were dispersed with water cannons and tear gas, curfews were imposed for the first time since the dictatorship, and protesters endured torture and sexual abuse at the hands of the Chilean national police force.[3]

Despite the government's repressive tactics, the protests persisted, and artists played a vital role in the growth and imagination of this movement. An explosion of graphic art covered the walls of Santiago, rejecting the current government, state violence, and neoliberalism, while inscribing utopic ideals across the city.[4] Though the theaters closed for performances, they opened their doors as spaces of refuge, serving as first aid stations for those injured during the demonstrations. Performances in the streets lent energy to the protests and provided a mechanism through which multiple demands coalesced and circulated.[5]

To quell the ongoing unrest, Piñera and Congress agreed to a referendum on whether to draft a new constitution. On October 25, 2020, 78 percent of Chileans voted in favor of doing so. Chile would have the opportunity to rewrite its constitution for the first time since Pinochet's dictatorship. Chileans would imagine their democracy anew.[6]

Embodied performance has the remarkable capacity to assert rights claims and synthesize demands while linking those demands to a larger, revolutionary struggle. Baz Kershaw has pointed to dramaturgy as a way to understand how performances configure the symbolic and the real to make such "synecdochic" moves, while also highlighting the theatricality of state power—thereby rendering it contingent and subject to change.[7] In the case of *Un violador en tu camino*, LASTESIS marshals a feminist claim alongside a wider denunciation of state violence—the urgency of which was felt throughout the protests. The black blindfolds worn by the women symbolized not only the judicial system's blindness to gender violence but also referenced the many demonstrators who suffered eye injuries from rubber bullets during the protests.[8] Furthermore, by claiming "the oppressive state is a macho rapist," LASTESIS challenged the fundamental structures of Chilean society.

Performances such as this constitute powerful acts of radically democratic citizenship. Throughout Chile's transition to democracy, artists have used performance to reimagine, rearticulate, and engage in acts of democratic citizenship. Whether during Pinochet's dictatorship, when democracy was a hoped-for future or, following the democratic transition, as a present yet incomplete reality, Chilean artists have harnassed performance's capacity to imagine new worlds and relations to the state.

However, this process is not unidirectional, as LASTESIS's performance also illustrates. Much of the way that *Un violador en tu camino* produces meaning—at the intersection of aesthetic composition and explicit content—emerged from necessity: its move to the street, its intersectionality, its references to police violence, and its simplicity and replicability. A work's dramaturgy, the ways it configures the symbolic alongside the real, is profoundly influenced by the political, economic, and institutional structures that facilitate its production. Political performance, as both an aesthetic category and a mode of political engagement, is produced through a dynamic relationship to the state.

This book investigates that relationship, exploring how the production and aesthetics of theater and performance intertwine in processes of democratization, notions of citizenship, and the development of cultural policy in Chile. Though this question is grounded in the context of Chile's democratic transition, it emerges from larger theoretical questions concerning the relationship of theater and politics, specifically: how can we nonreductively conceptualize the dynamic linking political discourse, institutions, art making, and artistic agency? Furthermore, how can politics be meaningfully be enacted within the theater? Whereas much scholarship on Latin American performance, and political performance more generally, emphasizes either artistic resistance to or complicity with the state, this can obscure the way political theater is made and functions. A dramaturgical consideration of the works here reveals a complex, interdependent, and mutually constitutive dynamic. As the state has advanced shifting conceptions of Chilean citizenship, the relationship of artists to the state has also changed, transformations reflected in theatrical dramaturgies. At the same time, these dramaturgies call for, and at times enact, new modes of citizenship, revealing moments of resistance, complicity, crisis, and revolution. By examining how Chilean artists have advanced modes of democratic citizenship—and how the dramaturgies of those enactments are shaped by the state—this study elucidates the connections between aesthetics, state power, and the art's capacity to imagine a new politics.

New Dramaturgy

This book's project is both historical and theoretical. On the one hand, I trace the ways artists and the state have collaborated in a dynamic process of nation building and citizen-subject formation in Chile. This historical trajectory illuminates how particular political aesthetics have become dominant in contemporary Chilean theater.[9] At the same time, the artistic works considered here demonstrate remarkable acts of creative agency. In posing questions that traverse the realms of governance and art making, I heed Nikos Papastergiadis's call for "an expanded field that requires a new cross-disciplinary analysis" in which the scholar's task "is not only to reflect on art but also to see how a representation is both transformative and constitutive of subjectivity."[10] To account for the ways that art making is both reflective of its context and acts on it, I turn to the analytic paradigm of "new dramaturgy." A new dramaturgical framework, applied to historical questions, is uniquely suited to illuminate the dynamics in which political discourse, policies, and artmaking shape each other.

Theater is a collaborative art. Usually the collaborations referred to in this claim are those of the creative team: the director, writers, actors, and designers who contribute to the artistic "object" that appears onstage. However, as Diana Taylor has argued, performance is not only an object but also a "socially and politically embroiled" way of knowing, doing, and being in the world.[11] Scholars such as Shannon Jackson, Patricia Ybarra, Jen Harvie, Jean Graham-Jones, Marcos Steuernagel, and Sarah Wilbur have explored how infrastructures and material realities are woven into the aesthetic fabric of any work of art.[12] In this understanding of theater, numerous other collaborators enter the scene: the audience, the presenting institutions, the state that structures these relations, political events, and discourses. New dramaturgy helps to explicate this complex web of influences, not as overdetermining factors but as collaborations.

Marianne Van Kerkhoven coined the term "new dramaturgy" in a 1994 essay that describes process-oriented dramaturgical practices that are responsive to changing modes of theatrical production circulating in Europe at the time.[13] Whereas traditional dramaturgy—in the lineage established by Gotthold Lessing in his *Hamburg Dramaturgy*—had been largely concerned with textual analysis, new dramaturgy asserts the importance of process, collaboration, and affective experience in producing a work's meanings. This attention to process refutes the idea that an artwork can be separated from its mode of creation and explores how a work's meanings are marked by multiple collaborations, as well as by infrastructural contingency, as Konstantina Georgelou, Efrosini Protopapa, and Danae Theodoridou remind us.[14] Maaike Bleeker asserts that the practice of new dramaturgy involves a response-ability to what is immanent in a performance as well as to what emerges from the collaborative space where authorship becomes unattributable and collective.[15] Cathy Turner and Synne Behrndt note that by attending to this "complex web of elements," dramaturgical analysis can "reveal the implicit ideological, compositional, philosophical, and socio-political ideas that drive this performance."[16] Dramaturgy is thus, as Peter Eckersall elucidates, a practice fundamentally concerned with theater's connection to the social world.[17] A new dramaturgical analysis charts the process by which the aesthetics, structure, and text of a performance intersect with its environment and spectators to produce meanings. It traces how the real and symbolic are conjoined.

However, because this conceptualization of dramaturgy emerged directly from the practice of theater makers operating in a continental European context, those working with a new dramaturgical paradigm tend toward a presentist relationship to politics. As this book will illustrate, it also functions as a generative paradigm through which to frame historical questions. However, as Taylor has cautioned, one should be wary when applying artistic categories emerging from US or European contexts to Latin America.[18] Such applications risk collapsing modes of practice, creation, and self-understanding. The term "dramaturgy"—as I use it—is not a concept widely used in Chilean theatrical practice. Though in recent years *dramaturgismo* has been increasingly practiced in Chile—thanks in part to the influence of practitioners such as Soledad Lagos, who studied in Germany, as well as the international travel of a number of Chilean theater companies—it is not an explicitly named part of the creative process in the works I consider here.[19] Nevertheless, the artists discussed here all work in what I consider to be new dramaturgical ways—they create works specifically for performance that are highly collaborative and engaged with social questions and processes. However, the use of dramaturgy throughout this text is my own imposition to provide a framework elucidating the ways this work is politically embroiled.

To that end, I will here define a few related terms as I use them throughout my text. Throughout my analysis I will refer to "dramaturgical tactics." Drawing from Michel de Certeau's account of everyday expressions of individual agency within capitalist-ideological systems, dramaturgical tactics are the ways artists intentionally deploy artistic processes and aesthetic elements to communicate the work's metamessage or produce a particular experience or relationship to the work.[20] These dramaturgical tactics feed into, but do not fully compose, the larger dramaturgy of a piece, which I view as inextricably collaborative within a larger social totality.

I also center my analysis around what I call "dramaturgical acts." The dramaturgical act constitutes an instance when the dramaturgy of a work crystallizes in a moment of imaginative transformation. In these dramaturgical acts, as with Jill Dolan's concept of the utopian performative, the performance becomes performative and "intersubjectively intense," taking on a social life of its own.[21] Such moments may be fleeting or enduringly transformative, but they are the instances when the ontological status of the work shifts into the real. These are moments when performance transforms our sense of what is politically possible.

Finally, when I discuss the dramaturgy or "dramaturgies of . . ." (convivencia, solidarity, etc.), I am referring to a series of dramaturgical tactics that intersect with a larger social context to produce an ideological-aesthetic constellation that posits a way of relating to the state. These dramaturgies are produced by artworks but also by the aesthetic compositions of the social. In this conceptualization, I build upon Marcela Fuentes's notion of the "performance constellation": a means of understanding how contemporary political performance employs an expansive conceptualization of performance to incorporate embodied, ephemeral actions alongside online circulations and activity.[22] Here I consider dramaturgical circulations across distinct artworks and alongside political discourse and social performance as part of a larger political process that unfolds over time. The dramaturgies that compose this larger constellation are at once reflective and constitutive of social and political structures and discourse.[23] Their reperformances further contribute to this constitutive effort, and in the Chilean case, allow emergent dynamics to coalesce into the political demands and concrete imaginaries that lead to changing visions of citizenship.

Citizenship, Democracy, and the Politics of Political Art

My understanding of citizenship's relationship to performance is underlain by two central premises. The first is that citizenship is not a stable concept but is instead produced by the interactions between individuals and the state. It is, as May Joseph has pointed out, "a performed site of personhood that instantiates particular notions of participatory politics."[24] The second is that, like Emine Fisek, I consider theater and artistic performance to be an "embodied social practice" that is also fundamentally imaginative, thus constituting a site where citizenship is at once expressed, envisioned, and enacted.[25] Citizenship is both a performed and performative mode of subject formation through which individuals navigate their relationship to and agency within the state.

This book draws from the expansiveness of recent literature on citizenship, in which citizenship is conceived as both a status and a practice, a subject position and a claim, and a way of understanding oneself and of relating to the world. Not only is it, to follow T. H. Marshall's classic model, a constellation of rights and duties determining the individual's relationship to the state, but it is also a claim for the very *right to have rights*. It is at once a legal and bureaucratic category, a felt sense of belonging, a set of everyday practices, and the proposition of an ethical relationship to others.[26]

I strive to uncover how theater making is shaped by official understandings and discourse surrounding citizenship and public participation, as well as the infrastructures conditioning the production of artworks in Chile. I am therefore concerned with how art making becomes part of the everyday habitus of Chilean citizenship. At the same time, I examine how artists seek to transform those conditions and produce works that make new claims to citizenship. Such cases constitute what Engin Isin and Greg M. Nielsen have called *acts* of citizenship—a notion that informs the understanding of dramaturgical acts I elucidate above. These are moments that "disrupt habitus, create new possibilities, claim rights and impose obligations in emotionally charged tones; pose their claims in enduring and creative expressions; and, most of all, are the actual moments that shift established practices, status and order."[27] Such acts of citizenship circulate within wider understandings of citizenship—emerging from sets of practices while also creatively transcending them. They are performed and performative—creating new configurations of the real and the symbolic, exposing the disconnect between lived experience and changing ideological frameworks, and creating repeatable dramaturgies through which new relations to the state can be forged and eventually lived. By connecting acts of citizenship to *dramaturgical* acts we see the transformative political potential of performance itself. Yet the cases here also illuminate the ways both citizenship and theater are categories mutually determined by the state, even in moments where they offer ruptures with hegemonic forces. I therefore follow Jennifer Ponce de León to make the claim that political theater is a dynamic site of struggle over the meaning and forms of citizenship in Chile.[28]

Democracy, like citizenship, is another site of struggle. The term can stand for and legitimize a range of political practices. Wendy Brown observes that it can connote "everything from free elections to free markets, from protests against dictators to law and order, from the centrality of rights to the stability of states, from the voice of the assembled multitude to the protection of individuality and the wrong of dicta imposed by crowds."[29] Judith Butler contends that it might, then, be tempting to take a nominalist approach, defining democracy as that which calls itself democracy.[30] To some extent, I explore the discursive formulations that would constitute a nominalist approach, particularly as I consider democracy's definitions and redefinitions through Pinochet's dictatorship, Chile's democratic transition, and the estallido. However, while I do consider democracy to be an open and contestable concept, like Brown and Butler I locate it as a claim for the sovereign authority and agency of the people—"whoever the people are."[31] By focusing on dramaturgical acts of democratic citizenship, I attend to works that expand the notion of the people and assert their right to act and appear politically.

To identify these moments of democratic citizenship, I frequently draw from the political and aesthetic philosophy of Jacques Rancière and Nelly Richard, who each contend that the operations of power and politics are fundamentally aesthetic.[32] For Rancière, power, in the form of the police, is the ability to configure and maintain the "distribution of the sensible," or the way society is structured and behavior is regulated.[33] Such distributions are democratically disrupted when a group or individual that has been denied equal participation in society makes a claim to equality. Such a claim—which Rancière identifies as a moment of dissensus—reveals the inequality that has previously underlain the social order and thus asserts (like the theater itself) the "presence of two worlds in one."[34] It is the moment when LASTESIS proclaims that the rapist state has denied full personhood to women while simultaneously manifesting an assembly of women in the public space. If we consider the expression of power to be tied to the aesthetic task of ordering reality, then theater's ability to produce its own configurations of the sensible, as well as its ability to highlight their simultaneous aestheticization through its very theatricality, provides it with its ability to contest and enact power.[35] This political understanding of aesthetics helps to explain how the democratic engine of theater can be engaged in multiple contexts.

However, an emphasis on rupture risks advancing a politics that is neither sustainable nor generative. In focusing on dissensus, performance scholars risk losing sight of how performance can contribute to better systems of governance and neglect how performance is marked by contingency.[36] How, then, do we account for what Claire Bishop describes as performance's "double ontological status"?[37] On the one hand, theater and other performance-based participatory forms are "real" in the sense that they are made of real objects, bodies, and time. On the other, they exist, conceptually at least, in a quasi-autonomous realm. This seeming contradiction produces what Patrick Duggan has called a "mimetic shimmering": an experience in which the spectator is simultaneously aware of theater's reality and unreality.[38] Following theorists of theater of the real, I understand theater's unique relationship to reality as a central element of its political capacity.[39] Theater is both real and unreal, politically engaged and outside of politics. But it not only does this in an aesthetic sense—it does so as a social activity unfolding in time and space. I seek to connect the aesthetics and practice of theater to demonstrate that what is unreal *can be* real, *has been* real.

Political Theater and Cultural Policy in Chile

According to the playwright and director Guillermo Calderón, "in Chile, all theater is political. If you are not making political theater, it's as if you are not making serious theater."[40] In recent years, political theater has become a dominant aesthetic paradigm in Chile, a trend Camila González Ortiz calls the "citizen's turn," which she locates as a response to theater's engagement with twenty-first-century social movements.[41] Calderón connects a work's political engagement with its cultural capital—an elision that partially accounts for both the prominence of political theater in Chile, as well as its uneasy position within a market. In Chile today, there is both a personal and structural pressure on artists to create political works. This results in a kind of "political imperative," a product of the country's unique political and theatrical history, the development of contemporary cultural policy, and the disillusionment that many citizens have felt following Chile's incomplete transition to democracy.[42]

It is therefore important to first situate this study within a broader history of Chilean theater. Historians typically date the foundation of modern Chilean theater to 1941, with the creation of the first university theater, the Teatro Experimental de la Universidad de Chile (Experimental Theater of the University of Chile).[43] Prior to the university theaters,[44] the performing arts in Chile consisted primarily of either elite high art forms or popular entertainments such as opera, zarzuela, variety theaters, circus, pantomime, and mask.[45] The university theaters sought to reform Chilean theater from within official educational institutions. These reforms responded to demands from a rising middle class that had, with European migration to Latin America during the world wars, been recently exposed to European art-theater movements. The Chilean reforms consisted of the creation of a noncommercial theater, the renovation of playwriting and staging practices, public education about the theater, and the creation of theater schools.[46]

In 1955, theatrical reform expanded beyond the universities when several students from the Universidad Católica formed Teatro Ictus, an independent theater company. The students sought self-management and new ways of working. Ictus subsequently presented some of the nation's most important playwrights, such as Jorge Díaz, Marco Antonio de la Parra, and Juan Radrigán. Soon, other companies followed suit, and the independent theaters proceeded, in tandem with the universities, to consolidate the professionalization of Chilean theater—a process that followed a European, particularly French, model.

In 1960, Isidora Aguirre combined the quality and institutionalism of the newly professionalized theater with the spirit of earlier popular entertainments to create *La pérgola de las flores* (*The Flower Market*). A musical comedy in the zarzuela tradition, the play, produced by the Teatro de Ensayo de la Universidad Católica, depicted the story of urban flower sellers trying to save their market. The play combined music, composed by Francisco Flores del Campo, that incorporated popular forms with recognizable Chilean character types and light comedy to convey a message about economic exploitation and champion the working classes. The play drew massive national audiences and was one of the first Chilean plays to tour internationally.

La pérgola de las flores also reflected the profound social changes in Chile at the time. The 1960s and early 1970s saw agitation for political and economic equality and, consequently, a restructuring of Chilean society. In 1964, President Eduardo Frei, of the Christian Democratic Party, embarked upon the *revolución en libertad* (revolution in liberty). This program consisted of sweeping reforms, such as the agrarian reform and the 1967 educational reform, which restructured the university system and therefore transformed the university theaters. However, these reforms did not satisfy those hungry for greater change, and in 1970 Salvador Allende was elected, vowing to enact the radical, yet democratic, *vía chilena al socialismo* (Chilean road to socialism).[47]

During this period, artists across disciplines instrumentalized their art in support of the leftist political cause. Social changes were reflected in modes of theater making, outreach to audiences, and the increased representation of marginalized characters. Companies, such as Ictus, began to experiment with collective creation. The number of amateur and workers' theaters grew dramatically.[48] There was also a trend in theatrical, political, and civic performances toward mass spectacle.[49]

However, as Daniel Mansuy points out, Allende's coalition was always fundamentally weak. In the general election, Allende won a close three-way race, with 36.2 percent of the votes. Since no candidate had a majority, there was a runoff in Congress. Following negotiations between Allende's coalition, the Unidad Popular, and the Christian Democrats, Congress voted to install Allende in office. The combination of this tenuous coalition, close electoral margin, and divisions within Allende's own party did not amount to the political capital necessary to enact the programs he envisioned. So, when the initial economic gains of the early years of his administration gave way to inflation, the price of copper fell, and international actors pursued policies that weakened the Chilean economy, the ensuing domestic unrest—and the international support of the United States—emboldened those on the right to embark upon a coup.[50] On September 11, 1973, the military bombed the presidential palace, a siege that resulted in Allende's suicide and the installation of the dictatorship of Augusto Pinochet.

The military coup installed a repressive civic-military regime that imprisoned, tortured, murdered, and disappeared thousands of Chileans between 1973 and 1990. It also transformed all aspects of society, including the artistic landscape. Immediately following the coup, nearly all theatrical activity stopped, as many artists, because of their real or perceived connection to Allende's project, were detained, killed, exiled, or tortured. Most theater companies disbanded (with the notable exception of Ictus), and the university programs were restructured. The theater emerging from official institutions, including the universities, consisted of a benign classical repertoire. However, as early as 1974, an alternative theater began to assume a critical position toward the dictatorship. Beginning in 1983, the dictatorship loosened its repressive hold, and protests became more common. Theater more overtly denounced the regime's abuses, and some artists returned from exile. These artists, inspired by their aesthetic experiences abroad, shaped by the contingencies of censorship, and a desire to differentiate themselves from earlier "committed" artists, looked for new theatrical languages.[51] This led to a decreased emphasis on text and realism in favor of a theater that emphasized space, corporeality, and psychology, and symbolic and imagistic forms of expression.[52]

In addition to these theatrical innovations, the theater spaces themselves became sites of resistance. One of the most notable was Ramón Griffero's El Trolley. A repurposed trolley station, El Trolley became the clandestine center of activities for Griffero's company, the Teatro Fin de Siglo (End-of-the-Century Theater). Griffero and the company raised money for their activities by staging Saturday night parties (the only night without a curfew) that featured performances and music expressing opposition to the dictatorship. These parties became spaces to share in the camaraderie of their resistance.[53]

As I will explore in chapter 1, artistic countercultures constituted a major site of resistance to the regime, offering communities of solidarity and dramaturgies of resistance. Such dramaturgies would reach a mass audience in the opposition's television campaign leading up to the 1988 plebiscite. In the 1980 constitution, the military government had stipulated that a plebiscite would be held in 1988. A "yes" vote would ensure Pinochet eight more years in office; a "no" would require democratic elections the following year. Though the regime had not intended the vote to be a genuine contest, grassroots organization, international pressure, and an effective advertising campaign—significantly benefiting from the contributions of artists—emboldened Chilean citizens to vote against the regime.

Following the 1988 plebiscite, Chileans embarked upon a process in which democracy and citizenship were redefined. As this process of "redemocratization" unfolded, successive presidential administrations began to rearticulate and institutionalize cultural policy. As Toby Miller and George Yúdice define it, cultural policy consists of the "institutional supports that channel both aesthetic creativity and collective ways of life."[54] These supports can be discursive and material, are exercised explicitly and implicitly, and may or may not achieve expressed goals. I follow Néstor García Canclini in extending my understanding of cultural policy to include an artwork's embeddedness within a wider cultural field shaped by governmental policies.[55] My understanding of cultural policy is inflected by a Bourdieusian approach to the cultural field in which a work's dramaturgy is tied to its contingency, which I understand as its relative position, dependency on, and relationship to other artworks, state structures and discourse, material circumstance, and notions of capital and prestige.[56]

Chile's postdictatorship cultural policy included placing artists previously marginalized for their anti-dictatorship work into major institutional positions. These artists went on to establish cultural institutions and educational programs, develop funding structures, run major international festivals, and award prizes. As Arturo Navarro has shown, the explicit development of this cultural policy involved an intentionally "mixed" model. Whereas Allende's government created structures to facilitate the production of state-sponsored art in support of the socialist cause, during the dictatorship, art making was constrained and funded insofar as it was politically acceptable. Throughout the transition, the government explicitly sought to affirm culture as a right and to support a pluralist and democratic cultural institutionality that drew from both public and private support.[57] Artists who had previously situated themselves in opposition to the dictatorship had to reposition their work and navigate this developing cultural policy apparatus, leading them to think of their relationship to the state in new ways.[58] The director and playwright Ramón Griffero describes an artistic identity crisis following the 1988 plebiscite:

> Entering the democratic transition was an artistic shock to everyone. In Chile art had always been linked to cultural life with political commitment. When the political commitment disappeared, many artists, including me, didn't know what to do. . . . Before, I wrote from my opposition to Pinochet, from my ideological position. It was firm territory that others shared, so not only did I know where I was writing from, but I also knew for whom I was writing. . . . Our creative challenge is to reposition ourselves. Where I was no longer exists, where I talked from no longer exists.[59]

The confluence of negotiations and redefinitions provided by the Chilean case therefore offers a unique opportunity to analyze the connections between performance, political ideas, and institutions as they developed alongside each other.

Transitions, Transformations, and the Political Imagination

This book's trajectory traces the relationship between notions of citizenship, cultural policy, and theatrical aesthetics, as the early euphoria of Chile's democratic transition gave way to disillusionment, and as new citizen-actors emerged that were no longer defined by their relationship to the dictatorship. I construct an alternate periodization to previous studies—which tend to focus on either the dictatorship or postdictatorship periods—to elucidate the continuities and ruptures that emerge as performance aesthetics respond to changing state structures. This periodization is in line with the ways scholars such as Idelber Avelar have problematized the notion of the "transition." Avelar argues that the truly epochal Chilean transition was not from dictatorship to democracy but rather the aggressive shift from state to market ushered in by the neoliberal economic policies of Pinochet's dictatorship and sustained through the "return" to democracy.[60]

My long view of the Chilean transition therefore begins with the art actions of the Colectivo Acciones de Arte (Art Actions Collective) between 1979 and 1985 and continues to the 2019–2020 protests—artistic interventions that occurred as new constitutions were imposed and imagined (the 1980 constitution under Pinochet, and the 2022 Constitutional Convention). Each chapter is grounded in a case study focusing on an artist or dramaturgy, which I fold into a broader examination of cultural policy. In addition to situating my case studies within this history, I link them to flashpoints in the development of democratic citizenship: the implementation of Pinochet's 1980 constitution; the 1988 plebiscite; attempts at truth, reconciliation, and memorialization; the 2006 and 2011 student protests, and the 2019–2020 social movement and constitutional plebiscite. The case studies in this book are artistically innovative, connected to cultural institutions and funds, and tied to key debates or moments in the formulation of Chilean democratic citizenship. My case studies draw from works that have emerged primarily (though not exclusively) from the nation's capital, Santiago. Santiago is home to nearly 40 percent of the nation's population, and much theatrical activity is centered there, thanks in part to cultural policy, institutions, and the historical allocation of cultural resources.[61] My focus on Santiago is an acknowledgment of the centrality of the capital in Chile's theatrical landscape—however theater takes place around the nation, a fact I do not wish this study to obscure.

In chapter 1, I ask what was artistically possible in the context of Pinochet's dictatorship. I focus on the dramaturgy of resistance developed by the Colectivo Acciones de Arte (CADA), an interdisciplinary collective creating multimodal art actions in the urban environment of Santiago. I explore how CADA's dramaturgy emerged in response to the regime's repressive apparatus and vision of citizenship (manifest in the constitution of 1980), as well as from the networks of artistic countercultures that arose in this environment. Drawing from Chantal Mouffe's theory of agonism, I explore how CADA made use of the repressive environment to highlight its contingency and demonstrate that it could be otherwise. In doing so CADA invoked the artistic imagination as a means of creatively redefining citizenship. I consider how CADA's work reverberated in later protests against the regime and, in the next chapter, explore how their dramaturgical tactics were marshaled in the 1988 plebiscite campaign that ousted Pinochet.

Chapter 2 focuses on the way artists and the state collaborated in a process of redefining citizenship at the moment of democratic "transition." I chart the development of a dramaturgy of convivencia that circulated in political performances as well as in Andrés Pérez and Gran Circo Teatro's *La Negra Ester* (1988), arguably the most popular play produced in Chile. With a text written in *décimas* by Roberto Parra and a street-theater aesthetic, the show's dramaturgy intersected with desire for a more inclusive body politic, national consensus, and joy. However, I also explore how this dramaturgy veered toward apoliticism and upheld a patriarchal, heteronormative status quo—limitations that would lead to disillusionment with the democratic transition. I turn to Pérez's later work—clandestine parties and countercultural performances—that disidentified with the state and presented a queer challenge to its patriarchal foundations. The state's response to this work reveals official homophobia and a fundamental failure to institutionally support artistic *life*.

In the next chapters, I explore how the next generation of artists, who came of age during the transitional period, reckoned with new concerns surrounding the legacies of dictatorship and democracy. In chapter 3 I consider how *Prat* (2001), a play developed by Manuela Infante and a group of university students that would become Teatro de Chile, sparked public debate over history, memory, and arts funding. The play reimagined the legacy of a military hero, Arturo Prat, creating a dramaturgy of anachronism that brought the right to frame memory discourse and construct alternative histories center stage. I examine how the play was instrumentalized in broader cultural debates over free speech, censorship, cultural pluralism, truth and reconciliation, the military, homosexuality, and nationalism. Because the scandal preceded the play's premiere, it became a fundamental part of *Prat's* dramaturgy, transforming the play's enactment of Chilean citizenship and politicizing the work in ways unintended by its creators. Thus, this chapter reveals not only the political implications of anachronistic dramaturgies but also the way political theater is produced by its social and political environment.

Then in chapter 4, I turn to how Guillermo Calderón has wrestled with the notion of political theater within neoliberal cultural circuits and an environment of constrained political possibility. I examine how his works intersect with a new generation's political demands: specifically, the student protests of 2006 and 2011. Additionally, I consider how the political capacity of his work is embedded in the neoliberal structures Calderón seeks to resist, specifically through his alliance with the Fundación Santiago a Mil, an organization that hosts one of Latin America's most significant theater festivals, as well as a wider international festival circuit. In Calderón's work, citizenship becomes the challenge of redefining political engagement in a time of postpolitics.

The final chapter, drawing from the work of LASTESIS and KIMVN Teatro, explores the emergence of dramaturgies of solidarity alongside the estallido and proposed constitution of 2022. These dramaturgies—manifest in the theater, on the streets, and in the 2022 constitutional draft—reconceive and reimagine the state in ways that are incorporative of feminist and Indigenous subjectivities, theoretical frameworks, and cosmovisions. They challenge the physical, psychic, and economic violence of Chile's colonialist capitalist heteropatriarchy and, through their dramaturgies, strive toward a revolutionary, solidary future.

This book charts a new history of recent Chilean theater, proposing deep connections between the development of official understandings of postdictatorship Chilean citizenship, cultural policy, and the aesthetics of political theater. I consider artistic works that have not always been read alongside each other: art actions, protest performance, political events, and traditional theater, elucidating the connections between cultural policies and the dominant aesthetics of performance in Chilean artistic circuits. This constitutes an effort to illuminate how theatrical aesthetics in Chile have come to be what they are. This project necessitates my second offering: a methodology—through the application of new dramaturgical analysis to historical questions—that links aesthetics and politics in tangible ways.

Finally, I offer a meditation on political possibility refracted through the imaginations of artists. One of the reasons I embarked on this project was that I wanted to write about work that I loved. The inchoate attachments guiding this impulse are the foundations of my research and infuse every page of this book. But over the course of my writing, I've had to reckon with what those attachments mean and, crucially, with what they obscure.

I was first introduced to Chilean theater through the playwriting of Calderón. I was drawn to his work because it felt unflinchingly political and positioned, but not in the flatly propagandistic way that operates only on the level of explicit discourse. Rather, it was political in ways that enlivened his aesthetics and forged a theatrical language that I found unique. My sense in reading his work was that this was a theater desperate to burst out of the theater but that was also unabashedly theatrical. Something about this tension spoke to my own ambivalence about choosing a life in the theater in a world where state violence, injustice, capitalist exploitation, ecocide, and colonialism were rampant, as well as my discomfort with theater's status as a commodity. I knew theater could do something more, but so often it did not. I sensed from Calderón's plays that he knew that too.

Between 2016 and 2018 I spent over a year in Chile, conducting much of the research on which this book is based. I remember those nights attending the theater vividly: theaters in gorgeous, but crumbling, patrimonial buildings, theaters in state-of-the-art cultural centers, theaters in converted bodegas and in plazas, and my favorite little theater built on a bridge over the Mapocho River. As I sat in those theaters, I let myself get caught up in the political hopes of the performances I witnessed. And, when the estallido erupted in 2019, I let myself get caught up in the idea that Chile might see a revolution. Perhaps, as the former student activist turned president of Chile, Gabriel Boric, claimed, Chile, once the cradle of neoliberalism, really could be its grave. Yet the estallido and constitutional convention it birthed did not produce a constitution that would be implemented. Instead, Chileans voted emphatically against the draft proposed by that first convention, and in 2023 they elected a right-wing convention that holds the potential to draft a document even more neoliberal than the one currently governing Chile. The events of the last few years have both confirmed what I had learned from artists and forced me to reassess what I thought I understood about Chile, about the role of the arts in its politics, and about the dreams of its Left. It urges a confrontation with the profound reactionary power and the epistemological hegemony that patriarchal-colonialist neoliberalism wields on a global scale. It has forced me to confront the attachments driving my scholarship: the ways I looked to artists and the Chilean Left for hope that a different kind of world really was possible.

Chilean feminist philosopher Alejandra Castillo argues that the notion of a political imagination exists in a double bind: on the one hand, the imagination is always bound to the familiar. There is no way for the imagination not to be predetermined on experience. Furthermore, politics is concerned with reenactment: of accords, agreements, and contracts. In this way the political imagination cannot take us much beyond what is currently possible.[62] It is perhaps why when it stretches too far it is almost always jerked back to the familiar by a reactionary tether.

Yet faced with the multiple manifestations of injustice and exploitation that our current politics supports, we know we desperately need a transformative political imagination. Castillo argues that feminism offers an imaginative supplement that reconfigures who is imagined to be the body politic. In Castillo's formulation it functions as a loose leaf—inserted into the book, but that flutters out, untethered, and disturbs the coherence of the whole.

I propose here that theater and performance, as embodied imagination, also behave in supplemental ways and push what is imaginatively possible in expansive directions. As political dramaturgies circulate over time, the political imagination is transformed and expanded. These imaginings are always bound to experience, but by building imaginaries on imaginaries—embodied and brought to life through dramaturgy—they expand our sense of the possible, they leave residues of other worlds, they increase what has been experienced and allow the tether of the imagination to stretch farther and farther. They become capacious playgrounds for difficult narratives, for processing violence, for exploring irrationality, testing radicality, emboldening action, and dreaming of the utopian. If we view political art making not as tied to a single artist but rather as an unfolding process in conversation with other works, as well as with social dramaturgies, we have a different sense of the political efficacy of that art. This book's trajectory illuminates how artists push against the colonialist-patriarchal nation-state, offer expansive visions of the body politic, and ultimately intimate new conceptualizations of state or nonstate formation. Macarena Gómez-Barris cautions against "overinvestment in any one model of political change." Instead, she encourages scholars to "reach beyond the crashing ebbs and flows of national elections and political defeat to instead perceive how art and social movements fundamentally remake the world."[63] What I offer here is a documentation of these emergences, tangible evidence of a politics of imaginative hope: as an act of aftercare, an act of solidarity, and a provocation. One of the most powerful political potentialities of theater is in its capacity to tangibly expand what can be politically imagined, as dramaturgies circulate and transform, in repertoires, in memories, in dreams, in play, and in plays. They are the real, collective manifestations of a revolution. A revolution that almost came, perhaps. A revolution that never came, perhaps. A revolution that is yet to come, perhaps. But one that is also, already, here.

Chapter 1

✦

Dramaturgies of Resistance

CADA and Artistic Countercultures against the Dictatorship

At eleven o'clock in the morning on September 11, 1973, the Chilean air force bombed the presidential palace, La Moneda, as part of an attack that ended the Allende presidency, suspended democracy, and initiated the civic-military dictatorship of Augusto Pinochet. On July 12, 1981, at almost the midpoint of the dictatorship, six airplanes again flew over Santiago in military formation. This time, however, the planes did not drop bombs. Instead, they scattered four hundred thousand pamphlets with a text that called Chileans to view their lives as an act of creativity (see fig. 1). This art action, titled *¡Ay Sudamérica!* (*Oh, South America!*) and orchestrated by the Colectivo Acciones de Arte (henceforward CADA), subversively re-created a central moment from the violent history of the military coup in order to articulate an alternative course for that history and call for a new work of art: the creation of a new life. CADA challenged the regime's conception of citizenship by calling for an expanded space of existence and invoking the possibility of an artistic subjectivity within everyone.

¡Ay Sudamérica! was part of a series of actions created by CADA that, through interventions in the urban space of Santiago, sought to redirect history, reframe citizen subjectivities, and provide avenues for resistance to Pinochet's regime. Though the collective was active for a relatively short period (1979–1985), the dramaturgy they created had a profound impact on Chilean art, performance, and politics, reverberating in the surge of mid-1980s protest to the regime and ultimately the 1988 plebiscite that ousted Pinochet. In reflecting on the significance of the collective's work, member Raúl Zurita claims, "We showed what could be done."[1] Zurita's assertion provokes several questions: What, exactly, is artistically and politically possible within the context of authoritarianism? Relatedly, how might the constrained conditions of possibility brought about by dictatorship be marshaled to create an expanded sense of that possibility? And, furthermore, might considering such questions in the context of CADA's

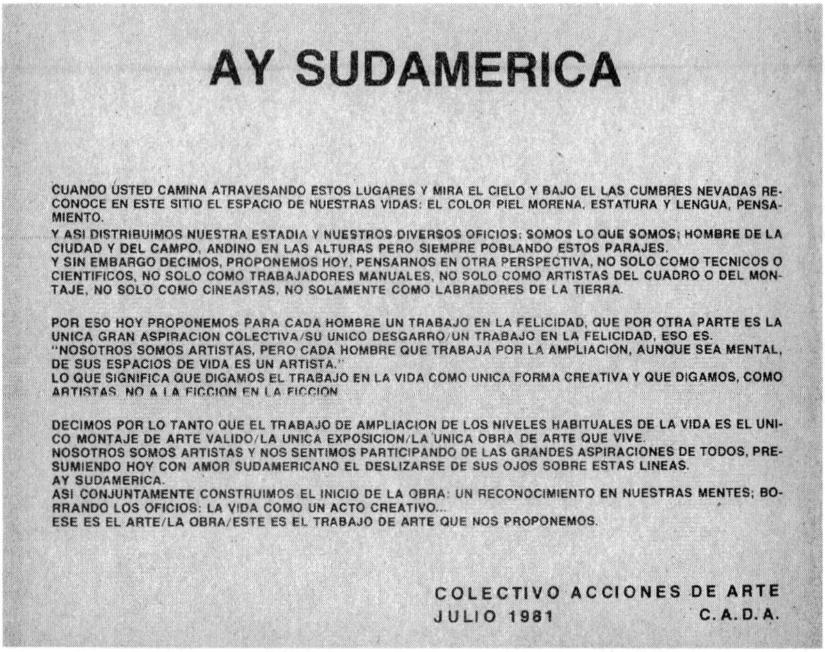

AY SUDAMERICA

CUANDO USTED CAMINA ATRAVESANDO ESTOS LUGARES Y MIRA EL CIELO Y BAJO EL LAS CUMBRES NEVADAS RECONOCE EN ESTE SITIO EL ESPACIO DE NUESTRAS VIDAS: EL COLOR PIEL MORENA, ESTATURA Y LENGUA, PENSAMIENTO.
Y ASI DISTRIBUIMOS NUESTRA ESTADIA Y NUESTROS DIVERSOS OFICIOS: SOMOS LO QUE SOMOS; HOMBRE DE LA CIUDAD Y DEL CAMPO, ANDINO EN LAS ALTURAS PERO SIEMPRE POBLANDO ESTOS PARAJES.
Y SIN EMBARGO DECIMOS, PROPONEMOS HOY, PENSARNOS EN OTRA PERSPECTIVA, NO SOLO COMO TECNICOS O CIENTIFICOS, NO SOLO COMO TRABAJADORES MANUALES, NO SOLO COMO ARTISTAS DEL CUADRO O DEL MONTAJE, NO SOLO COMO CINEASTAS, NO SOLAMENTE COMO LABRADORES DE LA TIERRA.

POR ESO HOY PROPONEMOS PARA CADA HOMBRE UN TRABAJO EN LA FELICIDAD, QUE POR OTRA PARTE ES LA UNICA GRAN ASPIRACION COLECTIVA/SU UNICO DESGARRO/UN TRABAJO EN LA FELICIDAD, ESO ES.
"NOSOTROS SOMOS ARTISTAS, PERO CADA HOMBRE QUE TRABAJA POR LA AMPLIACION, AUNQUE SEA MENTAL, DE SUS ESPACIOS DE VIDA ES UN ARTISTA."
LO QUE SIGNIFICA QUE DIGAMOS EL TRABAJO EN LA VIDA COMO UNICA FORMA CREATIVA Y QUE DIGAMOS, COMO ARTISTAS, NO A LA FICCION EN LA FICCION.

DECIMOS POR LO TANTO QUE EL TRABAJO DE AMPLIACION DE LOS NIVELES HABITUALES DE LA VIDA ES EL UNICO MONTAJE DE ARTE VALIDO/LA UNICA EXPOSICION/LA UNICA OBRA DE ARTE QUE VIVE.
NOSOTROS SOMOS ARTISTAS Y NOS SENTIMOS PARTICIPANDO DE LAS GRANDES ASPIRACIONES DE TODOS, PRESUMIENDO HOY CON AMOR SUDAMERICANO EL DESLIZARSE DE SUS OJOS SOBRE ESTAS LINEAS.
AY SUDAMERICA.
ASI CONJUNTAMENTE CONSTRUIMOS EL INICIO DE LA OBRA: UN RECONOCIMIENTO EN NUESTRAS MENTES; BORRANDO LOS OFICIOS: LA VIDA COMO UN ACTO CREATIVO...
ESE ES EL ARTE/LA OBRA/ESTE ES EL TRABAJO DE ARTE QUE NOS PROPONEMOS.

COLECTIVO ACCIONES DE ARTE
JULIO 1981 C.A.D.A.

Fig. 1. The pamphlet dropped by planes in *¡Ay Sudamérica!* The text calls citizens to recognize "life as a creative act . . . / This is the art / the work/ this is the work of art that we propose." Archivo CADA, donated by Lotty Rosenfeld and Diamela Eltit in 2016. Courtesy of the Museum of Memory and Human Rights, Santiago, Chile.

work during the Pinochet regime illuminate how, specifically, performance can generate new avenues for political engagement?

In *¡Ay Sudamérica!*, an individual spectator may have only witnessed the planes overhead or encountered a pamphlet on the ground. Even considered in its entirety, the action's meanings are difficult to parse. These are dramaturgical tactics born out of a relationship to the dictatorship: the collective had to navigate precarious conditions and avoid censorship, or worse. Yet in each of CADA's works the collective highlights the ways the regime's continued power is not inevitable and calls Chileans to see the world otherwise. CADA's actions constitute an invocation of the political imagination. This is, for CADA, "the only work of art." The stakes and significance of such an invocation cannot be understated. After the destruction of Allende's socialist dream on the one hand and in the face of fear, intimidation, and extreme vulnerability on the other, CADA's dramaturgical act of citizenship was to propose the possibility of possibility. In doing so, CADA proposed nothing less than a new politics.

But what are the contours of this imaginative invocation? What possibilities does it point to and what, if anything, does it foreclose? In this chapter, I trace the ways that CADA's works emerged both in response to the discursive and material realities of the dictatorship as well as to the countercultural networks of artistic production operating at the time. This complicates an understanding of political artworks that are underlain by binary assumptions about artistic autonomy and heteronomy—in which a work's ability to resist state power is defined by its agency, disruptiveness, or purity, or in which a work's complicities negate its political engagement. Any artistic act of resistance is shaped by that which it seeks to resist, just as it shapes that which it resists. Rather than compromise a work's political capacity, I argue, drawing from Chantal Mouffe's theory of agonism, that this contingency enables and, in fact, constitutes the political valence of CADA's work. For it is through contingency that the work highlights the mutability of power and the agency of citizens; it is through contingency that the work bleeds into the creation of life itself; and it is by navigating contingency that the work—and the artists that make it—persists and survives.

CADA executed eight art actions between 1979 and 1985. Because my analysis centers on the dramaturgy of the group's actions as a practice of democratic politics, I focus on the four of these actions that unfolded in the public space of the city. These include *Para no morir de hambre en el arte* (To not die of hunger in art), *Inversión de escena* (Inversion of scene), *¡Ay Sudamérica!*, and *No +*.[2] I explore how, in their art actions, the artists of CADA made use of and highlighted both their works' and the dictatorship's contingency. CADA did so through collective collaboration and an embrace of pluralism, as well as by engaging with the urban environment in Santiago. The group challenged the Pinochet regime's attempts to structure space and human relationships, advance a linear historical narrative, and legitimize its power. Their work marshals these constrained conditions to show that they are not inevitable, and the future is not predetermined. That they do so through performance makes their work difficult to pin down (and helps to avoid censorship), but it also establishes a dramaturgy that operates in ongoing, affective, and rhizomatic ways. CADA enacted a vision of democratic citizenship characterized not by the pursuit of a particular end but by the unfolding creative process of remaking Chilean society. It established a dramaturgy of doing so—modeling collectivity, participation, creative contingency, and radical critique—that could shape-shift and reverberate beyond the present, giving it after and future lives.

Reframing Citizenship: The Repressive Apparatus

CADA's work was enmeshed in the political, material, and structural realities of Chile during the Pinochet regime. During the Allende period, art making had been supported by the state and linked to an explicit political goal: the advancement of the socialist project. However, following the September 11 coup, this artistic positioning—and the aesthetics and modes of working it birthed—had to be completely rethought. Artists who wished to politically engage had to contend with a new official conceptualization of citizenship and democracy, the disarticulation of state cultural support in favor of privatization, as well as a multifaceted repressive apparatus that targeted artists and constrained any forum for participatory engagement.

Immediately after the coup, the regime declared a "state of siege."[3] The military disbanded Congress and banned independent political organizations.[4] During this time, repression (including arrest, torture, and executions) was overt and indiscriminate, justified as necessary during a state of war. Political parties were suspended, labor unions were restricted, and neighborhood councils and professional associations were controlled by the government.[5] The intended effect was to render the population apolitical and atomized. A key element of this strategy was a series of constantly shifting curfews, a spatiotemporal policing that insisted the citizen's place was not at the scene of politics and that domesticized an entire population during curfew hours.[6] The curfews also gave the government free reign to terrorize the population through home raids and disappearances. Thus, at the same time as the curfews depoliticized the public space of the city, they politicized domestic space by rendering the home an apparatus of incarceration. The curfews also made it difficult to attend artistic events during nonworking hours, and established a framework in which leisure and creativity were disconnected from the public sphere.

Among the regime's most urgent aims was the elimination of political adversaries, particularly those who had supported Allende's efforts to create a democratic path to socialism. Allende and the Unidad Popular—the coalition of left-wing parties in support of his presidency—had sought to democratize the cultural sphere and to encourage art that advanced a leftist political consciousness. To this end, they supported publishing houses (Quimantú), record labels (IRT), and film studios (Chile Films).[7] Numerous artists took up political causes in their work. Musicians denounced social and economic injustices in their songs, theater companies worked to mobilize popular sectors and labor unions, and muralist collectives such as Las Brigadas Ramona Parra painted graphic murals on walls throughout Santiago, supporting Allende and envisioning a communist society.[8] The Pinochet regime targeted artists linked to Allende. The result was a total disarticulation of the cultural apparatus and the creation of a culture of fear.[9] Just as the regime sought to disentangle the notion of citizenship from its political or collective dimensions, it also worked to depoliticize and isolate the cultural sphere.

Shortly after the coup, the regime began to articulate a new vision for Chilean culture. On December 10, 1974, Decree Law 804 created the office of cultural adviser to the government junta, headed by Enrique Campos Menéndez. In 1975, Menéndez issued the first concrete expression of the regime's cultural policy, in the *Política cultural del gobierno de Chile* (Cultural policy of the government of Chile). This document advanced a vision of culture that was at once the moral expression of a national will (as defined by Pinochet), elite, and apolitical. The government policed the cultural sphere through the imposition of taxes, censorship, and intimidation. At the same time, the regime's broader efforts to reconfigure the Chilean economy according to neoliberal principles led it to cede public support of the arts to private industry, which favored elite forms, considered artistic expression a commodity, and could be mercurial in its support.[10] These cultural policies were linked to an overall reimagining of democracy—what Pinochet referred to as "nueva democracia" (new democracy).

On July 9, 1977, at Chacarillas Hill in Santiago, Pinochet advanced his plan to institutionalize nueva democracia—a vision that would culminate in the constitution of 1980. Steve Stern observes that the speech outlined that Chilean democracy would be "authoritarian, protected, integrated, technocratic, and with authentic social participation."[11] The speech asserted that freedom and democracy were vulnerable, justifying the state's containment of dissidence. It emphasized the importance of democracy's "integration," conveying a unifying antipluralism: citizens ought to be united in serving the National Objectives defined by the military junta. Meanwhile, its reliance on technocrats conveyed an ethos of modernization and social engineering. Finally, by asserting that social participation must be "authentic," Pinochet invalidated forms of participation that did not serve this vision of democracy, characterized by an apolitical civil society. Furthermore, this participation was tied to creative freedom—which he defined as freedom from political commitment—and economic freedom. The citizen was cast as an apolitically engaged but active participant in the neoliberal economic model.

The speech also launched an effort to establish democratic legitimacy for this authoritarian vision. One of the most enduring mechanisms by which it did so was through the drafting of a new constitution. This document, which would replace the constitution of 1925, granted the president centralized power and ensured the military's influence via its presence on a National Security Council and as appointed senators. It restricted political parties and freedom of expression, granting the president and military the "tutelary" power to enact those restrictions. In addition, the constitution established the "principle of subsidiarity," which bound the state to a neoliberal economic model. Whereas Allende had sought to nationalize key industries (copper) and services (health, banking), this principle (advanced in articles 1, 9, and 19) stipulated that the state could only provide a social right if a private entity, such as a corporation, could not do so. This has resulted in the privatization of public goods such as water, which has, over time, led the state to eschew communities and side with global agribusiness conglomerates engaged in resource extraction. The result has been the high cost of drinking water and water scarcity, which has exacerbated extreme drought and related wildfires in regions such as Valparaíso, and dispossession and violent conflicts with the Mapuche populations in the south.[12] Additionally, the constitution asserted a right to health care and social security, with the option to choose between public and private options. This ensured the privatization of both the health and pension systems and situated citizens as consumers within this privatized system.[13] The constitution was ratified via a referendum, in which the opposition had few avenues to campaign and in which there were no electoral registers.[14] Further, the 1980 constitution stipulated that Pinochet would remain in office at least through 1988, when a plebiscite would be held to determine whether he would serve an additional eight-year term.

Countercultural Artistic Circuits

The regime's vision of democracy and culture was guided by a conceptualization of citizenship as apolitical, consumerist, and part of a unified national body helmed by technocratic authoritarian leadership. However, in privatizing culture and moving it out of the public space, the regime also made it difficult to police. Additionally, beginning in 1977 and throughout the 1980s, the regime made a concerted effort to institutionalize and legally justify itself. This, combined with a citizenry, church, and press increasingly willing to contest the regime's human rights abuses led to what has been called an "aperture" of the repressive apparatus: a loosening of the harshest forms of repression that created the opportunity for collective organization and eventually protest.[15] In the second half of the 1970s numerous cultural organizations emerged, many of which created communities united by a shared political struggle.[16]

These groups collapsed the boundaries between art and politics, as well as between the artistic disciplines, as the space of art making became a space of free expression in which alternatives to the dictatorship could be imagined. The realities of the repressive and economic environment meant that many of these groups were short lived; nevertheless, they fostered a space to imagine alternative realities and began to experiment in the articulation of resistant demands.

Responding to the regime's vision of citizenship and culture, many groups worked to reconstitute an artistic, politically conscious civil society. They strove to make culture accessible and collapsed the boundaries between art and politics as well as between the artistic disciplines. For example, the Grupo Cámara Chile, an independent choir, debuted with a cycle of concerts performed in Cerro San Cristóbal, a public park that gave their performances greater popular reach than a more traditional venue would have afforded. In 1975 they expanded the reach of their work to various working-class and poor neighborhoods around Santiago. An account of their artistic activities in 1978 describes choral and instrumental performances, various theatrical group meetings and performances, classes in music, and a workshop fostering the investigation of the cultural life of Chile. These activities reflect a desire to foster cultural life outside of elite circuits, in rural areas and workers' unions, and among students. Their home at Miraflores 544 provided space for other artistic and political groups to meet, fostering a sense of community.[17]

Grupo Cámara de Chile was notable in the scope of its work; however, many cultural organizations also functioned in socially oriented, interdisciplinary ways. They included Taller Contemporáneo (Contemporary workshop) the Unión de Escritores Jóvenes (Union of young writers), Taller 666 (Workshop 666), Agrupación Cultural Universitaria (University Cultural Group, henceforward ACU), the Unión Nacional por la Cultura (National Union for Culture, henceforward UNAC), Nuestro Canto (Our Song), Centro Cultural Mapocho, magazines like *La Bicicleta*, *Apsi*, and *Análisis* and research groups such as Sur, CENECA, and Galería Imagen. Many of these groups focused on building a larger artistic community and forging an alliance between artistic creation and political struggles.[18]

Cultural organizations sought to offer an alternative community and sense of identity through art making and solidarity. In a declaration issued by Taller Contemporáneo on April 27, 1979, the group critiqued the insufficiencies of the Chilean cultural movement and expressed a desire to create a robust cultural environment. They wished to be a home to many manifestations of culture, and to incorporate professionals and amateurs into the group. Throughout the document, there is an awareness of both the seriousness and the scale of the work they are undertaking. The Centro Cultural Mapocho (1980–1989) sought to have a similarly expansive reach. They hosted a variety of artistic events, including exhibitions, performances, and workshops. Like Grupo Cámara de Chile, they had their own space, and provided a meeting place for many different groups, including political activists.[19] The artistic life and community of the center provided the impetus to persevere in dire circumstances. It also provided a sense of community and common purpose under a regime that sought to isolate individuals from each other. Rodrigo Vidal recalls,

> I think Pinochet isolated everyone, more or less. He individualized us. . . . In the Mapocho Center things were done in a team, they were done in consultation, in conversation, in consensus, but this did not represent a kind of censorship or saying, "you can do this" or "you can't do this." No, it was simply to say, "This is going to be done."[20]

In some instances, groups allowed participants to forge a subjective identification with the collective and offered, in their private spaces, models of participation that were curtailed by the regime's articulation of "new democracy." The ACU, for example, provided a forum for students to artistically express themselves, but also to identify their common concerns through dialogue. Representatives of the ACU describe their Saturday meetings as a place where art and political aspirations converged: students talked together about their lives, struggles, and hopes for a better world. The group's representatives expressed that "the conversations are long, sometimes too much so. Perhaps because this is the only way to hear all the voices. Even the shyest and newest to the group speaks. The dialogue is an absolute necessity . . . everyone is aware that they are necessary as a person, with their ideas."[21] They describe a space in which dignity is given to everyone, and pluralist dialogue is paramount to the functioning of their group.

Other groups, such as UNAC, sought to foster solidarity and build a cultural network through collective organization that was tied to the larger international community and human rights. UNAC also sought to articulate an alternative cultural policy in direct response to the regime. It outlined its objectives as uniting and coordinating groups and people in distinct artistic areas, offering a unified expression of the interests and concerns of the cultural movement, explaining and advocating artistic creation's service to man, promoting and protecting the rights of artists, incentivizing the development of professional and amateur audiences, and creating opportunities for reflection and analysis over cultural problems.[22] It contested the privatization of culture and education, censorship and taxes on books and performances, the unemployment of artists (due to blacklists, lack of resources, and fear), the limitations placed on unions, the exile of artists, and the detention and disappearances of cultural workers.[23]

In the face of culture's privatization, these groups were sustained by an economy of solidarity. They supported themselves with exhibitions and classes, and artists often volunteered their time, personal finances, and skills.[24] When cultural groups were in crisis, the community came to their support. In 1978, for example, Grupo Cámara Chile's work with the working-class and rural populations, as well as its advocacy for human rights, drew suspicion from the government. The Institute of Rural Education withdrew support for its project "El arte en el campesinado chileno" (Art in the Chilean countryside), because, according to the institute, the project conspired against the government. After two newspapers deemed Grupo Cámara Chile's work "subversive," the group was unable to obtain financial patronage from private companies, and it encountered obstacles in publicizing its activities in the press.[25] *La Bicicleta* issued a call to the community to support the organization, and the group raised enough money to continue functioning.[26]

Many groups also fostered international solidarity. International artists and organizations contributed to the activities of the Chilean groups, holding exhibitions in support of the artists, while several groups in Chile contested the exile of artists overseas. UNAC situated its work in an international context, invoking UNESCO and the Catholic Church's positioning of the free expression of culture as a human right.[27] Internationally, groups such as the Centro por la Defensa de la Cultura Chilena more boldly denounced the dictatorship and offered material and moral support for groups operating within Chile. In a document outlining its goals, it asserts:

> In this battle for a new democracy, culture has a foundational place. In Chile, it assumes innumerable clandestine and semilegal forms. Outside, the cultural workers that have been exiled or expelled have continued their search for words, for music, for color . . . the Center for the Defense of Chilean Culture was born to affirm that Chilean culture lives and in order to resist their attempts to shut our voices and so that we continue caring, creating, promoting. The center meets in and outside of Chile. . . . Its specific goals are to stimulate and materially support from abroad a varied range of cultural expressions that develop with difficulty in the interior of the country.[28]

Thus, in addition to the networks developing within Chile, cultural organizations operated in solidarity with a vast international network seeking to support Chilean culture against the dictatorship.

As a collective, CADA emerged directly out of these alternative cultural networks and was inspired by their interdisciplinary response to a shared political struggle. The writers Diamela Eltit and Raúl Zurita met in an Artaud workshop in 1974 at the University of Chile. Separately, in 1977, visual artists Lotty Rosenfeld and Juan Castillo met as part of a group of artists opposed to the regime. Though this particular collective was short lived, it provided Rosenfeld and Castillo with a formative experience in political art making. The two later met Zurita and Eltit at a Goethe Institute exhibition in which they were all participating. The artists were fascinated with one another's work and began collaborating following the exhibition. Later, the sociologist Fernando Balcells joined the group to give CADA's work theoretical grounding and articulation, and at times the collective collaborated with Chilean artists in exile—most notably Cecilia Vicuña in Bogotá—to create interrelated works in solidarity.[29] The group's interdisciplinarity—united in a sense of political urgency—and desire to have its work deeply and theoretically engage with society are reflective of the operations of the wider artistic counterculture and are elemental components of the dramaturgy they would create.

CADA and Agonism

Although the regime had sought to build a striated, orderly system and to advance authoritarian democracy, it had not done so in a linear or consistent way, policing public and private space, time, bodies, associations, and interactions. The structure of the repressive apparatus, in combination with the cracks it began to show at the end of the 1970s, led CADA to meet its repression with a dramaturgy of resistance that was similarly plural, rhizomatic, and temporally engaged.

Writing contemporaneously to CADA, Nelly Richard has set many of the terms of the group's subsequent analysis. Richard frames the dictatorship's project in terms of aesthetics and has explored the ways CADA's work has intervened in that aesthetic project. Richard argues that the dictatorship sought to disarticulate entire systems of signs present in Chilean society and to rearticulate those signs as it reconfigured society in authoritarian terms. She contends that CADA's work—which she classifies as part of the *escena de avanzada* (advanced scene, or vanguard)—intervened in official sign systems to produce ruptures and spaces for creativity amid a heavily stratified system.[30]

The thirty-year commemoration of the coup in 2003 renewed a consideration of CADA and its relationship to the dictatorship, sparking a debate between Richard and the philosopher Willy Thayer. Thayer situates the aesthetic gesture of the coup's rupture as both the culmination and the "point of no return" of Chilean vanguard art's commitment to nonrepresentation. Thayer proposes that the totalizing effects of the dictatorship predicated CADA's efforts and made them aesthetically complicit with the dictatorship. Furthermore, Thayer contends that Richard's canonization of CADA is therefore also complicit with the dictatorship project of disarticulation and its continued legacy in Chilean society.[31] Richard responds that Thayer's is a nihilist and totalizing perspective that neglects artistic agency and "dilutes the tension between the context (the social historical: the dictatorship) and text (the cultural-aesthetic: the neovanguard experiment)."[32] Richard situates the debate within the larger theoretical conundrum of art's relative autonomy and heteronomy. However, Richard's analysis emphasizes how the artists highlight these tensions and makes implicit assumptions of artistic autonomy in service to a heroic narrative of artistic struggle against oppression. To fully account for this tension, however, a consideration of CADA must heed Thayer's provocation and not simply ask questions about how the artists negotiated these tensions; it must also interrogate how these tensions—and the dictatorship more generally—prefigured and shaped the aesthetics of the artwork. I posit that it is precisely through its work's contingency that CADA enacts a politically resistant project.

As Miguel Valderrama has observed, the debate between Richard and Thayer takes place primarily on an abstract, philosophical-theoretical plane.[33] My goal here is to reengage a close historical reading of CADA's work, foregrounding the contingency of performance and its material conditions, to explore how such a reading might reconfigure this debate. I follow scholars such as Diana Taylor, Eugenia Brito, and Francisco González Castro, Leonora López, and Brian Smith who have begun to view CADA's work through the lens of performance, focusing on the body and its engagement with urban space.[34] Taylor, Castro, López, and Smith have done so with the caveat that contemporary notions of performance and performance art carry connotations of Western hegemony, the resistance of which was a part of CADA's project.[35] Indeed, Eltit has strongly emphasized that its work not be considered performance, preferring instead the terms "actions" or "interventions." She rejects performance as a retroactively imposed generic category emerging from Western art traditions, as well as its positioning within a protected or rarefied sphere. The term "action," she feels, better links CADA's art to its political intentions and engagement (and therefore vulnerability) with the space of the city.[36] Therefore, while the generic category of performance should probably be dispensed with in considerations of CADA, an analysis through the lens of performance is helpful in foregrounding its use of bodies and engagement with the materials inherent to performance including, time, space, movement, and spectators.

These latter elements lead me, with similar caution and caveats, to employ the analytics of performance in a consideration of CADA's actions to attend to the ways its works develop a dramaturgy. To facilitate an analysis that traverses artistic autonomy and heteronomy in complex ways, I draw from the political theory of agonism advanced by Chantal Mouffe. Mouffe posits a theory of politics, developed with Ernesto Laclau, that asserts that all orders are hegemonic by nature.[37] Mouffe contends that there is no escaping the fact of hegemony—to deny it would be to relinquish organization of the social. However, Mouffe also argues that this hegemony is also always contestable. Therefore, thinking politically "requires recognizing the ontological dimension of radical negativity."[38] In this formulation, all assertions can be negated, there is no objectively agreed-upon truth, and "antagonism is an ever present possibility."[39] Rather than seek to reconcile this fundamental antagonism, Mouffe argues for a democratic order that does not deny radical negativity, but that navigates this "terrain of conflictuality" via agonism.[40] Agonism differs from antagonism in that it recognizes the contingency of all orders and is therefore "compatible with the recognition of pluralism."[41] In an agonistic model, "others are not seen as enemies to be destroyed, but as adversaries whose ideas might be fought, even fiercely, but whose right to defend those ideas is not to be questioned."[42] An agonistic order would therefore consist of the constant assertion, contestation, and rearticulation of hegemonic structures through an egalitarian process of contention.

Bonnie Honig points out that this has a constantly evolving, performative dimension, as it is a "practice of (re-)founding, augmentation, and amendment."[43] This is in stark contrast to Pinochet's view of democracy and citizenship, in which strong authoritarian leadership was not to be contested and the orderly structures of society were thought to be fixed. Though CADA's work was decidedly *antagonistic* to Pinochet, a reading of its dramaturgy as *agonistic* elucidates how the group's collaborative, plural, and polyvalent acknowledgment of contingency advanced a model of an alternative, radically democratic, political process. With an aesthetic and working process inflected by the alternative cultural sphere from which it emerged, CADA formulated resistance as a process in which the world is continuously contested and remade.

Collaboration, Care, and Pluralism: *Para no morir de hambre en el arte*

Imagine this page completely blank

Imagine this blank page
reaching all the corners of Chile
like the daily milk to be consumed

Imagine each corner of Chile
deprived of the daily drink of milk
like blank pages to be filled.[44]

On October 3, 1979, CADA distributed one hundred bags of milk to residents of the working-class La Granja neighborhood in southern Santiago. The bags were printed with the words "1/2 litro de leche" (1/2 liter of milk), referencing Allende's promise to deliver a half liter of milk to every child each day.[45] The group requested that the recipients return the bags later so that they could be incorporated into an art exhibit. This was the first stage of CADA's action *Para no morir de hambre en el arte*. That same day, they placed an advertisement in the national magazine *Hoy*, with the above poem, urging readers to imagine the page as blank as the corners of Chile deprived of daily milk. In addition to the ad, CADA played a prerecorded speech, "No es una aldea" ("It Is Not a Village") in five languages—Chinese, French, Russian, Spanish, and English—in front of the United Nations' Latin American Economic Commission (CEPAL) building in the upper-class Vitacura neighborhood. Throughout the rest of the month at the Galería Centro Imagen, the group exhibited video documentation of the action alongside a clear box with empty milk bags inside of it, a copy of the *Hoy* ad, and the tape recording of "No es una aldea."

This inaugural action's dramaturgy emerged out of a collaborative and interdisciplinary creative process. In interviews, the members of CADA affirm the collective nature of their work. Though their individual contributions were informed by their own disciplinary backgrounds, their unified theoretical vision led them to an open collaboration in conceptual input and labor. Similarly to groups like the ACU, they emphasized the importance of open dialogue and pluralism. Eltit recalls:

> From the beginning, it was really a question of addition. Someone would say, "I want," another would say, "to eat," and another would say, "sandwich." Another would say, "you all would like a sandwich." There was not much specialization in anything. I know that might seem difficult to understand but really it was a collective work, very conceptual.[46]

The dialogue as method of creation becomes, under dictatorship, a transgressive act of democratic citizenship, by which social creation is generated in a pluralist process. While CADA's work was inspired by international artists creating participatory art, such as Wolf Vostell in Germany and Marta Minujín in Argentina, their project is clearly influenced by the interdisciplinary, politicized artistic groups forming in Chile throughout the second half of the 1970s. The decision to call their works "actions," emphasizing the political stakes and vulnerability of their engagements, underlines how CADA's shared political purpose gave their work an *a priori* political instrumentalization, from which the aesthetic of the action emerged. The politicization of their work contrasts with the regime's efforts to depoliticize both art and citizenship.

According to Eltit, the name CADA emerged out of a desire to convey the collective nature of the group's work. The full name, Colectivo Acciones de Arte, conveyed the organizational nature and medium of the work, while the acronym CADA provided an element of anonymity and created an open space in which content could proliferate.[47] The dual meaning of the word *cada* as "each" and "every" contains a tension inherent in egalitarian pluralism. "Each" allows for a retention of individual identity—an acknowledgment of hegemony and representational identity—while "every" conveys a broad inclusivity. When used as a signature, CADA is both inclusive of the specific members of the group and retains each individual identity, but it can also be read to include the spectators and citizen collaborators involved in the process of the group's unfolding actions. The tension between the individual and collective implied by the dual meaning of "cada" positions the art action as the product of an agonistically pluralist process in which the integrity of the individual is respected as it contributes to a larger structure and is therefore also part of a collectivity.

CADA's collaborative process is also evident in the formal elements of its actions. The multiple components of *Para no morir de hambre en el arte* fragment the work—it cannot be experienced as a totality—and bring multiple areas of the city together.[48] That these neighborhoods ranged from upper-class Vitacura to working-class La Granja further underscores the universal-individual duality inherent in the word "cada" and Mouffe's concept of agonism. While the regime fostered private, elite culture, CADA sought to bring Santiago's poorer neighborhoods into a community through art making. CADA's efforts were thus part of a larger project within the alternative cultural sphere of reconstituting an artistic, politically conscious civil society.

Additionally, *Para no morir de hambre en el arte*'s use of various mediums gives the work a polyphonous nature, literalized in the recording of "No es una aldea" in five languages. This speech explores the agonistic tension between individual and collective life. It calls for a new conception of human existence, one with great political urgency given the violence of the Pinochet regime:

> It is not a village, the place from which we speak, it is not only that, but rather a location, where the landscape, like the mind and like life, are spaces to amend. We are not talking about a forgotten place, or a place poorly remembered many times, but rather of the life that is shaped [by that place], of each [*cada*] sign that structures the life that is shaped. Each [*cada*] human life in the cut-off wasteland of this Chilean country is not only a way of dying, it is also a word, and a word within a discourse. To understand that we are also a word to be heard is to understand that we are not here just to face death.[49]

The speech rejects atomization, provincialism, and the idea that the structures of existence are fixed. It emphasizes collective humanity through the interconnectedness of structures, lives, and words, as well as the contingent nature of experience on earth and human vulnerability. Although the speech is generally referencing death, considering the violence experienced under Pinochet, it is also a call for solidarity and a confrontation with, rather than acceptance of, death.

The speech continues, asserting the aesthetics of political life and calling listeners to a creative engagement with their lived experience: "To correct life is a work of art, which is to say, it is a work of social creation of a new sense and a new collective form of life. The production of life and not of death: we are speaking of this as the only meaning that the words art, science, politics, and technique can have for us."[50] The interdisciplinary work calls for a more *human* interdisciplinarity required by the production of life. The community is both enlarged and fragmented by the translation of the speech into five languages. The translations expand the sphere of comprehensibility to an international audience, and this underscores the text's claims to a universal human purpose. By playing the recording in front of the CEPAL building, CADA positions the speech as a call for international recognition and ethically obliges the international body to respond (either by ignoring the action or engaging with it). But the translations also fragment the community of listeners, separating them through the distinct linguistic iterations of the speech. It thus performs a linguistic pluralism that is itself an agonistic double move: it champions pluralism while also highlighting the isolation and division that results from a multilingual world in which hierarchies of language are reified.

These theoretical and political expressions are reinforced by material components of the action. In requesting the return of the milk bags for inclusion in an exhibit, CADA sought to combat social isolation and build a community connected through caretaking and art making. The nurturing, subsistence-level symbolism of the milk is also layered with the political symbolism of Allende's presidency, policies, and suicide. Allende had striven to radically reorient the Chilean economy, pursuing policies to improve the welfare of Chile's poorest citizens. Among these policies were food distribution programs—specifically, the distribution of milk to families with children. The distribution of the milk bags hearkens to this policy, this care for Chile's poorest, but also conjures up memories of the larger loss of Allende and what his presidency promised.

As the military besieged the presidential palace, Allende addressed the Chilean people over the radio, vowing not to resign. He concluded with a call to continue the fight for his legacy:

> Surely Radio Magallanes will be silenced, and the calm metal of my voice will no longer reach you. It does not matter. You will continue hearing it. I will always be with you. . . . Workers of my country: I have faith in Chile and its destiny. Other men will overcome this dark and bitter moment in which treason seeks to prevail. Go forward knowing that, sooner rather than later, the great avenues will open again where free men will pass through them to construct a better society.[51]

Shortly after this speech he took his own life. Daniel Mansuy contends that the combination of the speech and suicide constitutes a powerful political act in which Allende created a mythology of his presidency as a movement to be resurrected for the people to construct a better society.[52]

The distribution of the milk evoked the memory of Allende and what he came to represent, and it highlighted the lack of caretaking by Pinochet's government. These layers of meanings connect the philosophical to the political and to the exigencies of daily survival. It was a micropolitical

Fig. 2. A member of CADA distributes milk bags in *Para no morir* . . . Archivo CADA, donated by Lotty Rosenfeld and Diamela Eltit in 2016. Courtesy of the Museum of Memory and Human Rights, Santiago, Chile.

act of resilience—carrying the dreams of the socialist Left forward despite their attempted annihilation. The exchange of milk bags was an act of life-sustaining care, an attempt to awaken a political utopianism and criticality, and an invitation to creatively collaborate in the exchange of caretaking and art making (see fig. 2).

CADA invited other artists to engage with the theme of hunger both in and outside of Chile. In Bogotá, Cecilia Vicuña performed *Vaso de leche*, an art action in which she tied a red string to a glass of white paint and spilled it onto the pavement with a pull. Next to the milk she wrote a poem in chalk, asking: "The cow / is the continent / whose milk / (blood) / is being spilled / What are we doing / to our lives?" The connections between these works demonstrate the participatory dimensions of CADA's creative invocation, and how their collectivity operated in generative ways, creating a larger dramaturgical constellation marked by collaboration, intersection, and transformation. Here, Vicuña, from exile, takes up the symbolism of the milk to situate CADA's provocation about caretaking and sustenance in the Colombian context, where several thousand children had died from milk contaminated with paint due to corporate malfeasance. In this piece, as well as several others, Vicuña's work intersects with CADA's to demonstrate the expansive possibilities of CADA's collective, participatory dramaturgy and to speak to the experience of exile as well as to unique local contexts.[53]

Similarly, the *Hoy* ad was a creative invitation. The text called readers to *imagine* the white or blank page, to imagine Chile as that page, and to imagine that Chile was deprived of life-sustaining milk. This invitation, and its placement in the magazine, prompted a broader community of readers to engage their imaginations to contemplate Chile's care. Implicit in the ad's text is an ethical call to responsibility. For after imagining Chile deprived of sustenance, it remains to imagine how it could be otherwise.

Para no morir de hambre en el arte operated through a dramaturgy that produced meaning through complex intersections: of creative process, of aesthetic form, and of its situation in the social and political field. Whereas Pinochet sought to depoliticize public space and isolate Chilean citizens, CADA repoliticized art making to reimagine and pursue the production of life. It called citizens to creatively engage in the world and modeled a practice of citizenship that was collaborative, plural, and guided by an ethic of mutual care. The group's interdisciplinary, agonistic dramaturgy developed in response to the interrelationship of political urgency and alternative cultural networks responding to that urgency. It emerged in a repressive, dictatorial environment within which it both innovated and was dependent on the structures it sought to subvert: in other words, it was fundamentally contingent.

Censorship, Contingency, and History: *Inversión de escena* and *¡Ay Sudamérica!*

Throughout the dictatorship, artists faced multiple modes of censorship.[54] Since culture was subject to the market, the regime used it as a vehicle to exercise ideological control, which it did through a legally justified and arbitrary imposition of taxes that rendered performances, books, or exhibitions financially prohibitive to their potential audiences.[55] In more direct and intimidating forms of censorship (the exile and torture of artists, destruction of spaces or artistic works), the government also followed a somewhat arbitrary logic, contributing to a climate of pervasive danger.[56]

It is therefore not surprising that when CADA approached the magazine *Hoy* for *Para no morir de hambre en el arte*, its editors were cautious. CADA originally proposed printing a blank, white page, with only its signature in the lower right-hand corner. However, the editor was anxious about publishing a page without content and refused.[57] The editor's refusal illustrates how pervasive the culture of censorship was: *Hoy* opted to censor not objectionable content but the absence of content. It also highlights the transgressive power of empty spaces in a society in which the hegemonic strategy is to construct the image of regimented order. To work around these constraints, CADA incorporated its failure to secure the page as desired into the work itself, and the call for readers to imagine the blank page emerged. CADA thus highlighted its own lack of agency and the curtailment of even empty expression while also demonstrating its ability to creatively transcend that failure.

In nearly all its actions, CADA's dramaturgy was marked by its negotiation of its dependencies—on the urban environment, on the Pinochet regime—and by an effort to reveal the contingencies therein, both as a challenge and call for collective community. Mouffe's recognition of hegemony as ever present involves a simultaneous recognition that it is ever contestable: it always depends on surrounding structures and it could always be otherwise. Agonism marshals the tension of hegemony's contingency to remake hegemony again and again.

By highlighting multiple aspects of contingency within society, artistic works might, as Shannon Jackson puts it, "provoke reflection on larger systemic assemblages."[58] In addition to provoking reflection, by foregrounding contingency, artistic works model how such relations might be reformulated. Such revelations are particularly potent in cities, in which social and infrastructural dependencies exist at high density. Furthermore, the revelation of contingency is particularly subversive in the context of a dictatorship that grounded its legitimacy on a sense of its own necessity or inevitability.

CADA's actions required a great deal of coordination and cooperation with both willing and unwitting parties and provided a means for the further revelation of contingency. By considering its interventions "actions," CADA drew attention to the entire process surrounding its works. Therefore, the social dependency predicating these actions was as crucial an element of CADA's dramaturgy as any "object" it produced. This dependency functioned agonistically, challenging the regime's isolation of its citizens as well as highlighting the contingencies of the regime's "order." Furthermore, it modeled how one might creatively engage with the repressive apparatus rather than simply take one's place within it.

On October 17, 1979, CADA staged a parade of ten Soprole milk trucks for *Inversión de escena*. After driving through Santiago, the trucks parked in front of the Museo Nacional de Bellas Artes (National Museum of Fine Arts) (see fig. 3). They covered the entrance of the museum with a large piece of white fabric in a gesture that both literalized the regime's culture of censorship and turned spectators away from the museum, suggesting that the real art was in the streets. To realize this action, CADA had to engage in deception. To acquire the trucks, the group persuaded the manager of the Soprole dairy company of the aesthetic beauty of the trucks parading through the city. When the company executives later realized that they had been complicit in a politically critical work, they tried to purchase the video documentation of the action to hide their participation. Failing that, they changed the logo on their entire fleet of trucks—an extreme reaction that highlights the potency of the image and the danger of political protest.[59]

Fig. 3. Milk trucks lined up in front of the National Museum of Fine Arts. Image: Archivo CADA, donated by Lotty Rosenfeld and Diamela Eltit in 2016. Courtesy of the Museum of Memory and Human Rights, Santiago, Chile.

The second part of this action also required coercion. To cover the facade of the art museum with the cloth, the artists needed to use the flagpole in the front of the museum. According to Rosenfeld, they knew that the museum director would be out of office on October 17 recovering from surgery, so they selected that day to execute the action. When they began to use the flagpole, they were confronted by museum guards. The artists explained that they had the director's permission and that they were honoring the museum's centennial. The guards could not check with the director since he was home, so they allowed them to proceed.[60] Though spectators would not have been privy to the deception required to stage the action, the unusual nature of the images might have prompted an awareness that transgressions were taking place, and word of mouth may have alerted them to the mischief behind them. The process of executing the actions disrupted the city by highlighting its contingency, upending the social structure by embarrassing those in authority, and demonstrating the agency that resulted from creative disobedience.

The cloth in *Inversión de escena* highlighted the contingency of censorship. The museum represented the elite institutional art apparatus. By hanging the white cloth (again conjuring milk imagery) in front of the museum's entrance, CADA executed a double move. First, it alerted spectators to the presence of censorship. Second, Richard points out that in blocking the museum entrance, CADA executed an inverted censorship of the national institutional art apparatus that prompted spectators to focus their creative engagement on the street.[61] This image, like many of CADA's complex metaphors, has a polyvalent function. Not only does it challenge the regime's notion of culture, but in framing the city itself as art, the action prompts an estrangement of spectators from both city and museum. In addition to calling attention to censorship, it highlights both the ways the regime has aestheticized life and the immanent artistic capacity of city dwellers. The city's residents become both the objects and creators of art, as well as subjects and active citizens. The role they take on is contingent on their subjectivity and complicity.

In its 1981 action, *¡Ay Sudamérica!*, CADA executed an even riskier engagement with infrastructural authority. This action required the recruitment of pilots with access to planes and permits to drop pamphlets throughout Santiago, a delicate task given that municipal authorities were not likely to be sympathetic to critical artworks (see fig. 4). Eltit considers this task itself part of the work:

> Obtaining permission was part of the work, because it seemed impossible that the Chilean air force would give us permission to take six airplanes that were going to drop pamphlets over the city of Santiago with an anti-dictatorial proclamation. It was almost unthinkable! . . . Therefore, having these mind-boggling conversations with people in the mayor's office, and convincing them to allow it, that was already a work of art. When the airplanes flew it was a miracle. . . . This was so subversive, but really subversive and crazy, because the permission had to be given by the authorities.[62]

To get permission, they situated themselves within the artistic elite, foregrounding their international fine art bona fides to appeal the regime's cultural priorities. In a letter to the Dirección de Aeronáutica, Rosenfeld emphasizes these elements: "Said work is situated within the category of ecological arts. The tradition of land art, or ecological art, practiced mostly in Europe, the United States and Japan, works with and within the landscape. Following this artistic line over the last two years, CADA has been invited to many international biennials representing Chile."[63] To bolster their high art affiliations, they also submitted letters to the Aviation Office from the Contemporary Art Institute vouching for the importance of their work.[64]

The surprising combination of complicit individuals required to execute the action was not lost on observers at the time. In *Hoy*, Ana María Foxley describes the logistics required by the action: "The Office of Aviation had given permission to fly, the armed forces permission to film and photograph from the air, and the municipality issued the permission to drop the pamphlets. Mayors, municipal secretaries, pilots, policemen, workers, and

Fig. 4. The planes used to drop pamphlets in *¡Ay Sudamérica!* Image: Archivo CADA, donated by Lotty Rosenfeld and Diamela Eltit in 2016. Courtesy of the Museum of Memory and Human Rights, Santiago, Chile.

artists collaborated together in the course of an artistic activity realized by CADA."[65] This odd assortment would have tied that community together but also introduced a rupture by coercing institutions linked to the military government to participate in a subversive action.

Another tactic CADA used to highlight contingency and combat the narratives and structures of the Pinochet regime was the exploitation of the unique presence of the past in the urban imaginary. Andreas Huyssen contends that the city is an unstable palimpsest, where physical traces and historical memory interact with the urban landscape.[66] The urban palimpsest is a temporal manifestation of agonistic plurality. This interaction of the materiality of the urban space with its imaginary via the subjectivity and memories of its citizens uniquely situates the urban as immanently agonistic. The regime's efforts to striate space, control bodies, and rewrite memory as a narrative pointing toward a single end (the stability and prosperity of the dictatorship) ran counter to agonistic politics to the unique temporal situation of the urban.

One of CADA's resistant tactics made frequent use of the city's relationship to time by invoking historical memories and then challenging that history by connecting those memories to new possibilities. Not only did the regime police present political engagement and citizen subjectivities, but it also policed the past—reframing the history of the coup as salvation from a socialist crisis.[67] CADA challenged that narrative. By returning repeatedly to the milk promised by the Allende government, CADA evoked its nurturing symbolic connotations alongside its continuing political valence within Chile's history. If a key tactic of Pinochet's regime was to cast the Allende period as a time of famine and chaos, repeatedly referencing this milk punctured the regime's version of history, illuminating instead a history of social caretaking and support, undermining Pinochet's claim to power. Other actions reimagine violent histories to reclaim the past for the future: the milk trucks parading through city streets in *Inversión de escena* may conjure images of advancing tanks, and the planes flying over Santiago in *¡Ay Sudamérica!* resurrect memories of the planes that bombed La Moneda. But these trucks carry milk and the planes drop utopian pamphlets, highlighting that even these acts of violence do not have predetermined outcomes. These images challenge old memories and create new ones, a layering that suggests that historical memory and trajectories can be reconfigured, as can the social order.

In their actions CADA conjured memories of the past, punctured the present, and acted into the future. Such actions contrasted those of the military regime, which sought to enforce a regular temporality through the policing of bodies in space with bans on public assembly and constantly shifting curfews. By inserting its art actions into the public space of the city, CADA contested the regime's domestication and privatization of the population and the cultural sphere. The instrumentalist politicization of these actions also repoliticized the public space that the regime had worked to vacate of politics.

CADA used the characteristics inherent to the urban environment to rupture the image of the orderly quotidian that the regime sought to perpetuate. Spectators might have only experienced part of CADA's actions. They might have seen a parade of milk trucks or witnessed planes flying overhead. They might have experienced it as ephemeral, as a present fleeting into the past and fading into memory. They might not have been able to clearly "read" CADA's symbols, but they might nevertheless have experienced a rupture or inversion—visually, spatially, and temporally—in the orderly image of the city and in that way might have become aware of its contingency.

Radical Negativity's Double Move: *No +*

CADA's work grew bolder in response to changes in Chile's political landscape.[68] In 1983 and 1984, as Chileans were increasingly willing to protest, CADA staged *No +*, an action many members of the group consider to be their most significant.[69] For this action, members of the group, along with other associated artists, would write the phrase "No +" on

Fig. 5. *No +*, hung on the banks of the Mapocho River. Image: Archivo CADA, donated by Lotty Rosenfeld and Diamela Eltit in 2016. Courtesy of the Museum of Memory and Human Rights, Santiago, Chile.

walls throughout Santiago. Then they, or other citizens, could complete the phrase with declarations of resistance to Pinochet's regime, such as "No + dictadura," "No + tortura," "No + desaparecidos" (No more dictatorship, no more torture, no more disappeared). As graffiti or banners multiplied throughout the city, the work was both permanent and ephemeral, simultaneously contributing to the plurality of the urban palimpsest and highlighting contingency. In one iteration, CADA hung a banner that read *No* + and an image of a gun over the banks of the Mapocho River in central Santiago (see fig. 5). In the video documentation of the action, the banner itself is striking, but even more so is the moment the police remove the banner and are thus incorporated into the work. Those passing at this moment would have witnessed the presence of multiple worlds in a single moment: the world in which the banner hangs freely and the world in which it is removed in an act of censorship. The action thus demonstrated the contingency of the present moment.

The action's many iterations also highlighted the relationship between contingency and radical negativity. In Mouffe's formulation, radical negativity is the acknowledgment of the contingency of hegemony and the constant process by which that hegemony must be critiqued. Furthermore, Mouffe's radical negativity does not operate as an isolated move. Since agonism acknowledges that hegemony is ever present, it allows the rejection to exist alongside the articulation of an alternative. Similarly, CADA's dramaturgy operates both as a rejection of the regime and an invitation to spectators to reframe their subjectivities as citizens and creatively engage in restructuring their lives and the world. CADA dramaturgically manifests the process by which an agonistic order would function.

The apparent simplicity of the rejection of Pinochet in the *No +* action belies a more complicated, expansive move. In many instances CADA did not sign its inscriptions. Both the action's simplicity and CADA's relinquishment of authorship invited spectators into a collaborative community. It allowed them to think creatively, to conjure their own rejections. In the open-ended call to engaged reactions, spectators were brought a step closer to imagining the reconstitution of a new order. The simplicity of *No +* meant that it was an easy formula for citizens to reproduce, which they did on walls and banners throughout Santiago. It provided a medium and language by which a plural, agonistic community could develop.

Many of CADA's longer texts also employ the generative capacity of rejection. The speech "No es una aldea" departs from an initial rejection—"It is not a village"—to create an expanded space whereby resistance might be possible. The pamphlets dropped in *¡Ay Sudamérica!* echo many of that speech's themes. This text also resists atomization and suggests solidarity through negation, asserting a way of thinking that goes beyond individual occupations and forms the basis of more collective ways of being. The pamphlet states, "And nevertheless we say, we propose today, to think of ourselves in another perspective, *not only* as technicians or scientists, *not only* as manual workers, *not only* as painters or montage artists, *not only* as filmmakers, *not only* as workers of the land." The collective dream they envision is one of joy, in which all work to expand the space in which life is lived. Anyone who works toward this spatial, and mental, expansion is an artist: "'We are artists, but every person who works for the expansion, even if it is mental, of the spaces of life is an artist.' Which means that we talk about work in life as the only creative form, and that we speak as artists. No to the fiction in the fiction."[70] The final sentence in this passage suggests the contingency and unreality of the society constructed by the regime and a rejection of its aesthetic formulations. Spectators and artists must instead strive for the creation of new forms of reality, which can only be achieved through the amplification of physical and mental space.

With *No +* CADA initiated an action that has become part of the dramaturgical constellation of Chilean protest. The combination of rejection and creative invocation was a tactic used a few years later by the No campaign in the lead-up to the 1988 plebiscite.[71] As I will explore in chapter 2, the coalition of opposition parties turned the rejection of Pinochet into an open, pluralist, positive vision of the Chilean future. It did this out of necessity—this was the position to which they had been assigned by the terms of the 1980 constitution. But by using the rejection as a creative, collaborative inspiration, the No campaign created a positive ad campaign that significantly contributed to the successful overthrow of the dictatorship. Since then, the No + inscription continues to echo on walls and protest signs throughout Santiago, renewing the call to radical negativity: a no reverberating hopefully with the history of the dictatorship's end.[72]

CADA's Afterlives

In 2017, on one of my final days in the archive at the Museum of Memory and Human Rights, I met Miguel Angel. In his adolescence he had participated in Santiago's underground punk scene. He came of age during Pinochet's dictatorship, frequenting clandestine parties and music venues, cultural centers, and performance events. Shortly after our meeting, it became apparent that his memories of this time were vivid and overflowing, and one line of thinking spun off into another as he tried to reconstruct the complex network of cultural resistance to the dictatorship. As he whispered to me animatedly in a half-hearted attempt not to disturb the other researchers, he kept repeating,"Estuve allá." I was there. For him, this was not a story of suffering and trauma—though his reminiscences were not without these darker elements— but of enthusiasm and pride at having been part of such a vibrant, diverse, and innovative cultural scene.

Our conversation continued after the archive's closing, as we walked through Barrio Yungay in the cold evening air. Miguel Angel led me to Avenida Portales 2615, the current home of Centro Cultural Taller Sol, a cultural center that opened in August 1977 and remains active to this day. We were invited in by one of the center's members, who described the center's current activities (performances, writer's groups, an anarchist school), emphasizing its autonomy and self-management. It had survived without any financial support from the government—"not a single FONDART"—a political stance and a source of pride.[73] Instead, the center's member described a budget cobbled together through performances and parties, book sales of tiny, banned communist texts, passing the hat, and barter—an economy of solidarity.

We were interrupted by the center's director, the visual artist Antonio Kadima, and his tall and gregarious friend, who, when introduced to me, immediately proclaimed that he had been a member of the MIR and a tortured political prisoner, and that Kadima had saved his life years ago by giving him a place to hide from the military police.[74] When it became apparent that we had not brought anything to eat, we were chastened and sent back out for bread. Not long after, we were drinking tea and eating marraqueta and cheese, discussing underground, popular, and elite performance circuits, political torture, and Chile's current cultural policy. The *apagón* (a journalistic term coined during the dictatorship to describe an ongoing "cultural blackout"), Kadima asserted emphatically, was a lie, and the artists I mentioned being interested in were only the "tip of the iceberg."[75] He proceeded to describe the center's archive upstairs. It was an archive of resistance, in contrast to the archive of memory I had been visiting a few blocks away.[76] The difference, he said, is that "theirs is an archive of death and ours—well, there is death and suffering too—but ours is of perseverance, of resistance."[77]

Resistance, perseverance, independence, vitality, pride, solidarity, and refuge: for my companions that evening, these were the dominant qualities their recollections of dictatorship culture evoked. CADA's work reflected many of these qualities, but Kadima cautioned me not to let my focus on their work overshadow the heterogeneous field it emerged out of. He was wary because CADA's aesthetic influence in Chile has, since the fall of the dictatorship, become canonized and in some ways hegemonic. In the third edition of her essay collection, *Márgenes e instituciones: Arte en Chile desde 1973*, Richard reflects on the canonization of CADA and the escena de avanzada, brought about in part by her work. She acknowledges the movement of these artists from the margins of the anti-dictatorial struggle to a place of institutional centrality.[78]

Many of CADA's members went on to have highly successful, institutionally embedded careers. In the early 1990s, during the first years of the democratic transition, Eltit served as a cultural attaché in Mexico. Since then, she has solidified her reputation as a renowned novelist and teaches one semester every year at New York University. Rosenfeld continued her work as a visual artist, for which she received numerous grants and awards and participated in international exhibitions and biennials, until her death in 2020. Zurita was also appointed cultural attaché to Rome during Patricio Aylwin's presidency, has taught at Chilean and US universities, been granted two Chilean honorary doctorates, and received many awards for literature. They are politically outspoken and able to wield their cultural and moral authority to significant effect. As these accolades and activities demonstrate, CADA's members have navigated a transition from margins *to* institutions. They voice resistance through positions of cultural, moral, and institutional authority.

Further, CADA's work was not without real, democratic limitations. Indeed, many of these limitations, as well as much of their success, can be attributed to their ability to appeal to official understandings of culture. They emerged out of, and made use of, an elitist milieu that fit the dictatorship's vision of cultural production, which was tied to its vision of authoritarian democracy. They were university-educated artists of European descent with enough resources to implement their actions. They often made use of their elite art connections. Though they did seek to reach residents of marginalized neighborhoods in their actions, this was a largely unidirectional process. Their work went into the poblaciones, rather than emerging from the *pobladores* (residents of the poblaciones). Furthermore, CADA's work was intentionally obscure and contained the possibility for multiple readings, a tactic that did open a space for a kind of pluralism but that was also an aesthetic that perhaps made it inaccessible or incomprehensible to individuals unused to reading such forms. In addition, their work's ephemerality and localization (which allowed them to avoid censorship) diminished its accessibility and, arguably, impact.

I do not wish to undermine the significance of and very real danger present in CADA's democratic dramaturgy, but I do wish to point out that political performances function in a dialectical relationship against that with which they rebel, and therefore, they are always also on the verge of their own demise. These dialectical relationships establish a horizon of democratic possibility. Tony Fisher notes that agonism allows for precisely these failures: "One way its radicality emerges is in the way that such a conception compels us to confront the dimension of the political as precisely bound up with the inherent possibility of failure insofar as it embraces the ambiguity and the exigency of human action."[79] By focusing on the plural and the processual, agonistic practices of art making or citizenship allow for the inevitability and multiplicity of temporary failures.

As a consideration of CADA's work has shown, the aesthetics and form of its actions were inextricably tied to the conditions in which they were produced. CADA's agonistic dramaturgy highlighted this fact and demonstrated the possibilities for creative agency within the heavily regulated world of the dictatorship. But not only did it demonstrate possibilities, it invited their proliferation, complementing the group's collectivity with collaborative calls to its spectators. In Zurita's assessment that it showed "what could be done," the efficacy of CADA's work lay in the action's intervention in visible, public space. However, this was not a closed or predetermined efficacy; the conditional possibility implicit in the word "could" positions its work as a point of departure, a springboard for other, undetermined interventions. Agonism allows for an efficacy that can be undone, binding efficacy and inefficacy together. Thus, CADA's dramaturgy highlights the interconnections between aesthetics, dominant structures of power, and the contestation of those very structures. In this way, CADA models a process by which the world might be creatively, democratically, and contingently remade.

Chapter 2

Dramaturgies of Reencounter

Andrés Pérez, *Convivencia*, and the New Body Politic

During the summer of 1988, in an open-air circus tent in Puente Alto in the southern outskirts of Santiago, audiences witnessed a joyful depiction of what it was to be Chilean. *La Negra Ester*, performed by Gran Circo Teatro (GCT) and directed and adapted by Andrés Pérez from a poem by Roberto Parra, depicted the love story of the picaresque musician Roberto and the beautiful prostitute Ester in the port city of San Antonio in the years prior to World War II (see fig. 6). Populated by a motley cast of characters and incorporating popular music and verse forms, the play displayed a distinctive dramaturgy that critics hailed as initiating a new phase in Chilean theater. Following its brief run in Puente Alto, *La Negra Ester* transferred to the city center, on Santa Lucía Hill, where audiences watched the love story unfold as the sun set over Santiago. There, *La Negra Ester* played to sold-out crowds. The company subsequently embarked on national and international tours. Since then, more than six million spectators have attended the play, making it the most viewed work in Chilean theatrical history.[1]

La Negra Ester was an ebullient play for an ebullient time. Two months prior, in October 1988, Pinochet had been defeated in a plebiscite intended to legitimate another eight years of his rule. But instead, for the first time in twenty years, Chileans would vote for their president. To accomplish this feat, the coalition of opposition parties ran a campaign based on the promise of happiness.[2] Their slogan, "Chile la alegría ya viene" ("Chile, happiness is coming"),[3] was a self-fulfilling prophecy: the campaign's victory brought the happiness it had promised. *La Negra Ester* tapped into this festive spirit, as well as the desire for a new, more inclusive body politic.

Amid this festivity, however, there was uncertainty. Many wondered whether Pinochet would cede power to the elected government. Even after the Christian Democrat, Patricio Aylwin, assumed the presidency in 1990, the country remained divided, and Pinochet and the military remained

Fig. 6. Rosa Ramírez, Boris Quercia, M. José Núñez, Alejandro Ramos, Pachi Torreblanca, Ximena Rivas in *La Negra Ester,* 1989. Design by Daniel Palma, José L. Palma, and Andrés Pérez. Photo: Jorge Brantmayer. Courtesy of the Brantmayer Photography Collection, Archivo de la Escena Teatral Universidad Católica, Santiago, Chile.

a powerful force. Furthermore, Pinochet's government had relied not only on the military but on numerous civilians to function. These civilians would be working and living alongside those whom the dictatorship had repressed. The new president found himself with a complex citizen constituency and limited ability to enact change. In response to these pressures, Aylwin opted for a strategy of gradualism and consensus building, or *convivencia*—a term Steve Stern defines as "living together in peace."[4] Casting himself as the sacrificing, ever-rational father figure, Aylwin promised to guide the Chilean family to democracy and justice *en la medida de lo possible* ("to the extent possible").[5]

In this chapter I explore the relationship between artists and the state as it developed through the process of redefining democratic Chile. Whereas CADA and the countercultural artistic milieu working during the dictatorship had a clearly resistant relationship to the Pinochet regime, the relationship between artists and the state became much more complex in the early years of the democratic transition. In the first part of this chapter, I chart the way artists and politicians allied in a project to defeat the dictatorship and rebuild Chilean democracy. In this process they construct a "dramaturgy of convivencia," which is evident in political performances as well as in Pérez and Gran Circo Teatro's *La Negra Ester*. As it is manifest in *La Negra Ester*, the dramaturgy of convivencia reflects the Concertación's efforts to reconceive citizenship, facilitate national reconciliation, and shore up the fragile democracy. This dramaturgy is framed around a joyful sense of reencounter with the nation and features a nostalgic celebration of a distinctively Chilean popular culture.

However, as Aylwin's phrase "to the extent possible" suggests, there were limitations to convivencia as a democratic principle. While the dramaturgy of *La Negra Ester* would align with these constraints, in later work Pérez would challenge them, bringing him into conflict with the Concertación. In the second part of this chapter, I examine the limitations of convivencia and turn to the ways Pérez's dramaturgy shifted in later projects: plays, parties, and countercultural performances, as well as efforts to economically sustain his art making. In these works, a disidentification at the heart of Pérez's dramaturgical project becomes apparent, which recasts some of the same dramaturgical tactics present in *La Negra Ester* into a more resistant and socially transformative dramaturgy. Whereas the Concertación sought to marshal the dramaturgy of convivencia in support of a patriarchal, capitalist, and heteronormative status quo, the reencounter Pérez staged revealed a very different possibility for Chile: a Chile that was hospitable to the flourishing of queer lives, that allowed space for politics and contentious memory, and that did not alienate artistic life from artistic work.

This chapter interrogates what the extent of the possible was for citizenship during the transitional moment and the dramaturgical mechanisms by which these possibilities were imaginatively transformed. In my analysis, I make three interrelated claims. First, I contend that the relationship between Pérez and the state reveals the patriarchal, heteronormative, capitalist ideology at the heart of the new state's vision of democracy and citizenship. This resulted in a cultural policy fundamentally aligned with artistic works, not artistic lives—a distinction that would have tragic consequences for Pérez. Second, an analysis of the dramaturgy of convivencia demonstrates how artists like Pérez helped to create the dramaturgical aesthetics of this ideology at the same time as they developed tools to challenge it. Finally, by engaging with Pérez's later works and rereading this dramaturgy as a mode of disidentification, we glimpse the possibilities it opens for solidarity and queer world making.

Redefining Democracy and Culture

La Negra Ester premiered in the period between the 1988 plebiscite and the installation of democracy. It offered a new vision of citizenship precisely when Chileans sought to turn the page of the dictatorship. Beginning with the campaign in opposition to Pinochet, the parties that would head the transitional government worked to reframe citizenship and promote national reconciliation, a project reflected not only in policy but also in political performances and discourse, establishing many of the conventions of the dramaturgy of convivencia.

The regime had set in motion its own remarkable end. The constitution of 1980 had been intended by the government to institutionalize authoritarian rule. Among its requirements was that a 1988 plebiscite would determine whether Pinochet would continue in office: a "yes" vote would prolong the dictatorship for eight years, whereas a "no" vote would require democratic elections the following year. As Stern has noted, those in the Pinochet regime had never meant the plebiscite to be a genuine contest. Instead, it was intended as a performance to confer legitimacy on the dictatorship in front of a national and international audience.[6]

For twenty-seven days prior to the vote, each side was given fifteen minutes of television airtime between 10:45 and 11:15 P.M. The campaigns produced short programs, or *franjas*, combining news broadcast, political advertisements, musical performances, and comic sketches. The late hour of the broadcast was selected to minimize viewers. Nevertheless, the franjas garnered unexpectedly high ratings. On the day of the plebiscite, the No campaign carried 54.7 percent of the vote.

The television programs were the mass media complement to years of resistance, protest, and grassroots organization. The No campaign's success required voter mobilization and poll watching, as well as citizen participation. Nevertheless, the franjas, watched by nine out of ten Chileans, significantly influenced the election, particularly in rural areas not reached by on-the-ground opposition efforts.[7] They therefore represented a key site in which the opposition articulated its vision for Chilean democracy. They also represented the first collaboration between the soon-to-be-elected government and the cultural sphere.[8]

Though the opposition won the plebiscite, the military ensured that it would retain influence in Congress and that Pinochet would remain commander in chief of the military. When Aylwin won the 1989 presidential election, he faced significant obstacles to democratic reform: a divided nation, a right-leaning judicial system and legislature, and Pinochet's continued official and symbolic power.[9] As Aylwin's administration set about the difficult task of governance, it worked to redefine Chilean democracy. In one of its first major events, on March 12, 1990, the new government held a massive inaugural celebration, called the Acto Nacional. Seventy thousand people filled the National Stadium—a former center of detention and torture—to witness the performance. The event culminated in a speech in which Aylwin articulated his vision of Chilean democracy. This vision, guided by convivencia, was like the No campaign: joyful, inclusive, and in pursuit of social justice and repair.

Toward a Dramaturgy of Convivencia

Through political performances such as the 1988 plebiscite and the Acto Nacional, a dramaturgy emerged in support of Aylwin's project to establish convivencia. A key feature of this dramaturgy was an emphasis on joy and festivity. This began with the No campaign, which cast the election as fundamentally about affect, specifically *alegría*: "joy" or "happiness." The campaign's slogan, "Chile la alegría ya viene," tapped into a widespread longing after years of repression. The slogan framed a positive ad campaign, which incorporated colorful imagery, music, and comic skits to promise a Chile in which citizens could freely express themselves and live together joyfully.[10] When Aylwin assumed power in 1990, the Concertación continued to emphasize alegría in its performances. The Acto Nacional was billed as a "fiesta por la democracia" (party for democracy). Hundreds of performers staged an ebullient series of skits, songs and dances, including a rendition of Beethoven's triumphant "Ode to Joy."[11]

The Acto Nacional also provided the opportunity for Aylwin to discursively define the new democracy, a task he connected directly to alegría. In his speech he declared,

> This is Chile: The Chile we long for, the Chile for which so many throughout history have given their lives; a free, just, and democratic Chile. A nation of brothers. We come together this afternoon with hope and alegría. With hope because we have finally begun, with a fraternal spirit and with longings for liberty and justice, a new stage in the national life. With alegría because—for the first time in twenty years—we have embarked on a path that we ourselves have consciously and voluntarily chosen. . . .[12]

In this invocation he linked alegría to a new beginning and nostalgia as well as to collective free choice. He thus framed alegría as part of Chile's history and the democratic sovereignty of the people. Alegría was both an end itself and a by-product of freedom and democracy.

In addition to staging alegría, the performances of convivencia represented a more diverse vision of Chilean culture than had been advanced by the dictatorship. The first episode of the No campaign's television franja began with the construction of a rainbow as singers sang, "Chile, happiness is coming." Once the rainbow was complete, the word "No" was written in bold letters in front of it. In this opening section, the campaign established its fundamental tactics. The rainbow implied the celebration of difference—the potential for pluralism—and the hope at the end of a storm. In the campaign's rejection of the dictatorship, it did not define a practical platform for the future, focusing instead on the affective desire of alegría. The campaign promised a hopeful future in which there might be a space for diversity and difference.

After the campaign's teaser, the newscaster Patricio Bañados appeared.[13] He explained that this was the first time in fifteen years that the opposition had a national media platform. His very presence reminded viewers of his own marginalization throughout Pinochet's regime. By reintroducing bodies into spaces from which they had been excluded, the campaign altered the paradigm of public discourse. It challenged the exclusions that prevailed during the dictatorship and modeled the possibility that viewers might participate in the public sphere. The franjas featured Chileans from a broad range of backgrounds, including rural workers, women, and Indigenous people. This reframed the composition of the public sphere. Chileans across the country might have seen someone to whom they could relate and whose inclusion might encourage them to vote.

The Acto Nacional also emphasized this pluralism. Part of the performance consisted of an origin story, invented specifically for the performance, that depicted the convergence of multiple rivers. Through a series of vignettes, the performance incorporated regional and ethnic identities and included Mapuche, Rapa Nui, and Andean music and carnival, popular traditions, contemporary dance, circus, and the appearance of Chile's two most important soccer teams. As one scene transitioned into the next, the artists hugged each other, embodying the new culture of convivencia. The performance represented a Chile that was pluralist and multicultural, as well as artistically driven and diverse, festive, and warm.

Following the individual performances, the entire cast sang, "Chile, nuevamente Chile." The nuanced connotations of "nuevamente" as both "again" and "anew" evoked the idea that Chile was both returning to its past and being reborn. An enormous Chilean flag was unfurled as the orchestra played the national anthem. In its performance the anthem constituted a site of revision and reencounter. During military rule, the regime had incorporated a verse into the anthem extolling the strength of the armed forces. In this version, however, the lyrics were restored to their precoup version.[14] The rendition of the anthem thus constituted an expression of patriotism, a break with the regime, a new beginning, and a return to Chile's national past. This gesture would contribute to an overall narrative in which the dictatorship was framed as anomalous in Chile's history.

Ultimately, the Acto Nacional constructed a narrative in which pluralism coalesced under the paternalistic leadership of Aylwin. After the group performances, a young girl came onstage with her mother. She approached Aylwin and gave him a box containing poetry (the national literature), a seed (the future), and a mirror (so Aylwin could see his reflection). Aylwin hugged the child and her mother warmly, conveying the image of the ultimate father figure embracing Chile's vulnerable, hopeful, and innocent future.

In his subsequent speech, Aylwin was clear that convivencia was not to operate agonistically but was instead a consensus that must subsume differences.[15] Social conflicts—and even social justice—that threatened that consensus were to be avoided. The Concertación's goals were measured and in many ways in continuity with the military regime's, including economic growth, the restoration of Chile's international standing, liberty (with order), and social justice "to the extent possible."[16] By acknowledging that he would cater to the constraints of the "possible," Aylwin ensured that the dictatorship's legacy would continue to influence politics.

Aylwin's understanding of convivencia sought to preserve the status quo through consensus and was not open to contentious politics. Aylwin blamed the coup on ideological commitment, writing that political slogans, such as that of Allende's Unidad Popular, "replaced rationality, tolerance and disposition toward dialogue."[17] Aylwin rejected strong ideological commitments in favor of gradualist, consensus governance. Thus, while the No campaign hinted at the possibility of a potentially agonistic pluralism, the pluralism Aylwin envisioned was fundamentally depoliticized.

Toward a New Cultural Policy

This official dramaturgy of convivencia carried over into the Concertación's cultural policy, influencing the structures and resources available to artists. In both the No campaign and the Acto Nacional, artists and cultural workers collaborated with the political sphere in some of the most visible expressions of the new democracy. Arturo Navarro, an early architect of Chile's cultural policy, argues that the campaign provided artists—many of whom had been operating on the countercultural margins—with a new place of prominence in the cultural and political life of the country.[18] Through their participation in the No campaign and the Acto Nacional, artists contributed to the construction of the new government's vision of democracy. They shaped a vision in which artistic expression became a right and expression of Chilean citizenship.

As early as 1990, Aylwin called for the development of an official cultural policy that reflected values linked to convivencia: specifically, he hoped to incentivize a broad range of cultural expressions, to further the development of popular culture, and to facilitate broad and equitable audience access.[19] Throughout the 1990s the government established the fundamental building blocks of Chile's current cultural policy. In addition to the goals expressed above, the government and the cultural workers they collaborated with, wary of both authoritarianism and the directed culture of the Allende era, sought to establish a horizontal rather than vertical model of cultural management. This horizontal model slowed the centralization of cultural institutions, eschewed a strongly directed cultural effort, and favored public-private funding structures.[20]

The first task—of "incentivizing" creativity—took the form of financial support through a "mixed model."[21] To encourage private support of the arts, the government made cultural donations tax exempt and created the opportunity for private-public partnership in cultural financing. The government also resurrected a dictatorship-era program, FONDEC (Fondo Nacional de Cultura, National Culture Fund), which funded artistic projects the government deemed enriching to national heritage. Under the 1992 Budget Law, the Concertación renamed the program FONDART and created a system for artists to apply for state support of individual projects.[22] The fund was administrated by an advisory council of cultural managers and artists. Rather than providing artists with long-term, institutional, or developmental support, FONDART employed a capitalist logic carried over from the dictatorship that focused on individual works, rather than artistic careers, and subjected artists to a competitive adjudication system.[23]

During this period the government also founded the first cultural center: the Centro Cultural Estación Mapocho (Mapocho Station Cultural Center). The center, a converted train station, was managed under a private-public model, marking the first time a public building came under nongovernment control. This center, and the others that followed (Matucana 100 [2001], Centro Cultural Gabriela Mistral, or GAM [2010]), operated primarily as performance venues and producing organizations and could only support the short-term development of artists working on individual productions.

In this incipient cultural policy, there were a few logics at work. On the one hand, as in the dramaturgy of convivencia, there was a valorization of popular culture, of reclaiming public space, and of democratizing access to culture. On the other hand, there was a desire for a horizontal, private-public institutionality that funded works via the capitalist logic of competitive contests and developed institutions allied with but independent from the state. This latter aspect of the transitional government's cultural policy was an attempt to break with the authoritarianism of the dictatorship but was also a continuance of the dictatorship's neoliberal reorganization of the economy—an example of the ways neoliberalism came to be linked to notions of democratic freedom. This early cultural policy was thus emblematic of convivencia in its efforts to establish a more democratic society while also retaining many of the dictatorship's structures and policies.

Andrés Pérez Araya

Born in 1951 in the far south of Chile, Pérez came of age in a changing political and cultural landscape. In 1970, he enrolled at the University of Chile, when university theaters were experimenting with collective creation. In 1972, he married the actress Rosa Ramírez, in a short-lived romantic relationship but a long-term artistic collaboration. On September 11, 1973, the day of the military coup, Ramírez gave birth to their son. The dual tumults—of parenthood and political upheaval—led Pérez to take a hiatus from university.[24]

When he returned to the University of Chile in 1975, he participated in the performing arts. He joined the Teatro Itinerante in 1977, a traveling theater company administrated by the Catholic University and financed by Pinochet's Ministry of Education and the Banco Concepción. The company primarily performed classic plays. But its director, Fernando González, found ways to transcend official constrictions, staffing the company with young artists inclined to experiment. The company toured the country, reaching audiences with limited access to theater. Participating in Teatro Itinerante, Pérez encountered some of his generation's most important theater artists.[25] He also developed an interest in a visual and corporeal theater that spoke to popular audiences.[26]

In 1980, Pérez left Teatro Itinerante to dedicate himself to street theater.[27] Incorporating pantomime, mask, and other circus techniques, Pérez and his collaborators adapted classic texts into a theatrical language that could be read by large audiences on urban streets. Later, Pérez recalled, "One of my greatest theater schools was having worked making theater in the street, out of a necessity that was as much economic as it was political. This world of urgency, this permanent contact with the reality of citizens, with their contradictions, taught me the beauty of the present."[28] Working in the street, Pérez honed a dramaturgy directly related to theater's social function and an active relationship to citizenship.

During a performance in Santiago, the French cultural minister, Claire Duhamel, was impressed by the company's promise. She offered Pérez a grant to study with Ariane Mnouchkine and the Théâtre du Soleil in 1983. With Mnouchkine, Pérez encountered a company that rehearsed consistent hours, had a clear rehearsal process, operated via a structured hierarchy, and had a space in which to work. Pérez was struck by how the company's professionalism was made possible by the cultural support available in France.[29]

Pérez returned to Chile to vote in the 1988 plebiscite.[30] Upon his return, he marshaled his artistic talents in the service of his citizenship. He directed an interdisciplinary performance called *Sí-No* (Yes-No) in Bustamante Park. The performance, which involved over one hundred artists in various disciplines, emphasized the significance of the vote—depicting the choice between "yes" or "no" as a choice between death and injustice or peace and liberty.[31]

The success of the No campaign ushered in another artistic and cultural sea change in Chile. While the end of the dictatorship had long been a dream of resistant artists, it also led to an artistic identity crisis. There was no longer a clear enemy to oppose, and the fall of the Berlin Wall meant there was no socialist utopia to which to aspire.[32] This led many artists who had been actively resistant to the dictatorship to enter a period of reflective silence. Some companies disappeared; others eventually returned with a focus on their "classic" works.[33]

Some younger artists, who had spent time during the dictatorship in Europe, navigated the transition more easily. They formed theater companies that, like their predecessors, sought to avoid a text-based, realistic theater, but did so in works that dehistoricized and denationalized social conflicts, advancing a "universal" vision of the popular and incorporating international influences, particularly from France.[34] Such companies included Laura Pizarro, Jaime Lorca, and Juan Carlos Zagal's La Troppa, Mauricio Celedón and Claire Joinet's Teatro del Silencio (Theater of Silence), Alfredo Castro's Teatro la Memoria (Memory Theater), and Andrés Pérez's Gran Circo Teatro.

Pérez's artistic formation was forged within institutional structures developed prior to and during the dictatorship. He began his artistic work in a theater culture that had a strong sense of political commitment and that emphasized experimentation. Following the coup, Pérez worked under the constrained conditions of the dictatorship and within networks of countercultures, adapting classic texts and developing theatrical languages to evade the repression of the regime. His work abroad exposed him to new aesthetics, rehearsal processes, and the institutional supports required to create such work—experiences that shaped his expectations for cultural policy. When he returned to Chile, it was to participate as a citizen—a role that he would enact not only as a voter but also as an artist.

La Negra Ester

Upon his return from France, Pérez reconnected with his former collaborators, among them the actors Willy Semler and María Izquierdo. He proposed that they develop a play based on the nineteenth-century Chilean president José Manuel Balmaceda (1840–1891). Balmaceda's political reforms led to conflict with Congress, civil war, and his eventual suicide—a history that could be read as analogous to that of Allende. However, Semler and the others were resistant to doing a work with contemporary political resonance. Unlike Pérez, who had had respite from the dictatorship in France, they were exhausted from living under the military regime. Semler said to Pérez:

> Look, it's just that we, and this country, have had enough of political theater, man . . . democracy is coming, or at least the

> unstoppable fall of the [military] regime, and we are exhausted, man. We've been doing guerrilla theater for more than ten years [and] we have been talking about the same themes during all this time and we want to liberate ourselves from this thing.[35]

They longed to do something joyful, and they told Pérez, "We want to do a story of love, man."[36] Semler then described a project the group had worked on the previous year, a theatrical adaptation of Roberto Parra's poem "*Décimas de la Negra Ester*."[37] Intrigued, Pérez met with Parra and the two began developing a stage adaptation. The group started rehearsals, and six days after the plebiscite, on October 11, 1988, they founded the company, the Gran Circo Teatro.

Initially, GCT planned two months of performances in different neighborhoods, financed by the French Cultural Embassy and the personal savings of company members.[38] As was the case with Teatro Callejero, the performance was shaped as much by necessity as by an aesthetic vision. Gustavo Caprario, a "man of the circus," lent them a tent and other props, providing the show's primary aesthetic frame.[39] The only space they could obtain was a plaza in Puente Alto, a neighborhood far outside the city center. According to one of the play's producers, Andrés García, "The project consisted of twelve itinerant performances in various *comunas* in Santiago; if we did well, we could think about having our own tent, and perhaps traveling."[40] The show indeed did well. It transferred to the center of Santiago, where it performed to sold-out audiences. It subsequently embarked on national and international tours, performing in major cities and venues, as well as in public spaces and towns that rarely hosted theater.

In its very inception *La Negra Ester* reflected the dramaturgy of convivencia. It was shaped by the collaborative input of the company—a collaboration marked by their relationship to the dictatorship, the politicization of the cultural sphere in which they worked, and the practical circumstances that conditioned their resources and possibilities for production. Many of the play's collaborators longed for a joyful creative process to escape the repressive environment of the dictatorship. Like the architects of convivencia, the artists rejected a legible politicization; the coming democracy instead heralded an opportunity for citizens to reencounter each other on a more affective level.

La Negra Ester depicts the story of Roberto, a traveling musician who loves a prostitute, Ester. At first the penniless Roberto struggles to win her over, but eventually the two fall in love. However, Roberto's alcoholism and attempts to make a living in spurious pursuits lead him to abandon Ester. After his family confronts him with his love for Ester, he woos her more seriously. However, she is in a relationship with an abusive client, Lacho. Roberto challenges Lacho, and during their ensuing knife fight, the *transvestite* prostitute, Esperanza, intervenes and is killed at Lacho's hand.[41] Following Esperanza's death and the departure of Lacho, Ester tells Roberto that she longs for a more stable life with the kindly, widowed shoemaker, Barahona. Recognizing that he cannot give Ester what she needs, Roberto arranges the match and attends their wedding. Later, pulled by nostalgia, Roberto returns to San Antonio, where he learns that Ester has died, presumably from a broken heart.

Much scholarly and theatrical criticism of *La Negra Ester* situates the play as a theatrical "phenomenon" before and after which Chilean theatrical history would be divided.[42] Juan Andrés Piña, María de la Luz Hurtado, Marco Antonio de la Parra, and Sergio Pereira Poza attribute the play's significance to its recuperation of the popular and marginal into a conception of the national.[43] De la Parra writes, "It has become a kind of national reliquary, where it had to necessarily change our aesthetic, ethical, and even ideological ideas, where our language, our idea of country, our conception of mankind was revised."[44]

While much scholarship on the play verges on the hagiographic, others have grappled with the ideological contradictions of the play. Boyle suggests that the play's depiction of the popular provided a pluralist challenge to the transitional government's attempts to bring the story of the dictatorship and the transition to democracy into narrative coherence,[45] whereas Juan Villegas suggests that Pérez "has constructed . . . a theatrical poetics concomitant with national social changes . . . and that corresponds, at the same time, to the cultural policies of the hegemonic sectors of society and the Chilean policies of reconciliation and national agreement."[46] Cristián Opazo concurs with this assessment, but adds nuance to the argument by considering *La Negra Ester* within the context of Pérez's larger body of work, noting the tension between official support for *La Negra Ester* and official relinquishment of support in the case of his later work.[47] Anna Harcha Cortés emphasizes that *La Negra Ester* is a hybrid work that draws from a number of understandings of the popular, and that the hegemonic alignment critics like Villegas perceive does not stem from apolitical complicity but is instead a form of pluralist micropolitics that must be understood within the context of the play's development in the repressive environment of the dictatorship.[48]

I build on the arguments of Harcha, Villegas, and Opazo to consider the ways *La Negra Ester* corresponds to the cultural priorities of the transitional government. In many ways, the play operates via a dramaturgy of convivencia. Key aspects of this dramaturgy include an affective emphasis on alegría; a nostalgia for an earlier Chile that must be reencountered alongside an idealization of the future; a democracy that incorporates popular and marginal sectors in its self-definition; an understanding of democracy based on consensus and gradualism and that rejects that which poses too significant a challenge to the status quo; a democracy that is guided by a self-sacrificing, rational, paternalist leader; and finally, a desire to restore Chile's international standing. *La Negra Ester*'s enactment of the dramaturgy of convivencia helps to explain the play's extraordinary success and status as the emblematic theatrical production of the transition.

Alegría, Festivity, and Reencounter

As the No campaign promised, a spirit of joy swept through Chile following the plebiscite and infused every aspect of *La Negra Ester*'s dramaturgy. Ramírez, who played Ester, recalls, "It was like part of this panorama of 'happiness is coming' "[49]—linking the play directly to the No campaign's slogan. As in Aylwin's discourse, this joyfulness was connected to a deep human need and a reencounter with the Chilean nation. Pérez conceived of festivity as a profound expression and experience of one's humanity. He explained, "I want and conceive of a theater that has anthropological information about the human soul, of its emotions, its fears and joys. A theater that is a party of the spirit . . . a popular theater in which neither the soul nor the body are forgotten."[50] For Pérez, fiesta was connected to the popular and was part of both the corporeal and spiritual aspects of human existence.

The play's alegría began with the rehearsal process. Pérez recalled that "we had a great time, we had a joy in creation."[51] Post show partying was a fundamental element of the play's life, as well as part of the cast's practice of self-care. Accordingly, he told the theater critic Eduardo Guerrero:

> I said to the actors that we would later end the shows so that we could go party afterward. When the play was in performance, the work finished around eleven at night, and from there we would go to life as well, because that is another form of caring for ourselves. . . . The best aspect of *La Negra Ester* is that it was a show made in total joy, without any expectations and with long nights of partying.[52]

The show's ebullience emerged from a joyful creative process that characterized not only the work of rehearsals but also of self-care. Partying was a liberatory and necessary practice of one's rights as a citizen in a society that, until recently, had been marked by repression.

Audiences attending *La Negra Ester* also participated in this practice of festive, communal self-care. Performed in public spaces, the play was a social event. Long, twenty-minute intermissions (rare in Chilean theater, especially when performances needed to end before curfew) and food and drink vendors offered audiences opportunities to socialize. Though the sociality of the play took on a different tenor based on where it was being performed at the time, the festive spirit remained. In Puente Alto, for example, the performance provided a unique local event for a community to assemble, facilitating an exceptional festive space in areas underserved by official cultural circuits. At Cerro Santa Lucía, the play required a pilgrimage to a site outside of one's usual circulations—not to mention a long wait in line—heightening the audience's sense of camaraderie. No matter where it was performed, the show provided the opportunity to exercise the right to assemble in public spaces, a practice of democratic citizenship curtailed during the Pinochet regime.

Though this social atmosphere was intended by the company, it was heightened by serendipity and the continued need to navigate the military regime's bureaucratic infrastructure. According to Semler, Pérez initially wanted to perform in a park just outside the National Museum of Fine Arts. However, the Pinochet-appointed mayor of Santiago, Gustavo Alessandri, disinclined to give the play a central location, instead offered the Terraza Caupolicán, on Cerro Santa Lucía, on the condition that GCT not say anything against the military government.[53] At the time, the hill was a marginal space populated by sex workers and drug users. Yet it had been a key site in the founding of the city.[54] Attending the show provided audience members with an opportunity to reencounter a historic site and reconstruct a historic national imaginary. It also provided a beautiful backdrop for the play. Semler ascribes the success of the show, in part, to the serendipity of this setting:

> Our being placed there was part of the phenomenon. That is to say, pure coincidence was part of the phenomenon of [the show's] success, because the people had to make a pilgrimage. They had to arrive at a place that turned out to be very charming. We began the show when the sun was setting, and from the stands the people saw the sun setting over Santiago down below.[55]

The play's location, a critical part of its initial success, cannot thus be ascribed only to the artistic choices of Pérez and the company. Even after the 1988 plebiscite, artistic creation—much like Aylwin's policy of convivencia—remained contingent on the dictatorship.

Despite this contingency, the play's joyful tone broke with the oppressive atmosphere of the dictatorship. Like the performances at the Acto Nacional, the play's dramaturgy combined nostalgia and a popularly inflected nationalism in its joyful vision. At the play's opening, the band, consisting of Guillermo (Cuti) Aste, Jorge Lobos, and Álvaro Henríquez began to play the Chilean national anthem, situating the play in the tradition of the popular circus and as an expression of national identity—an "Acto de Chile" (Act of Chile)—in Pérez's words.[56] However, the anthem soon transitioned into an upbeat jazz *guachaca* that became the leitmotif of the play's protagonist, Roberto.[57] Played by Boris Quercia, Roberto entered with the jaunty walk-dance of an inveterate drunkard: knees together, movements hunched forward and lithe, hands grasping in front of him. Roberto's entrance undercut any seriousness that might accompany the anthem's gesture by transforming it into a fun, jazzy, *Chilean* party. Theater critic Juan Andrés Piña suggested this moment constituted a joke on the audience, leaving them unsure whether to respectfully stand or to sit and enjoy the performance.[58] This moment thus connected official Chile to popular culture, and by toying with the audience's responses to the anthem, established a jesting, participatory relationship with its spectators. Vicuña notes that the anthem's interruption also represented a transgression of the sacredness of national symbols, an act unthinkable prior to the 1988 plebiscite. Vicuña also contends that implicit in the transgression was that there was another future for Chile.[59] This was a simultaneously nostalgic, recuperative, transgressive, and future-oriented approach.

As with the Acto Nacional, in *La Negra Ester*, the anthem was a loaded symbolic gesture, a direct assertion of one's right to redefine the Chilean nation. Pérez explained:

> Yes [the reencounter with popular, critical Chile] was a necessity. Including . . . a moment in which we were discussing including or not including certain stanzas or beginning with the first chord and with the final chords and distorting them in between. It was our vision of Chile, what we believe ourselves to be, how we behave. That what could be recovered again. There is a very nostalgic idea in there too, that has to do with the truth: that if something once was, it could return to be, the good as well as the bad.[60]

The opening moment of the play thus established several dramaturgical tactics permeating the work: the idea that the national could be recovered, an inclusion of popular and previously marginal sectors of society in that conceptualization, an emphasis on joyful affect, and the participation of the audience in the project of redefining the Chilean nation.

Lo Popular: A Hybrid Sphere of Reencounter

The official dramaturgy of convivencia celebrated a more diverse vision of Chilean culture than under the dictatorship. In many ways, this idealized vision was plural and heterogeneous, mixing popular, regional, Indigenous, and European cultures. Similarly, *La Negra Ester* invited audiences to imagine a more inclusive Chile, one that celebrated popular culture and that incorporated previously marginalized populations in its vision of the nation.

The popular was the framework through which Pérez and GCT enacted their citizenship by reimagining Chilean society, and it was the principle through which Pérez invited audiences to enter that society. Pérez explained, "Our concept of contemporary popular theater . . . passes through the entirety of the theater's structure, from its production to the place where it should be done, the scenic design, the price of tickets, workshops in the locations where we present the work, [and] the integration of the environment in the atmosphere of the work."[61]

At its most basic level, the play's democratizing impulse was about the way the play was made accessible and legible to audiences and about the way citizens assembled in public space. By performing outside of traditional artistic circuits, GCT reached, according to Pérez, "sectors that had not seen the theater and that had fewer economic resources."[62] With affordable ticket prices ranging from 400 to 1,200 pesos (~US$0.70–US$2.00), these performances were accessible to those not only around the capital city but also throughout the country. On its national tour, the production visited areas far from the central metropolitan region where theatrical activity was concentrated.[63] According to Marie-Christine Rivière, the director of the Chilean-French Cultural Institute, "We want to make a theater that goes to the spectator, that inverts this usual situation. This is a much more democratic form of carrying out cultural production."[64] It put the spectator-citizen at the center of the play's dramaturgy and expanded the scope of who that spectator might be.

In addition to the company's desire to reach a broad audience, the desire to create a popular theater shaped the play's generic referents. As Harcha notes, the concept of the popular in Chile is a complex constellation at times equated with the national, the folkloric, the massive, and the marginal.[65] In *La Negra Ester* the representation of the popular traverses these categories, drawing from multiple influences to create a hybrid dramaturgy that provided numerous reference points through which spectators might relate to work. This gesture democratized the work on the level of access as well as on the level of representation, portraying an image of Chilean culture that is itself hybrid and broadly inclusive.

The play's primary generic referents—circus and melodrama—represented key links to a plural understanding of the popular. Both were flexible, hybrid forms. Chilean circuses not only encompassed traditional acts, such as gymnastics, contortion, and clowning, but also included folkloric performances, or pantomimes treating Chilean history or politics.[66] By incorporating elements of circus, *La Negra Ester* signaled that it was a place where the audience could reencounter its living national traditions.

The play's melodramatic plot also accounted for the show's broad appeal.[67] Jesús Martín-Barbero notes the "obstinate persistence" of melodrama in Latin America. He suggests that melodrama's endurance lies in its operations as a mediator between folklore and popular-urban spectacles.[68] Soledad Figueroa and Javiera Larraín emphasize the populist, democratizing impulse inherent to the melodramatic form.[69] Through the incorporation of both circus and melodrama, *La Negra Ester* becomes both an expression of and a vehicle for a popular culture that is tied to the marginal, the festive, and the plural.

The commitment to a popular theater also shaped the textual components of the play. By celebrating marginal figures as national types, the play reconfigured the image of Chilean society in more inclusive terms. This was a democratic impulse that implicitly supported the validity of marginal communities' claims to representation within society.

The text of the poem and the theatrical adaptation were written in *décimas*, a verse form derived from oral poetry prevalent in both rural and urban areas since the conquest.[70] Poetry's oral transmission allows for sociality, improvisation, and the incorporation of Chile's inventive vocabulary of colloquialisms and vulgar language. As a form it invites revision and world making. Pérez's adaptation of Parra's verse forms maintained the style and spirit of the décimas.[71] The play begins with Roberto describing Ester:

La Negra Ester cosquillosa	The ticklish Negra Ester
no aguanta la barreta	doesn't tolerate abuse
guen chancho bonitah tetah	good ass, pretty boobs
su carita como rosa	her face like a rose
como espiga de orgulloso	ike a proud stem
Pero no le vale nada	but it's not worth anything
porque está muy deshojada	because she is leafless
como la pana en Otoño[72]	like a grapevine in autumn

The text thus establishes the local dialect (the h's added to the ends of words, such as "bonitah"), as well as its colloquialisms and vulgarity, propelled by the popular meter of the décimas.

The play's score also incorporated popular forms, including the jazz guachaca and the *cueca*—a musical genre linked to the national imaginary. Though origins of the cueca are unclear, by the nineteenth century it was firmly established in the country where it developed in cantinas and taverns.[73] The dance is thought to depict the mating ritual between a rooster and a hen and has a wide variety of regional iterations. Pinochet declared it the national dance of Chile in 1979,[74] and the "official" cueca became, according to Harcha, a form that was "sterilized, neutralized, its vocabulary and texture politically correct."[75] Nevertheless, unofficial versions of the cueca continued to be danced, and it became a site of revision during the dictatorship and transition.[76] Perhaps the most notable revision was the *cueca sola* (cueca alone)—a version that was performed in both the No's television campaign as well as in Aylwin's Acto Nacional. This version was first performed in 1978 by members of the Association of Family Members of the Detained and Disappeared.[77] In the cueca sola, a woman danced alone wearing a picture of her disappeared family member, as a chorus of women, also wearing photos of the disappeared, sang elegiac lyrics. The dance—known as a courtship partner-dance—emphasized the absent partner. It became a powerful expression of personal and collective loss, danced as an act of resistance during the dictatorship, and as an act of mourning and healing during the transition.

In *La Negra Ester*, Gran Circo Teatro also reinterpreted and reclaimed the cueca, yet in more festive fashion. One of the play's composers, Cuti Aste, explains:

> We revived the cueca . . . not the cueca that you heard on television or in mass media, because that was a cueca, a cueca of the boss. That was the cueca the dictatorship used to show the typical language of Chilean patriotism. It wasn't the cueca of the people, it wasn't the cueca of the country, it wasn't the original cueca.[78]

The play incorporated popular renditions of the cueca. These included the *cueca chora*, the *cueca brava*, and, according to Aste, the "cueca of the prostitute with her short skirt and high heels."[79] Incorporating these versions of the cueca was a both nostalgic and revisionist gesture, finding in the country's musical traditions alternative versions that contain the potential for resistance to Pinochet's understanding of culture.

This recuperation of cueca forms also represented a pluralist vision, in which multiple variations could be included in the national repertoire. This pluralism was further advanced by the score's incorporation of other popular musical forms including tangos, boleros, Peruvian waltzes, polkas, and foxtrots. Juan Pablo González writes that the music "shows Chile as a mestizo country, where the foxtrot meets the cueca, and poetry goes hand in hand with scribbling. There could not be a wider or more real identity reference for a nation that needs to believe more in its own achievements and to find within itself its destiny and reason for being."[80] This mixing was tied to a sense that a lost past could be recuperated. The show musically reinforced the sense of a Chilean reencounter by incorporating popular songs. At times these songs were diegetic, allowing the audience to sing along. The music fostered the sense of reencounter, a sense of pluralism, as well as a sense of community.

Throughout *La Negra Ester*, the "popular" served as a multimodal category through which the national community could be reencountered and reconfigured. For Pérez, marshaling the popular constituted a dramaturgical tactic by which he and the company enacted a vision of their own citizenship through a process of reimagining the nation, an exercise of their right to construct, imagine, and reencounter Chile on their own terms.

For its citizen-audiences, the company's commitment to the "popular" allowed for greater access on practical, representational, and interpretive levels. Audiences had easy and affordable access to the play and—via the play's festive, social atmosphere—to their own communities. The play also provided multiple frames of reference through which spectators engaged with the work—they might have seen someone like themselves onstage, recognized a poetic or musical form, or had familiarity with a particular genre. The play thus invited many different publics into an inclusive community that celebrated marginality, folklore, and pluralism. In this way the play's dramaturgy aligned with the official dramaturgy of convivencia, in which a more inclusive, popular, and heterogenous understanding of culture replaced the ordered, authoritarian, and elite official culture of the dictatorship.

The Paradoxes of Convivencia

However, it is important to note that this broader inclusivity was carefully calibrated not to disturb the ideology of the patriarchal, heteronormative nation-state. The dramaturgy of convivencia marshaled the popular toward multiple ends: as a democratizing impulse, but also in the maintenance of a status quo that enforced certain exclusions. Both the play and Aylwin's policy privileged unity and reconciliation over a democratic politics that risked contentiousness. The universalizing focus of convivencia thus contained within itself significant democratic limitations, particularly regarding rights claims that might challenge the patriarchal, heteronormative status quo of the nation-state. I turn now to the contours of these contradictions to illuminate the ideologies at work in elevating *La Negra Ester* to a status emblematic of both Pérez's work and newly democratic Chile more generally. The inner contradictions at work in this dramaturgy underscore that democracy must be conceived of as an ongoing process rather than an end. This processual understanding of democracy in turn offers a clearer view of the dramaturgical transformations necessary to imagine and enact the alternative modes of citizenship and world making that characterized some of Pérez's later projects.

The play's title, *La Negra Ester*, translated literally as "The Black Ester," itself establishes aspects of the play's inclusive popular appeal while illuminating the hegemonic universalism at work in its formulation of the popular. *Negra*, meaning "black," is not here intended to suggest that Ester is racially Black, but is a descriptive term of endearment often used in Chile (and across Latin America) for anyone with darker skin or hair. As used here, the term might carry vague connotations of indigeneity and would map on to a class status that is poorer than someone with lighter skin or hair. The Negra Ester, the object of endearment, is a romanticized vision of marginality manifest in the idealization of the character of the prostitute Ester. However, it is important to note that these racial and economic connotations are vague precisely to foreground a mestizo identity rather than a specifically Indigenous or Afro-Chilean identity. As scholars such as Ezequiel Adamovsky have pointed out, the circulation of "negra" as a term of endearment erases racial differences and claims to representation in favor of a mythology of a national mestizo identity.[81] Whereas an acknowledgment of specific Indigenous identities, or the Latin American history of slavery, might call into question the foundations of the Chilean nation-state, mestizaje offers a racially inclusive concept on which the nation can be justified. Thus, in the play's title the popular is marshaled at once to create space for and lift marginal identities in a manner that neutralizes them into a mythos that in fact undergirds the very legitimacy of the nation-state.

In addition to erasing and co-opting Black and Indigenous identities into a universalized mestizaje, convivencia also advanced a distinctly patriarchal, heteronormative conceptualization of the nation. Pinochet's regime had linked homosexuality and gender nonnormativity to the ideological Left and had made it a matter of political persecution. The military aggressively policed gender norms, giving buzz cuts to male students who had long hair and requiring female students to wear skirts or dresses.[82] Though a nascent LGBTQ political movement had emerged in 1973, it was forced underground for the duration of the dictatorship, as with all other political activity.[83]

In the ebullience of the advent of democracy, as well as with the urgency of the AIDS epidemic, queer culture began to reemerge, and LGBTQ activist networks began to form openly. However, Aylwin was not keen to incorporate homosexuality or nonnormative expressions of gender into the Concertación's conception of citizenship. As Óscar Contardo notes, while Aylwin denounced discrimination based on sexual identity, he did not consider sexual orientation as a framework through which to consider individual rights, nor was he willing to express personal "sympathy" for homosexuality. Homosexuality was considered a "theme" or "problem," not a locus for rights claims.[84]

Because of convivencia's ostensible inclusivity, its exclusions were not always overt, operating instead via pressure, omission, and co-option. Aylwin's response to an artistic intervention at one of his campaign events is emblematic of this dynamic. In an event at the Teatro Cariola, Pedro Lemebel and Francisco Casas, as the performance duo Yeguas del Apocalipsis (Mares of the Apocalypse), interrupted the proceedings in jackets, heels, and corsets and carrying a sign that said "Homosexuales por el Cambio."[85] The goal of this interruption had been to insert homosexual identities into the space of political appearance and to locate gay rights as part of the human rights violated during the dictatorship. The vague campaign platitude "change" gained a potency when paired with the assertion of homosexuals as a political constituency, quite literally rejecting a perpetuation of the status quo and the current composition of the body politic. Following their interruption, Lemebel and Casas were quickly ushered off the stage. According to Lemebel, Aylwin applauded their appearance with good humor, mitigating its recognition as a rupture. However, he instructed the press not to report on the event, excluding the performance from the official record and rendering the action's aim—to become part of the postdictatorship political dialogue—mute.[86] Ironically, in a later analysis by the CNCA, the sociologist Bernardo Subercaseaux casts this event as paradigmatic of free speech in the new democracy, revealing the limited parameters by which the Concertación framed pluralism: an apparently good-natured tolerance of difference that it seeks to sweep under the rug so as not to upend the status quo.[87]

Like Aylwin's convivencia, although *La Negra Ester* reached broader audiences by performing in public, peripheral, and marginal spaces, its occupation of these spaces contained a logic of exclusion. This is present in the production's transformation of Santa Lucía Hill. When GCT installed itself in the park, it was a marginal space. However, shortly after *La Negra Ester's* performances began there, the park began to transform. Initially, those who inhabited the hill did not welcome the intrusion. García recalled,

> We didn't know the new challenge we were going to encounter was a tenacious opposition from those who inhabited the hill: prostitutes, delinquents, and drug addicts. But just as with Puente Alto, we negotiated with them, we spoke to them of the good of the project, we invited them to participate, and finally, we put them in charge of the security of the enclosure.[88]

The incorporation of the hill's habitués into the performance event is a complicated gesture. On the one hand, it is a well-intentioned attempt to avoid a one-sided act of gentrification. Yet gentrification was nevertheless the consequence: the participation García mentions is to provide, rather than receive, a service: the show's security. Just as the Concertación would later incorporate the interruption of the Yeguas del Apocalipsis into its narrative of cultural tolerance and free expression, the inhabitants of the hill are incorporated, but not in egalitarian terms. Instead, they are mobilized to transform the space, rendering it safer for audiences.

The hill was further transformed by the municipality. Pérez recalled, "The municipality of Santiago began to worry, they put in lamps, later they added a funicular. . . . The hill stopped being a den of thieves, the dark and dangerous place it was. The theater achieved a real urban and social transformation of the space, recuperating it for the people."[89] While Pérez correctly asserted that the show recuperated the space for "the people," making it hospitable to theater audiences, the category of "the people" here suggests certain exclusions. Pérez's and García's recollections privilege a culturally elite population, in which "the people" are theatergoers. Granted, this is a broader demographic group than would be present at many shows, but it is still a self-selecting population. On the other hand, those constituting the "den of thieves" are erased from an understanding of "the people," illuminating that how the show's inclusiveness excludes the "real life" versions of the characters *La Negra Ester* depicts.

The marginality and popular culture represented by the play ultimately did not unsettle the status quo. The characters who could most threaten it—the travesti Esperanza (who threatens gender normativity) and Ester (who threatens the Parra bourgeoise as a love match)—die. They are included in the world of the play but at its end have been tragically purged (and, in the case of Ester, reformed and reconciled along the way). Nor did the marginality represented by the play necessarily serve as a vehicle for a critique of marginalization. Vicuña notes that if the play were a realistic depiction of life in a San Antonio brothel, it would have represented the precarity of that life and its dangers in serious terms.[90] However, except for Esperanza's murder, the danger in the play is depicted comically. Instead, the play's depiction of its marginal characters functions more as a blanket homage to inclusiveness. Semler recalls, "It was important to introduce *La Negra Ester* to the public in terms of love and simplicity, in terms not of reform, but of reencounter with a vital and creative impetus."[91] Rather than face Chile's complex reality—a divided nation in which a dictatorship had been supported by a vast civic-military apparatus—there was a nostalgic call to envision an idealized, ahistorical Chile.

To achieve this love and simplicity and facilitate reencounter, official calls to convivencia asked Chileans to put aside social conflicts, including demands for social justice, that might threaten consensus. The emphasis on reconciliation over reform is a defining feature of *La Negra Ester*, which employed a carefully calibrated nostalgia to appeal to audience members across the political spectrum. The play's setting in the 1930s was distant enough so as not to provoke controversy. This time is framed as the time of the true Chile: before the country was engulfed in political strife.

Like Aylwin's rhetoric, the play's nostalgia is underscored by a belief a universal Chilean experience. This is scenically manifest in the open-air circus tent, conceived by Pérez "so that the characters would see the same sky as San Antonio over their heads."[92] This sense of universality was preserved by the play's interpretive slipperiness. Pérez links the play's openness to his understanding of the return of democracy. Now that the dictatorship was over, theater no longer had to be teleological in its aims. He maintained, "Recently, today, thanks to the plebiscite and the latest elections, I would say that, as a country and as a people, we are not accounting for the endings we want and the ones we do not want."[93] Accordingly, the plot of the play could be read in multiple ways. Stern suggests that in one reading Ester might be interpreted as Chile: she is betrayed repeatedly by men and requires someone to sacrifice himself for her so she can move toward redemption. In another reading, Roberto could stand for Chile: charming but irresponsible, he needs insight and maturity to grow. In any event, Stern notes that the cycle of betrayal and tragedy always leads to forgiveness and reconciliation, to food, song, and partying.[94] The return to joy would allow those who wished to ignore the darker elements of the play to do so and enjoy the entertainment. For his own part, Pérez demurred on interpretive questions, invoking, in the true fashion of convivencia, universality and nationalism. He stated, "It was typical of people to ask what the play's text meant: *idiot, what have you been thinking doing this to Negra Ester*. Who was Negra Ester? Was it all of us or someone in particular? It surpassed all of our capacity for analysis, I think, because it was concrete, it was universal, and it was Chilean."[95]

Aylwin felt that consensus could best be achieved when the country was guided by a self-sacrificing, paternalistic leader. At his inaugural address he promised to be "like a good father of the family that puts his utmost diligence, abnegation, and authority into laboring for the good and happiness of his people."[96] Just as Aylwin sought to achieve democratic convivencia through an ostensibly inclusive, paternalistically guided process of consensus governance, the play also enacted a collaborative, seemingly inclusive, yet at times paternalistic dramaturgy. Aste is adamant that the show's collaborative elements are fundamental to the play's character and success. He insists that the play should not be ascribed to Pérez's singular vision but viewed as a collaborative work.[97] Parra's text had indeed been shepherded into its theatrical life by Pérez, but also by Rojas, Semler, Izquierdo, Ramírez, and the rest of the cast. Nevertheless, Pérez did exercise a strong directorial vision and authority in his leadership of the company and the creation of the work, and paternalism found its way into the content of the play.

The rehearsal process was highly collaborative and constituted, in many ways, a "living together." The company worked long days and, in the style of Mnouchkine, ate common meals prepared by members of the company. This remained true for all of Pérez's rehearsal processes. The actor Cristián Soto, who frequently worked with Pérez (though not on *La Negra Ester*), relates the creative process directly to convivencia, which he casts in egalitarian terms:

> One of his great strengths was how he integrated a group into its own kind of convivencia of a marginal Chile. . . . In this way the common kitchen is part of a communion that strengthens a team,

> where actors, stagehands, costumers, scenographers were equal in terms of relationships, and certainly, they were responsible for carrying out the work.[98]

This equality extended to the actors' work with their roles. Each day the actors would improvise with text in hand, collectively creating the physical life of the piece. Initially roles were not assigned, and everyone tried each role. Such collaborations led to some of the play's most defining moments. For example, in rehearsal Semler played Ester, which led to the idea of including the travesti prostitute Esperanza in the cast—one of the play's most humorous and affecting characters.[99]

Ultimately, however, this collaborative environment—like Aylwin's Chile—was overseen by a strong leader in Pérez. Semler asserted that Pérez was unequivocally the director with the final word on the show. Ramírez described Pérez as "my professor, my guide, my teacher, my director."[100] Pérez asserted as much as well, suggesting that adhering to this role was part of the artistic maturation he had undergone while working with Mnouchkine. Pérez explained that this vertical structure was, in fact, inhibited by Chile's authoritarian government and more possible in a democratic environment. He described the lessons he learned in France:

> In Chile, we lived in such an authoritarian system that in our groups we rebelled against this by operating in a total democracy. This was a mistake. It is good to be an apprentice. Even in one's share of the economic participation. There will come a time when one will more fully participate in decisions and with money, but that has to do with the time that you have put in. Also, with the roles you play, because those are cooperative.[101]

Rather ironically then, working under democracy provided the pretext for a less democratic mode of working, including hierarchical financial structuring.

This paternalist structure also shaped the play's plot. The story is largely driven by Roberto's actions. When Ester does express agency, she chooses submission. When she decides to end her relationship with Roberto, preferring instead to be with the shoemaker, she tells Roberto: "I already love the New lover / one that is always by my side / I will respect the agreement / that puts conditions upon it / so that God will forgive me / I want a tranquil life/ I will not step out of line / I do not have pretensions."[102] Her decision to embark upon a new relationship involves renouncing her profession to conform to the social expectations of Christian womanhood. Marginality, though first celebrated, is incorporated into respectability. Furthermore, though it is Ester who makes this decision, it is Roberto who arranges the match with the shoemaker. He does this as a business transaction, assuring Barahona that everything will turn out well: "Then let's have a drink / let's have an agreement / that everything will come out precisely / I have accomplished my task / I say however / It is a safe marriage / It will not involve much trouble / I will be your witness / I tell you as a friend / That this is not a dark business."[103] Then, like a father giving his daughter away, he attends Ester's wedding with a sense of bittersweet self-sacrifice. The play is resolved not by conflict but by negotiation and reconciliation, by consensus. Like Aylwin sacrificing himself for the Chilean nation, Ester's redemption requires Roberto to make the rational, self-sacrificing gesture for the larger good.

By almost any measure, *La Negra Ester* was a tremendous success. At a time when Chileans desperately needed something to be proud of, when there was a desire to break with the country's most recent history, and the government sought to increase the country's international standing, the play provided a vehicle that could satisfy these desires. Critics praised the show, calling it "one of the most significant shows in the recent history of Chilean theater," "the biggest theatrical event in the last fifteen or twenty years," or "the most beautiful and innovative show in recent years."[104] Some remarked upon the play's ability to do the consensus-building work of Aylwin's convivencia. Eduardo Guerrero del Rio writes, "La Negra Ester has marked a milestone in the Chilean theater of the 1980s, it has injected vitality into our theater, it has achieved a large consensus (in and of itself always difficult) in a public that feels amazed at what it has witnessed."[105]

The play's success was reinforced by its international tours, which provided the show with a metric of success that intersected with the aim of the new democracy to restore its standing in the international community. In the press coverage surrounding the show, much was made of Pérez's time studying with Mnouchkine in France.[106] It gave his work an elite cache in Chile, and his travels were represented as a national triumph. For example, Anita Klesky wrote, "There [in France] our compatriot triumphed and returned to apply what he learned here."[107] Similar language pervaded journalistic descriptions of the show's tour. Headlines such as "Andrés Pérez: From the Street to the Conquest of the World"[108] and "La Negra Ester Conquers Europe"[109] cast the show's tour as one of conquest, a kind of Chilean cultural colonization.

Many directly linked the play's success to the restoration of democracy. A 1990 headline from *Fortín Mapocho* proclaimed, "With the Gods of Theater and Democracy, 'La Negra Ester' Will Keep Living Its Fiesta."[110] The show, cast as a transitional moment in Chilean theater, provided evidence that the country was, in fact, in transition. That it did so while displaying clear indicators of success (large audiences, long runs, tours) confirmed the success of the transition itself. Stern notes, throughout the period, a tendency toward *exitismo*, meaning an emphasis on and extreme pride taken in success. Though Stern is cautious about providing a reading of the period that imposes too much psychologization, he cites Marco Antonio de la Parra, who contends, "*Exitismo* has to do with a kind of manic repair of the sorrow of Chile. . . . The exitismo is the equivalent of saying 'all that we suffered has a meaning. We are good exporters, we are the best in something, we win.'"[111] Perhaps, then, some of *La Negra Ester*'s success stemmed from its ability to absorb the cultural anxieties around the conflict and fragmentation of the dictatorship period and assuage them with catharsis, joy, and reconciliation.

Alternative Dramaturgies of Citizenship and the Limits of Convivencia: *Época 70: Allende*

Following *La Negra Ester*, Pérez continued to have a well-respected career but never again achieved the same level of success or institutional support. Instead, he repeatedly tested the limits of the developing democracy. In his later dramaturgies he enacted a process of reencountering and reimagining Chile through its history, through the free expression of sexual identities, and through a push for artistic agency and self-management. The official response to these moments demonstrated the limitations of the Concertación's conceptualization of democracy to reckon with history, be inclusive of identities that might threaten the patriarchal, heteronormative status quo, and create the structures to support the long-term artistic development of the artists.

As GCT embarked upon its next project—a historical investigation of the Allende presidency—Pérez sought an artistic home. He found the Teatro Esmerelda, an abandoned, early twentieth-century theater in the center of Santiago, which he and García got in working order, laying floors and wiring the electricity themselves. After the success of *La Negra Ester*, Pérez had expected that they would easily obtain the financial support to maintain the patrimonial space, but this was not the case. Pérez maintained that after they renovated the theater, the whole neighborhood transformed, much like Santa Lucía Hill. The area was better lit, children played in the streets, and a dance club opened next door. However, they never received state support, so Pérez took out an enormous loan and the company had to rely on ticket sales, personal financing, and fundraising to pay the rent and rehabilitate the space, all of which put the company in a precarious financial position.[112]

Since his return to Chile, Pérez had wanted to create a theater that was more directly engaged with politics. On October 2, 1990, GCT premiered its next play. *Época 70: Allende* was a collaboratively developed documentary piece tracing the period from Allende's inauguration to his suicide during the military coup. For this work they consulted sources across the

Fig. 7. A performance in the Fiestas Spandex, directed by Andrés Pérez Araya. Photo: Víctor Calzadillas, ca. 1990–2000. Courtesy of the Víctory Calzadillas Photography Collection, Archivo de la Escena Teatral Universidad Católica, Santiago, Chile.

political spectrum and relied heavily on verbatim text to construct the script. Though they did not seek to advance a political position regarding Allende's presidency, his very representation was contentious and fraught with emotion.[113]

Allende had a complicated relationship to the Concertación and in particular to Aylwin, who claimed to respect his democratic legitimacy but had been adversarial to his governance.[114] At the same time, he was a potent political symbol for the Left, a martyr and a lost ideal. Though Allende had urged Chileans in his final speech not to forget his legacy, as Tomás Moulian, María José Contreras and many others have pointed out, the Concertación had a vested interest in its forgetting.[115] The play's climactic moment consisted of a simple staging of Allende's final speech. This was a reencounter with the Chile that the Concertación did not wish to conjure: on the one hand, so as not to alienate the Right, and on the other because it was not the dream they were building upon. To depict Allende was to dissensually reintroduce a potent political figure into the space of appearance in a move that ran counter to a consensus aimed at leaving precisely that history behind (see fig. 7).

Época 70: Allende departed from the dramaturgy of convivencia by invoking the country's painful history. But this did not cause the play to be entirely unsuccessful: in Santiago and on tour it initially played to full houses. However, it received a very different, more politicized reception. Leonel Cornejo, a member of the company's production team, recalls:

> It was very strange because people came to the shows and filled the theater and Allende the character entered but it was Allende the president. And [the audience] applauded and shouted. Members of the Communist and Socialist Parties came . . . it became another thing. It was not a play; it was something else.[116]

Similarly, Aste recalls that in the northern mining town of Tocopilla they were met with a moving display of the flags of left-wing parties that had supported Allende and the UP. He remembers receiving the strongest applause he had ever heard in a theater, one that was qualitatively different from that of *La Negra Ester*, because it was "a political applause." However, Aste also maintains that "it wasn't the political moment to do it."[117] *Época 70: Allende* received largely negative reviews, with headlines calling it "distressing," "slow," and "strange."[118] Some questioned the wisdom of mounting such a divisive piece. Rosario Guzmán Errázuriz noted in her critique that it also received an official snubbing, writing that "some from the Concertación have shown a decided lack of interest in attending a play that . . . does not appear appropriate or opportune."[119]

More detrimental than the reviews, however, was the company's sense of vulnerability. A few months after the opening, in December, Pinochet and his son were embroiled in accusations of financial malfeasance.[120] In response, Pinochet ordered troops to report to their units within two hours on December 19. The presence of soldiers in the streets was a harrowing echo of the military coup, and many feared Pinochet was preparing to retake power. Aste recalled the military exercise sending the company into panic. Several members of the company met at his house to discuss what they would do, "because if Pinochet retakes power, which was something everyone was feeling . . . and we are doing a play about Allende, we are going to be the first ones shot."[121] Though Aylwin deescalated the situation, the mobilization frightened the company. At a meeting a few days later, the group decided to close the show.[122] The short life of *Época 70: Allende* illuminates the ways in which Chile was politically constrained and unable to confront its past.

The Fiestas Spandex

To boost the morale of the company, Pérez suggested they return to safer territory in the form of a Shakespearean double bill (*Richard II* and *Twelfth Night*). To do so GCT needed to raise money. They therefore turned to the repertoire of the dictatorship era's resistant solidarity economy. Inspired, in part, by the overnight parties at Ramón Griffero's Trolley, Pérez approached scenic designer Daniel Palma about producing a series of parties called the "Fiestas Spandex." The parties would be held on Saturday nights in May and June 1991, after *La Negra Ester* came down, and would continue until four in the morning. On a given night, anywhere from eight hundred to four thousand people attended the Fiestas Spandex. They paid an entrance fee of CLP 1,000 (roughly US$1.20 today), proceeds that would go to funding the costumes for their next shows.

For the most part, the parties staged a queer, disidentificatory agonism. As I outline in chapter 1, agonism is a process by which the contingency of existing structures and constraints is incorporated in a process of remaking those structures. In this way it operates complementarily to José Esteban Muñoz's concept of disidentification, which marshals contingency as a mode of subject formation. Muñoz posits disidentification as a process of identity formation in which the hybrid cultural logics that "undergird state power" are navigated and resisted in "subcultural circuits" that "strive to envision and activate new social relations."[123] It is a process of identity formation that is neither socially constructed nor essentialist, that resists fixed identifications and that is characterized by the ways minority subjects "work with/resist the conditions of (im)possibility that the dominant culture generates."[124] By enacting a number of disidentificatory practices, the Fiestas Spandex engaged in both a process of identity formation and a process of queering democratic citizenship that, working within the constrained conditions of possibility of the transitional period, would challenge the patriarchally guided, consensus-based vision of democratic citizenship advanced by the new government. When these disidentificatory practices fundamentally challenged the existing social structures, the new government censored the parties.

In staging the parties, Pérez and Palma applied a neoliberal capitalist logic (commodifying pleasure) to a problematic brought about by the absence of cultural supports engendered by a nascent neoliberal cultural policy that was itself the legacy of dictatorship. The agonistic, disidentificatory gesture arose from the way Palma and Pérez worked within the logic of what was available to them at the same time as they defied those conditions of possibility. By drawing from the repertoire of parties in opposition to the dictatorship, the Fiestas Spandex would have contained traces of a resistant stance. And although the parties were fundraisers, they staged a disidentification with a purely capitalist economy. No one was turned away at the door. Those who couldn't pay were put to work (the punks worked the coat check) or paid for by someone else in line. This led to what many recalled as one of the parties' most remarkable and democratizing aspects, or what Palma referred to as the "crazy mix" of people.[125] The parties were a heterogeneous, pluralist social space where difference was respected. At *Spandex* one might have encountered artists, members of the LGBTQ community, punks, new wavers, university students, socialites, entertainment professionals, and politicians. One of the parties' attendees, Ema Pinto, recalled that "it was incredible, in Chile there was no other thing, there will not be another thing like *Spandex*. It was the union of communities, and it was the concrete practice of respecting difference, of the respect of a punk dancing alongside a *cuico* with a lot of money."[126]

Unlike the parties at the Trolley, which were predicated on a shared sense of resistance, the Fiestas Spandex, like *La Negra Ester*, tapped into the transitional moment's spirit of alegría. Palma conceived of Spandex as a "party party party party party." The parties were ebullient because "we [were] a free country, a free society, alegría [was] coming and we [had] all of the marvelous future ahead of us."[127] That freedom manifested itself in free expression and a cathartic, corporeal release. Alcohol and marijuana were consumed openly and Palma described dancing and experiencing "the body as sensuality and the body as an object of pleasure" in a process of "democratizing the senses."[128] Accordingly, there was no set way to experience sensual pleasure. Cornejo recalled that "if you didn't want to dance you could go to the bleachers above, or be with your partner." Furthermore, "everything happening, in the open, as many gay partners as hetero and nothing was a problem. Living or seeing it was super nice."[129] The parties offered what Kemi Adeyemi, Kareem Khubchandani, and Ramón H. Rivera-Servera see as the promise of queer nightlife: "that feeling of being swept up in spaces and communities that make us believe in our bodies and affirm our desires" (see fig. 7).[130]

If the dramaturgy of convivencia staged the democratic transition as a Chilean reencounter with itself, the Fiestas Spandex also staged a reencounter. But unlike the nostalgic reencounter of *La Negra Ester*, this was a reencounter that fundamentally shifted one's understanding of the Chilean community. Palma recalled, for example, the joy he felt running into old friends at the parties and realizing for the first time that they were gay.[131]

Like the Chile imagined in convivencia, the Chile of Spandex was a heterogeneous community, but at the parties this community was constructed via disidentification. It was not the pluralist reencounter envisioned in *La Negra Ester* and the Concertación's political performances, nor was it the utopian community imagined in the nostalgic recollections of the resistant Left. Palma and Pérez rejected an aesthetic in which popular culture was equated with folklore, marginality, or economic precarity, favoring instead a cosmopolitanism. Palma recalls, "My primary requirement was I said I do not want that kind of *charango* [a small Andean guitar] thing . . . all the nostalgia of the coup, or this leftist aesthetic . . . goodbye . . . goodbye to that poverty thing." While the Acto Nacional had showcased folkloric performances, the Fiestas Spandex featured go-go dancers, drag performances, contemporary bands, and raunchy stand-up comedy (see figs. 8 and 9). The popular culture they drew inspiration from was not a

Fig. 8. Andrés Pérez prepares a performer in the dressing room at the Fiestas Spandex, 199?. Photo courtesy of the Víctory Calzadillas Photography Collection, Archivo de la Escena Teatral Universidad Católica, Santiago, Chile.

Fig. 9. A performance in the Fiestas Spandex, directed by Andrés Pérez Araya. Photo: Víctor Calzadillas, 199?. Photo courtesy of the Víctory Calzadillas Photography Collection, Archivo de la Escena Teatral Universidad Católica, Santiago, Chile.

traditional culture but a culture of the street. Palma asserted, "The street was very present . . . it was our school, our inspiration . . . there we discovered our aesthetic lines, our subjects, the street was our street."[132]

Whereas convivencia aimed at re-creating the national space, the Fiestas Spandex constructed a cosmopolitan, deterritorialized space. Palma insisted the parties serve imported Absolut vodka and that the events be modeled as much on the Trolley as on Studio 54, the Factory, and Blitz. The parties thus turned to an aesthetic forged through the dual experience of exile (Palma had spent time in the United States and Pérez had spent time in Europe during the dictatorship) and neoliberal globalization—forces both the dictatorship and democratic governments welcomed—as a means of escape, disidentifying, in a way, with the experience of exile. Palma maintained that after years of living under dictatorship, underneath the alegría there was great sorrow and constrained conditions of possibility. He explained, "[You] wanted to leave Chile because you wanted to be an artist, because you were gay, because you wanted to breathe, because you wanted to see something else, because one was exhausted here. It was very unpleasant to live in Chile. It was a very sad society."[133] The parties transported their attendees out of this "sad society." Palma recalled walking into the first party and thinking, "Wow . . . another country."[134]

The parties also allowed attendees to gauge their agency as citizens. This power was tested on May 25, when the police arrived following a minor altercation. While this could have been a flashback to dictatorship raids, the party's attendees asserted their rights. Palma recalls one woman boldly chastising a police officer for touching her. When the police began checking IDs they asked the men to line up on one side of the party and the women to line up on the other. One attendee, whom Palma describes as a *loca*, mischievously asked, "And what about us? Where do we line up?" and started a line in the center.[135] He was joined by several others, and Palma remembers everyone—including the police—laughing at the gesture. For Palma, these small acts of agency—through the assertion of spatial ownership, personal boundaries, through humor and a rejection of clear gender identities—constituted a rite. He asserts that it was "the first time that we had this experience of democracy and of experimenting with the power that democracy gave us as citizens."[136]

Yet, as Adeyemi, Khubchandani, and Rivera-Servera remind us, "The club must always close, and 'closing time' works to inscribe revelers back into hetero-capitalist temporal order."[137] A few weeks after the incident with the police, Palma and Pérez had lunch. Pérez gave Palma a choice: he could either continue with the Fiestas Spandex, or he could design sets and costumes for the theater company. GCT, however, would no longer host the parties at the Teatro Esmeralda. Palma felt confused and betrayed. The parties were bringing in much-needed income for the company. Furthermore, for Palma, they represented a utopian democratic vision. Palma later learned that Pérez had been called by a government official and told that he would not continue to receive funding for a tour of *La Negra Ester* if the parties continued. This act of censorship demonstrates the Concertación's efforts to promote the dramaturgy of convivencia, at the expense of a more transgressive democratic dramaturgy. It also demonstrates Pérez's choice to side with official culture, which Palma attributes to a desire he had to participate in the development of a ministry of culture.[138]

Palma opted to leave the company. He moved the parties to the Teatro Carrera in the Concha y Toro neighborhood,[139] where they continued, though some of the "red set" aura had worn off. Nevertheless, they attracted crowds from all over the country. Palma used the parties as a forum for AIDS education and prevention in the form of a *Show de condón* (Condom Show) and in collaboration with activist groups in public spaces, such as operating a safe-sex booth in Santiago's O'Higgins Park.

Eventually, Palma was approached by the student federation of the University of Chile (FECH) and asked to collaborate on an AIDS education campaign. FECH held a press conference announcing their partnership. Immediately after the press conference, Aylwin himself summoned the leaders of FECH into a meeting. According to Palma, at this meeting, Aylwin held up a FECH newspaper, which had an article about Fiestas Spandex, and disapprovingly asked, "'Does anyone know about these Fiestas Spandex? Who of you have gone?' . . . like Dad asking."[140] This alliance—between students and Spandex—was more than Aylwin could tolerate. In going outside of the party, in collaborating with students to acknowledge the reality of AIDS, and furthermore in doing so not by policing sexualities but by facilitating them safely, *Spandex* had threatened the Catholic, patriarchal, heteronormative state.[141] The event was canceled, and the landlord refused to allow the parties to continue at the Teatro Carrera. Palma realized that the pursuit of justice and social reorganization "to the extent possible" really meant a Rancierian distribution of the sensible: "Each person in their corner. The *colas* here, the punks on their street corner, the university students in their classroom."[142] For Palma, the radically democratic reconfigurations the parties' disidentifications facilitated revealed the superficiality of democracy as convivencia.

The parties were over. Opazo interprets the censorship of the Fiestas Spandex as an attempt to "disrupt the branches of solidarity, that, from an abandoned theater provide shelter, education, financing, memory, pleasure, and therapies to a community of university students, *colas*, and *punkies*, rebelling against the factions that instructed them to remain isolated."[143] These reconfigured branches of solidarity constituted a series of disidentifications that posited and enacted alternative understandings of Chilean culture, of cultural policy, of the body politic, of corporeal freedom, and of the rights and agency of citizens. They carried with them the utopic promise of radical democracy, which was precisely why they could not coexist with the consensus the architects of convivencia sought to create.

Matucana 100

GCT could no longer afford the Teatro Esmeralda and gave it up. They continued developing new productions and touring. In 1994, however, Pérez ended his personal relationship with technical director Ignacio Miranda and felt emotionally unable to continue working with the company. He announced that he was dissolving the company while they were performing in Brazil and took a break to recover.[144] In 1995 Pérez resumed work, participating as a director in the first Muestra Nacional de Dramaturgia, a government-sponsored festival of new Chilean playwriting. He revived GCT and directed for other companies in theater and opera. Occasionally, his work received official support (he received FONDART grants for *El desquite* [1995], *Cartas para Tomás* [1997], and *Nemesio Pelao ¿qué es lo que te ha pasao?* [1999]), though just as often it did not.

Throughout this period Pérez was critical of the underdevelopment of the Chilean cultural policy and the way the country's main cultural center, Centro Cultural Estación Mapocho, was run. He objected to its management as a public-private partnership that based its decision-making more on economics than artistry.[145] He continued to dream of a self-managed cultural center. In 1997 the company petitioned the mayor of Santiago, Jaime Ravinet, to use an abandoned theater in Barrio Yungay. Cornejo recalls that Ravinet was initially enthusiastic and promised the company the theater in their meeting. However, a week later Ravinet announced that the city would take possession of the theater and develop it as a cultural space.[146]

In 2000, Pérez found another space for recuperation: the abandoned bodegas at Matucana 100. Again, they petitioned the city of Santiago for use of the space. The city deferred their petition but granted the company temporary permission to occupy the space in December. Cornejo recalls the space being filled with trash and abandoned buses. Yet again, Pérez and the company set about cleaning and outfitting the venue for theatrical production. At the same time, they put together a detailed proposal for the space's use as a cultural center, in collaboration with architects and several other theater companies.[147] There, the company presented pieces from their repertoire, as well as a new play, *La huida* (The escape), written by Pérez. *La huida* was a poetic reflection on persecution of homosexuals during the dictatorship of Carlos Ibáñez del Campo in the 1930s. Pérez had written the play at twenty-six because he saw resonances between the historical period and his own life during dictatorship. Just a few months after the premiere, in April of that same year, the company was asked to turn the space over to the state for its development as a multidisciplinary cultural center administered, like the Centro Cultural Estación Mapocho, as a public-private partnership. Pérez resisted returning the space in a series of negotiations, suggesting that a public contest be held in which artistic companies could apply to administer the space. The contest was agreed to but never actually occurred. Instead, the space was placed under the leadership of a government functionary.

The reasons the state denied Pérez the artistic directorship are not entirely clear. Was it that the state was committed to reproducing the version of public-private management exemplified by Estación Mapocho? Was it that Pérez's *La huida* had, yet again, tapped into Concertación homophobia as Opazo suggests?[148] Or was it that Pérez was a disorganized financial manager, as Andrés García and Cuti Aste conjecture?[149] Whatever the reason, Pérez asserted that his proposal, which he considered an attempt to render the cultural infrastructure more plural and democratic, and his person did not fit into the government's vision. He maintained

> the proposition . . . that there should not be just one way of cultural management seen; that is to say, not only corporations administered by cultural managers named by the government, but also that [for] these public spaces belonging to all Chileans, artists could apply to administer them . . . this has not yet been validated, I think, because either the entirety of this proposition or we (Gran Circo Teatro and I) do not enter . . . I do not fall within the government's trusted parameters by which it would allow this kind of space to be directed.[150]

Ramírez attributes this to a failure of the Concertación's democracy to fully trust its people, arguing, "There was never any confidence, not just in us, there was never any confidence in the people who have autonomy of thought."[151] Pérez's last performance—in April 2001—therefore took the form of a public protest at Matucana 100. GCT staged scenes from its plays and read an "Open Letter to Public Opinion," which called for a more democratic cultural policy. Pérez hung from a beam as though being executed and read sections of the letter, which stated,

> This project responds to the need to recuperate public spaces . . . What we want is to give the community and our country an open center that with the management of artists accepts the suggestions of its living environment. . . . We recognize that there is an official point of view about cultural management. However, we believe that in this century, and in democracy, cultural policy should be renovated.[152]

The protest contested the top-down bureaucratic administration of culture in favor of a model that emerged from the artists themselves.

Pérez and Gran Circo Teatro were not granted the administration of the space. This outcome left Pérez disillusioned, not only with cultural policy but also with the Concertación's enactment of democracy. He explained,

> I felt that we were in a democracy, that the democracy was for everyone. I felt that everyone in the dictatorship—artists, politicians, common people—had dreamed of what they could not do. In the darkness, everyone filled their notebooks with petitions. I felt that we should do what we could not do during the dictatorship. Now I realize that the politicians feel they are the only ones with the right to place their notebooks of petitions into practice.[153]

Ramírez echoes these thoughts, casting the Concertación's democracy as a betrayal: "It was a betrayal in the end. . . . It's not a democracy for us, for the people, it is a democracy in the service of the economic powers."[154]

In the same month that he was asked to leave Matucana 100, Pérez was diagnosed with AIDS. The combination of the diagnosis and the failed bid for the cultural center sent Pérez into a depression and he became gravely ill, even refusing to see his closest friends.[155] He died on January 3, 2002, of respiratory complications attendant to AIDS at the age of fifty. He had been hospitalized in bed number 8 of the intensive care unit at the San José Hospital. Three other people had died in that same bed prior to Pérez, all from complications arising from a faulty oxygen connection. After Pérez's death, the mortality number in bed number 8 had climbed to twenty-two before the error was discovered.[156] It was an early, unjust, and possibly preventable death for one of Chile's preeminent theater artists.

Following his death, the theatrical community came together for a large funeral on January 4, 2002. His coffin was driven through Santiago in one of the abandoned buses from Matucana 100, now covered in brightly colored flowers. Hundreds processed on the street alongside the bus. On January 7, *La Negra Ester* was performed in Constitution Plaza, directly in front of the presidential palace. A popular initiative, led by GCT, declared his birthday, May 11, the National Day of Theater. The Senate made this designation official on December 26, 2006.[157]

Even in Pérez's death there is a tension between the way the state and its infrastructure failed him and the way he was officially endorsed and embraced. *La Negra Ester* became the emblematic play of the transition precisely because it enacted a dramaturgy in line with the government's vision of democracy—a dramaturgy of convivencia, a dramaturgy of profound paradox and democratic limitations. The tragic events that mark the end of Pérez's life lay bare the core inhumanity at the ideological heart of the transitional government's cultural policy. This was a policy that supported artistic works but did not support artistic *life*, a crucial distinction that here amounts to a necropolitics.[158] For in this reading of the dramaturgy of convivencia, a dramaturgy that sought, through joy and a celebration of the popular, to bring about a renewed, more inclusive Chile, we also read the state's assertion of patriarchy and heteronormativity as ideologies fundamental to governance, its rejection of contentious politics or ideological commitments, its homophobic response to the AIDS epidemic, and a cultural policy—powered by a capitalist ideology—that alienated artistic makers from their works, all while celebrating them as part of the larger Chilean national project. We thus see the dynamics at work in what would lead to increasing disillusionment with the transitional project—for Pérez and the wider Chilean population.

But what should we make of Pérez's collaboration in the creation of the dramaturgy of convivencia? While Aylwin and the Concertación governments sought a reification of this dramaturgy in order to preserve the tenuous status quo and legitimacy of the transitional nation-state, Pérez marshaled this dramaturgy, repeating it with difference, to explore the ways it might continue to expand the body politic and reforge the nation. This process proceeded in fits and starts, as Pérez tried to navigate his own ambitions, precarity, and artistic vision within this new state. This ultimately led him to an agonistic disidentification with the state that inflected and transformed the mechanisms of the dramaturgy. The unfolding of Pérez's dramaturgy over time reveals the imaginative accumulations that power the transformative political potential of performance.

Chapter 3

Dramaturgies of Revision

Teatro de Chile's Reimagination of History

In 2001, Manuela Infante and Héctor Morales, acting students at the University of Chile, were brainstorming in their shared apartment: What if they made a play? Could they depart from classics like Shakespeare and Chekhov and put something onstage that they would enjoy, that represented them? This impulse led to *Prat*: a thirty-minute play based on a script by Infante that incorporated material devised by the actors. The play took the martyrdom of the Chilean military hero Arturo Prat Chacón (1848–1879) in the nineteenth-century Battle of Iquique as its starting point, but it had no ambitions of historical accuracy. The students instead depicted a fictionalized Prat, employing him as an allegorical figure to reckon with their own coming-of-age and question the objectivity of official historical narratives. What if Prat hadn't wanted to be a hero? the play asked. What if heroism was a role forced upon him? Instead of representing Prat according to official history—as a thirty-one-year-old lawyer and veteran naval officer who sacrificed himself for his nation—the play portrayed Prat as a scared sixteen-year-old with a sophomoric sense of humor, an inability to hold his liquor, and a reluctance to claim his own independence (see fig. 10).[1]

The play premiered at the Víctor Jara Festival of Playwriting and Directing at the University of Chile, where it won both Best Actor (Morales) and Best Show.[2] The students were invited to perform it the following year in the fifty-eight-seat Sergio Aguirre Theater at the University of Chile and were encouraged by their professors to apply for a FONDART grant. On June 24, 2002, they learned they had received CLP 2 million from FONDART (around US $3,000). When the award was announced, letters arrived at newspapers expressing concern about the representation of the military hero. This ushered in a snowballing controversy. The students were accused of distorting and dishonoring history, of portraying Prat as drunk and as homosexual; groups of former naval officers were furious the government would fund such a show. The press inflamed the controversy,

Fig. 10. A poster for the production of *Prat*. Courtesy of Manuela Infante.

publishing the script without Infante's authorization. Right-wing groups and descendants of the naval officer filed cases against the students, former military officers demonstrated in the Senate, and neo-Nazi vigilantes terrorized the students. Some within the government distanced themselves from the play; others supported the students, casting the event as a battle over the autonomy of the cultural field, censorship, and freedom of expression.[3] Eventually, the director of FONDART, Nivia Palma, resigned her post in support of the students.

Like the Prat depicted in their play, the students had been thrust into a symbolic role they hadn't asked for in a battle they didn't fully understand. Debates about the play, a work very few had actually seen, became a stand-in for debates about the nation, about the relationship between history and memory, about freedom of speech and cultural policy, and about the legacy of the dictatorship and the status of the military—its vision of masculinity and its heteronormative, patriarchal values.[4] The dramaturgy of the play was thus embedded in a larger cultural crisis surrounding the legacy of the dictatorship and the limitations of the democratic transition.

The scandal surrounding *Prat* reveals how, after over ten years of Concertación rule, theatrical dramaturgies were enmeshed in the fundamental failure of the consensus on which convivencia had been predicated.[5] In the previous chapter, I examined how theatrical works—in dialogue with an official dramaturgy of convivencia— reimagined citizenship and the body politic at the moment of democratic transition. Now, I turn to the ways a younger generation of artists, coming of age in the postdictatorship period, reckoned with their relationship to citizenship, national identity, and history.

To do so, I first attend to the ways tensions over memory and history illuminate the fundamental failures of consensus-based convivencia as a democratic principle. I contend that this crisis of consensus and the particularities of the Chilean memory environment intersected with the anachronistic proposal of Infante's play to produce a scandal far out of proportion with the scale of the play. Drawing from repertoires of memory performance circulating within official circuits as well as the activist networks of a younger generation of Chileans, the play inserted the dramaturgy of memory (fractured, subjective, absurd) into the purview of official history (linear, objective, significant), producing an anachronistic allegory about coming of age in a militarized, patriarchal society. This dramaturgy of anachronism troubled the fundamental ideology at stake in the very premise of history, in turn challenging the ideologies of Chilean nationhood. It made the political claim that history could be reimagined to forge a new relationship to present and future Chile.

However, I am not only concerned with the ways the play itself produced a dramaturgy of anachronism, but with the ways this dramaturgy was distorted during the scandal. Because the scandal preceded the play's premiere, it became an integral, almost *a priori* component of the play's dramaturgy, transforming the way the play enacted Chilean citizenship. Not only did the play enact the students' right to reimagine their national history, in the scandal it became a symbolic assertion of the right to freedom of speech, of cultural pluralism, and of the autonomy of the cultural sphere. By considering how *Prat*'s dramaturgy, political capacity, and enactment of citizenship emerged at the intersection of the artistic intentions of its creators and the public controversy, this chapter reveals not only the political valence of a dramaturgy of anachronism but also the ways political theater is produced by its social and political environment.

This approach locates the play's dramaturgy as emerging from the interaction of its aesthetic proposals with its material, political, and cultural context. I conclude with a consideration of how this feedback loop propelled the students toward what I view as their most profound act of democratic citizenship: the decision to name themselves Teatro de Chile. In this choice of name, made with irony and humor, they claim the state for themselves and reject the instrumentalization of their work by those opposed to the play as well as by the cultural institutions that held them as symbolic of their own project. This gesture asserts the possibility of an alternate role for cultural production: not as an object reflective of national values, but as an organism fundamental to the life and identity of the state.

Memory, History, and the Problem of Consensus

Paul Connerton, Andreas Huyssen, Steve Stern, and others have demonstrated how memory work is central to establishing the legitimacy of new political orders, particularly those that emerge in the wake of violent or authoritarian regimes.[6] Whether through the construction of official narratives, musealization and commemoration, truth and reconciliation, or pacification and forgetting, it is, as Connerton argues, "surely the case that the control of a society's memory largely conditions the hierarchy of power."[7] As the work of scholars such as Elizabeth Jelin, Brenda Werth, Idelber Avelar, and Noe Montez demonstrate, memory shapes and charges struggles over power, as well as collective identity in both state and nonstate formations.[8] This helps to explain why the dramaturgy of a small student production was a practice of citizenship that triggered intense debate about the values and role of the state itself.

The relationship between memory and history is a series of constant negotiations—the two are not one and the same, nor can they be separated from each other. Furthermore, the nature of this relationship depends on one's definition of both terms. Nevertheless, the Chilean state faced the challenge of whether and how memory—open, subjective, embodied, and ongoing—could, or indeed *should*, be converted into a particular kind of history—official, archived and archival, pedagogical, significant, *past*.[9] In other words, it was a question of whether and how memory might achieve consensus.[10] Rancière's consideration of history helps to further illuminate the political valence of history by suggesting that not only does the dramaturgy of history involve a linear and horizontal ordering of events (i.e., chronology) but it also involves a vertical ordering. By this, Rancière means that the logic of historical organization is underlain by a truth claim. History is thus composed according to various "regimes of truth," such as an epoch guided by a Christian concept of eternity, of human causality, of progress, of change over time, or of human rights. Avelar contends that the epochal logic undergirding the post-dictatorial period is that of supremacy of the market and the commodification of all areas of life.[11] History's predication on a vertical relationship to time illuminates how historical discourse is a discourse of power. Consensus and democracy in Chilean postdictatorship serve the "epochal" logic of market supremacy and the privatization of social life.

Yet memory does not easily acquiesce to such formulations of history. Richard contends that memory runs counter to the Rancierian proposition of history as it "stirs up the static fact of the past with new unclosed meanings that put recollections to work, causing both beginnings and endings to rewrite new hypotheses and conjectures and thereby dismantle the explanatory closures of totalities that are too sure of themselves."[12] As Avelar points out, memory resists the epochal logic of postdictatorship and the "eternal present" of market dominance—which seeks to constantly "forget" old commodities to necessitate new consumption—insisting on the traces of the ruins of the past, ruins that rupture the accords of the present.[13] Memory is operationally contingent and as such is a fraught terrain in which to attempt consensus.

Accordingly, Stern understands Chile's memory environment as a conflictual terrain of "competing selective remembrances."[14] Despite the Concertación's emphasis on convivencia, throughout the nineties the memory environment was marked by a fundamental lack of consensus. This shaped *Prat's* dramaturgy. I would therefore like to broadly chart this memory environment, highlighting how it created the conditions in which both the play and the scandal would be produced.

Richard maintains that for the Concertación, consensus meant "neutralizing differentiating counterpoints, antagonistic stances, and polemical demarcations of contrary meanings through an institutional pluralism that obliged diversity to become 'noncontradictatory.' "[15] Richard thus argues that the Concertación's pluralism was fundamentally depoliticized. The pursuit of consensus often eclipsed the need for justice and a break with the military regime, limiting the government's ability to address the dictatorship's human rights violations. Manuel Antonio Garretón argues that the Concertación forged an "illusion of consensus" that, bolstered by demands for economic and political stability, masked a lack of debate over "the broad issues that define society and the foundational bases of democracy."[16]

Perhaps more than in any other arena, the memory environment revealed the inability of the transitional government to achieve consensus. In the early years of the transition, the Concertación grappled with how to frame the history of the military coup and the memory of the dictatorship period so that it would not threaten the fragile democracy. This was a challenge, according to Richard, of memory's "pacification, when today, a community divided by the trauma of homicidal violence must be reunited on the postdictatorial stage, suturing the edges of a wound that separates punishment from forgiveness."[17] Accordingly, Aylwin staged a series of official memory acts aimed at using memory to promote reconciliation and convivencia among Chileans.[18] In these acts, memory was contained, serious, and disciplined, and history was pedagogical. Memory was invoked as part of a cleansing ritual and was framed as a journey from sadness to joy or from rupture to repair, and history was staged as a lesson in democratic civility.

The Alywin administration used key symbolic moments to bring the contentious and subjective aspects of Chile's collective memory into a clear narrative of significance. It was a dramaturgy that was Aristotelian in its structure and that focused on catharsis and social cohesion.[19] Aylwin's inaugural celebration, which I discuss in chapter 2, staged a linear movement of sorrow into joy, creating what one spectator called a "collective exorcism."[20]

Later that year, Aylwin staged a national funeral for Allende, an act he referred to as "a ceremony of reparation, of reencounter, and of peace."[21] Allende remained a highly contentious figure—and a symbolic locus for the divisions still present in Chilean society. In the public ceremony, Aylwin gave a eulogy acknowledging his differences with Allende but framed them not as destabilizing, but as part of democratic discourse.[22] The president used the ceremony as a pedagogical moment to model how respectful disagreement could take place in a society guided by convivencia.[23]

The government's first efforts at truth and reconciliation had similarly ritualistic and reparative components. In 1990, Aylwin commissioned a report, helmed by Raúl Rettig, to investigate political violence during the dictatorship. The Rettig report documented over two thousand cases of death and disappearance. As the first large-scale record of the crimes committed during the dictatorship, it was a powerful document. It offered incontrovertible evidence that the deaths and disappearances constituted a systematic violation of human rights.[24] After the 1,350-page report was delivered to Aylwin, he addressed the nation, asserting the importance that the crimes be recognized and acknowledging that forgiveness and pardon would be a personal and difficult process. Stern recounts a rather remarkable moment, in which Aylwin took responsibility for the dictatorship's crimes and said, with tears in his eyes,

> When it was agents of the State that caused so much suffering, and the capable organs of the State could not or knew not how to avoid it and punish it, and when there was also not the necessary social response to stop it, the State and the whole society are responsible, whether by action or by omission. It is Chilean society that is in debt to the victims of violations of human rights. . . . That is why I venture, in my capacity as president of the Republic, to assume representation of the entire nation in order, in its name, to ask forgiveness from the relatives of the victims.[25]

It was a gesture drawn from Christian ritual, invoking the surrogacy of sin and the importance of forgiveness: Aylwin took on the sins of the dictatorship to heal Chilean society. Though Aylwin acknowledged the difficulty of forgiveness, and the necessity of social and structural efforts at repair, the presidential address also created a symbolic moment in which responsibility was assumed and forgiveness could happen; it was a ritual aimed at moving the country toward healing.

In the early years of the transition, the Concertación advanced dramaturgies of memory that made use of symbolism and ritual to bring memory into a larger narrative of democratic transcendence. Richard writes that such efforts aimed "to turn the page, to close the chapter . . . figuring memory as a book, narrative, and archive."[26] Yet these efforts ran counter to the subjective and fragmented operations of memory. Furthermore, these official dramaturgies of memory contained crucial omissions—omissions aimed at fostering consensus, but that made the likelihood that counter-memories would haunt the public sphere far higher. The Rettig report only investigated cases of death or disappearance and did not report on tortures, nor did it name those who had committed the crimes. It therefore was not a complete acknowledgment of the dictatorship's crimes, nor did it provide an avenue for the justice that many desired.

Despite official efforts to channel memory into a cathartic, ritualistic, and pedagogical narrative, memory frequently convulsed the public sphere. Alexander Wilde refers to these events as "irruptions of memory," which he defines as "public events that break upon Chile's national consciousness, unbidden and often suddenly, to evoke associations with symbols, figures, causes, ways of life which to an unusual degree are associated with a political past that is still present in the lived experience of a major part of the population." Such events might include the discovery of unmarked graves, the declassification of CIA files, national holidays, or new evidence of past dictatorship crimes. These irruptions revealed fundamental disagreements about the past and the superficiality of consensus.[27] Some viewed the military dictatorship's crimes as necessary, an unfortunate price to pay for peace in the context of the Cold War. For others they were inexcusable: human rights violations unjustified regardless of the political context.

Realizing that they could not impose a dramaturgy of consensual significance on Chile's collective memory, the Concertación retreated from its efforts at commemoration and memorialization.[28] The abandonment of commemorative efforts contributed to the association of consensus with forgetting and to increasing cultural disillusionment as the century ended.[29] However, Stern notes that after 1998, Chileans nevertheless found themselves in a "new memory environment," in which some of the old impasses began to give way.[30] During this period the impunity around Pinochet and the military regime was less assured and justice for dictatorship-era crimes increasingly possible. There was a growing acceptance of memory and history as subjective coupled with an ongoing privatization of culture. Meanwhile a younger generation—without direct memories of the Unidad Popular period or the military coup—came of age in this new environment, among it a group of theater students at the University of Chile.

Perhaps one of the most intense and transformative irruptions of memory took place while Infante and her colleagues were at university. On October 16, 1998, Pinochet was arrested in London under an international warrant issued by Judge Baltasar Garzón of Spain. The warrant requested Pinochet's extradition, and he was charged with ninety-four counts of torture of Spanish citizens, the assassination of a Spanish diplomat, and conspiracy to commit torture. The arrest sparked demonstrations in Chile, with some advocating for Pinochet's release and others hopeful that he would finally stand trial. The Concertación president, Eduardo Frei, opposed the arrest, arguing that any trial of Pinochet should take place in Chile.[31]

Six days later, London's High Court ruled the extradition request invalid. However, the House of Lords continued to debate the case, and Pinochet was placed under house arrest in London. Though President Frei advocated for Pinochet's return to Chile, the veneer of Pinochet's immunity had broken, and the arrest emboldened efforts to try his crimes in Chile. In addition, it increased a desire for personal justice where official justice failed and marked a shift in the way memory and history would henceforth be conceptualized.[32]

While under house arrest, Pinochet sent a public letter asserting that he had done what was morally necessary to prevent Chile from falling into chaos and communism.[33] To bolster the argument that the military regime acted out of necessity, the conservative newspaper *La Segunda* ran a series of supplements by the historian Gonzalo Vial Correa that detailed the "crisis" of Chilean society during the 1964–1973 period.[34] Though Vial had served on the Rettig Commission and condemned human rights violations in that capacity, Stern notes that in this analysis he advanced a hegemonic vision of the historical narrative that served as an apologist's explanation for the regime's actions.[35]

In response, eleven historians issued a "Manifesto of Historians" challenging Vial's interpretation of history and the assertion that the coup was unavoidable. Stern observes that the manifesto and the debate that followed illuminated the problems of determining a historical truth and demonstrated the ways such "truths" were politically motivated.[36] It also thrust the debate into a moral and philosophical register about the rights of man and of citizens. The manifesto concluded:

> History is not only the past, but also, and primarily, the present and future. History is projection. It is the social construction of the future reality. The most important human right consists in respecting the capacity of citizens to produce for themselves the future reality that they need. Not to recognize this right is to usurp or adulterate this right and to impose, above all, not the truth, but the historical lie. It is to empty the true moral reserve of humanity.[37]

In this final assertion, the manifesto collapsed past time into an urgent political present with implications for the future, connecting the writing and interpretation of history to both human rights and the rights of citizens.[38]

As this debate took place, there was also a move toward what Stern calls "a more privatized culture of plural memories."[39] Stern cites the creation of the "Dialogue Table" by the Frei administration in August 1999 as emblematic of this shifting culture.[40] The table brought together a range of stakeholders, often with clashing understandings of the coup. It asked human rights advocates and military actors to work together to provide answers about the fate of the disappeared and locate and return their remains. It would require that the opposing camps listen to each other and confront some of their fundamental disagreements in a common purpose.

I dwell on these events to point to the ways that there were newly emergent dramaturgies of memory and history in both official and nonofficial spheres—dramaturgies marked by contention and subjectivity, creating the space for a more personal writing of history. Stern points out that in the opening ceremony for the Dialogue Table, Sol Serrano explained, "It is not a text of consensual history that we want, but rather sources for history, for reflection about the past."[41] Approaching the past required a process of reflection on moral responsibility, acts that did not require a shared historical interpretation. In Frei's address to Congress on May 21, 1999, he echoed this understanding of history, asserting that Pinochet's arrest "has shown us that there are pending problems, that there are distinct visions of our recent history. Let us accept this reality and renounce the desire to impose on others our own points of view with respect to the past. There cannot be official histories or gross denials of the facts."[42]

The shifting dramaturgical paradigms surrounding memory and history were manifest and further elaborated in activist youth culture and their pursuit of justice. The failure of the truth commission to bring about meaningful justice led some to take matters into their own hands. Inspired by activist organizations staging *escraches* in Argentina and motivated by the absence of systematic redress of human rights violations, groups of young Chileans convened to stage *funas*, a Chilean slang term derived from the Mapuche language Mapudungun meaning "to reveal or display something." The first funas were coordinated in September 1999 through a Chilean branch of the transnational activist group HIJOS, the group Acción, Verdad, y Justicia, and members of the Agrupación de Familiares Detenidos Desaparecidos. By October the funas were coordinated by the Comisión Funa. The funas were public actions outing the perpetrators of military crimes in noisy, often festive, street happenings.[43] They would target individuals who had participated in the detention, torture, and murder of Chileans, but who now worked in civil society as doctors, managers in telephone companies, farmers, and so on—highlighting the scope and ongoing legacy of the *civic*-military dictatorship.[44] As ephemeral urban interventions aimed at social transformation, the funas shared a legacy with CADA but also represented a stark contrast to the culture of fear and the clandestine resistance of the dictatorship years. At the same time, they were a bold refutation of convivencia, an act of shaming both the perpetrators of violence and the current state, as Temma Kaplan observes.[45] The coordinating institution's name, "Comisión Funa" was a clear reference to and play on the "Comisión Nacional de Verdad y Reconciliación (National Commission of Truth and Reconciliation). This act of naming challenged the work of the state's institution and staked its own claim for legitimacy in the project of transitional justice. They rejected the larger culture of forgetting and insisted instead upon accountability. They took acts meant to deprive individuals of political agency (the repression of the regime in the case of the original trauma, the insistence on consensus and reconciliation in the second case) and, according to Taylor (writing about the Argentine case), turned "personal pain into the engine for cultural change."[46]

The funas were predominately a youth movement, led by the children of the disappeared, signaling a new relationship to the dictatorship. This was a generation whose experience was marked by what Marianne Hirsch terms "postmemory." In Hirsch's formulation postmemory is an experience in which the traumatic memories of a previous generation are so imprinted upon subsequent generations that they become their memories as well, even though they were not directly lived. The concept of postmemory captures the increasing chronological and experiential distance but persistent legacy of these memories.[47] We might say it is an anachronistic perseverance of the past that assures that history will remain personal and immediate. Postmemory also allows for the possibility that past events will not easily be formulated into "history," but will persist with the dramaturgy of memory. At the same time, however, because this generation was not itself directly a target of the military regime, it might have felt less vulnerability confronting the state. The funas signaled that a new generation was willing to constitute Chile on its own terms. They offered a ritual, marked by repetition, affect, and efficacy, which in their coordination and institutionalization challenged the state's hegemony in dispensing justice. The funas established a youthful dramaturgy of direct action that brought the past into the present, critiqued the failure of the institutionalized state, and provided their own form of justice. History, memory, and justice each became personal and plural acts. In many ways *Prat* would reflect these new dramaturgies of history and memory, particularly in the ways it offered a radically subjective and anachronistic engagement with history, marshaling it to speak to the students' personal experiences in the present.

Prat, History, and Anachronism

If the contentiousness of the memory environment in Chile emerged because of disagreements about the legacy of the dictatorship, why did a student play about a nineteenth-century military hero become a heated locus for these disagreements? While there was an obvious symbolic connection between Prat and the military, an implied critique of the military does not account for the scale of the scandal and its perceived threat to "national values." Why could the play not be dismissed as fiction, or even as harmless historical error? Why could it not be taken simply as a piece of criticism, to be refuted rather than censored? Why did those driving the scandal refuse to see the artistic intent behind the play's anachronistic moves? What was so potent about the play that its premiere had to be stopped?

The play's political potency lay not only in its unflattering depiction of Arturo Prat—a uniquely beloved national figure—but in the intersection of that depiction with the play's dramaturgical act of anachronism. The play provoked a scandal because it challenged notions of historical truth and authority. It posited citizenship as a right to rewrite history, and to establish a subjective relationship with national mythology. Furthermore, it posed these challenges in an allegorical register that spoke to contemporaneous debates about historical authority and intervened in those questions in ways that touched on the policies of a government that was still defining its fragile democracy as well as institutionalizing its cultural policy. The tensions that surfaced in Chile's memory environment were about the impact of the dictatorship and about truth and reconciliation, but they were also about the power of citizens and their right to answer such questions.

In Chile, the figure of Prat sits at the intersection of national history and mythology.[48] Prat's name christens streets, and his figure adorns plazas in nearly every city in Chile.[49] He is part of the obligatory curriculum in elementary schools, and his martyrdom is commemorated as a national holiday on May 21. In 1973, the historian William F. Sater dubbed Prat a "secular saint," a term Sarah Misemer suggests denotes figures who "[embody] modern secular notions we ascribe to the understanding of icons as a marker of a plurality of discourses."[50] Such figures are, as Jean Graham-Jones points out, both "cultural agents and cultural products." She further contends that, as such, "icons are very personally, politically, historically, culturally, and generationally grounded, and that contextual ground is constantly shifting."[51] Accordingly, Prat's symbolic image has traversed shifting moral and nationalistic values.

Agustín Arturo Prat Chacón (1848–1879) was a Chilean lawyer and naval officer. During the War of the Pacific (1879–1884), a dispute over taxes and border claims with Bolivia and Peru, he was assigned command of the *Esmeralda* warship. Though the *Esmeralda* was poorly equipped, Prat was charged with sailing the ship, alongside the Chilean *Covadonga* (commanded by Carlos Condell), north to take some Peruvian warships by surprise.

The Chilean forces were met by two much larger Peruvian ships, the *Huáscar* and the *Independencia*. The *Covadonga* fled south, pursued by the *Independencia*, but the *Esmeralda* engaged the *Huáscar*. After exchanging fire, the Peruvian ship rammed into the *Esmeralda*. Recognizing their imminent defeat, Prat rallied the sailors with a speech. As the *Huáscar* collided into the *Esmeralda* a second time, Prat famously proclaimed, "¡Al abordaje muchachos!" ("All aboard, boys!") and boarded the ship, fighting until he was gunned down. Meanwhile, Condell took advantage of the fact that the Peruvian ship had crashed in its pursuit of the *Covadonga*, and he and his crew were able to destroy the Peruvian vessel.[52]

Following the battle, Prat became a hero, eclipsing even Condell, who had sustained the battle's only victory. Prat's defeat became credited with the moral victory that rallied the Chilean troops and led to their eventual victory in the war five years later. Fernanda Carvajal observes this anachronism: "Against all evidence of the facts, Prat's leap is a victory in the official history."[53] Sater contends that Prat's immediate heroism was cast in terms of Christian martyrdom, one that made redemption possible through victory in war. Later, he argues that Prat's image was symbolically deployed on account of his civilian virtues, in particular his dedication as a husband and father, to bolster middle-class moral reform. At other times, Prat's popularity has risen for reasons of political expediency, as his image has been used by political factions to critique the corruption or incompetence of those in power.[54]

Although Prat's image had been used for political purposes and had nationalistic implications, Morales, who played Prat in Infante's production, contends that his figure is symbolically flexible and does not have obvious partisan associations. He is almost universally beloved—an attachment that begins for many at a young age. For Morales, Prat was a "very blank figure and associated with every Chilean's childhood." He was "the first superhero that every child had," and his heroic act was "very metaphoric."[55]

Though the play's scandal was largely driven by those on the political right, Prat's universal, nonpartisan associations enabled the scandal's scale. Prat could function as a less freighted symbol for the military honor now that many, including on the right, had begun to distance themselves from Pinochet following his arrest. Perhaps because Prat was strongly associated with the military, but was *not* Pinochet, those on the right felt free to deploy him as a surrogate in defense of nationalistic, patriarchal, heteronormative values and to assert their continued authority in national life.

Yet the scandal was not about Prat's legacy alone, nor even the legacy and status of the military. As it was debated in the media, in the Senate, and in the courts, it became about power, rights, and who possessed them, about democracy and cultural pluralism, about freedom of speech, and about national values. It became about these things because in addition to invoking the figure of Prat, the play invoked him anachronistically—a move that has deep political potency.

In a 1996 essay, Rancière cites Lucien Febvre's provocation that anachronism is an unforgivable historical sin. He proceeds to explore the ways anachronism unsettles a concept of history, and the political implications of this disturbance. Rancière contends that the establishment of history as a scientific discourse actually "involves a knot of philosophical questions about the relations of time, speech, and truth."[56] The challenge anachronism poses to history is not that it mistakes chronology, but that it unsettles the relationship of time to truth. It might do this, as *Prat* does, by bringing two different value systems together, undermining the hegemony of either. According to Rancière, an anachrony is "a word, an event, or a signifying sequence that has left its time, and in this way, is given the capacity to define completely original points of orientation."[57] In this way, anachronism operates similarly to memory. Richard describes the anachronistic moves of memory, writing that rather than freeze the past in time, memory reestablishes the past as a "field of citations" marked by both continuity and discontinuity to create "discordant temporalities."[58] The logic of memory and anachronism are similar: both irrupt into the present, eschew linearity, and foreground the subjective. Both trouble the concept of a hegemonic truth, threatening the ideology that undergirds the legitimacy of the nation and its ability to incorporate history. I dwell on Rancière's formulation because I wish to emphasize how a dramaturgy of anachronism is tied to the logic of memory, as well as how, especially in the Chilean case, it constitutes a claim, which I consider to be a foundational gesture of citizenship. In the case of *Prat's* anachronism, it inserts a subjective experience into the historical space of appearance (a claim to agency). It insists on questioning the values of that history and their relationship to the present.

Prior to the play the figure of Prat had dwelt in a mythic "regime of truth"—in which Prat could stand for unquestioned national values like military, masculine heroism, patriarchy, family, and heteronormativity. The play's dramaturgy of anachronism brought Prat into a regime guided by memory, in which subjectivity determines truth. It turned Prat from symbol—which Avelar contends privileges timeless images—into allegory: "a trope that thrives on breaks and continuities." Avelar demonstrates that this turn to the allegorical is part of a larger trend in Latin American post-dictatorial literature, a trend marked by the difficulty of identifying clear enemies to oppose and the need to speak from an estrangement with the present.[59] *Prat's* anachronism asserted individual agency and disputed powers that sought to contain and structure time. It involves a relationship to the past that also unsettles a relationship to time itself. Infante suggests that it is precisely this tension between different concepts of time—brought about by generational change—that provoked the scandal:

> The theme of the objectivity of reality is so political. All the historical impositions from the most ferocious dictatorships . . . are supported by a worldview that believes in objectivity, that believe that there is a truth. And I think that the commotion over Prat

> had more to do with the fear of realizing that there is a generation that is beginning to read things differently, than that it touches a particular figure.[60]

The fact that a younger generation was being funded by the government to assert its power as citizens to reimagine national history and to posit a subjective relationship to the nation was unsettling those who wished to impose a nationalist, authoritarian structure of power or simply preserve the status quo.

FONDART and Its Controversies

The 2002 FONDART awardees were announced on June 24. Since its inception in 1992, the program, the Fund for the Development of Culture and the Arts, has been one of the Chilean government's primary means of artistic support. As I describe in chapter 2, the fund had its antecedents in a short-lived dictatorship program, which sought to use government funds to promote state-sanctioned art.[61] The 1992 version of the program was established as a gloss in the Budget Law and was administered through the Ministry of Education. The fund's aim was (and is) to contribute to the development of culture and the arts in Chile, adjudicating its resources—which came from taxes and donations—via an open public competition.[62] In its first ten years, FONDART distributed CLP 16,669,233,685 (over US$24 million) to 5,199 projects in categories including visual arts, audiovisual arts, theater and dance, music, literature, patrimony, integrated arts, interregional events, and first people's arts.[63] Proposals were first evaluated by a committee of artists in the relevant discipline, and then juried by a panel of artists consisting of representatives from each area as well as a representative from the private sector.[64]

As the Concertación's primary mechanism of artistic support, FONDART was situated at a complex intersection of postdictatorship culture and politics. Emerging from the same logic of dictatorship-era proposals, it was, on one hand, another site of continuity with the military regime, imposing a competitive, individuating, capitalist model on artists. As I argue in chapter 2, this model did not provide a system by which a company could be sustainably supported and thus facilitate its longer-term development. Carvajal and Van Diest contend that this led most companies to conceive of themselves as independent, marked by the requirement that they must generate the resources to create work every time they wished to embark upon a new project.[65]

Both FONDART and the artists it funded operated within an environment in which freedom of speech remained significantly constrained. Many had expected that the end of the dictatorship would augur the end of a culture of censorship. However, the entrenchment of authoritarian enclaves combined with the desire for consensus meant that freedom of speech was one of the most compromised rights of the democratic transition.[66] Film censorship continued to emanate from executive authority, and the courts operated as an arena through which other forms of censorship could take place.[67] In such cases, freedom of speech was most commonly curtailed because it came into conflict with other rights and laws, in particular an individual's right to "honor." Additionally, the general culture of consensus presented a major stumbling block to the establishment of free speech and debate, encouraging a continued climate of cautious self-censorship.

Yet, at the same time as FONDART was an outgrowth of a dictatorship-era logic and operated within a culture still shaped by a climate of censorship, FONDART was also intended as a mechanism to resist authoritarian, "directed" culture and to promote freedom of expression and cultural pluralism. The fund's adjudication by committees of independent artists aimed to ensure autonomy. Often the artists composing these panels were known for works that had resisted the dictatorship. The panel that had awarded the FONDART to *Prat* consisted of Fernando González—the former director of Teatro Itinerante—and Diamela Eltit, also a member of CADA.[68] The fund's director since 1993 had been Nivia Palma, a member of the Socialist Party who also represented a wing of the Concertación coalition that was further left than that represented by presidents Aylwin and Frei, or Palma's supervisor, minister of education Mariana Aylwin (the daughter of Patricio Aylwin). Palma herself was invested in supporting works that might critique or question Chilean society. Of *Prat*, Palma asserted, "It seems wonderful to me that among other things, FONDART projects questioned a historic affirmation of what it is to be Chilean."[69]

Given FONDART's complex position within postdictatorship culture as well as its willingness to fund provocative works, it is unsurprising that prior to *Prat*, the program had multiple controversies. Often these controversies revolved around representations of national or Latin American identity, in particular those that touched on questions of gender and sexuality. In 1994, the program funded the reproduction of Juan Dávila's *El libertador Simón Bolívar* (1994), a work that depicted Bolívar—a hero of South American independence movements—with aspects of a female body and dress and making an obscene hand gesture. The work subverted militant, patriarchal notions of heroism and Latin American identity, inserting the feminine, the queer, the popular, and the profane into its history. The following year, Juan Pablo Sutherland's "erotic biography of the city," *Ángeles Negros*, came under fire for its homosexual themes,[70] and in 1999 the municipality of Machalí protested the public installation of a four-meter, eight-ton penis financed by FONDART. In 2000, FONDART financed *Nautilus, la nueva casa trasparente* (Nautilus, the new transparent house), also called "Casa de vidrio" (Glass House), a project in which a young woman lived her daily life in a transparent house built in a vacant lot a few blocks away from the presidential palace. The artists intended to draw attention to the lack of transparency in Chilean daily life and politics.[71] However, the young female actress, Daniela Tobar, attracted throngs of leering men to the house. As would occur with *Prat, Nautilus* provoked a media firestorm. Letters to newspapers and editorials condemned the piece as pornographic, and several legal cases were filed to stop the work and "safeguard the basic principles of [Chilean] society."[72] Fearing for her safety, Tobar withdrew from the piece. When she was replaced by an middle-aged man the throngs of voyeurs disappeared.[73] The piece thus raised questions about political and social transparency alongside complicated questions about sexual politics, gender, and voyeurism.

Each of these works challenged Chilean national and sexual values, and surely would have been apparent in their grant proposals. In funding such works, FONDART demonstrated that it valued critical, provocative art and art that unsettled the heteronormative patriarchy. It did so by asserting its rejection of censorship and its commitments to freedom of expression and the autonomy of the cultural sphere. At a roundtable concerning the Dávila and Sutherland controversies, Palma asserted, "The State cannot determine the ethical or aesthetic contents of art because in our democratic society it is free men and women who judge the works." She thus posited artistic discernment as part of democratic liberties. Nor would FONDART consider "extracultural" criteria in the selection of its artist-evaluators: "Despite the artistic qualifications of a possible FONDART evaluator, were they excluded for belonging to a particular political party or for their sexual preferences . . . or lists of 'dangerous artists' for the system—that same day this fund will have lost all meaning."[74] For Palma and by extension FONDART, culture in democracy was to be facilitated but not determined by the state. However, in her statements Palma overlooks the ideological bias inherent in any evaluation of artistic "qualifications." In their evaluators, FONDART seemed to privilege elite artists who had been resistant to the dictatorship—artists and critics such as Eltit, Rosenfeld, and Richard—individuals whose tastes likely tended toward contestatory art making. Despite its efforts to the contrary, FONDART could not help but be ideologically, politically, and aesthetically positioned. This, in combination with its complicated imbrication in postdictatorship culture, made the fund ripe for controversy.

Prat and Its Controversies: Toward a Dramaturgy of Anachronism

When the 2002 FONDART awards were announced, Morales recalled *Prat* described as a work that "questions the heroic image of Arturo

Prat."[75] Following this announcement, the students were besieged in the press, Senate, courts, and streets. At first, the controversy was driven by hearsay, as only a small university audience had seen or read the play. When the script was later printed in the press, the controversy escalated and the play's attackers latched on to specific elements of the play, many of which they misinterpreted.

The scandal began in and was primarily driven by the press—in particular the conservative paper *La Segunda*. There, the controversy was fueled by anxieties coalescing around the play's challenge to national "values." The play was perceived to threaten the patriarchal, heteronormative status quo, undermine the military, and challenge a hegemonic notion of history. This latter challenge positioned the play within debates in the realm of memory. Like the Manifesto of Historians and the premise of the Dialogue Table, the play's rejection of a singular historical narrative challenged those who used such narratives to justify and explain the military coup.

Following the FONDART announcement, outraged letters arrived at various newspapers, condemning the students, as one letter put it, for "smearing the cultural and historic values of the Chilean navy." In such letters, Prat was defended as the paragon of patriarchal heteronormativity. Accordingly, Prat was "a perfectly normal man, simple, Christian, father, husband, son, lawyer, and officer of the Chilean navy, who made the decision to offer his life for his country, for his honor, and for the defense of the most precious values rooted in his sailor's soul."[76] Implied in such statements was that to represent Prat otherwise was to represent something aberrant, and to threaten the Christian, patriarchal, and martial values of the country.

For some, the threat to these values represented a significant political threat. The spokesperson for the retired naval admirals, Jorge Swett Madge, condemned the play in terms reminiscent of dictatorship-era fear-mongering. According to Swett, the play constituted part of a larger effort to destroy Chilean cultural values and take power.[77] On September 6, such a perceived threat led the prodictatorship group Corporación 11 de septiembre (September 11 Corporation, a name that commemorates the date of the military coup) to demand that the Ministry of Education stop the premiere, invoking the Law of State Security.

The students tried to focus on their work. In the introduction to the published text, the company wrote, "We were afraid, we felt anger, and we protected ourselves in the world constructed in our rehearsals, that for us was more real than what was going on outside."[78] However, the students could not isolate themselves entirely. In September, a reporter disguised as a student from the Catholic University approached Morales and told him that they wanted to discuss the play in their class. Morales and the company agreed to share the script with them.[79] Shortly thereafter, on September 17, 2002, a day before the Chilean national holiday—a time

La Segunda ESPECIAL

EXCLUSIVO
Texto íntegro de la obra de teatro "Prat" que financió el FONDART

Ha crecido en las últimas semanas la controversia pública sobre la obra de teatro "Prat" que recibió el apoyo del FONDART y el respaldo teatral de la Universidad de Chile. No sólo la Armada, a través de los canales institucionales de la Defensa, ha reclamado por la tergiversación de la figura de nuestro héroe má-

Tercer Festival de Dramaturgia y Dirección Víctor Jara de la Universidad de Chile que tendrá lugar en octubre—ganó el Fondart regional que le asignó dos millones de pesos. La mitad de esta cifra fue entregada en julio pasado. El jurado que decidió apoyarla fue presidido por el director de teatro Fernando González.

Rechazo del primer recurso.

Fig. 11. A special section of *La Segunda*, September 17, 2002. The headline reads, "Full Text of the Play 'Prat' Financed by FONDART." Courtesy of the Compañía de Teatro de Chile Collection, Archivo de la Escena Teatral Universidad Católica, Santiago, Chile.

when nationalism was on high display—the unfinished script was printed in a special section of *La Segunda*, without their permission (see fig. 11).

The text published in *La Segunda* was fundamentally incomplete. As a rehearsal draft, it contained many typographical errors, a fact pointed out by the newspaper in a note appending the play with the false implication that the printed text had been approved by the author, and that those authorial wishes had been respected.[80] More significantly, the script represented only a small part of what would be seen onstage. The text had functioned as a guide for an improvisational rehearsal process.[81] Accordingly, the stage directions were scant, and much of the dialogue and action of the performance was not represented by the text. Therefore, the artistic intentions of the students could not possibly have been gleaned from the text alone, a fact that was not noted by any of the play's critics. When the company later published the script, they acknowledged even its incompleteness by subtitling the printed version *Guide for the Creation of a World*.[82]

The first thing a reader of *La Segunda* would have encountered was the character list, which specified that Prat was sixteen years old, an obvious factual inaccuracy as Prat had been thirty-one at the time of the battle. This list was followed by a prologue, which further served to establish many of the play's anachronistic moves, moves that traversed the realm of both verifiable facts and unverifiable subjective experiences, and that posited time as epochal:

> There was a time in which we feared the Peruvians. There was a time in which we feared the police, there was a time in which we feared technology. . . . Of course we were afraid of unidentified flying objects. . . . We were also afraid of AIDS. There was one time, as well, in which we feared the horizon. We were very afraid of mistaken crucifixions, afraid that a bomb would fall on us, there was also a fear of fire. . . . We were afraid of Chupacabras, of Charles Manson, but let's leave the individuals behind. Fear of eating uncooked lettuce, fear of having a Star of David on the lapel. Many times we had a fear of cold. Well. There was one time, I swear, in which we were afraid of the Peruvians.[83]

Prat's prologue situates the play within an epochal time bound by belief—in this case the nationalistic fear of the Peruvians that justified the War of the Pacific. With this first statement, the audience is positioned outside of time and able to look, like a discerning historian, on those within that time. This historic detachment is immediately undercut by the prologue's address to a collective "we" that fears in the *imperfect* tense (the conjugation of *temíamos*—we feared—implies an ongoing emotional state), suggesting that the historic boundaries of this fear-guided epoch do not have a clear ending point. Accordingly, the opening sentence also evokes a fairy tale or story structure—"Había una época" ("There was a time"). The play—and Prat—are framed as being part of a mythic time, situating the historic Prat as part of a national mythology, in contrast to a more historic factuality. The prologue proceeds to tease out anachronistic connections, linking real and absurd fears (many of these expressed in the more finite preterit tense, a grammatical inconsistency that calls attention to the multiple past tenses' relationship to the present): a fear of the police, technology, UFOs, meteorites, AIDS, Chupacabras, and having to wear the Star of David. The free association of these fears—some of which convey vivid and specific historical association (the Carabineros and the dictatorship, the Star of David and the Holocaust, as well as dictatorship antisemitism), others of which are more general—brings the past into the present and the present into the past, establishing that this story transcends a particular historical epoch in its connection to the subjective and collective experience of fear. The prologue's linguistic repetition and elaboration establishes and highlights poetic techne, rendering the relationship between history, mythology, and poetics apparent—and asserting the contingency of a nonanachronistic history. The prologue concludes by returning to the fear of Peruvians, and the "we" (the national body), again addressed in the imperfect tense, are never defined explicitly as Chileans, but conjured implicitly through nationalistic fear of the other.

The prologue demonstrates that the formulation of a historic narrative is a poetic act and is tied to a national mythology that emerges from subjective emotional experiences. This establishes the contingency of history and the ideology that undergirds it. On another level, the play's anachronism makes connections that trouble clear periodization, suggesting that historic figures are bound to their time's regimes of truth. The prologue brings Prat into the present so that the actors and audience might interrogate their own relationship to what roles may be expected of them. Finally, the prologue's foregrounding of fear insists on fear not only as part of Prat's story but also as a fundamental part of national identity: the "we" has been constituted by fear of the Peruvians. This follows Mouffe's assertion that all groups are predicated on a "constitutive outside," in which a community, in this case a national body, is formed by that which it is not.[84]

The play's subsequent temporal structure disrupts the linearity of the Prat myth's "historical" narrative. The play is not structured as a chronological sequence of events leading to Prat's heroic martyrdom. Set on the days leading up to the battle, between May 18 and 21, scenes often take place in short fragments, small snapshots of mundanity. At times, one scene will end and the next one will begin where the previous one began, doubling back to depict the same segment of time on a different part of the ship. During these scenes the sailors pass the time drinking, playing soccer, and discussing banalities. The sailors often have conversations about different things at different times. and fragmented human relations parallel the sense of fragmented time. Later, the play takes temporal leaps forward, and there is increasing crisis, fear, and drunkenness, though the play's absurdity does not diminish. As the moment of battle arrives, for example, rather than mobilize, two sailors, Bucarest and Juárez, discuss whether to let the birds trapped on the ship go free, or whether they risk being hit by a cannonball. During this conversation, one sailor impulsively threatens Juárez with a potato. Any sense of the temporal drive toward the play's impending crisis is undercut by the play's humorous absurdity.

Structurally and generically the play created the surprising connections characteristic of anachronism. In the text of the play, the scenes are given an exact time and place, such as, "The Esmeralda. Sunday, 18 May. 7:30 P.M. Dining Hall. After the meal." These scene headings, alongside the representation of quotidian mundanity as well as the randomness of the conversations and scene selection, give the script a documentary feel that works in tension with the play's overt fictionalization. Perhaps this is why many readers of the text in *La Segunda* perceived the play as anachronistic and political rather than as a work of fiction.

However, the play's connection to fiction is evident in the play's representation of Prat as sixteen years old—an obvious, verifiable error. Nevertheless, it is the *unverifiable* that constitutes the play's primary anachronistic gestures—specifically, its representation of the youthful Prat as a reluctant hero who rejects the role he is forced to play. Throughout the play Prat infantilizes himself, spending much of his time onstage looking for his mother. In an early scene, he stands at her cabin door begging her to come out:

> Mommy, I promise you that there is no other place I could be, I have thought a lot, and nothing occurs to me, and it was you who told me that you wanted to be with me. Look, as soon as I can we'll get you off the ship, I promise that I don't have strength, I promise, Mommy, that I don't have will, I wouldn't do anything stupid, ma, because I would not do anything.[85]

Prat here is unable to take responsibility for his life or act according to his own will.

Just as he rejects his own heroism, Prat also rejects a historical narrative that attributes heightened significance to events and that connects them to a regime of truth that would endow them with meaning. He tells Robinson, "This history is not key, there are no key histories, just as there are no key battles,"[86] undermining a nationalistic narrative in which the Battle of Iquique has long figured prominently. Further, he wishes Robinson was captain instead because he (Prat) is "not old enough for honor. I am not old enough to love another woman besides my mother."[87] Prat's rejection of his own authority prompts Robinson to punch him. Robinson thus violently enforces the patriarchy, heroism, and history.

Shortly thereafter, a conversation between Bucarest and Juárez emphasizes that the hero is a narrative construct dependent on the role one arbitrarily plays; meanwhile, the rest of the historical figures are supporting actors:

> JUÁREZ: You came looking for me so we will be heroes.
> BUCAREST: No, Juárez, the hero is always the captain.
> JUÁREZ: And the cook?
> BUCAREST: He's the one who nourishes him to become a hero.
> JUÁREZ: And the engineer?
> BUCAREST: He's the one who calculates so he can be a hero without a mishap.[88]

As the hopelessness of their position becomes apparent, Prat's rejection of honor turns to rage at the way the battle—and the state—is consuming Chile's youth. He sees a young sailor attempting to shoot a cannon without cannonballs. Outraged by the futility of this act, he confronts the boy:

> Come here, boy, let the boys shoot the cannons without balls. That's it, the children of who knows who, shoot the cannons without balls. Come on, son, light the wick; shout, son, shout,

> Viva Chile! Each time the canon explodes, let the boys shout, Viva Chile! Long live the boys of Chile! Long explode/exploit the boys of Chile! Long live Chile without boys![89]

This is Prat's moment of greatest agency and clarity. He proclaims the nationalistic cry, "Viva Chile," anachronistically transforming the call into a passionate tirade against state violence and its consumption of the country's youth, inverting Prat's dedication to his nation and his values. Robinson punches Prat again, knocking him to the floor and silencing him. Forces stronger than Prat control his life; his own critique will be erased by history.

Prat next appears alone, rehearsing his famous speech. He makes it clear that this is a fictionalization of his life by connecting his personal narrative to a larger, more archetypical narrative. He says, "My father died of an illness in the southern countryside," then ironically adds, "like fathers die." He continues to discuss his siblings: "The first died because he was born prematurely, like the first ones are born."[90] The darkly ironic repetition linking the deaths and births to a universalized master narrative renders Prat's own story part of a larger fiction in which his own future was fated: "And I, who did not get to know anyone, was born a hero. 'Avenge the blood,' they said." He goes on to emphasize that his own conditions of possibility were limited by his life story, elaborating with ironic dark humor: "When one has had brothers like that, you cannot play dumb, you cannot die of cancer, no sir, you must eat and shit the role, the role, the role, the role, the ROLE, if I say it enough times I bet it sounds like another word. They should have called me Rolando."[91] Prat has been consumed by his role, a word, a notion so redundant that it has come to be meaningless. He is not a key figure in a key battle, but a consumed figure in an all-consuming battle with a nationalistic narrative. He again pronounces, "VIVA CHILE," a phrase now transformed by his earlier tirade about state violence and its cannibalism of youth; he too is a youth consumed by Chile so it may endure.

The following scene with Prat's closest friend, Graziet, begins with the stage direction "(*drunk*)." This stage direction and the ensuing scene would prove to be one of the most controversial: the drunkenness an affront to Prat's heroic gesture and the affection the two men show to each other evidence of Prat's homosexuality (an interpretation Infante would refute as never something they had intended). In a moment of quiet before his martyrdom, Prat, inebriated, childlike, and unable to find his mother, asks his friend to pat him on the head. When Graziet asks Prat to reciprocate the gesture, Prat again rejects his own agency and asserts self-doubt, telling his friend, "Because when I do it, I always think that I am doing it badly." Graziet responds that Prat will be important, and the two adolescents reflect on the nature of Prat's heroism:

GRAZIET: You are going to be important, Prat.
PRAT: Yes, I know, Graziet.
GRAZIET: And why you, Prat?
PRAT: I don't know, Graziet. . . .
GRAZIET: Are you going to jump, Prat?
PRAT: I think so, Graziet.
GRAZIET: You are going to be a hero, Prat, a martyr. Do you want that? Does that serve us?
PRAT: Look me in the eyes, Graziet. (*He takes his face in his hands.*) I don't know.[92]

Prat's assertion that he does not know the value of his own heroism implies a larger critique of nationalistic histories: What end do such narratives serve, particularly when they involve loss of life and when they bolster fear of the other and nationalism?

The scene shifts and Prat prepares to jump aboard the enemy ship. However, Jean Crisp notices Prat's jacket is missing a button. Prat is hardly the image of the dignified hero: he is unkempt and must borrow a jacket from the boy sailor. That done, he cannot remember what he was going to say, and Jean Crisp whispers the famous words of his speech into his ear. Before he can jump, he notices that the ship is moving and, unsettled, asks who is at the helm. The boy sailor replies that it is Prat's mother. The ship lurches and Prat is thrown onto the enemy ship. He is still fully dependent on his mother, and he is not afforded the agency even to jump and realize his defining heroic act.

The script published in *La Segunda*—a partial representation of the play's dramaturgy—enacted several anachronistic gestures. First was the fundamental factual inaccuracy: the play plucked the Prat of historical record out of the story and in his place inserted the sixteen-year-old boy, which both factually and in Chile's national imaginary he could not have been. It compounded this verifiable inaccuracy with the unverifiable: a representation of Prat's subjective experience. This exploration of Prat's subjectivity, the proposition that Prat was unready for heroism, challenged the "regime of truth" that had long governed Prat's history. His history belonged to a mythic time; his iconic figure had contributed to the maintenance of certain national values, and to complicate this story with a different subjective experience was to bring one regime of truth into another—in which the world was a more complicated place, nationalism and the state were subject to critique, and memory and history were subjective experiences. The students thus asserted their right as citizens to reimagine national history, to claim such histories as their own, and to consider how they might define their own futures. In the scandal following the script's printing, the nuances in these anachronistic gestures were lost, though the fundamental anachronism was not. This anachronism was simplified, heightened, and distorted in ways that would inextricably shape the dramaturgy of the play and its impact.

The script was published alongside an article by the Vial, the same historian whose apologist supplements outlining the unrest of the predictatorship period had accompanied Pinochet's "Letter to the Chileans." Vial condemned the show in a critique tinged with homophobia and political grievance. Vial asserted the authority of factually based history. By refusing to consider the student's artistic intent in fictionalizing Prat's life, Vial could only view the play through the lens of historical accuracy and heteropatriarchy. In his critique of the play, Vial thus affirmed Rancière's understanding of anachronism as a fundamentally political act. For Vial, the play's anachronism threatened Chilean values, an act that justified the curtailment of certain democratic rights of the citizen-artists.

Lest it was unclear that Vial's critique was steeped in residual political divisions of the dictatorship period, he suggested that artists would never have depicted a "drunk and drugged Salvador Allende."[93] He went on to argue that such false depictions were a slippery slope and could lead to the same treatment of "Allende, or with Orlando Letelier, Víctor Jara, or Tucapel Jiménez, or with the detained and disappeared."[94] He thus concluded his critique by threatening the sanctity of the memories of the Left and—in defense of a silencing consensus—by arguing that the state should not foster divisiveness by funding such plays. Though the play is about Prat, Vial firmly situated it as part of the memory battles over the legacy of the dictatorship. In doing so, he implicitly advocated for the maintenance of consensus at the expense of cultural pluralism and asserted a hegemonic interpretation of historical narratives.

A few days later, the minister of education, Mariana Aylwin, distanced herself from the play. In a statement, Aylwin emphasized the panel's autonomy. While the ministry would uphold the panel's decision, she was clear that the play did not reflect the thinking of the ministry itself. Aylwin asserted, "We understand that from the perspective of the Ministry of Education we have to reconcile that [the commitment not to censor] with the protection of values that preside over our national convivencia."[95] This statement belies the limits placed on cultural pluralism in favor of a national convivencia.

Palma, the director of FONDART, was more vociferous in her support of the play, and she participated in an event in solidarity with the students. At the event, Palma connected the play's funding to the principles of a democratic society. The real threat was not posed by *Prat*, she argued, but by those who would censor it:

> In democracy . . . a fundamental principle is the unrestricted respect for freedom of creation. We understand that people and institutions such as the September 11 Corporation, which backed

> the military dictatorship for so many years in Chile, which applied a systematic policy of censorship, may have a hard time understanding the cultural dimension of democracy. However, as a cultural program of the State we cannot accept that one would try to prevent the premiere of a play because one does not agree with its contents, precisely because we must protect compliance with the fundamental democratic principles in the cultural field.[96]

Palma's less measured stance conflicted with Aylwin's equivocations. When a FONDART celebration in Valparaíso was canceled due to naval resistance and Aylwin asked Palma not to attend the premiere of the play or speak to the press, Palma accused Aylwin of caving to the September 11 Corporation and resigned:

> The defense of these principles and the right to premiere the play, *Prat*, are more relevant and urgent, when it is your knowledge that the playwright and director have received grave threats to stop the premiere of the play. More so, when the questioning and pressure come from an institution that glorifies the Military Dictatorship of General Pinochet, and a branch of the armed forces that was part of a government that applied a systemic policy of censorship.[97]

The tension between Palma and Aylwin also reveals the splintering support among the Concertación coalition for a consensus-based project.[98] Palma accused Aylwin of being too conciliatory to the authoritarian enclaves within Chilean society—a critique that implicates the larger policy of convivencia—and of also demanding self-censorship. The play was thus enmeshed in multiple conflicts touching Chilean democracy: those surrounding the status of official history, those surrounding the legacy of the dictatorship and the status of the military, and those surrounding the efficacy of the Concertación's transitional project. Meanwhile the content of the play and intent of the authors was severely distorted or ignored.

Palma's resignation did not de-escalate the conflict. On October 2, 2002, four hundred military officers packed the Senate galleries to protest the play.[99] The ensuing Senate debate put the rights of citizens and the role of arts funding into contention and cast the conversation in constitutional terms. In the debate, the preservation of national values—here conceived as patriarchal, heteronormative, and militaristic—was pitted against cultural pluralism and free speech. Even more than in the press, the debate in the Senate made it apparent that the play had become a stand-in for a much larger conversation about arts funding, the nature of Chilean democracy, and the legacy of the dictatorship.

Senate member Jorge Arancibia Reyes, a former naval officer and adviser to Pinochet, introduced the topic, framing his comments as part of a larger critique of FONDART and attacking Mariana Aylwin.[100] There was a strong undercurrent of political partisanship throughout his commentary, reflecting a tension between the military and the architects of the democratic transition. Arancibia argued that FONDART had gone against its constitutional duty to "honor the country and preserve the essential values of the Chilean tradition."[101] The document Arancibia invoked, of course, was the constitution of 1980, put in place by the military regime to institutionalize its rule under the notion of a "protected democracy." Arancibia thus employed the notion of Chile's "essential values" to limit the pluralist free expression of democracy.

According to Arancibia, the values requiring protection were represented by the military hero. He rejected Infante's depiction of Prat, which he said characterized Prat as "a despicable youth, who refers to his mother as 'the female [bitch] who gave birth to this street dog,' who despotically and rudely treats his subordinates, who displays homosexual tendencies and is unable to pronounce his immortal speech because he is drunken and semiunconscious during combat." Like Vial, Arancibia rejected an image of Prat that did not conform to patriarchal heteronormativity by appropriately respecting his mother, exercising his authority correctly, and living with moderation.

He rejected Aylwin and FONDART's commitment to cultural pluralism. He argued instead for limitations on freedom of expression and maintained that "cultural diversity" cannot be pursued at all costs, particularly when it threatens national history and "allows the hero of Iquique to be transformed into a drunk homosexual." Arancibia concluded by asking the president of the Senate to convey to the president, Ricardo Lagos, that his attention was needed "against a problem so large that it cleaves the national soul and the bases of our convivencia." This last statement moved the debate to the terrain and contentiousness of the memory environment. Arancibia here was quoting Lagos, who recently had said the same words to express his dismay at the air force's justification for intentionally obscuring information about the disappeared in a report mandated by the Dialogue Table.[102] Arancibia outrageously suggested that allowing *Prat* to continue was a problem of the same scale as the investigation of dictatorship human rights abuses.

Following Arancibia's speech, the session was suspended so that order could be restored. Upon the session's resumption, several parties continued the debate. Critiques on the right ranged from centrist objections regarding the public funding of the piece to extreme calls to limit pluralism and free speech. There was also an emphasis on national history and heroic, martial values as the basis of a fundamental national consensus.

Those defending the play were just as willing to insert the play into the memory environment and to invoke the specter of the dictatorship. Carlos Ominami Pascual, a former member of MIR who was exiled during the dictatorship, defended the play stating, "Consensual art does not exist, except in dictatorships. . . . Fortunately, we are in democracy."[103] Ominami asserted the right of art to neglect rigorous historicism or correspondence to "reality." Furthermore, he argued that artistic freedom is "a constitutional norm." In such defenses, the funding of the play and freedom of expression were conflated—to not fund the play in this case would be to censor the play, and censorship is antithetical to democracy. Jaime Naranjo Ortiz, a senator from the Socialist Party, conceded that though he had not seen the play, people did not lose their lives fighting for democracy for a play to be censored. Invoking the deaths, exiles, and disappearances during the dictatorship, he argued that democracy must allow for freedom of expression.[104]

The Left's defense of the show generalized the debate around issues of censorship and freedom of speech in democracy (invoking the moral authority that came with fighting for human rights) and did not take up the complicated question of whether not funding the show would amount to its censorship. This question of the relationship of arts policy to censorship and democracy went largely undebated, as both sides cast the debate in more extreme terms about national values and democracy.

As soon as FONDART announced the play, several groups tried to legally censor the play. The first effort to halt the play's premiere was initiated by the president of the September 11 Corporation under the Law of State Security.[105] This law, instituted in 1958, was vastly expanded during the dictatorship with provisions that allowed for the legal punishment of those who spoke against the president or the military. During the dictatorship, it became one of the primary legal mechanisms under which political censorship took place—a role it continued to play even into the democratic transition. However, the September 11 Corporation's complaint was ruled inadmissible because it had been incorrectly filed.[106] Shortly thereafter, an independent citizen filed a protective appeal arguing that the play was offensive to Arturo Prat.[107] That same week, five opposition parliamentarians asked the minister of education to suspend the premiere of the play. Their request was also refused, though the ministry did distance itself from the play.[108]

The most effective legal challenge to the play came in protective appeal filed by Prat's relatives. Their appeal asked the Appellate Court of Santiago to declare that the work was an arbitrary and illegal act and to prohibit its exhibition. The appeal asserted the authority of history and maintained that the play's depiction of Prat was injurious to him and his family. Anachronism here was not taken for its artistic intent but as an affront to honor.[109] The appeal directly referenced several scenes, refuting them by citing historical sources, most of which were drawn from the biography of Prat written by Vial. The appeal concluded that "we consider ourselves seriously offended in our honor, because we have always had and have our predecessor [Arturo Prat Chacón] as a notable man, of extraordinary human and professional virtues as father and, needless to say, as a patriot." In this appeal, then, anachronism was considered an affront to honor, and honor was posited as a value that superseded the right to freedom of speech.

In April, the appellate court rejected the Prat family's petition, stating that it contravened article 13 of the American Convention on Human Rights, which prohibits all censorship. The ruling was appealed, and on July 16 the Supreme Court upheld the decision of the appellate court.[110] The limited scope of these cases meant that neither the cases nor the court's ruling touched on the question of arts funding. Because the protective appeals constituted efforts to directly censor the play by impeding its premiere but not by revoking its funding, the play was legally embroiled in larger battles about free speech and human rights, justifying the court's ruling based on the *Convención Americana*. The fate of the small student production thus hinged on international law and was inserted into human rights debates. The play became a surrogate in the battle against censorship, a battle that was part of Chile's effort to rid itself of the authoritarian legacy of dictatorship.

The scandal did not just take place in state and civil institutions. It also invaded the students' lives in terrifying ways. Prior to the premiere, the costume designer's car was broken into, and the show's costumes were stolen. Infante and other members of the cast were harassed in public and physically attacked. On the day of the play's premiere, Morales recalls arriving at the university, at that point surrounded by police barriers. The street swarmed with press, and there were protesters and counterprotesters on the streets. Pamphlets had been thrown around the area calling Infante a lesbian and alleging the play was communist. Inside the school, the students had set up a dressing room in one of the classrooms. There they had installed their dressing tables, which were decorated with inspirational materials and presents they had given each other in an opening night ritual. About half an hour before the curtain, a military-tactical police force (GOPE) came into their dressing room and announced that there had been a bomb threat. The students were forced out of their dressing room as the GOPE stormed in. The tables were overturned, their opening night gifts ruined, and the costumes thrown on the floor.[111]

Morales suspects that there was never a bomb threat but that this was done to intimidate them and ruin their opening night. He recalls, "I always get emotional when I remember this because as young people we had been part of the history of this country. The coup was very strong for us, but one didn't . . . one didn't perceive the violence that existed. It was different living close to that."[112] The scandal brought the past into the present for the students in unsettling ways. Infante was also surprised to feel the presence of the dictatorship: "I am from a rather postdictatorship generation, and I didn't think these things happened. I was left with a certain fear of the press, I felt used."[113] The scandal was a wake-up call for the group, alerting them to the limits of the freedoms of their democracy. Infante recalls, "It is as if they had told us, 'Well, we are in democracy, and you are free to have opinions,' and we said, 'ah, OK.' . . . And what we ended up having was 'But no . . . no, no, no, no, no . . . not that much.' "[114]

Prat in Performance

For opening night, the students invited a small number of friends and acquaintances, hoping the event would not be disrupted. Prior to the premiere, Infante read a statement to the press: "This play does not attempt to re-create the biography of Arturo Prat, it attempts to re-create our biography. . . . These are my words and not those of Prat. . . . They are our fears and our pain. . . . We can only speak of ourselves."[115]

Indeed, the play emerged from a collaborative rehearsal process in which the actors engaged with their own experiences. Bringing the play closer to themselves was a key aspect of the play's dramaturgical anachronism—an aspect wholly overlooked by those on both sides of the controversy. The rehearsal process brought the history of Prat out of the past and into the present, not to destroy the image of Prat, but to intersect with the actors' subjective engagement in the creation of the work. In the director María José Parga's notes for their first rehearsal, she drafted a statement that she read to the actors asserting that "the directorial proposal for 'Prat' involves the work of the actors as a priority."[116] According to Parga, what this meant was a rehearsal process based on the actors' reading of the text, their improvisations, and character development. She went on to assert that the actors were not there to serve a hegemonic text, but instead the text would be viewed "as a REAL support of the acting work and not as an aesthetic or other pretext." Parga's notes detail extensive rehearsals refining improvisations depicting the daily life of the ship or the battle scene, and she documents the actors' attempts to channel a realistic sensibility rather than a historically accurate depiction. Accordingly, video documentation of the performance differs significantly from the written text of the script, and the performance of the play was peppered with dialogue, songs, and transitional scenes derived from the rehearsal process. Further, the notebooks document the way the characters were refined in conversations with the actors and in rehearsals.

In her notes Parga also makes clear that the play was intended as fiction and that notions of "obligatory heroism" or the "false hero" were key thematic pillars. She documents frequent conversations with the cast discussing the concept of the hero and the way notions of the hero intersected with ideas about the state and romanticism. Throughout their rehearsals,

Fig. 12. The cast of *Prat* in performance, 2002. Héctor Morales (*center*), José Miguel Jiménez, Juan Pablo Peragallo, Rodrigo Sobarzo, Eduardo Díaz, Eduardo Luna, Tomás Espinoza. Courtesy of Manuela Infante.

the company was not thinking of Prat as a purely historical figure but as a symbol to explore their relationship to the concept of nation. It became an anachronistic process through which they understood their own relationship to Chile's national myths, the roles they played in their own lives, and their relationship to the national body.

When the audience entered the Sergio Aguirre Theater, they would have heard a voice over a speaker recite the prologue printed the previous month in *La Segunda*. However, the fears listed may have certainly seemed more urgent given the recent experiences of the students, whose dressing room had been raided by the police moments before. The wooden planks of the dual-level set would have evoked the deck and cabins of the *Esmeralda*. Alexandra Ripp notes that velvet ropes surrounding the upper decks "like those protecting art in museums" would have served as a "nod to the narrative's seemingly untouchable status and value in Chile."[117] The actors onstage—all in their teens or early twenties—exuded a youthful energy, making it apparent that the play was a coming-of-age story (see fig. 12).

Morales recalled that the audience seemed confused following the play's performance. The scale of the scandal did not match what they had seen onstage. He remembers, "And the people were disillusioned. The people had come to see a play that had grown in public opinion." Now they were asking, "Seriously, they got all worked up for that?" People seemed to think it was a "very good exercise, but it has all the defects and all the errors and all the inexperience of twenty-year-old kids making theater. It's nice what they are doing."[118] The reality of the play's anachronistic premise—which brought the subjective experience of a group of young theater artists to bear on a mythologized national history—did not seem proportionate to the controversy. But as this premise intersected with the distorted accusations of those opposed to the play—who felt their authority threatened— the play's defenders, many of whom had an interest in preserving the nation's cultural institutionality, transformed its dramaturgical enactment of citizenship into an assertion of freedom of expression, a rejection of censorship, and a case for the autonomy of the artists and the artistic sphere.

Becoming the Theater of Chile

The scandal surrounding *Prat* reconfigured the play's dramaturgy and shaped the company's identity, inserting the artists into a more politically charged role than they had intended and ensuring that their work became legible as an assertion of citizenship. Rather than retreat from this phenomenon, the company acknowledged and incorporated the complex imbrication of their work in the larger political and cultural environment. Morales asserts that the scandal "completely decided and configured us."[119] This dialogue with their own positioning is apparent in one of the company's most foundational gestures: their choice to name themselves the Teatro de Chile (Theater of Chile).

Carvajal and Van Diest point out that the naming of a company is a performative act. It brings the company into existence. It allows the life of the group to be seen as shared and continuous, as part of the same entity.[120] This group of artists would no longer be a collection of students, but a company. Henceforward *Prat* and the scandal would become part of the company's identity and would propel its subsequent work. Morales recalled that several company members were sitting at a bar across from the university during the scandal, laughing about those who insisted that they were not Chilean. If they weren't Chilean, what were they, they joked with each other. In a gesture that struck them as both humorous and defiant, they decided to name themselves "Teatro de Chile."[121] The name—and by extension the company's identity—served as a response to the scandal and to those who would brand them as being antipatriotic. According to Infante,

> We invented the name in the middle of the polemics over *Prat*. And it was *a way to stand against that*. In the end, it was a way to unite it with the themes of the play about Prat, to ironize with respect to

> the mess that they were calling us unpatriotic and all those things, and it came out of that and there it stayed.[122]

Carvajal and Van Diest suggest that the name performed several moves. It asserted the group's ownership of and right to claim national identity, implying that their expressive works were just as reflective of national identity as any official history. It was at once a grandiose and micropolitical statement: the students were Chile, but it also suggested (as the play did) that there was no universal expression of Chile.[123] Carlos Labbé and Mónica Ríos point out that read another way, the name suggested that Chile itself was theater, tapping into the veneer of society under convivencia.[124] Additionally, the notion of Chile in the postdictatorship period was not necessarily a positive reference. It—and patriotism—were ideas freighted with the legacy of the dictatorship and the disillusionment of the transition; it was a way the group confronted their fear of the nation and asserted their place within it despite their fear. The name also situated their work in a lineage with other historic theater companies with similarly expansive names, such as Ramón Griffero's Teatro Fin del Siglo (End-of-the-Century Theater), a move that implied that the students were part of a tradition of resistant theater. Juan Pablo Peragallo observes that "the theater of the end of the century does not belong to Ramón Griffero, obviously not, and the theater of Chile does not belong to us."[125] The expansiveness of the name, which clearly eclipses the scope of the group itself, mirrored the expansiveness of what *Prat* came to signify. Like the Comisión Funa and its direct actions in pursuit of justice, Teatro de Chile instantiated itself as an alternative state institution, invoking an alternative state. In both cases it was not simply an imagined alternative but a present reality made possible by the artistic double life of performance in a way that bled into political life. Despite the efforts of those who would censor them, Teatro de Chile came into being. Such acts of naming asserted the presence *in this world* of *another world*. They are the manifestation of an expanded sense of what's possible, offering tangible evidence that the Concertación's "extent possible" does not define the only political horizon. This possibility, in the case of the Comisión Funa, was that justice was institutionally feasible through direct action, that the wounds of the past could be expressed, incorporated, and perhaps healed, through performance. This possibility, in the case of Teatro de Chile, was that a national arts might redefine who spoke for the nation. It was the possibility that a group of students might make art, ask questions, and engage with the past on their own terms. It was the prospect that the ideologies of the future were not predetermined by Chile's history, but that the present was contingent and the future was an open possibility.

Following *Prat*, Teatro de Chile created works that continued to explore similar themes. Subsequent works challenged history and mythology, addressing figures such as Joan of Arc (*Juana*) and Jesus Christ (*Cristo*) as well as philosophical perceptions of humanity and reality (*Rey Planta, Realismo*). Carvajal and Van Diest note that while the company's experience with *Prat* created a traumatic relationship between the company and the press, it could be considered to have had a positive impact for the group in artistic terms, particularly in the way that "in the memory of diverse legitimizing agents (critics, the academy, the consecrated agents of the field) the name of Manuela Infante and Teatro de Chile came to be associated with a milestone in the development of a more autonomous artistic field in Chile."[126] Between 2002 and 2017, the year the group disbanded, it was regarded as one of Chile's most important theater companies, touring festivals in Latin America, the United States, and Europe and garnering significant national institutional support through funding and residencies. The company received multiple FONDART awards and numerous national prizes, and in 2010 it was awarded a grant to support the work of the company for a period of two years—at the time, one of the largest financial supports ever granted by the Chilean Ministry for Culture and the Arts.[127] The earlier scandal—which had sought to silence the play— proved formative in the creation of the company's identity, an identity that was forever bound up in the history of Chilean cultural policy.

The anachronistic dramaturgy of Teatro de Chile's *Prat* intersected with the contentious memory environment of postdictatorship Chile to lead to a scandal that amplified the play's political capacity and positioned its performance as an act of democratic citizenship. Rather than use the social environment to simply contextualize the work, I have sought to reveal the ways dramaturgy and the political capacity of performance are products of both artistic agency and political contingency. The case of *Prat* also highlights the political challenge inherent in memory's dramaturgy—for in its irruptions we find not only forgotten histories or erasures, traumas, and present postmemories but also dramaturgical modes of relating to the nation and challenging the ideological apparatus on which it grounds citizen-subjectivities.

Chapter 4

Dramaturgies of Rebellion

Guillermo Calderón and the Paradoxes of Political Theater

The year 2013 marked the fortieth anniversary of the military coup. That January, Guillermo Calderón premiered *Escuela* (School). The play takes place prior to the 1989 plebiscite in a safe house where guerrillas train to resist the dictatorship. The actors each wear *capuchas*, masks made from T-shirts and folded over the face, and the characters' identities are kept secret from each other—and the audience—for their own protection. Each actor alternates playing the role of teacher as the group learns about firearms, psychological warfare, clandestine communication, and the ideology of the capitalist system they seek to overthrow (see fig. 13). By depicting the activities of a youth movement training to violently overthrow the dictatorship, *Escuela* troubles the story of peaceful, democratic triumphalism pervasive in official histories. At the same time, the play asserts that what was gained by this "democratic" process was not, in fact, democracy but a consolidation of many of the dictatorship's policies: "An unreal democracy. The same domination but with a white mask."[1] The play operates as both a revisionist history and critique of the foundational ideologies of the democratic "transition." Forty years after the coup, Calderón provocatively asked what, beyond political aesthetics, had *really* changed.

Escuela was produced by the Fundación Santiago a Mil (Santiago a Mil Foundation, FITAM). It had an initial sold-out run as part of the foundation's annual festival in January and was followed by runs in the foundation's "Teatro hoy" ("Theater today") and "40 años del Golpe" ("40 years since the Coup") cycles, as well as an international tour managed by foundation.[2] Since the festival's inception in 1994, FITAM has played an unparalleled role in the legitimization, production, and internationalization of Chilean theater. Its many civic partnerships allow it official privilege, and its public-private funding model strengthens its ties to the state while imbricating it within the private sector. Its role as producer, presenter, and facilitator of national and international tours

Fig. 13. *Escuela.* Photo: María Paz González / @polagonzalezfoto.

and commissions situates it as a primary agent of the theatrical market. According to Carvajal and Van Diest, their annual summer theater festival, Santiago a Mil, is "the event in which the theater comes closest to being conceived as a *cultural industry*."[3]

At the heart of Calderón's *Escuela*, then, is a paradox: the play is embedded in, and indeed owes much of its success to, the same system and structures it seeks to challenge. This is further complicated by the fact that these structures were themselves born of resistance and facilitate critique, albeit along a particularly circumscribed (and commodified) line. According to Carvajal and Van Diest, the construction of the larger Chilean cultural field has led to

> the dissolution of the traditional antinomy between institutions and dissidence: the same institution can finance projects that later question it, the same critic can write against the art that pleases the tastes of the market, and at the same time, feed its gears. What the institutions reproduce is the availability that all the objects, all equally rendered merchandise, have in the market. In the same space you can choose antagonistic alternatives.[4]

How, then, do artists navigate these paradoxes to create resistant political dramaturgies in societies that homogenize and neutralize real political engagement? Can theater, in this context, become a site for radical engagement with and reimagination of notions of citizenship? Or is it always overdetermined by neoliberalism? Has the neoliberal reduction of politics to aesthetics resulted in the reduction of aesthetics writ large?

These questions serve as the restless engine driving Calderón's dramaturgy. Their urgency has pushed Calderón to develop a prolific body of work marked by self-critique and revision in the pursuit of meaningful political aesthetics. At the time of this writing, Calderón has written over a dozen plays that together address interrelated themes traversing Chilean and global politics. These themes include militarism and the patriarchal nation-state, the efficacy of political resistance, the failure of Chilean democracy and neoliberalism, trauma and the legacy of the dictatorship, and art's capacity to meaningfully engage with politics. Whereas in the previous chapter I explored how Infante's *Prat* was politicized by outside actors in a larger battle over the legacy of the dictatorship, in this chapter I explore how Calderón has sought to politicize his work in a cultural field that, in many ways, works to depoliticize his work. To do so, I situate Calderón's work within the knotty paradoxes that characterize twenty-first-century Chilean politics, as well as alongside the resistance movements—such as the 2006 and 2011 student protests—that have also sought to negotiate such paradoxes and posit a new vision of citizenship. This analysis points to a processual and paradoxical dramaturgy in which Calderón's plays—driven by an ethical commitment to political resistance and responsive to the demands of an art market that positions political theater as a salable brand—reproblematize their political engagements with each new staging.

Calderón's plays posit citizenship through its very redefinition: audiences are invited to reimagine their political positioning, affects, and experiences in relation to the political frameworks that have been constructed by the transitional democratic project. In Calderón's dramaturgy citizenship becomes not a particular constellation of rights and duties but the challenge of redefining politics. Nor is this vision of citizenship tied to the nation-state: international audiences are also invited to recognize these aporias as they relate to their own political context, and the state itself comes into question. Calderón's plays thus seek to reforge citizenship in times of "postpolitics." According to Calderón, "When plays reach a dead end they can be about pessimism, but at the same time it's theater, it's art, so when political ideas reach a point of pessimism there's always a possibility of creativity, of gathering around the village to think collectively, feel emotions collectively, experience theater collectively."[5] The imaginative potential of Calderón's theater—the interstitial space where the audience meets performance in the dead end of despair—offers a fleeting glimpse of a new politics and strengthens the affective desire that sustains its pursuit.

Chile, Postpolitics

In Calderón's first play, *Neva*, set on the verge of the Russian Revolution, Masha would be a revolutionary. Yet this desire is difficult to sustain, especially when satiated by consumption, as she explains to Olga and Aleko:

ALEKO: Olga, sometimes Masha wakes up with the urge to kill nobles.
OLGA: Is that true Masha?
MASHA: Yes, but it goes away after lunch.[6]

In this small moment, Calderón, comically self-aware, critiques the neutralization of political desire. This reads as a commentary on Masha's uneasy commitment to her revolutionary ideals but also points to a larger critique of the systems in which she functions.

In the first decade of the twenty-first century Chilean democracy could best be described as a site of paradox. Successive Concertación presidents, guided by commitments to consensus and gradualism, had slowly eroded authoritarian enclaves, restored civil liberties, and begun to address and seek justice for human rights violations. Yet Pinochet never stood trial, and many who had committed the dictatorship's crimes remained free. As the *Prat* controversy demonstrated, freedom of speech was a fraught concept, and those sympathetic to the military regime remained a force in public life. In many ways, the Concertación governments had deepened the neoliberal economic model begun during the dictatorship, bringing a measure of economic prosperity to the country but further entrenching income inequality and attenuating social safety nets. Though some of the country's democratic processes—such as free elections—had been reestablished, they were undermined by disillusionment and declining political participation.[7]

The paradoxes that characterized Chilean democracy suggest that Chile had become a site of postpolitics.[8] Though postpolitics can take different forms depending on its context, according to political scientist Japhy Wilson and geographer Erik Swyngedouw, postpolitics broadly refers

> to a situation in which the political—understood as a space of contestation and agonistic engagement—is increasingly colonized by politics—understood as technocratic mechanisms and consensual procedures that operate within an unquestioned framework of representative democracy, free market economics, and cosmopolitan liberalism. In post-politics, political contradictions are reduced to policy problems to be managed by experts and legitimated through participatory processes in which the scope of possible outcomes is narrowly defined in advance.[9]

Postpolitics is marked by the assumption that ideological differences have lost relevance in the context of the global hegemony of capitalism. The seeming inevitability of market co-option becomes a profound ideological crisis. At its most extreme, it is encapsulated by Francis Fukuyama's assertion that the end of the Cold War marked the end of mankind's ideological evolution, terminating in the universalization of Western liberal democracies: "the end of history."[10] Postpolitics makes it such that, according to Fredric Jameson's famous provocation, it is "easier to imagine the end of the world than to imagine the end of capitalism."[11]

Florian Malzacher points out that in such an environment the question of political theater is particularly fraught.[12] Old ideological frameworks are no longer valid and artistic production is easily co-opted by market forces. The unmooring of ideology on the one hand, and the threat of market co-option on the other, is why it took Calderón—who felt a commitment to producing political theater—until his midthirties to begin to write plays, searching for an aesthetics that did not succumb to this banalization.

Though Calderón had been working in the theater as an actor and director, he attributes his late start in playwriting to an uncertainty about how to express his experiences of Chile.[13] Calderón was born in 1971, and the experience of growing up during the dictatorship and coming of age during the democratic transition left him unsure how to position himself. As an acting student at the University of Chile, one of the major institutional drivers of contemporary Chilean theater, Calderón had an early theatrical formation that was influenced by works such as Alfredo Castro's *La manzana de Adán* (Adam's apple), which Calderón admired and considered emblematic of "postdictatorship" theater.[14] According to Calderón, Castro's staging created a density of discourse such that its meanings could not be co-opted. However, Calderón maintains that as such works became the theatrical norm, they lost their political valence. He observes, "This theater transformed with time, into a kind of formula that was more hermetic and disconnected from the political."[15] At the same time as he rejected the hermeticism of this "postdictatorship" theater, he was also unwilling to turn away from politics, as younger colleagues seemed to him to be doing. A self-proclaimed "child of the dictatorship," he feels he must "insist on the political."[16] Calderón's writings thus emerged from two conundrums, that of "postdictatorship" and that of the "post-political": on the one hand, he did not identify with the political languages of postdictatorship because of their commodification and loss of political viability; on the other, he rejected the depoliticization that took place during democracy. To find a way forward, which for Calderón meant to "develop a more explicit theater in terms of political discourse," he first had to get some distance from Chile, so he studied in the United States and Italy.[17]

While Calderón was pursuing a master's degree in New York, two of his collaborators, Trinidad González and Paula Zúñiga, suggested that he direct them in a play. Calderón had an affinity for Chekhov: he empathized with the sense of defeat he read in Chekhov's work. Furthermore, Calderón had become obsessed with the uncertainty around Chekhov's death. He agreed to direct González and Zúñiga if they would allow him to write the play.[18] The result was *Neva*, which premiered in 2006 at Santiago's Teatro

Mori Bellavista. With its premiere the group formed the theater company Teatro en el Blanco (Theater on the target), and Calderón began to develop many of the elements that would thread throughout his dramaturgy. *Neva* can thus be read as a starting point, in which Calderón—positioning himself in a paradoxically dialectical relationship to Chile—began a project to interrogate and explore theater's relationship to politics.

Neva takes place in a St. Petersburg rehearsal room on January 9, 1905. Three actors, Aleko, Masha, and Chekhov's widow, Olga Knipper, have gathered to rehearse *The Cherry Orchard*. They huddle together on a raised stage, illuminated only by the light of a small heater. The surrounding, nearly enveloping, darkness hearkens to a dangerous and uncertain world outside their theater: Russia is on the eve of revolution. The rest of the cast is absent, presumably having become embroiled in the Bloody Sunday massacre taking place that day. As the actors await their colleagues, they gossip, discuss acting, and re-create the scene of Chekhov's death. Eventually, their conversation turns to politics, and the dialogue questions what purpose the theater serves when there is real political violence in the streets.

Though *Neva* is set in Russia, the two countries' shared history of political violence renders the Chilean parallels apparent. Alexandra Ripp contends that the connections between Chile and Russia are underscored by the play's central image: the titular river Neva, which runs through St. Petersburg.[19] The characters refer to the river as a site where bodies were deposited during the massacre that morning. For Calderón, this image evoked Santiago's Mapocho River, "a kind of moving cemetery" where discarded bodies would emerge throughout the dictatorship.[20] The countries are linked by the urgency of the political situations, but also by the mourning for the lost life in the cities' central rivers—sites that should be sources of life for the city but instead become sites of moving death. This anachronistic disjuncture invites the audience to see the darkness of their time and where the light (the river as a source of life) should have been.

The dialectic between darkness and light is literalized in the play's design. The action takes place on a raised platform, on which an electric heater provides the only illumination. The costumes are black and spare, yet connote a period-specific realism. The actors are isolated together, finding light and warmth in a hostile and unknowable world.

Despite the encroaching darkness, the play is comically seductive, mocking the self-seriousness of actors and theater world gossip. However, in the context of the political violence occurring outside, this preoccupation becomes ethically problematic. Soledad Lagos and Carola Oyarzún both observe that in *Neva* the relationship between the real world and the theater are at odds.[21] The actors must substitute experiences to perform experiences, but even these substitutions are false:

ALEKO: For example, Olga, if you have to say, "I love you" and you don't feel it, you remember someone you loved.
OLGA: A different person?
ALEKO: Yes. You replace them in your mind. . . . For example, . . . "Mother, forgive me, cut off my hand." [*Masha laughs*]
OLGA: No, don't laugh. Why are you laughing? That was very well acted. What were you thinking about, Aleko?
ALEKO: About my mother when I hit her in the face.
OLGA: You hit your mother in the face?
ALEKO: No, Olga, I imagined that too.[22]

Human experience has been co-opted by the work of the actor, highlighting the alienation born of co-option that characterizes postpolitics.

As the play proceeds, Calderón interrogates the viability of various ideological positions. Calderón's preoccupation with ideology, particularly the tenability of leftist ideologies, will pervade his subsequent work. It is fitting, then, that his initial theatrical proposal in *Neva* addresses Russian ideological positions at the turn of the century: a crucible and testing ground for the leftist ideological vision that the dictatorship would work to eradicate and that would drive much of the global Cold War, just as turn-of-the-century Russia was also a crucible for realistic playwriting and acting. In *Neva*, Aleko and Masha represent two strains of leftist thought. Aleko advocates for a retreat from society and a utopic return to the land. Masha advocates for a violent overthrow of the current system. Calderón's attitude toward these ideologies is complicated, as he sees both their appeal and their failings. Aleko's vision is too disconnected, and Masha's is too dangerous. Calderón does not resolve their debate but uses it to represent a fragmentation in his own thinking: "Just as I divided my thinking in two characters, one that is committed to the idea of rehearsing theater and the other that is committed to going in the street to participate, I also divided this political idea of the one that retreats to his books and the type that is politically active, even though it will be fatal."[23]

Calderón thus posits a relationship between political activity and annihilation. As the play concludes, Masha's ideological commitment transforms into affective overflow. She erupts in a verbose tirade asserting the meaninglessness of theater in the face of political violence. Masha rails, "Yes, Olga. Your husband died and you want to relive his death because you cannot act. Who cares?" As she continues, she grows increasingly apocalyptic, telling Olga and Aleko,

You want theater? You want to cry? I'll give you scenery and tears. We're going to die and they're going to forget about us. Love will end. The sun will never rise again for anyone. Russia will end, we will die to everything. . . . May the theater die with you.[24]

After this tirade, she drops off the stage and vanishes. Her speech is cut short by a surprising theatrical gesture implying the death of the revolutionary ideal, an ideal both compelling in its emotional force and comic in its extremes and contradictions. Aleko then uses the stove to shine light on the audience, implying a complicity and urging, perhaps, a responsibility. Then he and Olga drop off the stage and the play ends. Whereas Masha falls off the stage consumed by her passion, Aleko and Olga willfully choose a path of retreat: though their paths there are different, each of the characters meets the same fruitless end.

Calderón's first play concludes with a strange ambivalence. Masha's rejection of the theater creates a metatheatrical tension, as Calderón's actors gathered nightly to perform a play critiquing the theater to packed audiences. The presence of those audiences not only heightened the play's fundamental ambivalence but also embedded Calderón's work within a deeper crisis, as the play's very popularity threatened to vacate it of its political potential. Reflecting on *Neva*'s initial run, Calderón recalled,

> I swore that this play would be very provocative, but as it was pretty and well done it was co-opted and transformed into a kind of high-culture object. In that moment it lost its political edge. I found that *Neva* was the most political play of the moment, but at the height of its popularity, two of Pinochet's ministers attended the play at two different performances, and upon seeing them applaud and leave content, obviously I thought that the play was not as "heavy" as I thought. Then I realized that plays lose their critical potential when they become cultural objects.[25]

With *Neva*, Calderón wanted to foreground his political discourse in the realistic aesthetic of a period piece. However, the play did not resonate as he had hoped. Its co-optation, evident to Calderón when two of Pinochet's former ministers appeared to uncritically enjoy the production, was facilitated by the Chilean cultural sphere as well as by Calderón's dramaturgical choices. The Russian setting, which he hoped would foreground the play's politics, may have had a universalizing effect, tempering its political bite. Furthermore, the play's Chekhovian references, excellent acting, and appearance at Teatro Mori Bellavista (a theater that programmed largely commercial theater) may have contributed to its situation as an "art object." Following *Neva's* run, Calderón vowed, "I have to radicalize my work even more."[26]

With *Neva* Calderón initiated a project to find a political voice in the theater, which involved questioning theater's political capacity as its initial premise. He also established several of the characteristics that would define his dramaturgy: the creation of spaces set apart from their time and the cultivation of estrangement, a dismantling of the structures and relationships governing the status quo, an emphasis on ideological questioning and unresolved debate, a metatheatrical self-criticality, and a final annihilating gesture that allowed for a new, if troubled, space of creativity. *Neva* proposes a vision of democratic citizenship that is ambivalent, in which there is an ethical imperative to politically engage, but the path for that engagement is unclear.

Equally fundamental to this dramaturgy is Calderón's critical and institutional success, the paradox of his own position within the broken world. *Neva* received positive critical reviews, which while acknowledging the sense of theatrical crisis in the play and its sociopolitical context also emphasized the excellent acting and design, contributing perhaps to Calderón's sense that the work had been perceived as an art object.[27] The play was selected by the Art Critics' Circle as the best national premiere of 2006 and won Altazor Awards for Best Director, Best Playwright, and Best Actress (Trinidad González).[28]

The play's success vaulted Calderón into an international theater circuit that further contributed to the contradictory dynamics at work in Calderón's political dramaturgy. After *Neva*'s initial run it was selected as part of the 2007 Festival Internacional Santiago a Mil. First produced in 1994 by Carmen Romero and Evelyn Campbell, the festival grew out of "a desire to break away from the dictatorship" and to support the work of theater artists, according to Romero.[29] The festival's initial programming was designed to appeal to a young audience with substantive tastes and to resist the dominance of consumer culture.[30]

Today the festival is overseen by FITAM, a foundation funded by public and private entities and that plays a key role in shaping the dramaturgies of Chilean theater. Every year the festival features a presenters' week, through which artists secure international tours and commissions. For a 20 percent commission, the foundation will manage these arrangements. Graham-Jones notes that "born out of a need for artistic solidarity and cultural reclamation, today its overseeing foundation occupies the center of Chile's theatrical production and is regarded by many national artists as final arbiter and gatekeeper of their success, both at home and abroad."[31] Teatro a Mil is an embodiment of the contradictions of the Chilean cultural sphere: at once democratizing and elite, an advocate for artists and a gatekeeper, an expression of a commitment to public culture that marshals private funding. Though Calderón recognizes that the foundation's dominance of the theatrical environment is problematic, he asserts that for artists the only option is to "just join . . . don't fight them."[32]

Calderón did indeed "join." *Neva*'s selection as part of Santiago a Mil led to its international tour, during which Calderón wrote his next play, *Diciembre* (*December*). When Calderón returned to Santiago he developed *Clase* (*Class*), which premiered at the Teatro Mori in 2008 and was featured in Santiago a Mil 2009 (in which *Diciembre* also made its

Chilean premiere). The foundations of Calderón's playwriting career were directly tied to FITAM. All the plays that he has subsequently staged in Chile [*Villa* (2011), *Discurso* (2011), *Escuela* (*School*, 2013), *Mateluna* (2015), *Dragón* (*Dragon*, 2019)], and *Colina* (2023) have been featured in the festival, and Calderón currently sits on the foundation's board. FITAM has facilitated numerous tours and commissions for Calderón in Latin America, Europe, and the United States.

Calderón's explicitly political theater must therefore also be seen as responsive to the demands of an international market. He explains:

> The international festivals always invite two important groups, like the Schaubühne and the Wooster Group, that are expensive teams of thirty people. But they need diversity, so they invite the odd group from Lebanon, Malaysia, and Chile. But these productions have to be cheap. We participate in this world economy that is "not the main dish" but the "worthy side dish." . . . Now, that side dish has to be political. Because they like stuff from Chile or from Lebanon or from Indonesia to be about war, torture, memory, history, horror. So, if you don't fulfill that, then it's really hard to pull off a love story or something else, so they push you in that direction.[33]

Calderón's residency with the Royal Court Theatre in London—where he developed *Discurso* and *B*—is emblematic of this political imperative. Artistic director Vicky Featherstone's description of the program illustrates its logic: the program invites "emerging writers from across the world to make radical new work for Britain."[34] Calderón—one of Chile's most preeminent playwrights—is positioned as "emerging" (alongside other well-established artists from Global South countries, such as Lola Arias [Argentina] and Liwaa Yazji [Syria]), and his work is defined by both its radicality and its consumption by Britain. In such residencies and commissions, marketing materials and critical reviews always refer to Calderón as a "Chilean" playwright—even though he has worked and lived extensively abroad—rendering his nationality a brand. In writing plays that are largely about Chile's political situation and casting these political questions broadly enough to be relevant outside of Chile, he navigates this political imperative by deftly meeting its demands for a political and national theater with his own ethical commitments.

Dramaturgies of Process and Paradox: *Neva*, *Diciembre*, *Clase*

Neva premiered in a year of political milestones: the nation's first female president, an atheist, Socialist, former political prisoner and exile, and single mother, took office; Pinochet died; and across the country secondary school students protested the Chilean educational system. In many ways these events demonstrated how much had changed since the dictatorship. There were new kinds of leaders, new citizen-actors, and the former dictator was no longer in public life. Yet the fact that even these events did not augur significant change revealed how entrenched the condition of postpolitics had become. Pinochet's legacy continued to divide the nation, and his death meant that he could never receive justice. The inability of President Michelle Bachelet or the students to enact meaningful structural change or transform Chilean citizenship—despite the promise that both had initially offered—would provide the background, and the disillusionment, driving much of Calderón's subsequent dramaturgy.

Neva established the fundamental problematic that would be the engine behind Calderón's dramaturgy: What is the political value and capacity of theater? Calderón's desire to further radicalize his work is apparent in *Diciembre* and *Clase*, which spoke in increasingly explicit terms to the contemporary Chilean political context. Though these three plays were developed with different collaborators, Calderón intended them to operate together at an "unconscious level," creating a "narrative density" that allows them to speak "in contexts, in relationships that go beyond themselves."[35] Like Isabel Baboun Garib and Alicia del Campo, I therefore consider the ways these three play's dramaturgies work intertextually and metatextually.[36] Together, the plays take the possibility of coherent ideological resistance as one of their central concerns and can be seen as working through a crisis of resistance engendered by consensus society. *Neva* interrogates the value of theater in relation to politics, *Diciembre* questions the validity of the nation-state as a concept, and *Clase* questions the integrity and viability of political resistance, particularly when neoliberalism threatens its co-option. Together the plays constitute a radically negative critique of the theater, of the state, and resistance. They also constitute a site in which Calderón worked to balance his increasing success nationally and internationally with his desire to create politically radical work.

Calderón's plays return repeatedly to transitional moments—settings that allow him to work through the possibilities, paradoxes, and failures of Chile's democratic transition. *Diciembre* is set in a domestic dining room after Christmas dinner, in a dystopic Chile of the near future. Chile is engaged in multiple wars: one in the north with Bolivia and Peru, and one in the south with the Mapuche resistance movement. Santiago has become a ghost town, as all the men fight the wars, and those who have returned are disabled. Jorge has taken leave from the military to celebrate the holiday with his fraternal twin sisters, Paula and Trinidad. Despite the absence of sexually viable men, Paula and Trinidad are both pregnant. The play's plot surrounds Trinidad's efforts to convince Jorge to defect, a plan she tries to keep from her sister Paula. While the sisters are drawn into an ideological confrontation, Jorge longs for his compatriots in the military, to whom he has developed a homoerotic attachment. The play posits a breakdown of the patriarchy and suggests that militarism and imperialism have led to a crisis of the structures they seek to reify: heteronormative masculinity, the military, and the nation-state itself.

Clase even more explicitly addresses the contemporaneous political environment of Chile, and it foregrounds questions Calderón struggled with in *Neva* and *Diciembre*: specifically, how to enact meaningful political resistance. *Clase* is set in a secondary school classroom in 2006, when students across the country protested the educational system. The students' dissatisfaction stemmed from the persistence of dictatorship educational policy, which deregulated education, minimized public spending, and ensured that the profit motive would drive the educational system.[37] The initial movement was massive and radical: the students demanded free, unrestricted bus passes, free university entrance exams, and an end to the laws governing the educational system. In June, Bachelet formed a commission to address the students' concerns. As the movement became locked in the specifics of these negotiations, the public demonstrations diminished. For a while at least, the students had been neutralized, caught up in negotiations with the government.

Though *Clase* takes place during the protests, its premise departs from this neutralization. The play begins as all the students are out protesting except for one, who attends class to deliver her paper on Buddha. The Teacher arrives late, with a head wound incurred in the tumult outside. In their subsequent conversation, he critiques the student movement, arguing that it agitates for better opportunities within the neoliberal system rather than a reconfiguration of that system. With bitter nostalgia, he reflects on his experiences resisting the dictatorship and admits his culpability in the present situation: he has failed to truly teach the students. Calderón's Teacher—a figure he admits is autobiographical—is unable to move beyond the past.[38] The play thus stages Calderón's generational disenchantment as a conflict without a solution: neither those resistant during the dictatorship, nor those engaging in the current resistance movements, have a way forward.

In Rancière's thinking, the political emerges when there is a fundamental disagreement over meaning.[39] It is an assertion of presence on the part of those who have been denied the space to appear and who have not been counted as equal members of society: the part who have no part.[40] The notion of a part that has no part is embroiled in two paradoxes. The first is that not having a part is itself a kind of part—a distribution of the sensible that is interrupted and redistributed in the moment of politics.[41] The second paradox is predicated on a fundamental contradiction that Rancière states is present in any social order: "In order to obey an order at least two things are required: you must understand the order and you must understand that you must obey it. And to do this you must already be on the equal of any person who is ordering you. . . . In the final analysis, inequality is only possible through equality."[42] The emergence of the political brings these paradoxes to light. It is, therefore, the "presence of two worlds in one."[43]

Calderón's dramaturgy is predicated on the potentiality of these liminal moments. Each of his plays takes place as tremendous shifts occur outside the space in which they are set: a revolution brews in Russia, wars threaten Chile on multiple fronts, student protests rock the streets. Calderón's plays occur at moments of becoming, in which politics have the potential to take place. The tsars might fall, the nation-state might dissolve, the students might reconfigure the educational system. Or they might not: these moments contain equal capacity to disappoint. Calderón revisits these transitional moments, in almost a traumatic recur, to ask how ideologies might find coherence. The settings of the plays thus reflect Calderón's preoccupation with the Chilean democratic transition and its central role in defining opportunities for political engagement. Calderón returns to such moments to search for a way forward. Yet the way forward is never clear, and his dramaturgy is subsumed by the double trauma of the dictatorship and the failure of the transition.

Although the plays are deeply embroiled in the actions taking place outside, they are not dramas of action. Instead, the plays occur at locations set apart from the events: a rehearsal room, a domestic space, an empty classroom. This leaves the characters suspended in a moment between past and future, allowing for a consideration of the deeper issues underscoring these events. These are heterotopic spaces, spaces that Michel Foucault writes "are something like counter-sites, a kind of effectively enacted utopia in which the real sites, all the other real sites that can be found within the culture, are simultaneously represented, contested and inverted."[44] Heterotopias, like Rancière's moment of politics, foreground the presence of two worlds in one. Calderón's heterotopic settings metatheatrically underscore the fact that the theater itself is a heterotopic space where more than two worlds are always present. Calderón emphasizes this theatrical dialectic with a design aesthetic that incorporates realistic elements but that does not seek to disguise the fact that this is a play taking place in a theater.[45]

By foregrounding theatricality, Calderón allows the characters' nonparticipation in the events taking place outside to highlight the audience's own nonparticipation. The normative imperative of democracy—the participation of its citizens—is turned on its head as the citizens sitting in Calderón's theater are invited into an act of nonparticipation, an act that resists co-option in the imperative of surface-level participation in postpolitics Yet it is also a nonparticipation that allows the status quo to continue outside the theater, and it is nonparticipation that allows his audiences to consider his work on formal rather than ideological terms and renders his dramaturgy paradoxically political.

Calderón complicates the explicitness of his politics by structuring his plays as unresolved dialectics in which the characters and conflict are defined by opposing ideologies. In *Diciembre* the central conflict revolves around Trinidad's attempts to convince Jorge to desert the war. Trinidad is a left-wing anti-militarist whose worldview, like Aleko's in *Neva*, involves escapism. She has spent much of her life traveling abroad and has a worldly elitism. Paula, meanwhile, is a racist nationalist who believes that war is necessary for a country's strength, and she would clearly turn her siblings in should Jorge defect. Though Calderón considers Paula's views reprehensible, he finds ideological coherence in them. Trinidad, on the other hand, is too detached from the world. According to Calderón,

> For me it was important that Trinidad, the idealistic character in the play, had this fundamental flaw. Paula, on the other hand, is a person that we don't want to sympathize with, but at the same time presents an ideologically coherent and committed discourse that many Chileans identify with.[46]

The weakness of leftist ideologies and the vulnerability of their co-option contributes to the central conflict of *Clase*, in which the dialectic is as much generational as ideological. The Teacher criticizes the student protests not for seeking to fundamentally change state structures, but rather for wanting more rights within a dysfunctional system:

> Professor: Your classmates outside are not earning anything. . . . / They want to be congratulated and to be given an A+ in fight and idealism. / I will give them an A+. / In opportunism. / An A+ in reformism. / An A+ in posing / An A+ in performing before the cameras. / They want capitalism to improve. / For it to become generous. / But don't be confused. / From this window it looks like an insurrection. / But from within it is conformism.[47]

The Student defends her classmates but is not interested in a political debate. She prefers to reconcile any disappointment with a detached Buddhist spirituality. In *Clase* the debate centers on both questions of idealism and compromise and—as in *Neva*—on questions of the value of political engagement versus detachment. These debates are never resolved. Though Calderón's ideological stances seem clear through his critique, his theater remains ambivalent.

In each of these plays, Calderón's dramaturgy stages a breakdown of the sensible, undermining the consensus upon which society has been built. The relations that structure the world, including professional, filial, and pedagogical ties are all on the verge of dissolution. Lies figure prominently throughout Calderón's plays, as communities and personal connections are undermined by uncertainty about what is true, underscoring the lies on which the Concertación's democracy was based.

In *Neva* the actors cannot connect on a human level because it is unclear where their performances begin and end. In *Diciembre* Calderón creates a world that is even more out of balance than revolutionary Russia. Calderón repeatedly returns to the image of the *hoyo* (hole), which encapsulates a grotesque spiritual vacancy:

> JORGE: And where are the men?
> TRINIDAD: No. There are none. They are all at war.
> JORGE: Right.
> TRINIDAD: And the few that return are disabled.
> JORGE: Like me?
> TRINIDAD: No. They arrive without legs and say that they have changed forever.
> JORGE: I have changed forever.
> TRINIDAD: Oh really? Well I have a friend who lost an eye.
> JORGE: He didn't cover it?
> TRINIDAD: No. He has a hole.
> JORGE: We all have a hole.
> TRINIDAD: Yes.
> JORGE [*touching his chest*]: Here.[48]

Upon Jorge's return, the connections between the family members have largely dissolved. The twins have no empathy for each other and operate at cross-purposes. Their conflict over whether Jorge should abandon the war is based not on connection to Jorge, but rather on their own ideological commitments. They frequently lie to Jorge, passing the deceptions off as "a joke . . . to relax you."[49] But these "jokes" underscore the larger lie of their pregnancies—which they use to manipulate him. But when Jorge reveals that he does not wish to win the war, but simply to die with his soldiers, Trinidad and Paula reverse positions. Paula wishes him to desert so as not to hamper the war effort, and Trinidad wishes him to stay because she views his presence as potentially undermining. Their attitudes toward Jorge stem from their agendas regarding the military exercise.

In *Clase* Calderón also presents characters who cannot connect. Over the course of the Teacher's ramblings, he concludes that he has nothing to teach the Student. Though he critiques the students, as Opazo points out, his criticism is contradictory, becoming a parody of itself.[50] He confesses that he has propagated society's myths: the myths of the Concertación, the myths of neoliberalism. He tells her, "I lie, I've lied to you. I told you that if one tries and works hard one can achieve anything in life. Well, it is not this way. It is not this way. There are people who try and work hard for all their lives and don't achieve anything. Neither effort, nor responsibility, nor being an optimist will do. Because I was that way and look at how that ended."[51] The Teacher's disillusionment stems from a paradox of equality: he recognizes a fundamental equality across humanity but realizes that it is unattainable because of the way society has been structured.

One of the dilemmas of postpolitics is the challenge of imagining an alternative future. Calderón's dramaturgy does not posit an alternative vision of the future, which he highlights by ending the plays with an apocalyptic gesture. In each case, these gestures are preceded by an effusive verbal outpouring by one or more of the characters. In these outpourings, the expression of political ideas defies the structures that govern political discourse, transforming into an affective logorrhea. This excessive language taps into a linguistic theatricality that runs through Calderón's plays, a tactic that Sofía Castaño observes emphasizes the metatheatricality of Calderón's work, and that contributes to an awareness of his plays as heterotopias.[52] These outpourings also underscore that politics do not take place on the logical level of discourse, but on a less rational, more affective level.

In *Diciembre* the sisters each have long monologues insulting the other, and this leads to Jorge's confession that although he initially joined the military thinking he might resist, he has converted into a patriot—not for political reasons, but for the love that has blossomed for his fellow soldiers.[53] Upon these revelations, the sisters reverse positions. Then they reveal that they were never pregnant as they open their fake bellies in front of the audience and allow hundreds of beans to fall onto the stage. For Calderón, beans are symbolic of the Chilean nation.[54] Their use in simulating the pregnancies suggests the deceptive qualities of nationalism, as well as the nation's sterility. Of the image, he tells Forttes, "The idea is that identity is trauma, and the (perhaps somewhat nihilistic) grand fantasy of the play is the destruction of Chile. In other words, the concept of Chile as a nation can cease to exist. I have never recovered from the trauma and I feel that this is a problem without solution. In the twenty years of the Concertación, I have not been able to reconcile myself to the idea of Chile."[55]

Clase ends in a similarly apocalyptic way, with ideology giving way to something more complex and resigned. The Student tells the Teacher that her generation too will be defined by the state's betrayal:

> My classmates outside look beautiful in the street. But the State is going to continue betraying them. And the history of this scam is going to continue forever. We are going to be the republic's new disillusioned generation. We are going to be like you, but with more laughter. And perhaps one day we will see the end of the ministries. The end of school. The end of classes. I am the Buddha.[56]

The Student stands, palms open, evoking the image of the Buddha. The lights go down, and backlit behind her are rows of chairs covered in student uniforms. As Ripp points out, the image is dialectic: it conjures masses of students marching, yet also evokes students sitting in regimented rows.[57] It suggests the hope of a mass mobilization, but it also implies that as they protest the students remain pupils of neoliberalism, and their demands fit into those structures.

With *Neva, Diciembre*, and *Clase*, Calderón established many of the tactics that would characterize his dramaturgy. The three plays operate together, in a process of radical questioning. They highlight the dialectic of the theater, introducing the presence of multiple words in a single space. They each wrestle with the failure of ideological coherence and the flaws of the Left. These ideological debates give way to political affects, which are subsumed in a final, apocalyptic gesture, leaving the audience to reckon with this unresolved conundrum. Citizenship is posited as a practice of critique and questioning, in which the structure that typically defines it—the state—even comes under scrutiny, therefore calling into question its viability as a category.

Mourning Politics: Forging Communities from Trauma in *Villa + Discurso*

With Calderón's next works he continued probing territory that explicitly addressed the Chilean present. *Villa + Discurso* constituted a double bill, coproduced with Santiago a Mil for their 2011 festival.[58] *Villa* dramatizes a debate among three women about how to transform Villa Grimaldi—a former site of political detention and torture—into a commemorative space. *Discurso* consists of an imagined farewell speech given by President Michelle Bachelet, who had been held at that same space. Though the pieces operate independently, they are richer as a diptych: together they address the fundamental inability of democratic processes to reckon with histories of violence. More than Calderón's previous works, both plays also—*Villa* through site specificity, *Discurso* through the portrayal of a real figure—engage the political by collapsing the boundaries between the heterotopia of the theater and the real world, creating a porousness and intimacy that serves to trouble, if not fully disrupt, the distribution of the sensible and forge a community in the theater.

The two plays were inspired by President Bachelet, a figure also imbricated in postpolitics. In many ways Bachelet's 2005 electoral victory demonstrated how significantly Chilean culture had changed. A former prisoner at Villa Grimaldi and a political exile, Bachelet was personally connected to Chile's traumatic memory. Her father was an air force general and opponent of the military coup whose torture and imprisonment led to a fatal heart attack. Chile's first female president, a member of the Socialist Party, an atheist, a single mother, and a feminist, she also embodied significant sociocultural changes. She valued participatory politics and promised that rather than rule by technocratic pacts her government would be "by the citizens, for the citizens."[59] She represented a new kind of hope, and when that hope was not realized for Calderón, an even greater disillusionment.[60]

According to Calderón, the premise for *Villa* emerged in part from the needs of *Discurso*:

> I wrote *Discurso* to be performed in Chile, but it needed a context. The fact that Bachelet had been tortured was very important for me. I thought about Villa Grimaldi, where she and her mother were held. And I myself had a direct relationship with that place. So I decided to use it as a context for *Discurso*.[61]

Villa Grimaldi was the site of a former nineteenth-century villa on the outskirts of Santiago. Between 1973 and 1978 it was occupied and run by the DINA as Cuartel Terranova. During that time, approximately 4,500 prisoners were tortured and interrogated there, 229 of whom were murdered or disappeared. Pinochet's troops destroyed most of the villa to eliminate evidence of the crimes. However, with the return of democracy, citizens petitioned to recuperate the site as a peace park. Calderón, whose uncle had been held at the villa, followed these memorialization efforts with interest, eventually writing audio guides for visitors. Today, the site contains an archive, re-creations of some of the buildings, a small-scale model of the villa as it once stood, and memorials. *Villa* is based on actual debates about the space that took place among those on the memorial's directory.[62]

Villa begins with a crisis of democracy, highlighting the relationship between past trauma and political processes. Three women, all the same age, all named Alejandra,[63] sit at a table holding a model of a nineteenth-century villa and fill out paper ballots (see fig. 14). They are voting, the audience learns, to determine how the villa should be transformed into a memorial site. The women write their selections on slips of paper and hand it to the chair of the group. The women were supposed to select from binary choices—A or B—but when the results are tallied it becomes apparent that one of the women has spoiled her ballot, writing the Mapudungun word *marichiweu* ("we shall triumph tenfold") on hers, nullifying the vote to the apparent exasperation of all three. When no one confesses to having done this, the women abandon the vote and try to come to an agreement via debate.

The play's action is thus predicated on the breakdown of democracy. The binary choices, like the binary of the 1988 plebiscite, present a limited

Fig. 14. *Villa.* Photo: María Paz González / @polagonzalezfoto.

set of options; real politics cannot happen under such constraints. In the play's first moments, Calderón stages a dissensual gesture: *marichiweu* is a claim for the "part that has no part"—in this case the Mapuche population that has endured centuries of ongoing dispossession by the Chilean political system. Ethan Madarieta points out that in the equation of marichiweu with a null vote "the play performs the Chilean erasure of the Mapuche from its memory and its nation."[64] Madarieta further contends that marichiweu and the presence of Mapuche absence will reemerge throughout the play, always as an irruption highlighting its erasure, always threatening any possibility of resolution via consensus.

Consensus, meanwhile, is framed as a coercive perversion of democracy, a "mind control."[65] However, in the play's debate, ideological commitments become hollow and insidious, as the characters argue for positions they may not agree with. One warns, "Be careful though, because sometimes you can say something you're not convinced of but you say it, like, clearly and you end up convinced of something you didn't think before, just because you've heard it so much."[66] Calderón thus portrays ideological commitment as both a requirement for real political engagement and as fundamentally in crisis—a position that allows him to critique Chilean politics as he critiques his own theater and to suggest a position without fully committing to himself to it.

The women have gathered because a larger meeting to determine an appropriate memorial erupted into violence the previous night. The space, as in Calderón's other plays, is configured as one in which debate and reflection can occur as crisis looms outside. The sense of being in an alternate world is underscored by the central scenic element, the enclosed white model of the villa (see fig. 14). The model is positioned as an object of contemplation, to be viewed with detachment. Yet this detachment is undermined by the fact that Calderón typically stages *Villa* (and *Discurso*) in former sites of detention and torture. The two plays' January 2011 Santiago premieres took place in Londres 38, a memorial at the site of a former torture center in central Santiago.[67] It has since been performed at other memorials including Villa Grimaldi, where the audiences were invited to explore the sites. By setting the play in spaces laden with traumatic history, Calderón invites his audience into an intimate community with his actors, a community that vibrates with a simultaneous sense of reality and unreality, of shared purpose and spectatorial detachment.[68]

The dialectical aspect of the theater is supported by staging elements that are at once hypernaturalistic and metatheatrical. The actors wear visible microphones, which render subtle shifts in voice and breath audible, giving the piece its intimacy. Yet at the same time, the timbre of the microphones highlights the voices' mediation and produces a distancing effect. As with all of Calderón's dialogue, the rhythms and colloquialisms of the dialogue here are at times highly naturalistic, though the language frequently veers into obvious theatricality through repetitive, quirky, and excessive usage. The play's combination of critique, leftist in-jokes, and self-ironization invites the audience into a community with the actors and with Calderón. As in *Neva*, the play's metatheatrical staging supports an interrogation of the meaning that art can give to past trauma. After one of the women suggests that "artistic art gives meaning to the thing in the end," the others respond with incredulity:

> CARLA: To what?
> MACARENA: To what happened in the villa. To what happened.
> CARLA: Oh.
> MACARENA: Yes, because this is such a big thing that it can't be understood, there's no justice right, so art does what art does and. . . . Well. You know what I mean; don't make me explain it. . . .
> FRANCISCA: It's just that it's not clear what art does.[69]

Ultimately, Macarena cannot answer what art does, and this question lingers throughout the play.

As with Calderón's other plays, *Villa* is driven by a debate, which parodies the ways other real memorial sites have been configured in Chile. The women critique, for example, the Museo de la Memoria that was opened in 2010. Francisca calls it "a politically correct, new-leftist version of history. . . . It tries to make out everything's finished with, like the wounds are all healing, like we're all so united as a country and we can spend money on a museum of memory that looks like a contemporary art museum."[70] The debate also highlights the tension of memorializing leftist struggles from advanced neoliberal environments. In one vision of the museum, Francisca describes

> a white room with a black-and-red banner that says: THOSE WHO DIED HERE WERE MARXISTS. Right. Powerful. Intriguing. That gives you an idea of what's in store. Because of course you're in a museum which is, like, white sort of with mirrors, like an international architecture competition, which is basically the aesthetic of modern-day capitalism. And you say, *this is very contradictory. Intriguing*. Right. And then you go into the museum sort of wanting to know who were these Marxists who died. And then they put you in a room with tables covered in Mac computers. With music, like that. And you can sit at the Macs and see lists of all the people who passed through the villa and died.[71]

The presence of the neoliberal economy threatens the banalization of the memory of the past traumas.

Even more than in his previous plays, here Calderón's characters are subsumed by the debate. It is difficult to track who believes what, and someone is certainly lying about having written marichiweu on her ballot. The indistinguishability of the women is made absurdly apparent by the fact that they all call each other Alejandra—a name that alludes to the infamous "flaca Alejandra," who was a political prisoner turned informant for the DINA.[72] Paranoia runs throughout the play; the women often conspire against each other. The Alejandras' mutual mistrust highlights Calderón's larger mistrust of democracy and consensus governance.

Near the play's end, Francisca confesses to voting marichiweu, and she gets the play's affective outpouring:

> Well, I vote Marichiweu. And I don't care if they punish me for the second time; . . . But I don't want to walk through the villa and feel all soft. I want to strike fear. I want to denounce them all. I want to be furious. . . . Because I'm from the nineties. I was bored at birth. I was sold at birth. I was strangled at birth. . . . There are people who tell me to change. But I want to stay suspended in the air. I want to be a photo. I want to die without changing. I can't stand happy faces. They'll call me, cow, misery, lefty, rabble-rouser. It doesn't matter. I'd rather stand waiting for the leader of the revolution. I can't stand the dawn. I can't stand happy endings. I'm the road not taken. I am bone. I am rock. I am cumbia. I am guitar. I

> am bullet. I am candy bar. I am little star. I am the people. I am the march. I am victory. I'm a walking political pamphlet. This is me. This is how I speak.[73]

Calderón thus associates living through the democratic transition (the nineties) as a formative political experience—one that has scarred and enraged Francisca. Francisca unabashedly asserts the politicization of her language, and the audience can infer that this perhaps is also Calderón refusing to apologize for teleologically political plays.

One of the play's nagging questions is why these women have been selected for this committee. Only at the play's end do they discover their connection: each of their births are products of rapes committed while their mothers were prisoners at the villa. The Alejandras share both history's wounds and a capacity for violence. This inheritance is not only the provenance of the dictatorship but also echoes Chile's foundational colonial violence, underscored by the fact that one Alejandra's (Francisca) mother was a Mapuche woman raped by a blond officer, who she speculates was German.[74] According to Grass, this gesture disturbs "the pact of silence that has existed for centuries in our country with respect to the Mapuche victims at the hands of the State."[75] For Madarieta, the rape by a German officer is "an always visible trace of internal and external colonial violence and of both Francisca's mother's and subsequently Francisca's trauma."[76] This revelation softens the women, and empathy and commiseration overtake the argument. Though they don't arrive at an explicit agreement regarding the site, they agree to respect that everyone responds to trauma differently. The play recognizes the impossibility of consensus. This is a pluralist, open vision, yet it is also a choice for the status quo, an acknowledgment that there is no adequate way to address the ethical dilemmas produced by national traumas. The play concludes with this acknowledgment:

> FRANCISCA: Yes. Because all tortured women react differently.
> MACARENA: Yes. There are women who never recover.
> CARLA: Yes. And there are women who organize and build museums.
> FRANCISCA: Yes. And there are women who become the president of the republic.[77]

With this observation, the women don the white jackets that had been hanging on the chairs throughout the show, under one of which is a presidential sash. The women then face the audience "invoking the image of Michelle Bachelet."[78] *Villa* ends with a segue into *Discurso*, where Bachelet will take the stage. The connection between the two plays established at the end of the first act emphasizes that her presidency was born of trauma.

Discurso is a poetic elegy, both to Bachelet's presidency and to the dreams of a socialist utopia. Written in blank verse, the text consists of a meandering goodbye speech by Bachelet at the end of her first presidential term. Though she does not mention the transfer of power specifically, in 2010 she turned the presidency over to Sebastián Piñera, the first right-wing president since the democratic transition. The changing demands within the Left coalition, their electoral weakness, and the rise of the Right marked the end of the Concertación as a viable coalition. Bachelet's speech reflects on the nation and its history with both pride and regret, mourning the failure of the socialist dream. It does so with a frankness that Calderón imagines is latent in the leader, giving her a voice that is not quite her own. Pottlitzer points out that the word *discurso* in Spanish has a dual meaning: speech and ideological discourse.[79] The play is at once Bachelet's speech and Calderón's ideological treatise.

In the Chilean production, the text was divided between the three actors who portrayed the Alejandras in *Villa*.[80] These divisions are not delineated in the published version of the text, and Calderón distributed them in rehearsal according to rhythm and desired emphasis.[81] This distances the audience from an easy connection with Bachelet as a character; it also highlights the play's theatricality and the presence of multiple words in a single space. At *Discurso's* outset, Bachelet establishes that this speech will be unusual, not only because it is a goodbye but also because someone is putting words in her mouth:

> Dear Friends: / I address you as president of the republic for the last time. / I'm here to say goodbye. / I know you think you know what I'm about to say. / . . . I know you expect sober words and hugs for everyone. / Like always. / But no. / Not today. / Today I feel like something's happening to me. / Before I came in, I took the speech that I'd written. / I read the first few words. / It's hard to explain. / I think that in that moment a shadow came in through the window. / And now I have a voice that isn't mine. / It's strange. / . . . today I'm going to be someone else. / Someone tougher. / And it's strange.[82]

Calderón thus emphasizes his own hand as a playwright. This disconnection illustrates the ways we put our hopes in leaders, the way we imagine them to speak, or at least think with our voices instead of with their own. According to Calderón,

> I wanted to write about Michelle Bachelet, who she is and who she was. I felt it was important that she was the first woman in Chile to be president and that she was also a direct victim of the dictatorship's human rights violations. I wanted her to defend herself

> against the many political attacks she received while in office. In reality, she never did so, but in my play she does. She never mentioned that she was tortured or spoke of her father, but in my play she does.[83]

The distance between Calderón's fantasy of Bachelet and the reality of her presidency becomes the subject of the speech, in which the utopic vision is always underneath the disillusioned reality. Here, Calderón's voice, and the critique of the democratic transition, is introduced as the part that has no part.

Calderón's Bachelet recognizes the fantasy that she could repair the damage done to Chilean society. Yet she also acknowledges that she was part of a system she did not have the power to change. By participating in the Chilean democratic process she would lead the neoliberal market economy and perpetuate the condition of postpolitics. Her primary significance would therefore be symbolic:

> And I was a good president. / Although we all expected more. / Always. / Even I did. / We all wanted an end to poverty. / Well. / Honestly, I did what I could. / I'm not to blame for everything. / Let's not forget the past. / I boarded a moving train. . . . But if you recall you didn't elect me to change everything. / You elected me for something else. / To give yourselves a treat. / . . . To have me be the best president in History.[84]

At times she frankly accepts this reality, while at others she reckons with her shame and guilt:

> Because all this business of being the daughter of a military man . . . / of having been a young socialist . . . / of having slept with the Party of the Vanguard . . . / of having been tortured, or not . . . / and then having changed so much. . . . / All of that is like a journey to the center of guilt. / Sometimes we victims feel that we deserve the violence.[85]

She apologizes for her imbrication in the capitalist economic model but does not renounce the trappings of it: "I sit and watch the lake sometimes. / I have a house by the lake. / It's an awkward subject I know. / I'm sorry for being rich. / Well. / I watch the lake sometimes and think, / 'Maybe capitalism is just a dark phase in human history. / Maybe the next phase will be all about cooperation. / Maybe life will be one big party. / And sex.' "[86]

Throughout the speech she wrestles with the identity of the Left. Though she feels as though people are "at least normal, leaning toward good,"[87] she cannot reconcile this worldview with the malevolence of those on the right. She is torn between her ability to empathize, her desire to rise above political violence and forgive, and the distinct feeling that forgiveness is a betrayal of the Left, of her principles, of herself: "Forgiving them is like betraying myself."[88] At another point she says,

> When you think I could have crushed the torturers with one finger. / But chose the smile and the warm embrace. / As a moral gift to History. / To make it clear that good and evil do exist. / And that I was good. / And that the others were the evil ones. / I forgave. / I was on the Left. / I am on the Left.[89]

The principles of convivencia and reconciliation are thus posited as a moral good and a fundamental failing of the Left, one of the reasons why the transition will always be a betrayal.

Throughout *Discurso*, Bachelet is frank about her failings. She apologizes to the students for the failures of the educational system and maintains that they are "right to rebel."[90] She questions whether schools are all just forms of subjugation, and indulges for a moment in an anarchist fantasy:

> When we go to school, we're taught to forgive everything. / Violence and brutality. / And that's the school of life. / Or at least the school of my life. / Learning to subjugate ourselves. / We know that by the age of seventeen. / Wait. / Maybe if there were no schools there'd be no violence. / Or subjugated people. / We'd all be rebellious and happy. / Maybe the anarchists who plant bombs in banks aren't that mistaken. / But I don't know if I really think that. / I'm not myself. / I feel like someone's putting words in my mouth.[91]

Again, the anarchist fantasy does not quite seem to be Bachelet's but Calderón's, allowing his voice, his critique, to be spoken by the outgoing president.

As she proceeds, she speaks about how her own trauma motivated her to become president. She asserts, "This story is like something to write a tragedy about. But playwrights aren't up to a story like this."[92] Calderón thus expresses his own inability to make sense of her story, and the play moves into a nihilistic register. Bachelet had offered hope, but still "there is no divine justice. / Or socialization of the means of production. / Men's exploitation of women will still go on. / Children will still be beaten. / Hearts will still be broken."[93]

The play ends as an elegy, and Bachelet tells the audience, "The time has come to say goodbye. / That is what I came for. / To say goodbye. . . . Everything ends. / And this is the September of my life."[94] Following these words, the table that held the model of the villa begins to shake, evoking a real-life natural disaster: the 8.8 magnitude earthquake that occurred on February 27, 2010, just over a week before Piñera was sworn in. Multiple water glasses—which now cover the table—begin to crash to the floor as the lights dim.[95] The only light is a small red light coming from within the model of the villa. The scene of the trauma remains, even as the rest of the world comes crashing down. Though Calderón's earlier apocalyptic gestures fostered alienation or critical detachment, this gesture brings the audience affectively together, uniting them through tragedy and mourning. The spectators feel themselves together in a crumbling world.

With *Villa + Discurso*, Calderón employs many of the elements that had come to characterize his dramaturgy: heterotopic spaces, ideological debate, a disturbance of the distribution of the sensible, and an apocalyptic final gesture. In addition, these plays follow *Clase*'s lead and speak with frankness to the Chilean present. Though Calderón foregrounds the intellectual debate over the plays' emotional register, these plays are undeniably more affective and personal than Calderón's previous works, reckoning with questions of trauma in the exact spaces where those traumas occurred. The site specificity would likely have drawn a sympathetic audience, and the sensitivity of being in such spaces, where trauma has what Paola Hernández calls a "power of presence."[96] The mourning evoked by the space would have combined with the elegiac frankness of *Discurso* to bind the audience together. Thus, as Calderón laments the breakdown of democracy and the dreams of the Left, he also brings the audience together in these sorrows, positing citizenship as an intimate community, bound together in relationship to the collective traumas of the dictatorship, the failure of democracy, and the failure of the Left.

Escuela and Mateluna: From Forging Community to Call to Arms

During Piñera's subsequent presidency, the student protests resumed with even more extensive demands. By this time, many of the students had entered the university. In 2011, the students again staged massive protests alongside a national strike. They demanded an end to "market education" and its replacement with universal, free public education. When the government declared that this was financially impossible, one of the movement's leaders, Camila Vallejo, suggested that it be paid for by renationalizing the country's natural resource industries (a key component of Allende's platform).[97] Thus the movement shifted away from educational demands and toward economic reconfiguration. Vallejo explained to the *New York Times* in 2012, "Having a market economy is really different from having a market society. What we are asking, via education reform, is that the state take on a different role."[98] Gabriel Boric—who had defeated Vallejo in the election for president of the University of Chile Student Federation—took a somewhat less radical tone but maintained that the students sought an overhaul of the educational system: "We're not taking an all-or-nothing stance. Our positions aren't maximalist. We understand that changes aren't accomplished overnight. But [real change] is going to require a willingness to transform the essence of our current education system."[99]

In addition to critiquing the Piñera administration, the 2011 student mobilization continued to critique the Concertación. Boric asserted that "nothing that is born of the Concertación is born with life."[100] The students refused to compromise their demands to align with either party's existing agenda. The students reimagined the resistant vocabulary of the Left in this rejection of the Chilean political system, reworking the historic chant *"el pueblo unido jamás será vencido"* ("The people united will never be defeated") as *"el pueblo unido avanza sin partidos"* ("The people united advance without parties"), and some factions went so far as to mount antivoting campaigns. They thus reconfigured resistant rhetoric, refusing to allow the specter of dictatorship and the political blocs established during the transition to dictate the intractability of neoliberalism in Chile. California Jackson emphasized: "We demand no more cosmetic changes in the Chilean education system but structural reform that leaves behind the 'consensus politics' that characterized Chilean politics for the last 20 years."[101]

The movement significantly impacted the following election. The Concertación dissolved, and a new coalition, the *Nueva Mayoría* (New Majority) emerged, with a more radical agenda. As the *Nueva Mayoría* candidate, Bachelet ran on three promises: education reform, tax reform, and the implementation of a new constitution. Citizenship was now framed around the right to education, economic egalitarianism (tax reform), and a reconfiguration of political representation (the new constitution). According to Calderón, the 2011 student movements constituted an "incredible political movement . . . where the students basically staged a revolution and Bachelet basically took office to enact the reforms that the students were demanding."[102]

Calderón's critique of the initial student movement in 2006 had been predicated on the fear that the students were not *political* enough, particularly in comparison to the movement he had been part of during the dictatorship and early years of the transition. He asserts,

> One of the problems with how the transition to democracy has written its own history is that it has whitewashed the movement. So basically, all the people who resisted the dictatorship have been painted as freedom fighters who were fighting for freedom against

> the dictatorship, people who were just innocent and pure and fighting for the freedom to vote and to just express themselves. But I belonged to the movement, and I can tell you that those protesters were people on the Far Left. The people who were eventually going to take advantage of the transition were people who stayed at home watching television or maybe enjoying the new bourgeois commodities brought in by the neoliberal revolution of the mideighties. So that of course is a source of frustration. The fact that people portray the resistance against the dictatorship as apolitical.[103]

With *Escuela* he worked to correct this apoliticism, to challenge this whitewashing, and to reinscribe revolutionary politics into that movement. Just as the 2011 student movement sought to reimagine resistance and the history of the Concertación, Calderón worked to repoliticize the history of resistant struggles and challenge the Concertación's narrative of the transition.

With *Villa + Discurso*, Calderón's dramaturgy forged intimate communities enmeshed in the ethical conundrums of the present: specifically, questions of memorialization, reconciliation, the breakdown of democracy, and the "reasonability" of power that all emerge from a shared history of political violence. In *Escuela* and *Mateluna*, Calderón further bring his Chilean audiences together into a community, which he accompanies with an increasingly tangible call to political engagement. This poses a challenge to his initial, albeit ambivalent, proposition with *Neva*, that theater is irrelevant to the life-and-death stakes of politics.

Escuela is set on New Year's Eve in a safe house, where a group of students—played by Luis Cerda, Trinidad González, Camila González, Francisca Lewin, and Carlos Ugarte—train to resist the dictatorship.[104] They learn to shoot firearms and arm explosives, how to communicate clandestinely, and about capitalist exploitation and psychological warfare. Each of the characters alternates playing the role of a teacher and student in an overlapping episodic structure depicting a series of lessons.

The play is a memory play, re-created from Calderón's own experience in resistance movements as well as the experiences of his contemporaries, such as Jorge Mateluna, who spent considerable time educating the cast during rehearsals.[105] For Calderón, working on the play was very personal, reconnecting him to the emotions of the period and his friends from that time.[106] The play offers a revisionist history, challenging the notion that the dictatorship was overthrown with a vote, and reinserting the part that has no part—the violent resistance movements to overthrow the dictatorship. Even this revisionist history, however, retains an element of obscurity. The actors all wear hoods, and their identities are not known to each other or to the audience. According to Calderón,

> For me it was super important to do this. Precisely because these people are invisible and as these people were never considered fighters for democracy, but because they were considered terrorists or extremists, they currently live in secret because you were a combatant for all your life. Despite the years this continues to be a secret, the identity is still not revealed because the dictatorship continues to be imposed in some form. And also because I think it is a sad, and uncomfortable theme and the play has to emphasize this. Finally, the political-military schools were like that, with faces covered. So, there is an issue with identity. Because the identity disappears as a person and you transform into a combatant bigger than a cause. And this is really nice, because it becomes a collective where identity disappears and you become something much bigger than it.[107]

The anonymity of the characters on one hand works to distance his audience and on another, invites them in, as they experience the same uncertainty the characters do. Throughout the play, Calderón employs the heightened naturalism of his previous plays: the set is simple (a few benches, a blackboard and projector), the actors wear microphones, and the dialogue is colloquial and, at times, circuitous. However, *Escuela* is less overtly metatheatrical, and the language is sparer. The humor of the play comes from the characters' reactions to the awkwardness of holding a gun or making a bomb, and much of the play's absurdity comes more from the fact that these are normal people training to commit violent acts and less from linguistic excess or other situational absurdities. In this play Calderón creates less space for ironic distance, and the audience is invited into the world and allowed to be seduced by its lessons.

As the play begins, one of the actors plays the guitar as the rest of the cast sings songs from guerrilla movements in Latin America and Spain. The songs encapsulate the idealism of the Left, emphasizing that these battles are not only national but are against capitalism and exploitation everywhere—political resistance to postpolitics requires global citizenship. As the final song concludes, one of the characters, Fidel, transforms into the instructor Zeta, donning sunglasses and taking out a bullet. He commences the first lesson on firearms. The lesson is interrupted as another character, Alejandra, arises and becomes the teacher, María, beginning instruction on capitalist exploitation. The lessons proceed accordingly—each one transitioning in medias res to the next—eventually circling back to resume where they had left off. This gives the play a fragmented sense of the student's continuing education and enacts a democratic structure as each actor alternates between playing teachers and students—a very different educational environment than the formal classroom of *Clase*.

The first series of lessons have a simple didacticism that troubles the boundaries between the theatrical event and real life, uniting the artists and audience in a common community. For just as the characters learn about the propulsion of bullets and the state's protection of capital, so too does the audience. The members of the audience are positioned at once as spectators and students in an ethical community with the theater makers. Calderón conceives of this relationship as a dynamic process of discovery, of coming together to think and feel and learn. He maintains:

> Because when you do a play you discover things that you felt and that you didn't necessarily know that you felt. And by exposing it in the theater you complete it with the reaction of the audience. It creates a sense of community because many people start to think what you think. . . . When the theater is full, I feel I am not alone. . . . For example, when you see onstage they are teaching how to use a weapon, you feel compelled to say something, to remain silent, to applaud, to be scandalized, to laugh. There is a feeling of discomfort because you do not know what others think. That secret disturbance, which forces me to negotiate what one feels with what one can express, is for me a minimal, but significant, way of re-creating what it means to live history.[108]

For Calderón playwriting is a practice of self-expression, of testing the limits of what one thinks, and through that process finding a community and reimagining oneself in history.

Eventually the lessons turn more affective and commemorative. An archival photo of members of a guerrilla group is projected on the blackboard (see fig. 15). In a lesson on bomb making, the instructor tells the story of sixteen-year-old Dani, a real member of the resistance movement that the cast's consultant, Jorge Mateluna, had known. While Dani was trying to plant a bomb to blow up a power line, he saw several people walking by, and, not wanting them to get hurt, hugged the bomb to his chest as it exploded.[109] Here Dani, who would have been marked by the government as a terrorist, is commemorated for his humanity, as one of the fallen in the fight for a true democracy.

With the story of Dani's death, the play shifts registers. The instructors are open about their disdain for and the cost of violence but are more vehement about the stakes of the struggle. One instructor, Marcela, tells them, "All this talk of war can sound disgusting. I know. But in truth I believe that we can win. The Chilean army are cowards. They kill civilians and hide. They are traitors. . . . For this I believe we can win. We can."[110] The play then moves from this affective, commemorative space into the ethical, as María makes explicit that any democracy following the

Fig. 15. *Escuela.* Photo: María Paz González / @polagonzalezfoto

plebiscite will be a continuation of dictatorial rule. This critique brings the play into the present, and the audience must reckon with their relationship to Chilean democracy, and whether they too should take up arms to fight the vestiges of the dictatorship. Though the answer for most will be no, more than Calderón's other plays, in which one can sit back and think critically, this play requires an ethical engagement. It forces a position. Can one accept one's own complicity? And how might one reject it?

Although Calderón forces an ethical engagement, he recognizes that the response will likely be ambivalence. He acknowledges that these dreams are too idealistic to be viable from the standpoint of governance. The political exists on the verge of its own demise. In her final lesson, María is asked what will happen after the revolution is won. She replies,

> I don't know. We will call for elections. I guess. And we will surely lose. Because we do not have the stomach to govern. The state disgusts us. We do not like power. Because what we have always wanted is simpler. We want to fight. And to create. A power that is popular. Popular. The simple power of the people. We do not want to make anyone a subject. We want. We want dignity, we want food. A stove in the winter. We want to go to the sea. We want liberty to live and to study. We want peace. Peace. But for this we have a long way to go.[111]

María thus recognizes the fundamental inequality upon which power is based: that it requires the subjection of some, and for this, she has no stomach; for this the revolution will always continue.

Despite the recognition that the guerillas' dreams are not viable from the standpoint of their institutionalization, there is a hopefulness to *Escuela*, and the play does not end on the same note of apocalypticism as many of Calderón's others. Throughout the play, the students have learned to fire a gun, but they have yet to shoot. They need practice, they suggest, and their instructor, Zeta, agrees. He hands each member of the group a gun and instructs them to shoot at midnight. Before they do, they dedicate themselves: one to "Bread. Work. Justice and Liberty," another to his father, and another to Dani, who died embracing an explosive.[112] They then count down, wish each other a happy new year, and begin to chant, "Yes. No. They are both the same thing. Yes. No. They are both the same thing,"[113] as they shoot their guns into the air. The gunshots blend into the sound of fireworks and from somewhere, a cumbia. Though the revolution will not succeed, perhaps like the 2011 student protests its pursuit augurs the hope of the new year.

Six months after the premiere of *Escuela*, Jorge Mateluna—who advised the cast throughout rehearsals—was arrested for robbing a bank. Calderón and the cast were shocked. Though Mateluna had participated in the armed resistance to Pinochet and been incarcerated for those activities, he had since dedicated his life to artistic and cultural activism. The company could not imagine Mateluna would risk his freedom and suspected his arrest had been politically motivated. Calderón wanted, urgently, to do something.

The resulting play, *Mateluna*, is emblematic of and exceptional within Calderón's body of work. Whereas *Neva* questioned theater's ability to engage with politics, *Mateluna* intervenes directly by increasing awareness of Mateluna's case and pressuring the judicial system for his release. Calderón's political engagement now incorporates a direct and unambivalent call to action. In staging this call to arms, Calderón both heightens the dramaturgical elements that thread throughout his works and breaks with them—confronting the aesthetic parameters of the political imperative as well as his own sense of the limitations of theater.

Frustrated that his plays' politics were received by spectators and critics as secondary to his artistry, Calderón felt compelled to "test the limits of political theater." Calderón explains, "I always got a similar review: Oh, it's good that he's doing this political theater thing, but the good thing is that he's not doing overtly political theater, he's not doing *panfletario*." Initially, Calderón took this distinction between his work and *teatro panfletario* (pamphlet theater)—a form of unambiguous, largely amateur, political theater that emerged in the streets and farms and unions—as a compliment. However, he realized that this distinction was "a dismissal of

Fig. 16. *Mateluna.* Photo: Guto Muniz / Foco in Cena.

the uneducated or the people who are doing theater that isn't commercial, people who haven't had the luck to go to Berlin or Paris and the people whose theater is not an end."[114] By inserting a more confrontational political theater into the cultural field he would insist on that theater's artistic legitimacy, challenging the aesthetic parameters implicitly policed by the political imperative.

However, while *Mateluna* was born of ethical and aesthetic commitments, it was also born of a commission. Calderón had been invited to participate in a festival commemorating Peter Weiss at the HAU Hebbel am Ufer Theater in Berlin. *Mateluna* premiered in October 2016 at that theater as part of the festival The Aesthetics of the Resistance—Peter Weiss 100. It subsequently premiered in Chile in January 2017, as part of the Santiago a Mil International Festival. Even as *Mateluna* challenged the co-option of political theater, it represented a response to a market demand for just such a challenge.

Mateluna stages an even barer theatricality than Calderón's previous works. Not only are the cables exposed but so is the computer that runs them: entering the theater, the audience sees some chairs and a computer on a makeshift worktable downstage, from which a company member will run the play's cues. A bottle of water and half-empty glasses placed haphazardly on the table convey that the audience is witnessing a work in process (see fig. 16). Much of the play consists of direct address calling the audience to participate in Mateluna's campaign.

At the play's outset, company member Francisca Lewin explains the cast's relationship to Mateluna and introduces an excerpt from *Escuela*. She then shows a video, released by the prosecutor's office, of a police lineup, in which Mateluna is identified as one of the assailants in the robbery. She thus introduces one of the play's primary dramaturgical tactics: the use of documentary materials alongside metatheatrical reflection. This tactic will be used both to prove their case in favor of Mateluna and to underscore the constructed, theatrical nature of police evidence and documentary materials.

Calderón's metatheatrical self-referentiality constitutes much of the first act's structure. The cast recounts their efforts to process and understand the events that led to his incarceration. At first, Francisca explains, they assumed he was guilty and embarked on a theatrical exploration of his relationship to violence. They present excerpts of these attempts—all absurd, metatheatrical reflections on violence. Though they are presented as real efforts, each of these plays is a mostly fictionalized artistic creation—and all are wildly inadequate attempts to reckon with Mateluna's relationship to political violence. Francisca explains that the third of these attempts, *Aesthetics*, is a nearly seven-hour adaptation of Weiss's novel *The Aesthetics of Resistance*. The excerpt they then perform renders the notion of resistant aesthetics ridiculous, poking fun at the commission occasioning the creation of the show. Francisca tells the audience, "We want to warn you that we speak very quickly, and that the subtitles will also pass very rapidly. It's best not to read them."[115] *Mateluna* parodies an serious international artistic circuit in which resistant aesthetics are oppressively long and require translation. By creating this consciousness of the festival and the tropes of the political imperative, Calderón situates his play within and outside of the commission.

The first act thus constitutes a microcosm of Calderón's own processual dramaturgy, highlighting that dramaturgy's absurdity and inadequacy. Francisca relates that each play ends with an incongruous non sequitur, as the characters sing Erasure's "A Little Respect," a queer eighties pop song about respect in love. In the first two plays the song was followed by an explosion and a waterfall of blood: a replay of Calderón's final annihilating gesture. She maintains, however, that none of these attempts helped them understand Mateluna. Furthermore, the song baffled audiences: "Why so sentimental? Why in English? It was terrible."[116] Making theater could not get them closer to understanding or helping Mateluna. However, as they were working on their third attempt, they received a letter from Mateluna prompting them to seriously consider his innocence.

In the second act, the play shifts tactics as the cast presents the exculpatory evidence in Mateluna's favor: materials provided by the defense team, as well as their own re-creations (see fig. 17). In the first act, the juxtaposition of the plays with the police evidence emphasized the theatricality

Fig. 17. *Mateluna.* Photo: Guto Muniz / Foco in Cena.

of state power. Now these juxtapositions demonstrate that theatricality's insidiousness by revealing the corrupt manipulations of that evidence. In the play's most damning moment they replay the video of the lineup, which clearly shows the eyewitness selecting a man who is *not* Jorge Mateluna. Though this error was made evident in Mateluna's trial—an audio recording then played for the audience—the judges presiding over the case ignored the video and allowed the police to submit equally dubious pieces of evidence. Upon these revelations the actors angrily throw the onstage chairs, and they project a photo of Mateluna as "A Little Respect" plays. The sound cuts out, the photo of Mateluna disappears, and in the darkness, reggaeton plays.

But the play doesn't end there. Calderón attempts to channel his play's despair into action. One of the performances I saw, in 2018 in front of a packed auditorium at the University of Chile Law School, was followed by a conversation with Calderón and Mateluna's lawyers about the status of his case. While *Neva* posited that theater had no role in the streets, *Mateluna* spills onto the sidewalks outside of the theater. There the exiting audience was given the opportunity to pose with a sign declaring "Mateluna Inocente" and encouraged to post photographs on social media. The play was thus directly connected to a larger social media effort and solidarity movement to support the campaign for Mateluna's innocence.

But what of "A Little Respect," the poppy refrain that haunts the play? Beyond the surface-level call for respect, the song has no apparent connection to Mateluna's predicament. It is a song about lovers, in English, from the 1980s. It is a jarring contrast. But by using it throughout the play Calderón inscribes Mateluna's story on to the song, which in the course of the play becomes an earworm; Mateluna's struggle and the song become irrevocably, if inexplicably, connected in the audience's mind. Calderón tells Opazo and Benítez, "The idea of using the song obeys the need to instill in the audience the memory of the 'case'; each time the song is heard, wherever it may be, we want the spectator to remember that Jorge Mateluna suffered an injustice, that he is imprisoned."[117] In some ways, this is the play's most subversive gesture. It uses a piece of pop culture and co-opts it for political ends, performing the opposite of the depoliticizing co-option that Calderón has contended with throughout his career.

With *Mateluna* Calderón received his most ambivalent critical response within Chile, with many lauding its political integrity but critiquing its lack of attention to form. Some contended that it could not be considered theater.[118] Outside of Chile, the work has met with varied responses, but not with the same questioning of its theatrical value: in Europe, its political valence was foregrounded because, according to Calderón, "Audiences were shocked to realize how openly unfair and corrupt the justice system was in Chile." However, he maintains that in places like Brazil and Mexico, where there is similar corruption, there was a deeper aesthetic consideration of the play.[119] Where the work is inefficacious (it cannot impact the case outside of Chile), it can be considered a viable work of art; where it has the possibility of genuine efficacy, its status as an art object as diminished. The political imperative thus posits real politics as aesthetics, co-opting not only works of art but also political struggles.

By 2018 the Mateluna Inocente campaign had taken significant steps forward but was still met with frustration. On December 17, 2018, the Chilean Supreme Court refused to reopen Mateluna's case. However, the play and the wider campaign had provoked the interest of President Bachelet, and in March of that same year, as one of the final presidential acts in her second term, Bachelet issued a pardon for Mateluna. However, her minister of justice refused to sign the order.[120] Searching for a way forward, Calderón and the company began to develop *Colonia*, a new play about freedom and incarceration, in collaboration with Mateluna. This work established *Escuela* and *Mateluna* as part of a larger trilogy, connecting the dictatorship to the present police state as well as a wider curtailment of freedom within Chilean society. As their work on this piece proceeded, the student activist turned presidential candidate, Gabriel Boric, made a campaign promise to pardon Mateluna. In 2022 he did so, also issuing pardons to twelve other political prisoners—protesters taken into custody during the estallido. This act, like the establishment of *Escuela, Mateluna*, and *Colonia* as part of a trilogy, situated Mateluna's legacy in a wider lineage of political resistance, connecting the dictatorship and postdictatorship periods to the present political unrest. However, this act was met with significant controversy, and a group of right-wing politicians tried several means to block the pardon. Amid this uncertainty—and unsure whether their production would put Mateluna in jeopardy—Calderón and the company canceled the initial run of the play, citing an infestation of rats in Matucana 100.[121]

Colonia finally premiered in January 2023, as Mateluna's freedom remained tenuous. Following the performance at Santiago a Mil, Calderón gave an emotional curtain speech, switching from Spanish to English in a simultaneous translation. The speech offered context for the international audience of presenters who might be considering the show (again, an art object) while it revealed Calderón's own attachments and deep concerns for Mateluna. In it he conveyed the contingency of the play itself, as the ephemerality of the theater intertwined with the ephemerality of the politics in the moment of an uncertain future. The conclusions of Calderón's works often dissolve into uncertainty, but here the stakes were higher as the life and freedom of a real human being hung in the balance. At the time of this writing (August 2023), it seems the Right has moved on to other concerns and will not pursue its efforts to overturn the pardon. However, that could easily change.

As Calderón's works have shifted from a project of compelling audiences to reflect and feel about political circumstances via stories set apart from their immediate urgency to works that press audiences and legal structures to act on present injustices, we are left with the question of how to think about the dramaturgy of works embedded in the terrain of a shifting political present. Are these plays, once they surprisingly fulfill their role of political efficacy, disposable? Or do they gain another status: as an archive of sorts, a trace of the political agency of theater? In Calderón's later works the contingency of present, life-and-death politics meets the paradoxical essence of theater to transform what it is that theater is and does. Calderón can delay a premiere, revise a work, transform the singular into a trilogy—and in these actions it's clear that the play's meanings are not always known, even to Calderón. Rather they unfold in a relational dynamic marked by urgency, affect, solidarity, vulnerability, and a need to sustain life. This has led him to a dramaturgy that is nimble and prolific, marked by contradiction and paradox, and an imperative to continually rework the theater, knowing that at any moment everything could change. Yet this dramaturgy persists as a mode of engagement, for these changes, seismic as they may be to one life, do not transform the essential violence of the nation-state, and Calderón's theater must pursue the shape-shifting evasions of postpolitics. This results in a theater that is messy, uncertain, and affective—whose meanings equally bear the potential for profound significance or obsolescence. In fact, it is the political efficacy of his theater that results in its obsolescence, and when Calderón's post-political dramaturgy really does find politics, it can only exist on the verge of its own demise. Calderón thus advances a vision of politics that is at once deeply pessimistic and fundamentally hopeful, that calls for revolution and mourns it impossibility, that posits the breakdown of human connections while working to build community, that laments the bourgeois co-option of artworks but relentlessly insists on the political engagement of theater. The dramaturgy of his works offers a road map of sorts, a way to transport Calderón's audiences into a space for reflection, where perhaps the will can be found to revitalize the present and start again, or at least, to feel oneself alongside others in the desire to build a better world.

Chapter 5

Dramaturgies of Revolution

KIMVN Teatro, LASTESIS, and the Solidary State

On October 7, 2019, a group of secondary school students began hopping turnstiles in Santiago metro stations, causing disruptions throughout the city. This fare evasion campaign was an immediate response to a thirty-peso metro fare hike implemented by the right-wing administration of Sebastián Piñera. In the coming days, the action gained momentum, causing damage and closures across the system. On October 18, the campaign ignited wider protests in downtown Santiago, leading to the suspension of the entire metro system. The police met the protesters with repression, deploying water cannons and tear gas. Uptown in elite Vitacura, President Piñera was photographed dining at an expensive pizzeria.

Later that night, Piñera declared a state of siege and heightened militarization of the state's response. The implementation of extreme repression alongside the heavily circulated image of Piñera's pizza-parlor indifference stoked collective outrage.[1] The imposition of a curfew in Santiago—an action not taken since the dictatorship—led people in other cities to take to the streets in solidarity. The protests in these cities, which did not have a subway, transformed the movement into a much broader, national expression of discontent. Chile "awoke."[2] Protesters torched metro stations and buses as the government imposed curfews across the country. The police shot rubber bullets at the protesters at close range, injuring and blinding many demonstrators. Many of those who were detained reported being tortured and sexually abused by the Carabineros.[3] On October 25, over 1.2 million people poured into the streets in Santiago and around the country, issuing a massive constellation of demands that touched the entirety of Chilean society: a transformation of Chile's systems of health care, education, and retirement; the recognition of Chile's Indigenous populations; an end to gender violence, patriarchy, and state violence; and the resignation of Piñera.[4]

On November 15, 2019, the Piñera administration and a multipartisan coalition of Congress signed the Agreement for Peace and a New

Constitution, in which they agreed to hold a referendum on whether and how to draft a new constitution.[5] On October 25, 2020, the measure was overwhelmingly approved by voters: Chile would draft a new constitution via a specially elected body.[6] Though this had long been a goal of activists, it had proved elusive: the document governing Chile had been drafted in 1980 under Pinochet and had been designed to ensure that it would endure.[7] Though it had been amended in the intervening years, it was still a text promulgated by Pinochet.[8] Yet the unprecedented scale of the protests finally broke the forty-year choke hold this document held on Chile. But despite the seismic nature of this shift, it is important to note that the new constitution was not a widespread part of the initial demands of the estallido. One of the reasons it was accepted was that it offered a way out for Piñera, who faced pressure to resign. It was thus on one level an institutional, top-down solution to the unrest.[9] The degree to which such a solution (facilitated by institutional, democratic mechanisms) could really offer the radical change demanded by the protesters remained an open question.[10]

It is also important to note that in March 2019 the Senate had approved bills to ensure an equal representation of genders and proportional representation of Chile's Indigenous population in any constitutional convention.[11] Therefore, the vote in favor of the constitution was, by extension, a vote for gender parity and Indigenous representation. Feminist and Indigenous activism had been a particularly potent part of the imagistic repertoire of the estallido: performances by collectives such as LASTESIS and Yeguada Latinoamericana created a repertoire of feminist resistance, and one of the most iconic images of the estallido consisted of a mass of protesters climbing atop a statue of General Banquedano and waving the Mapuche flag from there.[12] Feminist and Indigenous subjectivities had been major players in the movement on both practical and symbolic levels, and were poised to become central to any new vision of citizenship advanced by the 2022 constitutional draft.

In the years prior to the estallido, there had been an increasing effervescence of feminist and Indigenous theater-making within Chile's mainstream cultural circuits, an effervescence proceeding alongside the foment of activist movements. Alongside and following the 2018 *mayo feminista*, in which feminism revitalized the student movement with a demand for a nonsexist education, there was a surge of feminist theater, including the work of Nona Fernández, Flavia Radrigán, Isidora Stevensen, Trinidad González, Manuela Infante, and Carla Zúñiga. Their work builds on Chile's rich tradition of political theater, reconfiguring it through an explicitly feminist lens and developing distinctive dramaturgies. Similarly, in recent years, a new generation of artists—including Khano Llaitul, Ricardo Curaqueo, Seba Calfuqueo, Daniela Catrileo, Olivia Casagrande, Roberto Cayuqueo Martínez, Filutraru Pailafilu, and Millaray Jara—have foregrounded Mapuche identities and issues in dance, music, visual arts, film, and theater. Grass contends that these young, urban Mapuche artists "recognize their Indigenous identity, incorporate their material and immaterial patrimony in their work, and develop an acute critical discourse" in response to the systemic state violence against the Mapuche people.[13] In particular, these works have been tied to activist resistance to the application of the Anti-Terrorism Law to Mapuche efforts to halt extractivism in the Araucanía and to police brutality, as well as to movements for plurinationality, autonomy, the recognition of social and cultural practices, and the restitution of ancestral lands.

In this chapter I ask how dramaturgies created by Mapuche and feminist artists intersect with the 2019 estallido and the proposed constitution. To do so, I first consider the new vision of citizenship advanced by the constitutional process and resulting document. Drawing from the 2022 constitutional proposal that Chile be a "solidary republic," I offer a theorization of solidarity as a means of understanding the ways this new vision of citizenship is enacted. I proceed to trace the links between this vision and my two case studies. The first, *Trewa: Estado-nación o el espectro de la traición* (Dog: Nation-State or the specter of treason) premiered on March 29, 2019, at the Catholic University theater, eight months prior to the estallido. A multidisciplinary work by KIMVN Teatro, *Trewa* weaves an interlocking tapestry of Mapuche responses to real instances of state violence. Similarly, LASTESIS's *Un violador en tu camino*, first performed as a flash mob during the estallido, confronts both the specific abuses of the Carabineros throughout the protests and the systemic gender violence of the patriarchal state. In doing so, both KIMVN Teatro and LASTESIS create dramaturgies that are reflective and constitutive of the revolutionary spirit of the estallido and the constitutional process. These dramaturgies reject pervasive state violence with claims to citizenship that are at once grounded in specific identities and expansive. They employ performative enactments of theory alongside the lived experience of real, vulnerable bodies to expose and denounce injustices that are systemic and personally lived. They use multidisciplinary and multimodal dramaturgies to invoke alternative ways of knowing, thinking, and being to demand a radical new conceptualization the state. They create dramaturgies of revolutionary solidarity: dramaturgies that are not monolithic, but that, through their plural workings, set the stage for revolution and point toward a world to come.

Toward a Solidary State

In the previous chapter, I explored how Guillermo Calderón grappled with the paradoxes of contemporary politics in Chile. Numerous studies have noted a crisis of representation in Chilean politics, characterized by low levels of citizen participation and disaffection with technocratic governance and democracy.[14] However, as Sebastián Ureta and his coauthors note, the estallido offered a "radically different kind of participation."[15] This included a model in which citizens posed their demands not only directly in public spaces via massive manifestations but also through a proliferation of *cabildos*, small, open assemblies of people discussing and deliberating on a wide range of issues. The estallido offered the promise, at least, of a more radically participatory democracy.

The election of the Constitutional Convention seemed to reflect this spirit. Even beyond the requirements of gender parity and the proportional reservation of seats for Indigenous peoples, the 155-seat group was remarkably diverse. The establishment center-left and center-right parties both underperformed in the elections to the convention (giving the Right no avenue to reject proposals.). A majority of the seats went instead to parties aligned with the social movement, including feminist and ecological causes, as well as to independents. Many elected to the convention were not professional politicians, but rather schoolteachers, social workers, community activists, doctors, domestic workers, and a chess champion.[16] The convention's first president was Elisa Loncón, a linguist, Indigenous rights activist and feminist.[17]

The document itself proposed to enshrine a globally unprecedented number of social rights, including access to food and rights to housing, social security, health care, and work.[18] It stipulated that nature has rights and that the state must protect biodiversity and fight climate change. It required gender parity in state bodies and public companies. It compelled the state to eradicate and punish gender violence and ensured reproductive rights, including abortion. It would have created a plurinational state, formally recognizing Chile's Indigenous groups, guaranteeing their representation in legislative bodies and their rights to their lands and resources, and granting their justice system significant autonomy.

A comparison of article 1 of the two respective documents underscores the 2022 proposal as a direct rebuttal to the society envisioned by the 1980 constitution, as it is currently in effect:

1980

> Persons are born free and equal in dignity and rights.
> The family is the fundamental nucleus of society.[19]

2022

> Chile is a social and democratic state by law. It is plurinational, intercultural, and ecological.

The first proposal of the 2022 document is a reorientation around the collective and the centrality of democracy to the life of the state. Whereas the 1980 constitution leads with individuals and their rights—initially framed as the patriarchal "Men" and amended to "persons" in 1999—the proposed constitution asserts Chile's sociality and emphasizes that Chile must be a democracy.[20] The collective and its governance are situated as the core of the state. The 2022 proposal posits several characteristics of the state: it is plurinational, intercultural, and ecological. This establishes a state that recognizes its preexisting Indigenous peoples (explicit in article 5), establishes that its society is formed by multiple distinct cultures, and acknowledges its ties to nature—a vision of the state that must account for complex interrelationships between peoples and the environment. In contrast, the 1980 document emphasizes the family as society's nucleus, an individuating logic that implies a patriarchal heteronormativity.[21]

1980

> The State recognizes and defends the intermediate groups through which society is organized and structured and guarantees them the adequate autonomy to fulfill their own specific objectives.
>
> The State is at the service of the human person, and its goal is to promote the common good, for which it must contribute to creating the social conditions that permit each and every one of those composing the national community the greatest spiritual and material fulfillment possible, with full respect for the rights and guarantees that this Constitution establishes.

2022

> It is constituted as a solidary Republic. Its democracy is equal and recognizes as intrinsic and inalienable the values of dignity, liberty, the substantive equality of human beings and their indissoluble relationship to nature.
>
> The protection and guarantee of individual and collective human rights is fundamental to the state and guides all its activity.

The proposed document goes on to establish Chile as a solidary republic, implying that the state seeks to pursue a common good at the intersection of multiple peoples' interests. It continues to assert the equality of its democracy, again positing a fundamental connection to nature, and proposes the protection not only of individual but also collective human rights as fundamental to the state. This is a clear repudiation of the dictatorship and its human rights abuses, as well as any subsequent human rights abuses. Under this document no such government could be legitimate. In contrast, the corresponding stipulations in the 1980 constitution center the autonomy of social groups rather than solidarity and interrelated public life, and the document positions the state in service to the individual.

The notion of Chile as a solidary republic hearkens to the estallido, which emerged as a massive proliferation of demands united in solidarity for a radical overhaul of Chilean society. The document captures this both in the articulation of the solidary republic and in the more than one hundred rights it includes throughout the document. The concept of solidarity also stands in direct contrast to the notion of subsidiarity, a principle by which the 1980 document intractably connected the Chilean state to the neoliberal economic model.[22] This principle (advanced in articles 1, 9, and 19) stipulated that the state could only provide a social right if a private entity (such as a corporation) could not do so. In practice, the preservation of these markets was not only guaranteed by the 1980 constitution but also heavily subsidized (and therefore incentivized) by the state.[23] This ensured the privatization of both the health and pension systems and situated citizens as consumers within this privatized system.[24] As Fernando Atria, Constanza Salgado, and Javier Wilenmann explain, the solidary state is a fundamental reorientation of the Chilean state, a shift from a constitution aimed at protecting the functioning of markets to a constitution aimed at ensuring social rights.[25] Convention members María José Oyarzún, Giovanna Roa, and Beatriz Sánchez affirm this contrast, suggesting it implies a difference between horizontal and vertical models of governance.[26]

Arto Laitinen and Anne Brigitta Pessi note that "solidarity" is a slippery term employed to describe a range of macro- and microphenomena, relations, and affects.[27] In many ways the notion of solidarity evokes the very paradox of democratic governance. Solidarity implies solidity, stasis, heaviness. Yet in effective social movements solidarities are open and light, able to facilitate the proliferation of claims in their push for transformation. At its most basic, Sally J. Scholz defines solidarity as "some form of unity (however tenuously the members might be united) that mediates between the individual and the community and entails positive moral duties."[28] Jacques Rancière describes a similar paradox in his theorization of democracy. He understands democracy as the interplay between the people and the body in which they are unified.[29] But for Rancière democracy isn't the integration of people into a multitude, but instead the tension between an individual political subject and a collective.[30] Rancière understands democracy as having the potential to disentangle and dissolve the collective body, an action that, Todd May reminds us, is grounded in universal equality.[31] To follow Rancière, then, solidarity operates via an egalitarian claim that consistently challenges the relations between the collective subject and the state. However, given that Rancière claims "the essence of equality is in fact not so much to unify as to declassify, to undo the supposed naturalness of orders and replace it with the controversial figures of division,"[32] a collective subject acting in solidarity must operate through this tension and resist integration into a coherent whole. This implies a solidarity that is always a work in process, that is negotiated through the conflictual claims that arise from assertions of equality.

Feminist political thought elucidates how such a vision of solidarity allows for meaningful collective action—rather than slipping into the same atomizing traps of neoliberalism that Rancière's conceptualization might seem to risk. Jodi Dean contends that solidarity is fundamentally communicative and relational. Following Kathleen Jones, Dean sees solidarity as connected to interlocking responsibilities: the responsibility to act, and the responsibility to otherness.[33] Feminist theorists such as bell hooks and Chandra Talpade Mohanty illuminate bonds of solidarity emerging in and through the relationship between difference and equality, which address what hooks describes as the "interlocking systems of domination like sexism, racism, class oppression, imperialism, and so on."[34] Mohanty argues that this intersectional vision is not universalist in the sense that it negates difference, but is instead a way to make collective claims from situated difference. Solidarity is a communicative process, anchored in "relations of mutuality, co-responsibility, and common interests."[35] Further, it must emerge by attending to the "most disenfranchised communities in the world." Beginning an analysis there, Mohanty maintains, the workings of power are made most visible, and "we are most likely to envision a just and democratic society capable of treating all its citizens fairly."[36] Yet even the "most disenfranchised" are not monolithic, and solidarity requires what Nira Yuval-Davis calls a transversal politics. According to Yuval-Davis, transversality involves standpoint epistemology, which "recognizes that from each positioning the world is seen differently" and that each positioning is always an unfinished process. This is grounded in "difference by equality," which limits and orients the political possibilities that might emerge from this difference; at the same time, however, the political possibilities are never fixed.[37] Marcela Fuentes's notion of the constellation is an apt metaphor here, a framework that Fuentes draws from to consider the diverse activities of plural feminisms.[38]

A transversal, feminist solidarity grounded in equality is necessarily linked to decolonial projects. The solidarity Mohanty and others advocate involves thinking from the standpoint of those who have been excluded, an epistemology that reinstates that which has been erased or negated by the dominant epistemologies emerging from the modern or colonial project.[39] The concept of the solidary state works alongside and creates space for concepts such as the ecological state and plurinationality. Such concepts, emerging from Indigenous philosophy and activism, have precedents in the constitutions of Bolivia (2009) and Ecuador (2008) and suggest a configuration of the state that is radically different from the Western liberal model.[40] Such a configuration emerges from what Boaventura de Sousa Santos has termed "epistemologies of the South": ways of thinking and knowing that counteract colonial formations and exclusions.[41] The ecological state reconfigures the relationship to the natural world, not for its resources but for its rights—positing nature as having status that is equal to or greater than human beings.[42] This is a way of incorporating Indigenous philosophy, such as the Mapuche *itrofilmongen*, the Aymara suma qamaña, and Quechua sumak kawsay.[43] Itrofilmongen (also rendered as *ixofij mongen*) is often translated as "biodiversity," but more literally translates as "all beings without exception." It is related to the belief described by José Quidel Lincolneo, that "the Mapuche person is in a chain of living beings that profoundly interact with the rest of nature and the spirits that exist within them . . . the role of *che*—that is to say, the Mapuche person—is to maintain this equilibrium in nature, but with a criterion of reciprocity. Nothing is given, nothing is asked, everything implies a permanent exchange."[44]

Plurinationality—a demand of Indigenous activist movements across Latin America and the world—challenges the formulation of the modern state as based on a single civic nation that recognizes only the individuals deemed citizens. Instead, it proposes the recognition and sovereignty of ethnic-cultural nations, many of which can be present within the state. Santos contends that it would require new institutions, territorial organization, modes of democratic and economic participation, legal pluralism, and public policies. It is a direct challenge to the traditional Western conceptualization of the modern state.[45] The solidary state—plurinational and ecological—is predicated on ways of knowing and interrelated being that exist outside of Western cognitive hegemony and that run counter to capitalism, colonialism, and patriarchy.[46]

The final proposition of the submitted 2022 draft's first article is that it is the state's duty to generate the conditions and provide the goods and services for both the equal enjoyment of rights and the integration of individuals into the full life of the state.

1980

> It is the duty of the State to safeguard the national security, to provide protection for the people and the family, to promote the strengthening of the latter, to further the harmonious integration of all the sectors of the Nation and to ensure the right of persons to participate with equality of opportunities in the national life.

2022

> It is the duty of the State to generate the necessary conditions and provide the goods and services to assure the equal enjoyment of the rights and integration of people in the political, economic, social, and cultural life of the state for their full development.

The 1980 constitution hearkens to similar ideas; however, above these ideas it posits the duty of the state as the protection of national security.

This centralizes the state's security forces at the core of the state's mission and provides an implicit justification for repressive violence. Both documents reference integration. The 1980 document, however, proposes integration into the capital-N nation, a subsuming or homogenizing logic, whereas the 2022 document proposes integration into the life of the state, foregrounding the ability of citizens to participate in and direct the state, rather than their subsumption into the national body itself.

Toward New Understandings of Art and Culture

The 2022 document proposes to formalize a new relationship to art and culture that is reflective of the solidary state. As lawyer Jamie Bassa notes, arts and culture occupy a marginal space within the 1980 constitution.[47] The first reference is in a section largely dedicated to various property rights. A clause in article 19 asserts the freedom—and notably, not the *right*—to create and disseminate the arts, and it grants artists intellectual property rights over their works. The arts are framed from the standpoint of the creator, and there is no reference to access and enjoyment of the arts and culture. This is, as Manuel de J. Jiménez notes, a capitalist logic that directly links the arts to private property and implies a mode of singular authorship, rather than collective creation.[48] And though the artist is granted authorship rights, there is no guarantee to a just compensation for use. The second mention is in the context of the activities of the municipality—granting municipalities the right to integrate private nonprofit organizations with the objective of promoting and disseminating the arts and culture. What little attention is given to the arts and culture in the 1980 constitution is therefore directly tied to the notions of private property, and to the state's ability to outsource the function of the state to private entities.

The proposed constitution offers a more robust and complex consideration of the arts and culture, dedicating ten articles to them. In article 92, the proposed constitution introduces artistic and cultural creation and access as rights:

> Every person and community has the right to freely participate in artistic and cultural life and to enjoy its diverse expressions, goods, services, and institutions. They have the right to the freedom to create and disseminate cultures [*las culturas*] and the arts as well as to enjoy their benefits.

This would bring the Chilean Constitution in line with article 27 of the UN's Universal Declaration of Human Rights, which asserts that all have the right to participate in and enjoy cultural life and the arts. The constitution links art and culture with the right to "cultural identity," a key protection that is developed to preserve and protect Indigenous cultures (registered as well in the use of *las culturas*), among others. It additionally asserts that art and culture can take place in the public space—resisting the privatization of art and positioning it as part of public discourse. Further, article 92 links the creation of art and culture with ways of knowing:

> The State promotes, strengthens, and guarantees the harmonious interrelation and respect for all symbolic, cultural, and patrimonial expressions, be they material or immaterial, and access, development, and dissemination of the cultures, arts, and knowledges, attending to the diversity of culture in all its manifestations and contributions, under the principles of collaboration and interculturalism.

The document further develops the recognition of multiple, situated knowledges and implies the contingency of all knowledge:

> The State recognizes and strengthens the development of diverse systems of knowledge in the country, considering their different cultural, social, and territorial contexts. In addition, it promotes their equitable and open access, which includes the exchange and communication of knowledges to society in the most open way possible.[49]

The proposed constitution works against a monolithic understanding of culture and establishes art and culture as linked and pluralist activities that reflect and advance different kinds of knowledge and identity formation.

The 2022 constitution thus sketches a role for art that is in line with the notion of Chile as a solidary state. The making and enjoyment of art are protected as rights and are part of a recognition of both the diversity and contingency of cultural identity. To extrapolate the principles of the 2022 document—as they are connected to the 2019 estallido—into a dramaturgical orientation we might then expect to see dramaturgies that enact a multitudinous sociality and foreground interconnections, interrelationships, and interculturality based on a principle of radical equality; that reflect or make claims to the many social rights stipulated by and protected in the document; that facilitate autorepresentation and participation in public life; that constitute a kind of knowledge making; that foreground human rights and resist state violence; and that advance a vision of a collective guided by solidarity—not subsidiarity—integrated into the public *life* of the state, resisting a subsumption into the state itself and its privatization of individual rights.

KIMVN and LASTESIS

Both KIMVN Teatro and LASTESIS reflect such a dramaturgical orientation. Both groups advance an epistemically situated politics: KIMVN centers on exploring Mapuche identity, and LASTESIS was founded to render feminist theory accessible through performance. The artistry of their projects cannot be untangled from the activist elements of their work. Their dramaturgies assert radical equality and develop modalities of transversal solidarity that reflect the emergent dynamics of the estallido and the solidary state. Before I turn to a comparative analysis of the dramaturgies of solidarity advanced by KIMVN's *Trewa* and LASTESIS's *Un violador en tu camino*, it is therefore important to first preserve each group's differences by charting their respective artistic trajectories and contextualizing their work alongside the specific activist projects their dramaturgies touch.

KIMVN Teatro and Mapuche Identity

Today, KIMVN Teatro is a multidisciplinary collective that incorporates elements of documentary theater and theater of the real to develop performances that preserve and render visible Mapuche culture and political struggles. In an artist statement, they assert that their theater is part of a political project to recover memory; legitimize ways of knowing, being, and expressing; to bear witness; and to document resistance. They conceive of their dramaturgy holistically, encompassing the social and processual aspects of their work as much as the artistic and political elements that they weave together in multiple expressive modalities.[50]

Paula González Seguel founded the company in 2008 as part of a project for her theater degree at Santiago's Universidad Mayor. She and her sister and collaborator, Evelyn González Seguel, had been introduced to the arts through a rigorous study of classical music offered at a community center in their neighborhood. However, Paula González had not intended to pursue the arts professionally and initially studied the social sciences with the intention of pursuing a career in law.[51] One of her degree requirements was to memorize the Chilean Constitution, a document she quickly realized she could not dedicate her life's work to. She explains that because of its "neoliberal thought, also the inequality and injustices in Chile, I said, I can't."[52] Her turn to theater was thus motivated by a disidentification with the document that formed the legal basis of the Chilean nation-state and the citizens' relationship to it. Over time, the theater would become a means to reforge her sense of her own Chilean identity and a tool to critique the state.

Like most university theater programs in Chile, the Universidad Mayor's was based on a classical repertoire. Accordingly, she participated in a production of Aristophanes's *Lysistrata*. In rehearsal, the director asked each woman in the cast to explore a particular "type" of Chilean woman, assigning González to create a Mapuche character. To do so, González frequently went to her grandmother, the daughter of a Mapuche *machi* (a healer and ancestral authority) to ask her how to translate or pronounce words in Mapudungun. When she returned to rehearsal, the director was surprised to learn of González's Indigenous heritage and encouraged her to explore it beyond their production of *Lysistrata*.

This began a process of personal discovery for González. Growing up in Chile—first under the dictatorship, but later under democracy—she experienced a profound erasure of her Mapuche heritage, both in the public sphere and within her own family.[53] Until her director's encouragement, she had experienced her Mapuche identity in the theater as either silenced or the target of microaggressions and overt racism.[54] The Mapuche are the largest Indigenous group in Chile. They have faced two centuries of state policies and racism that have led to their discrimination, marginalization, and, often, criminalization. Macarena Gómez-Barris asserts that the sixteenth century colonial occupation of Mapuche territories (known as Wallmapu) initiated "a permanent war against Indigenous populations."[55] At the time of the Spanish colonization, they were largely concentrated in the southern Araucanía region. The Spanish forces were unable to subdue the Mapuche population, and during the colonial period the Biobío River formed a natural border marking the southern frontier. Eventually, a network of trade relationships grew between these societies. But historian Amie Campos notes that following Chilean independence in 1818, the new republic "began the process of consolidating its territory and redefining its relationship to the southern frontier."[56] Eager to exploit the region's economic potential the Chilean state fully occupied the Araucanía by 1880. The Mapuche were forced into isolated communities, retaining a small fraction of their lands, while European and Chilean settlers established farms on the most fertile lands. The conquest of Araucanía created what Patricia Richards describes as "a two-tier rural economy exacerbated by distinctions of race and culture." She continues that the "adoption of transnational racist discourse naturalized the power of fundo-owning colonos and the local representatives of the Chilean state, imprinting on the post-conquest Araucanía the unmistakable character of a colonial society."[57]

The "colonial character" of the Araucanía profoundly shaped the region throughout the twentieth century.[58] During the 1960s and '70s, some lands were returned to the Mapuche population and protected as communal settlements, in a process of agrarian reform initiated by Eduardo Frei and continued by Allende. Many Mapuche participated in the social and political movements connected to the Unidad Popular, and thus became a target of the repressive apparatus under Pinochet. Additionally, Pinochet's neoliberal policies reversed these agrarian reforms. The lands were stripped of their protected status, and their owners were no longer recognized as Indigenous, an invisibilization that allowed the land to be commercialized by private owners. Large timber corporations benefited from tax breaks and subsidies and caused environmental degradation of the land.[59] The invisibilization was formalized by the 1980 constitution, which is the only constitution in Latin America that does not recognize its Indigenous groups.

Following the transition to democracy, the government continued to promote the expansion of the timber industry and the construction of hydroelectric dams, incentivizing transnational conglomerates and razing entire ecosystems. This has led to conflicts throughout the region. Allied with human rights and environmental groups, Mapuche activists have staged marches, land occupations, and sit-ins, and launched legal actions. They have also employed more violent methods, including arson and equipment sabotage.[60] Though the Concertación made some efforts to recognize Indigenous rights and promote diversity, Richards notes that they "failed to address the ongoing colonial dispossession at the root of these conflicts."[61] These efforts are further undercut by the government's use of the Anti-Terrorism Act (promulgated under Pinochet in 1984) to prosecute Mapuche land and water defense efforts.[62] According to Helene Risør and Daniela Jacob, this "contributes to an extreme criminalization of the political Mapuche movement and helps to support the sustained presence of special forces that in the last decade has protected the private property of timber companies and large estate owners from land occupation by Mapuche communities who claim the land as theirs."[63] The day-to-day "securitization" of the region has been shaped by systemic racism and coloniality and has led to tragedies such as the murder of Camilo Catrillanca, who was shot by a police officer in the back while riding unarmed on a tractor with a fifteen-year-old.[64]

Until recently, Mapuche representations within official theatrical circuits have been rare or rendered largely invisible.[65] As Pía Gutiérrez notes, however, this does not mean they have been absent: they have been present both outside of official cultural circuits, as well as present—if overlooked or de-emphasized—within the works of canonical writers such as Isidora Aguirre and Juan Radrigán.[66] Nevertheless, Grass writes that the Mapuche representations that do exist within the dominant circuits—overwhelmingly written by playwrights who do not themselves identify as Mapuche—have been largely "racialized, exoticized, folklorized," or silenced.[67] This contributed to González's own sense of Mapuche cultural invisibility and motivated her professor to encourage her to explore her own Mapuche ancestry and identity in the theater "because there is no one in the theater who is doing it."[68] González recognized that theater offered her a tool to reconnect with her personal history and to make that history public.

In her final year at university, she began a project based on interviews with several Mapuche women in the El Bosque neighborhood of Santiago, among them her aunt. This project became *Ñi pu tremen: Mis antepasados* (My ancestors). In it, eleven older Mapuche women share the stage with three younger women between the ages of eleven and fourteen. None of the women are professional actors—many had never been to the theater—and all represent their own lived experiences. The women offer testimonies focusing on their experiences migrating from the country to urban Santiago. The play weaves the testimonies together, creating a story that reveals a shared multigenerational experience marked not only by violence, racism, and dispossession but also by persistence, joy, and strength derived from their Mapuche identities.

With *Ñi pu tremen*, González and her collaborators also began to develop the dramaturgy that would thread throughout KIMVN's work. Evelyn González explains,

> We were discovering a particular language for our artistic work: the documentary format brought to theatricality as much through body, text, music, and staging, to make visible and give an account of the testimony and the real, the diverse social, cultural, and political problems that the Mapuche people have confronted: territorial dispossession, poverty, marginality, and historical violence.[69]

The result was a dramaturgy that forged solidarity by highlighting universal experiences through difference and the autorepresentation of "real" people, that fostered intimate affective relations through testimony, and that revealed the interconnections between various manifestations of violence.

This piece—and many of KIMVN's subsequent works—was developed through a painstaking process of ethnographic research in which group members embedded themselves in Mapuche communities, forged affective bonds of kinship and friendship, and offered material care. For *Ñi pu tremen*, the sisters met weekly with the women for many months. They drew from Evelyn González's psychology training to build the trust that would allow for the women's testimony, some of which required a careful consideration of trauma and the ethics of witnessing. They shared food, checked in on the women when they were sick, and attended to their families—establishing relationships that existed beyond the project and that would extend for the years to come. After several months of working together and gathering testimonies, González suggested to the women that they might represent themselves in the piece.[70]

In the play, the women recount their fondest childhood memories, their experiences moving from the country to the city, when they met their spouses, and moments when they faced explicit racism and discrimination.

These testimonies are staged as part of a layered tapestry of cultural expressions, as the piece's multidisciplinary, multilingual dramaturgy surrounds the audience with sights, sounds, and smells. The audience hears both Spanish and Mapudungun, spoken and in song. They smell maté. The play incorporates music, dance, poetry, prayers, textiles, and metalwork.

At times these elements are presented with a pedagogical awareness for an audience that is presumed to be unfamiliar with Mapuche culture. The play is set in a *ruka*—a traditional Mapuche hut. To situate the audience within the space, one of the younger women verbally describes it in the first moments of the play. The description highlights the audience's distance from such a space—they cannot be assumed to recognize it—and brings them closer, allowing them to access its symbolic registers and functionality. At other times, elements go unexplained and Mapudungun untranslated. Patricia Henríquez Puentes and Mauricio Ostria González observe that the staging "contains a repertoire of scenic practices and documents of high ritual symbolic value that lead the viewer to dislocate vision and thought regarding Mapuche culture, to approach the deep and radical sense of its difference."[71] The play offers just enough context to understand some of the complex symbolic layers of these expressions, while leaving the audience with an awareness that there is much they cannot fully understand about this culture. By incorporating these elements alongside personal testimonies—of both a more universal nature (such as fond childhood memories or falling in love) and a nature more specific to the state violence experienced by Mapuche populations (such when Marisol Ancamil recalls her family's targeting by Pinochet's military police)—the play resists their romantic exoticization. At the same time the play does not attempt to collapse difference into universal sameness but rather works to preserve, and at times highlight, it.

The testimony of authoritarian, state violence is shared alongside the quieter, quotidian violence of cultural dispossession and assimilation. Toward the end of the play Elena Mercado Marileo brings her mother Rosa's xapelacucha onstage—this is a large piece of silver jewelry that represents her mother's Mapuche identity. She recounts how Rosa, a machi, used to play Mapuche instruments and pray to her god. However, her husband, who was not Mapuche, demanded that Rosa stop these practices.

> One day he came to my mother and said . . . Rosa, you cannot keep doing this, singing in front of your altar, singing with your *kulxun*, you cannot continue with this religion. . . . Think that our children are going to have their studies, they are perhaps going to travel to the city, I don't want them to be discriminated against. . . . And slowly my mom stopped playing her *kulxun* . . . our mom was a *machi* . . . but I think that when she died . . . in her heart . . . she never, never stopped being *machi*.[72]

In juxtaposing the sensational violence of the dictatorship with this quieter violence of domestic assimilation the play constructs a panorama of interrelated violence that it seeks to heal through recounting resistance and the rescue, via performance, of culture. After this testimony, the women appear onstage dressed in traditional clothing: "That which was dispossessed of them during the acculturation process that their bodies have lived."[73] They position their bodies in the direction of the sun. The three younger girls offer a prayer for their people and themselves. The prayer gestures to the sustaining ritual that connects them to their culture and the earth. In the final moment, music swells as the women dance, and Marlen, the smallest of the group, raises a Mapuche flag.

With *Ñi pu tremen* KIMVN began to develop a dramaturgy that served a project to rescue and render visible Mapuche culture and lives and that connected these lived experiences to politics and a call to resistance. Paula González recalls that for some who saw the play, it was not entirely legible as theater. The presence of nonprofessional actors, the layering of testimonies, the incorporation of real objects was relatively unique in Chilean theater at the time. González insisted on pursuing these dramaturgical tactics, and in subsequent works chose to deepen her exploration of the testimonies that arose in the rehearsal process.[74] The plays that followed, *Territorio descuajado. Testimonio de un país mestizo* (Dislodged territory. Testimony of a mestizo country, 2011) and *Galvarino* (2012), created a trilogy. Both drew from the testimonies of women who had participated in *Ñi pu tremen*, and they incorporated elements of documentary drama to construct affective responses to dispossession and violence.

In late 2013 and 2014 the company experienced several tragedies that led it to reevaluate its relationship to the Mapuche community as well as its way of working. Two of the company's collaborators—Reynaldo Cayufilo (who appeared in *Galvarino*) and Juana Huaquilaf (*Ñi pu tremen*)—passed away, a deep and personal loss. Additionally, a fire in El Bosque destroyed several of the Mawidache rukas. The spaces, where their collaborators and family had lived and welcomed them, where they had collected testimony and rehearsed for countless hours, represented a profound link to their Mapuche community and identity. Further, for the Mawidache community, the rukas were a haven from the violence and dispossession of colonialism and of their migration to the city, an assertion of their identity and of home.[75] These losses affected the company deeply, and they took time to process them.

In 2016, they changed the name of the company from Kimen Teatro to KIMVN. "Kimen," written in the Spanish alphabet, is a Mapudungun word meaning "Do you know me?" This question coincides with the first phase of the company's work, which can be largely seen as the sisters' efforts to unearth their family's Mapuche history. The word KIMVN, written in the Raguileo alphabet, means "knowledge."[76] This change, according to the company, reflected a shift in identity. The use of the Raguileo alphabet was meant to honor both their heritage and the creative contributions of the Mawidache community with which they had collaborated. The shift from the question "Do you know me?"—suggesting a process of discovery, of revelation—to knowledge indicates that their work is now concerned with reproducing Mapuche ways of knowing.

The company began new collaborations that injected energy into their creative process and expanded their dramaturgy. In 2016 they collaborated with David Arancibia Urzúa on *Ñuke—una mirada íntima hacia la resistencia Mapuche* (Mother—An intimate look at Mapuche Resistance). For this play, in which a mother deals with the consequences of her son's arrest, the company fully re-created a ruka. The re-creation of this space was meant as "a political and architectural testimony, interrupting the urban space and linking education and art."[77] The audience's immersion in the space was also meant to collapse the boundaries between the audience members and Mapuche culture and centralize Mapuche presence in Chilean identity. According to Evelyn González, *Ñuke's* project was

> claiming the memory of a people, giving space to express themselves, to raise their voice and interpellate the viewer, to generate a space of reflection and to go further and be part of a process of re-patrimonialization, where the spectator has the opportunity to value Mapuche culture and their people to begin the process of integrating it from empathy and an understanding of its people as part of themselves, not as part of a culture, breaking with the discriminatory and violent barrier between the Chilean and the Mapuche people.[78]

In this way, *Ñuke* aimed to do for its audiences what González's theatrical research had done for her: offer a reconnection to their Indigenous heritage that collapsed the distinction between Chilean and Mapuche, that allowed for a deeper understanding of the Mapuche presence in Chilean identity as well as a greater awareness of the violence that the barriers between those identities had created.

In tracing this brief trajectory of KIMVN's work prior to *Trewa*, I wish to highlight the ways KIMVN's dramaturgy is tied to the individual recognition of Paula González's own sense of her Mapuche identity and family history, as well as a close collaboration with Mapuche communities. These personal connections are dramaturgically expanded outward through research, the incorporation of multigenerational autorepresentation, multidisciplinarity, and artistic collaborations that illuminate the broader systemic issues at stake in these works. The plays forge solidarities with their audiences, offering opportunities for connection, identification, and immersion into Mapuche culture, while at the same time asserting difference allowing for unknowability. This sets the stage for the recognition of equality through both a personal connection to Mapuche claims to rights and a respect for difference. The works dramaturgically embrace the paradox of solidarity in which individual claims find strength and voice through a heterogeneous, situated, transversally oriented community.

LASTESIS and the Mayo Feminista

Like KIMVN, LASTESIS also conceives of art making as a tool in a larger political project that incorporates extensive research and multidisciplinarity. A Valparaíso-based collective, LASTESIS draws from theater, sociology, design, and literature to translate feminist theory into performance interventions. Lea Cáceres Díaz, Paula Cometa Stange, Sibila Sotomayor Van Rysseghem, and Daffne Valdés Vargas formed the group in spring 2018 (see fig. 18), amid what came to be known as Chile's Mayo feminista (Feminist May), a movement that revitalized Chile's culture of student protest with feminist dramaturgies particularly suited to resist their co-option into neoliberal policy "solutions" and that created space for heterogeneous solidarities.

The Mayo feminista began on April 17 in the southern city of Valdivia when a group of students occupied the Humanities Department at Chile's Austral University to protest the school's failure to respond to cases of sexual abuse. A few days later, in Santiago, the students at the University of Chile law school also staged an occupation. In the following months, students occupied campuses across the country. These occupations were accompanied by massive marches throughout Chile.

The Mayo feminista drew from the vibrant culture of protest established during the 2006 and 2011 student movement. It also took inspiration from international feminist activism, in particular Argentina's *Ni Una Menos* (Not one woman less) movement.[79] The occupations issued a number of concrete demands, ranging from the dismissal of prominent faculty members accused of sexual assault and the development of policies to address gender violence and discrimination, to the creation of gender-studies departments, parental support for students and employees, and the acknowledgment of name changes for transgender students and employees.[80] But more than these specific demands the students called for *una educación no sexista*: a nonsexist education. This negative demand aimed to unsettle the patriarchal ideological structure on which the entire educational system was based. Nelly Richard argues that this demand allowed the Mayo feminista a radicality and solidarity that the student movement had hitherto been unable to attain. She contends that the demand itself "constitutes an excess whose liberatory dimension cannot be absorbed by institutional politics."[81] The Mayo feminista thus combined demands for

Fig. 18. The members of LASTESIS. Photo courtesy of LASTESIS.

both concrete changes and a revolutionary overhaul of social structures. As I have argued elsewhere, it made these demands through performance: occupations performatively enacted alternative modes of organization and leadership within school spaces, and mass mobilizations situated specific demands within a broader movement. The slogan "*Nos han callado, ahora es cuando*" ("They have silenced us, now is the time") rejected women's silencing and patriarchal impunity, asserting that change would be now.[82]

LASTESIS's work similarly embraces the specific and the systemic to build solidarity and advocate for radical social change. They staged their first work, *Patriarcado y capital es alianza criminal* (Patriarchy and capital are a criminal alliance) in July 2018. This fifteen-minute performance was inspired by the Italian feminist Silvia Federici's *Caliban and the Witch*. In it, Federici employs a feminist-historical reconsideration of Marx to demonstrate the ways in which the subjugation of women and their reproductive function enabled the formation of the working class and thus lies at the base of capitalist exploitation.[83] LASTEIS's piece is fundamentally concerned with asserting the interrelatedness of class and feminist struggle:

> The class struggle cannot be understood without
> knowing that the working class is divided in two
> subclasses: men, privileged

women, dominated.
Hey you!
Private property.
My body will no longer be a pillar of capitalism.[84]

The piece combines music, chant, choreography, visual and aural collage, pop art, direct address, and agitprop to create arresting, pulsing visual and sonic images that distill and amplify Federici's argument, that point to its immediate manifestations, and issue a call to arms. The dramaturgical aim is to "translate" this theory into performance and thereby escape the hegemony of the text and reach audiences that might not otherwise encounter feminist thought. The result is a performance that is experienced both intellectually and affectively via multiple modalities.

The group works as a multidisciplinary collective in a dramaturgical reflection of their view of feminism as fundamentally communitarian and horizontal, ideals that speak to the proposed solidary state. Sotomayor explains:

> Feminisms have a history of a communitarian base, of putting the individual in the service of the collective and vice versa. We have been taught that historically they are activated from collectivity and also, frequently, from anonymity. For us, they operate from horizontality, networks, and cooperation. It is something that aids the movement and that responds to the neoliberal system that has rooted individualism in our forms of relating to each other and conceiving of ourselves as persons. In response, we always have to view things from the collective. In Chile we say that neoliberalism was born here and it is where it has to die, and we hope that this will happen soon.[85]

The group is intentional in its negotiations of the relationship to the individual and collective. Their manifesto, *Quemar el miedo*, begins with an introduction to "Nosotras" (Us). They assert that neoliberalism and patriarchy have isolated individual feelings and experiences. They claim a collective we/us as a "feminist political stance" to take individual experience as collective life.[86] Bernadita Llanos and Milena Grass Kleiner note, "LASTESIS's works display the shared experience of women and non-hegemonic minorities to create a sense of collectivity that goes beyond their artistic cluster."[87] This is not, however, an effort to collapse or homogenize individual struggles. Sotomayor contends:

> For us the struggle of women and disidencias and gender are inseparable. And this does not mean that it is homogenous, there are differences and distinct struggles, just as those crossed with

> race, class, or ethnicity. Reality is diverse, we cannot deny this and for this reason for us the feminist perspective cannot be any other way.[88]

Though at first glance KIMVN Teatro and LASTESIS operate in very different aesthetic registers and with unique political preoccupations, dramaturgically their works engage in the complex negotiations between individual struggles and those of the larger community. They create performances that recognize and illuminate the interlocking webs of oppression and state violence that render their claims and struggles shared while still allowing for individual and situated experiences. I now turn to a comparative analysis of KIMVN's *Trewa* and LASTESIS's *Un violador en tu camino* to illuminate the contours and commonalities of the dramaturgies of solidarity they forge and to link these to the reconceptualization of citizenship within the proposed solidary state.

Trewa and *Un violador en tu camino*

Both *Trewa* and *Un violador en tu camino* emerge from in-depth research projects exploring the systemic violence in the Chilean nation-state. *Trewa*'s central plot surrounds the aftermath of the real death of Macarena Valdés (1983–2016). An environmental activist, Valdés relocated with her young family from Santiago to southern Chile to live closer to nature and connect with their Mapuche roots. Once established near the Tranguil river, Valdés and her partner, Rubén Collío, became active in—and eventually leaders and spokespeople of—a Mapuche movement protesting the construction of a hydroelectric plant by the Austrian corporation RP Global. On August 22, 2016, Valdés was found by her eldest son hanging from the beams of her home in an apparent suicide. The only witness to her death was her twenty-month-old son. Collío and the community hired an independent coroner, who ruled that the cause of death was not in fact asphyxiation by hanging, but instead that she had died prior to her suspension from the ceiling. Despite this report, the state has not reclassified the case.[89] The play begins as several members of the community gather to help Collío with a ritual prior to disinterring Valdés's corpse for the independent autopsy. Among those who have gathered is the mother of another victim of police violence, Ada Huentecol, and Emiliano, a member of the community police force.

Trewa was the result of a 2017 collaboration between KIMVN and the Intercultural and Indigenous Studies Center (CIIR) at the Catholic University of Chile. There, the anthropologist Helene Risør, alongside sociologist Daniela Jacob, had been conducting an ethnographic study of the Indigenous Community Care Patrols (PACI), a community police force whose mission was to integrate with Indigenous communities and provide security and social services.[90] Often Indigenous themselves, members of the PACI were expected to establish trust with a community that they may be required to exert force on. Risør and Jacob concluded that as Indigenous officials working for a repressive state, members of the PACI were positioned in a potentially treasonous relationship to themselves, their community, and the state they served, illustrating how the burdens of facilitating an intercultural state are inequitably distributed.[91]

With *Trewa*, KIMVN collaborated with the research of Risør and Jacob, "[delving] into . . . the cruelty with which the security and order institutions of the State operate by sending people from the same community to carry out acts of violence against their own people."[92] In the process of conducting interviews for the project, a PACI officer remarked to González, "I know that I am a dog of the Chilean state." This comment led to the play's title, *Trewa*, which means "dog" in Mapudungun. It evokes a relationship that is both subservient and disrespected. The play's subtitle, *Estado-nación o espectro de la traición* (Nation-state or specter of treason), establishes the working assumption that the very construction of the nation-state carries with it the possibility, perhaps inevitability, of betrayal. The title also references, and therefore renders contingent, the notion of the "nation-state"—a concept that according to Pedro Cayuqueo is "a fiction created by 19th century Chilean elites that artificially equates the state with a single nation." Implicit in the attention called to this formulation is an alternative reality: "a land inhabited by at least a dozen First Nations that predate the state by centuries."[93] Similarly, Antonio Catrileo Araya, Manuel Carrión Lira, and Marcelo Garzo Montalvo ask,

> What happens when we consider $hile as an illusion, a fantasy created by *wingka* (non Indigenous) nation-states that are still occupying our territories? $hile is an unsustainable concept that was sculpted by settler relationships that divide humanity/nature, and define who is more civilized or barbarous. All are conceptions translated *from* Europe that have laid the foundations of this fiction that is $hile.[94]

The play unsettles this notion of the "reality" of the nation by using documentary techniques in an investigation of the PACI alongside an exploration of other instances of systemic violence against the Mapuche within the fictional frame of theater. At the same time, it offers the stage to another reality: Mapuche communities, customs, temporalities, and ways of knowing.

Like KIMVN did in its work on *Trewa*, LASTESIS also took inspiration from research emerging from academia and incorporated the work of its own investigative process. *Un violador en tu camino* had initially been intended as part of a larger performance, an investigation into the work of Argentine anthropologist Rita Segato.[95] Segato's work explores violence against women as an exercise of power in what she terms the "apocalyptic phase of capital."[96] LASTESIS aimed to combine Segato's theories with a critical investigation of gender violence and impunity in Chile. However, the demonstrations and curfews that began on October 18 made the performance's opening on October 24 impossible. The group was invited by the theater company La Peste to participate in a series of street interventions between November 18 and 23. They adapted a section of the piece to respond specifically to the police violence that had met the social uprising: the blinding of protesters with rubber bullets and the torture and sexual violence committed against detainees. The title of the work ironically alludes to a publicity campaign of the Carabineros during the height of the dictatorship—*un amigo en tu camino* ("a friend in your path"), implying a continuity between the police violence of the dictatorship and the present day. Just as *Trewa's* subtitle calls attention to the foundational social treason and violence at the heart of the construction of the nation-state, *Un violador en tu camino* foundationally rebrands the police force as rapists.

Trewa premiered on March 26, 2019, at the Catholic University Theater, one of the most important institutional theaters in Santiago. The first performance of *Un violador* took place later that year, on November 20 in Valparaíso in the streets at the Plaza Aníbal Pinto, with about forty people assembled from a call on Instagram (see fig. 19). Though *Trewa* is more legible as theater and *Un violador en tu camino* is a confrontational protest performance, both works forge dramaturgies linked by substantive, aesthetic, and processual commonalities. Both intersect with contemporary struggles against state violence, treat performance as a social activity that extends beyond the performance's frame, build space for heterogeneous community, offer avenues to make rights claims, and assert alternative ways of knowing and being. These dramaturgies of solidarity result in distinctive projects that are connected in their rejections of state violence and oppression, assertions of radical equality, and their collective hope for a better world. Their dramaturgies thus contribute to relational bonds and affective attachments that might sustain the difficult and ongoing work of constructing the world to come.

Interlocking Webs of Dispossession and Violence

A central premise of these works, and one through which they forge the possibility for solidarity, lies in the ways they illuminate interlocking webs

Fig. 19. LASTESIS's Instagram call. Courtesy of LASTESIS.

of dispossession and violence stemming from the imposition of the nation-state itself. Writing in the context of the feminist strike in Argentina, Verónica Gago and Liz Mason-Deese note that the

> work of weaving together different situations and struggles produces a political cartography that connects the threads that make different forms of violence operate as interrelated dynamics. . . . Tracing the modes of connection of different forms of violence allows us to build a complete understanding of the contemporary complex of capitalism-patriarchy-colonialism through its concrete manifestations.[97]

The dramaturgical weaves of *Trewa* and *Un violador en tu camino* do the work of forging solidarity, revealing the contingency and interrelatedness of the state's apparatus of systemic violence, and thereby calling for a radical reorientation of society.

Un violador en tu camino begins as a flash mob. As the participants assemble, one member of the collective plays a reveille on kazoo, and a driving beat plays on a speaker. The participants begin their choreography, shifting their weight from side to side as they chant:

The patriarchy is a judge
That judges us for being born
And our punishment
Is the violence that you don't see.

The patriarchy is a judge
That judges us for being born
And our punishment
Is the violence that you do see.

The lyrics slip deftly between metaphoric and concrete claims to illuminate the ways institutional systems are connected to ideologies with tangible consequences for human lives. The opening lyrics link patriarchy to Chile's legal and carceral systems. This connection operates on a broadly metaphoric level (patriarchy as judge, imprisonment, punishment) but is also grounded in a concrete claim (judge as direct manifestation and instrument of patriarchy), through which women are subject to multiple forms of private and public violence. This violence has many manifestations, which the performers directly name: femicide, impunity, disappearance, rape. Brenda Werth and Katherine Zien note that these slippages "[compel] a broader understanding of systemic sexual violence," underscoring that even domestic violence is state violence.[98] As the women name this violence, they chorographically reference the demeaning position women were forced to assume during police searches, bending their legs in a deep squat and placing their hands behind their heads. Furthermore, the blindfolds worn by the participants hold a double symbolism: first, the blindness of the state and its judicial system to crimes against women, and second, a reference to the number of protesters whose eyes had been wounded by rubber bullets in the previous month.[99]

The performance's dramaturgy demonstrates the interrelatedness of these manifestations of violence across multiple modalities. The performance's call on Instagram directly invited *mujeres y disidencias* (women and dissidents) to participate—the latter a term anthropologist Baird Campbell identifies as the "radical and anti-institutional" pole of the LGBTQ activist movement in Chile.[100] The piece thus situates itself within a wider activist movement surrounding gender and sexuality. The multitude of bodies present (about forty in Valparaíso on November 20, over two hundred in Santiago on November 25) testifies to the distinct, individually lived experiences of violence of each person there. By enunciating specific categories of violence (i.e., femicide, rape), while evoking present vulnerability to violence via the visual symbolism of the blindfolds and the choreographic gesture of the squat, the piece forges tentacles of solidarity. The lyrical framework situates all these manifestations in the inherent structure of the state judicial and carceral systems, unraveling, thread by thread, a tapestry of state violence.

With parts of its dramaturgy operating in a more explicitly narrative register, *Trewa* also stages interlocking instances of state violence, manifestations drawn from real events. It does so with an eye toward the explicit work of forging community. In an epigraph to the written text of *Trewa*, in what can be read as a guiding principle, González quotes a passage from Ileana Diéguez's *Cuerpos sin duelo* (Bodies without mourning):

> To narrate, to tell, to make visible are perhaps necessary actions to recognize and point out the vulnerability of life and the predominant place of trauma and pain in these times. . . . To claim, to document, to testify, to organize, to demand with tears and words, but also with actions, as the fathers and mothers of the thousands of murdered and disappeared have done, and continue to do so, in these times of sinister wars.[101]

As Ignacia Cortés Rojas and Ignacio Pastén point out, Diéguez proposes that through the representation of individual trauma, art can configure a *communitas* of pain. These representations create spaces of encounter where it is possible to "reimagine a community on the basis of vulnerability and loss."[102]

Trewa explores multiple manifestations of real cases of state violence: the troubling circumstances surrounding Macarena Valdés's death and the case of Brandon Huentecol, a seventeen-year-old shot in the back by police in 2018. At the time of the shooting, Huentecol had been trying to defend his younger brother, who was held by police officers at an identity check. After being subdued by police, he was shot with bird shot at close range. More than 180 pellets scattered throughout his body, and he suffered organ and nerve damage. Because the pellets are medically complex to remove, many remained in his body, leaking lead into his bloodstream. Though he remains alive, his mother Ada relates his suffering to the group, as well as the difficulty of receiving medical care, and the inadequate justice dispensed to the officer.[103] The officer, Ada tells the group, claimed the shooting had been an accident. Valdés's husband Rubén responds with incredulity, "How can it have been an accident, since the guns only shoot *lamngen*?"[104] His question underscores that this is racially targeted police violence.

Just as LASTESIS's work, by alluding to the dictatorship-era slogan of the Carabineros, connects present state violence to the legacy of the dictatorship, *Trewa* also draws these connections. Chachai Raimundo relates to Ada's suffering by recounting his own experience being abducted, tortured, and interrogated by the police during the dictatorship.[105] When he saw the officer years later, he realized that the officer was his neighbor and Mapuche. The officer claimed that he was compelled to torture Raimundo and that he was just doing his job. These layers of violence create a historical panorama to contextualize their systemic, ongoing nature as part of the function of the state. They also demonstrate the ways in which the state turns individuals against their own people in its violent operations.

This idea is explored in the play's central conflict, which is initiated with the arrival of Emiliano and his wife Marcela. The couple has presumably come to help with the ritual asking permission to dig up the corpse, and they express sorrow for Macarena's death. However, tensions rise as Marcela contends that the hydroelectric plant Macarena and Rubén had been protesting might be a positive development for the economy of the region. She asserts that those who have migrated to the region from the city cannot possibly understand what those who have lived all their lives in the south have endured and that these politicized values do not square with the need to mitigate the poverty in the region. The tension is heightened when Emiliano reveals that he is a member of the PACI.

After this revelation, the dramaturgical conventions established throughout the piece give way to two explosive monologues (first Emiliano's and later Macarena's) that rupture the world of the play with their affective power. As in the works of Calderón, the force of what must be expressed exceeds the bounds of the play. Emiliano puts on his uniform and the spectators hear an Offstage Voice, which gives a brief history of the PACI and pointedly notes that these forces operate alongside the frequent application of the Anti-Terrorism Law, applied disproportionately by the "democratic" governments to Mapuche communities.[106] Then, Emiliano breaks the fourth wall to address the audience, first in Mapudungun. He explains that he joined the PACI to work for his community, but that he has had "bad luck" with them. He has witnessed the worst of his community and dreams they will kill him. But, he asserts, he has been trained never to shoot someone in the back—as with Brandon Huentecol, Matías Catrileo, and Camilo Catrillanca.[107]

As the monologue reaches its climax, he continues in Spanish:

> I was there! . . . When they shot Brandon, I saw how my Seargent pulled the trigger and shot him. . . . I saw how the dogs [*trewa*] licked the blood of their son. I was there when they found sister Macarena. I saw how afterward the police made fun of her crying children, of you and the dead woman. . . . I saw how they manipulated the rope. . . . I was there and I stayed quiet. . . . I know that I am a TREWA, a dog of the bosses, of the businessmen, a TREWA of the Chilean State. I thought that working for the PACI would make everything calmer, but no. All the same they send us as special forces, all the same they send us to shoot at the communities, to throw out the abortion activists, to shoot people in the eyes but what am I going to do? What am I going to do? It's my job. It's my job and I can't say no.[108]

Like *Un violador en tu camino*, *Trewa* links multiple instances of violence to reveal a systemic panorama. Emiliano's speech demonstrates how, with initiatives like the PACI, the state off-loads the responsibility for violence on to the individual—with members of the Mapuche community forced to bear this guilt. Though the characters in the play do not forgive him, by staging an encounter between the audience and Emiliano, the play issues a call to empathy, or at least to understanding: a revelation that he too is connected to the other victims of state violence.

In weaving these instances of real violence together, *Trewa* creates an overwhelming tapestry of excessive state oppression in which even individual justice cannot solve the systemic burden of racism, discrimination, and violence. The violence stems from organs integral to the state as it is currently understood: its security forces, as well as the extractivist, capitalist economic system shaping Chile's governance.

The Body-Territory

Both pieces dramaturgically incorporate the body as a site through which claims are made, solidarity is forged, and knowledge is produced. Drawing on Gago and Mason-Deese, who themselves build on a lineage of feminist and Indigenous thought, Brenda Werth advances the notion of the "body-territory" as a means of thinking through feminist performance, linking the dispossession of bodies and lands in extractive, patriarchal-capitalist systems to both feminist and Indigenous claims for redress.[109] For Gago and Mason-Deese,

> the body-territory is a practical concept that demonstrates how the exploitation of common, community (urban, suburban, campesino, and Indigenous) territories involves violating the body of each person and the collective body through dispossession. And it is strategic: it links struggles to recuperate land and territory to struggles against both the violence of war and domestic violence, to struggles against neo-extractivist development—but again not based on victimhood but on a collective desire to live.[110]

Segato, on whose theory LASTESIS's work is based, draws similar connections, positioning the body, as Fuentes points out, as the very *territory* of war.[111] This is the product of what Segato claims is the apocalyptic phase of capital, in which

> the re-primarization of production, mega-mining, and extractivist agriculture are counterparts of the absolutist regime of the market and the fusion of political power with ownership, resulting in extreme aggression toward human beings and their environment, leaving behind only remains—the progressive exposure of life,

> merchandizing of everything, and reservation of exclusive security for property owners and controllers of the mechanisms of the state, and the radicalization of dispossession, ethnocide, genocide, and conquestiality.[112]

Segato follows Edward Said and other postcolonialist theorists in asserting that the scene of contemporary politics—a product of capitalism and attendant colonialism—in which there is "the universal subject, the generalizable Human" is underlain by the presence of the other ("the non-white, colonial, marginal, underdeveloped, deficient").[113] Any democracy grounded in such a system cannot be true democracy. Such a situation is resisted by dismantling the notion of the "One," reclaiming bodies and reforging he bonds of community, "so that a true plurality of spaces might emerge."[114]

In *Trewa* the body of Macarena Valdés is at the center of the play, both in the structure of the plot and as a spectral omnipresence. It is a body that, while living, threatened the extractivist ambitions of transnational capital and thus became the territory of war. It is a body that had been returned to the earth. It is a body that, after death, remains a territory of resistance, potentially offering forensic evidence revealing the criminal assemblage of state and transnational capital.[115] Macarena's Am, a life force or soul, here given physical form in the body of actor Paula Zúñiga, cannot escape the plane of the living. She stays on the stage: a refusal to acquiesce as well as the persistence of pain and the corporeal manifestation of Mapuche cosmologies surrounding death and mourning. The Am connects the present world to the world to come.[116]

As Gago and Mason-Deese assert, the bodies that comprise the body-territory are not only united in victimhood; they are also powerful. Zúñiga's physical presence emotes sorrow and rage and offers comfort and strength to her family through her gaze, through touch, and through song (see fig. 20). Her body is part of the larger community of bodies that fill the small playing space of the home: each with their own experiences of vulnerability of pain, each deriving power through their persistence, through their presence, and through their community. Like the participant's bodies assembled in *Un violador en tu camino*, the body is both a site of denunciation—the locus of the assertion of the illegitimacy of the state—and a source of power and hope.

After the participants in LASTESIS's chant call out the different modalities of gender violence, they march in double time, bending over and moving their hands in sync with their legs, in a free and almost joyous dance as they proclaim,

> And it's not my fault, not where I was, not how I was dressed.
> And it's not my fault, not where I was, not how I was dressed.

Fig. 20. *Trewa.* Photo: Sens Interdits Festival.

The Instagram call instructed the women to dress in "glam party clothes." Their attire and movements evoke a liberatory, festive atmosphere, as the women reject moralistic refrains that place the responsibility for violence on the victims themselves and not on the perpetrators of that violence. The women, the piece asserts, will still dance, will still live (see fig. 21).

For LASTESIS the choice to explore feminist theory through performance is a choice to foreground the body as an intersectional node where the personal and systemic, the feminist and the decolonial meet. As Argentine feminist María Pia López observes, when womanhood is conceived not as "a biological trait but a site of political articulation" for a "multitude of existences," the body can become a site from which to construct politics.[117] LASTESIS asserts the body as a site of knowing, a site from which to make demands, to issue *re*possessions, and a locus that connects their work to the historical struggles of feminism and resistance to colonialism. They write,

> This connection with the body, this demand for rights from the body, for the body, has been historic: the history of feminisms, of women and dissidents, of the sex-gender system, has been key. Also, the colonial discussion in terms of what we understand of valid knowledge, how do we understand this transmission of knowledge and in what spaces; how do we understand these embodied theories and how many times it is crossed with our own biographies.[118]

Fig. 21. *Un violador en tu camino* in Valparaíso. Courtesy of LASTESIS.

Gago and Mason-Deese assert, "The knowing-from-the-body challenges the colonial-capitalist-patriarchal unconscious by questioning preestablished identities and reactionary fears and creating new forms of desire and subjectivities."[119]

LASTESIS's exploration of feminist theory and KIMVN's collaboration with CIIR assert performance as a way to understand and create knowledge. Dramaturgically, KIMVN does so through a destabilization of the binary division of the "real" and the fictive, in the tradition of the theater of the real—particularly as it has been conceived in contemporary Latin America.[120] Weaving documentary materials, ethnographic research, and fictional stories together, *Trewa* highlights what Paola Hernández has described as the "liminality between factual and fictive, public and private."[121] In a note at the beginning of the text, González recontextualizes some fragments from Taussig's *The Magic of the State* to indicate that this blurring of boundaries establishes a dialectical process that illuminates the poetics of knowledge making as well as the construction of the state, the distribution of the sensible:

> The theatrical limits that this dramaturgical and scenic proposal touches—of fiction on the one hand, and the documentary genre on the other—are located in a space at the border of genres. The names of individuals have been changed to ensure their anonymity, their protection, but also to highlight the fictional gestures

> without which the documentary genre (including history and ethnography) would not be able to exist. In a similar way to the act of estrangement that Brecht speaks of, the act of renaming [characters] confers a more acute understanding of what we call history, as much in the events that make up its narration, especially when it comes to the stories of souls and the dead as symbols of a Nation and the State and their specific form of existence.[122]

By operating between fact and fiction, González seeks to tell a particular affective story dramaturgically constructed to highlight the contingency of the state and its dependence on the human lives on which it is built.

The tension between the real and the fictive also underscores the KIMVN's efforts to incorporate a Mapuche cosmovision in which porousness and interdependence characterize the relationship between human society and the natural world, between justice and mourning, and between life and death. An early exchange between Macarena's eldest son, Francisco, and Chachai Raimondo, an elder in the community, illustrates the interdependence of knowledge:

> FRANCISCO: Do you know what the birds say, Chacha?
> CHACHAI RAIMUNDO: Sometimes.
> FRANCISCO: It's that the other day Papay Rosa told me that if I take water from where the two arms of the rivers meet, I will learn to speak Mapudungun, and those that speak Mapudungun speak with the birds. This is why I want to learn because I could talk with them.
> CHACHAI RAIMUNDO: If Rosa says so it must be true.
> FRANCISCO: What is going to happen to the body of my mother, Chacha?
> CHACHAI RAIMUNDO: The day will come in which the roots will take the body of your mother.
> FRANCISCO: And that way she will go to the immensity of Kalfü?[123]
> CHACHAI RAIMUNDO: And she will turn to the dust of our dreams.[124]

The elders of the community offer an epistemology in which they do not transmit the knowledge content itself but rather the path to it, which exists in the individual's connection to the natural world. In this case, knowledge of the Mapuche language, Mapudungun, comes not from human transmission but from the intersection of river waters. This knowledge in turn enables communication with the animal world. The human body, placed in the earth, will be overtaken by the roots of the trees and so enter the spiritual plane, from which it will communicate to the living by dreams.

Dreams—often harbingers of death—figure prominently throughout the play, largely serving as warnings of impending violence.[125] The

Fig. 22. *Trewa.* Photo: Sens Interdits Festival.

connection to the earth and the afterlife is protective against hostile forces in the world. However, this connection risks being severed by the very forces enacting violence. As Cortés and Pastén point out, the proposed hydroelectric project would reroute the river, threatening not only the ecology of the region but also ways of being and knowing structured by the interrelationship of human and environment.[126]

Dramaturgically *Trewa* stages a porousness: of space, of spiritual planes, of theatrical convention, and of ways of knowing. The stage itself is divided into three spaces (see fig. 22). The largest area, which takes up most of the stage, is covered in a natural terrain. As the actors walk on it, the audience hears snow crunch underfoot. The space is peaceful, bare, and lonely: it evokes both the natural world and the supernatural, as it is the space where Macarena's Am spends most of its time. Upstage of this area are a series of semitranslucent scrims, behind which sit a group of musicians. At times the scrims are lit to be opaque, a backdrop for projections of snow, water, the sunlight coming through trees. At other times the scrims are lit transparently, and the audience glimpses the musicians or the wandering Am. They evoke a porousness between the physical and spiritual worlds, suggesting that this permeability is ever present if not always apprehended. The smallest space, stage right, is a home, designed in a conventionally theatrically realist style. It is cramped and warm, featuring a kitchen and dining area. A large table takes up most of the downstage space, where the children sit and do homework and the family eats and

Fig. 23. *Trewa.* Photo: Danilo Espinoza Guerra.

talks, as several women expertly prepare food upstage. The space is in fact too small to hold all the bodies that enter it, and they must spill out onto the natural terrain in the play's heightened moments, such as the ritual for Macarena and the play's final monologues.

KIMVN uses these three spaces to stage a multimodal dramaturgy. It combines the affective and imagistic in the natural projections, the music, and the wandering emotive figure of Macarena herself. As Grass observes, it also incorporates elements in a legibly "documentary theater" tradition: text projected onto the scrim contextualizes the play, recorded narrations explain concepts, and the play incorporates ethnographic elements and the real figures on which the play is based.[127] These figures, played by actors, inhabit the stage alongside nonprofessional actors, members of the Mapuche community, offering multiple senses of the real.

These disparate elements collapse in the staging of the ritual for Macarena, and the play becomes real in a different sense. All the actors assemble on the central, natural space of the stage, wearing elements of traditional Mapuche dress and playing traditional instruments. The ritual is led by Papay Rosa, played by Norma Hueche, a member of the Mapuche community with which González conducted her initial ethnographic explorations. Hueche takes over the play. The ritual is conducted in Mapudungun, and Rosa's body, which is not trained as an actor's, comports itself with the knowledge of age (see fig. 23). The participants stomp, dance, play their instruments, and ask Macarena for permission to disinter her body. As the ritual continues, the audience hears an Offstage Voice, which connects multiple threads of historic and present violence: the deaths and disappearances during the dictatorship, the inadequacies of the truth commissions, the recent deaths of environmental activists, the human rights violations of the Carabineros during the estallido. The ritual concludes with a denunciation from Rubén:

> I am Rubén Collío, spokesperson for the Newen de Pangui community, life partner of Macarena Valdés. They assassinated la Negra, they killed la Negra for being a woman, for being Mapuche, they killed her for daring to lift her voice, for defending life. The Panguipuilli Prosecutor's office, the Investigative Police have not done their job well. They have not done their job well! Work! Drones! Because we are not going to allow more deaths, we will not allow them! *Newentuleimvn Pu Peñi Lamngen!* [Have strength, my people!][128]

Just as the play stages scenic permeability, it also situates the relationship between performance and reality as porous. On the one hand, *Trewa* operates on the level of a legibly theatrical performance in both documentary and realistic modes—positioning the spectator in a reflective position vis-à-vis the pedagogical elements of the play. However, as the ritual commences, the modality of the dramaturgy shifts to the more performative, in the tradition of Austin and Butler. The ritual for Macarena, led by Norma Hueche, is *real*.[129]

Andrew Goldberg argues that a significant aspect of performance's political potential lies in its ability to interpellate the spectator. Drawing on the work of Louis Althusser, Goldberg defines interpellation as the way ideology—manifest in material institutions and embodied behaviors—is enacted through subject formation. Interpellation occurs when an individual is hailed as a subject—in both the sense of having autonomy and agency and in the sense of being "captured and beholden to the power of the State."[130] It thus offers a horizon of political action. The spectators of *Trewa*—as witnesses to this ritual—are interpellated into the ritual itself and thereby into the community supportive of Macarena and capable of political action. However, *Trewa* and *Un violador en tu camino* also perform another interpellation by shifting the object of the hail from the individual to the state. Dean and Mohanty both forge their concepts of solidarity via a relational triad: "I ask you to stand by me over and against a third."[131] The spectators, now *lamngen* and addressed in Mapudungun, are interpellated into a politically activated community, as the state is interpellated as the third. Rubén's final denunciation both forges solidarity and figures the state as subject to the citizen's claim to justice.

LASTESIS invites multiple audiences to engage with *Un violador en tu camino*, creating various modes and dynamics of interpellation. As a performance that, out of urgency and necessity, moved from a theatrical framework into the more open frame of the street, and then again to viral circulation on social media, the performance acts in the world in tangible ways. It performatively rejects women's culpability; it actively denounces the state. Through its direct references to varied manifestations of gender violence—including the recently experienced instances of police violence against protesters—its dramaturgy invites all those participating in the estallido into identification with the piece. Expanding further outward, many of the participants wear green bandanas, a symbol of the transnational Latin American abortion-rights movement. Individuals enter the performance through multiple avenues: they might perform the work in Chile, standing up directly for their own lived experiences; or they might act as spectator-allies, observing and documenting the performances and participating in its online circulations; they may be part of a wider community of spectators who are actively vulnerable to state violence; or they might compose a larger transnational audience, with the option to circulate the performance on social media or adapt and reperform the piece. In this way *Un violador en tu camino*—a multisited, multimodal performance that incorporates both online and embodied activism—is emblematic of Fuentes's performance constellations.[132] It allows heterogeneous groups of individuals that share in the work's claims and denunciations to participate in a network of solidarity.[133]

After the women reject their own culpability as victims of violence, the participants point directly in front of them and proclaim, "The rapist is you." On subsequent lines they point ahead of and behind them as they assert, "It's the cops / It's the judges." They then circle their arms around their heads declaring, "It's the state," and finally bring their forearms above their heads in an X, announcing, "It's the president." These gestures, like Rubén's call following the ritual, frame the state, its institutions, and its leadership as the rapist, transforming the state into a subject of its feminist citizens. This move—in which citizens interpellate the state, creating the triad of solidarity—hearkens to the gesture made by the first article of the 2022 constitutional draft, which positions Chile as subject to the constitution, as opposed to the individual of the 1980 document.

In its next move, the piece slips between the dramaturgy it has established as a choreographic chant—set within but lifted slightly apart from the marches taking place that day—to the more traditional dramaturgy of the protest march, as the women pump their fists in the air and chant, "The oppressive state is a macho rapist." They thus offer a script for the marches later that day. The piece then shifts modalities again, and the participants declaim an excerpt of a historic Carabinero hymn: "Sleep sweetly, innocent girl, without worrying about the bandit; that in your sweet and smiling dreams you see your carabinero lover."[134] This fragment links policing to the sexual objectification of women. LASTESIS rejects the hymn's infantilizing romanticization, asserting in the chant's final interpellation, "The rapist is you." Throughout *Un violador en tu camino*, LASTESIS produces the kind of "feminist aesthetic" outlined by Nelly Richard: "Postulating woman as a sign immersed in a chain of patriarchal forms of oppression and repression which must be broken, through coming to awareness of how masculine superiority is exercised and combatted."[135] Deborah Martin and Deborah Shaw note that the work "produces the female body as both subject and object, as both resistant and subjugated, and it references the trappings of femininity both for direct protest and as a means of 'staging' femininity in order to think about and critique gender norms."[136] *Un violador en tu camino* disrupts the chain of patriarchal forms of oppression by fostering awareness and reclaiming agency in its acts of interpellation.

Following its initial performances, the collective made the lyrics, musical beat, and choreography available online, facilitating its reperformance. It has subsequently been performed in cities around the world, including a performance translated into Mapudungun and performed by Mapuche women in Temuco in December 2019, illustrating its transversal resonance.[137] Javiera Manzi and Fernanda Carvajal note that the logic of the thesis—as an argument that can be applied—positions the piece as a "tool for articulating protest, making it possible to prefigure other political-affective territories that are not necessarily those of a nation or a political party."[138] Cometa conjectures that the work's transnational virality was "probably due to the virality of systematic violence that human beings have to live under the structures of the modern state . . . it was like a scream that we all have to give."[139]

Fittingly, then, KIMVN's *Trewa* draws to its conclusion with a scream. After Emiliano is discovered and expelled from the community, the Am of Macarena, silent for the entirety of the play, commands the stage. She lets out a long scream, filled with the rage and pain that have been visible throughout the play. She addresses the audience. She describes coming with Rubén to live in the south and the process of learning to live with nature. An attunement to nature, she contends, asserts different ways of knowing, grounded in radical equality—the basis of solidarity: "There is no wrong skin color if we close our eyes and feel. . . . Neither trees nor birds are more just than others. If the river bubbles and makes sound it is because it speaks to us in another way."[140] She references the pain and loss that have shaped this community. She died, she claims, for defending water, a human right. The state, and its alliance with extractive capital, is a murderer. However, she claims that she will live on "as the voice of the interminable wound of a people." Her monologue concludes and an ancestral Mapuche song rises from the divine plane of kalfü. A text is projected onto the scrim. It explains that upon reexamination of Valdés's corpse a forensic scientist concluded that her death could not have been by suicide, but that her corpse was hung after her death. Valdés, the play asserts, had been murdered.

Trewa and *Un violador en tu camino* both conclude with the assertion that the state is the source of violence. In *Trewa*, a text projects on the scrim: "Boys and girls from Mapuche communities live with the daily fear provoked by historical violence exercised by the institutions of power, the forces of security and order of our country."[141] *Un violador en tu camino*'s chant concludes, "The rapist was you." These final moments are powerful and power-full: in the sense of their affective impact on their spectators, but also in the way they invert the act of subjectification, giving power to the citizens. By rejecting culpability and asserting presence, by critiquing the state and performing liberation, they posit a claim to power. The state—named as the perpetrator of violence—is now subject to its citizens, hailed by them and subject to their justice. Such a state, the works posit, is fundamentally contingent. Underneath these final enunciations lies the possibility, indeed the necessity, of its transformation. The dramaturgies of solidarity that they create—which offer embodied modes of knowing and being—gesture toward intersectional and transversal ways of relating that might counteract the overbearing systemic violence and totalitarianism of neoliberal capitalism. They offer a processional framework to forge a new, more democratic, world.

Epilogue

✦

Dramaturgies of Defeat and Political Futures

I arrived in Santiago on a gray Wednesday at the end of August in 2022. It was the first time I had been back to Chile since 2018, and so much had happened: the heady explosiveness of the protests that convulsed Santiago in October 2019, the almost incomprehensible state violence and curfews that met the manifestations, the trauma and isolation of the ongoing pandemic, and the organizing and activism that had led to the constitutional proposal. Riding in a cab through the morning rush hour, I scanned the streets for visible traces of these events. The buildings, which had always been a canvas for graffiti, were even more densely covered than I remembered. The walls of the city were bursting with hope and rage. Layer upon layer of paint issued wide-ranging demands and denunciations: No + AFP; ACAB, Apruebo, Dignidad, No + Terrorismo del Estado, EVADE, and on and on (see fig. 24).

The proposed constitution reflected the proliferation of demands inscribed across the city. If ratified, it would fundamentally transform the economic and social model that Pinochet had implemented. Yet I knew, even before I boarded the plane, that the campaign for the constitution's approval was faltering. The convention had been plagued by scandals, and polls suggested a strong preference for the rechazo (reject) option. President Boric had stated that if the constitution was not approved, he would initiate a new constitutional process—a seeming admission of defeat. Nevertheless, those in favor of the apruebo (approve) seemed hopeful. At subway stops, campaigners played classic Los Prisioneros songs and handed out cheerful flyers highlighting the proposed constitution's contents. Grafitti, signs, and pasteups around the city highlighted the utopian vision of the apruebo (see fig. 25). The polls couldn't be trusted, friends told me, since it was the first time in many years that the vote would be compulsory—no one knew exactly what that would portend. Thursday night, at the closing campaign event, produced by FITAM's Carmen Romero, over four hundred thousand people filled the streets to hear popular artists such as Ana Tijoux and Francisca Valenzuela. In one of the evening's most powerful moments some of Chile's most renowned actors

Fig. 24. The entrance to the Banquedano metro station, closed at the time for repairs and converted to the *jardín de la resistencia*. Grafitti and memorials cover the space. Photo by the author.

read article 1 of the constitution, as Victor Jara's "La Partida," performed by Inti Illimani, played underneath. The combined effect of the sweeping instrumental music underscoring the actor's trained voices endowed the words with somber profundity. Dramaturgically, the campaign leaned heavily on the memory of resistance to the dictatorship. The music of both Jara and Inti Illimani had deep associations with Allende and the resistance to the dictatorship, as well as its atrocities. Many of the actors too (Alfredo Castro, Francisco Reyes) were known for their resistance to the dictatorship. The suggestion was that this was part of the ongoing struggle against the dictatorship, and a chance to finally leave that history behind. Farther west, the rechazo held their rally, to a far smaller audience numbering in the hundreds.

Around five o'clock on Sunday afternoon, I gathered with friends to watch the results. When the first votes came in from Southernmost Magallanes the mood in the room turned somber. As the polls closed across the country it was apparent that the rechazo was leading. Nearly everywhere. At nine o'clock President Boric addressed the nation to concede to the rechazo. He looked tense and pale, and his eyes clung to the teleprompter as he vowed to initiate a new constitutional process. My

Fig. 25. Pasteups advocating for a plurinational (*left*) and solidary (*right*) Chile. Photo by the author.

friends conversed intently with each other: some looking for sources of optimism, others grieving the apruebo's failure as Chile's best, perhaps only, chance for transformation. *We are not a society that values the collective*, one friend kept repeating. *We have chosen neoliberalism. We have chosen individualism.* All agreed that Chile's future was suddenly very uncertain.

I left the house and walked out onto Avenida Providencia in the cool evening air. I was met with an enthusiastic group of rechazo supporters flooding the streets—car horns honking, flags waving. I groped in my bag for my metro card but was unable to find it. I began walking toward the city center. As I neared Plaza Dignidad the back of my throat began to burn from the tear gas lingering in the air, and the pavement was slick from recently deployed water cannons. These police actions had mostly cleared the streets, but a few groups were beginning to reconvene and set small barricades on fire. Some threw glass bottles and rocks at armored police vehicles parked along the streets. As I turned off the main road, I was confronted by a woman who, upon seeing me, yelled, "The wealthy [los cuicos] don't walk here, only the poor walk here!" I wished I could communicate my solidarity, but I felt vulnerable and quickened my pace.

When I boarded my return flight there was no more certainty about where Chile would go from here. Would there be the political capital to elect *another* constitutional convention, to draft *another* constitution, to hold *another* vote? Or would the right-wing parties take control of the process, entrenching neoliberalism even further? Would the social movement regroup, or had Chile's appetite for social transformation been crushed? How did this defeat change the things I thought I had learned about this country, about its struggles and social movements, about its desire to leave the dictatorship behind, about the dreams of its Left? I had hoped to be writing a very different ending to this book. But the history of the dictatorship is not past, and Chilean citizenship stands to yet again be redefined.

I interviewed Paula González just days before the constitutional vote, and our conversation turned to whether a legal document or institutional processes really could address the intertwined crises of ecological collapse, state violence, and neoliberal precarity. She told me that regardless of the result of the referendum, her Mapuche ancestors "have known how to reinvent themselves. For example . . . to survive crisis, to survive war, to survive massacres, there is something to learn from them."[1] Throughout this book, we have glimpsed the tactics artists have used to resist and survive authoritarianism and its double, the totalitarianism of late-stage capitalism and the necropolitics of the nation-state. We have seen the ways artists engaged with cultural institutionality and political systems to forge new identities and paths. We have seen the ways artists make political claims in the face of state violence and the way their work can offer community and healing in the face of this violence while still pursuing antagonistic demands. Finally, we have seen the ways artists continue taking up their work in an ever-shifting political landscape.

The infrastructural relationships that constitute performance force us to reconsider and expand the web of collaborations composing a given performance, as well as to reconceptualize the notion of "artistic agency." This agency and these webs are impossible to fully untangle. However, the cases here affirm that these collaborations are agentive, and their work does coalesce in real, imaginatively transformative moments. Theater's unique ontological status as a real social activity and as an activity set apart from the everyday world grounds its political potentiality. It is at once efficacious and impossible. It can gesture toward a world to come while demonstrating that this world exists here and now. In this way it always points us toward a horizon of possibility. Furthermore, theater's unique status as both ephemeral and repeatable mirrors the fleeting nature of transformative politics. It spurs us toward a hopeful future, with the awareness that such futures are always on the verge of their own demise. The work must be taken up and rehearsed and performed again, each time for a different audience. By considering dramaturgy not as the purview of one artistic work but as part of a larger constellation of various kinds of performances, I have traced the ways political and aesthetic ideas travel, coalesce, and find expression. Attending to dramaturgy illuminates connections between performances that we might otherwise have missed and helps us to understand how the artistic imagination gives transformative politics its life and futurity.

Both KIMVN and LASTESIS draw on historical legacies of persistence, resistance, and survival. In the case of KIMVN it is Indigenous cosmovisions and Mapuche activism; in the case of LASTESIS it is the legacy of the feminist movement and the resistance to the dictatorship. They also draw from a long and deep legacy of politically engaged performance in Chile that, as this book as shown, has forged and reforged, configured and challenged conceptualizations of democratic citizenship in Chile. Though these conceptualizations have been shaped by particular horizons of aesthetic possibility—horizons conditioned by Chile's history, institutions, policies, and politics—they have all proposed a reorientation of the state: CADA's agonistic and plural collaborations, Andrés Pérez's reimagination of the body politic and cultural institutionality, Teatro de Chile's assertion of the right to reimagine history, and Calderón's efforts to reinsert dissensual politics into the political and cultural spheres have all imagined a world that could be otherwise, and thus posited a present moment that is contingent.

The demands of LASTESIS and KIMVN, emerging within and alongside revolutionary upheaval, are presupposed on the historical contingency of the state itself. González asserts, "We are a theater that seeks an origin that exists before the conception of the nation-state. We are a theater that is rooted in the true identity of the citizens of this territory."[2] Marking the contingency of the state allows these groups to reforge citizenship in a temporal register that spans past, present, and future. Their performances have a vibrancy in the present but are also oriented around a new notion of state, or perhaps nonstate, formation, or at least its possibility. And even though they may not demonstrate precisely what the future looks like, as the utopian performatives Jill Dolan charts, they gesture toward and enact what it might *feel* like: liberatory, communal, solidary.[3] As Sara Ahmed writes, "The moment of hope is when the 'not yet' impresses upon us in the present, such that we must act, politically, to make it our future."[4] While I must conclude this book with uncertainty about the direction of Chile's political future, I am certain that its artists will continue to impress the not yet upon the present, and in so doing, imagine its future.

NOTES

Introduction

1. This, and all translations unless otherwise noted, are my own.

2. In 2019, Sandra Cuffe reported that the performance had been staged in over two hundred cities. Sandra Cuffe, "Chile's 'A Rapist in Your Path' Chant Hits 200 Cities: Map," *Al Jazeera*, December 20, 2019, https://www.aljazeera.com/news/2019/12/20/chiles-a-rapist-in-your-path-chant-hits-200-cities-map.

3. See "Chile: Eventos de 2019," Human Rights Watch, accessed November 21, 2020, https://www.hrw.org/es/world-report/2020/country-chapters/336397#.

4. Carla Pinochet Cobos, "Disrupting Normalcy. Artistic Interventions and Political Mobilisation against the Neoliberal City (Santiago, Chile, 2019)," *Social Identities* 27, no. 5 (2021): 538–554, https://doi.org/10.1080/13504630.2021.1931091.

5. Other notable performances during the *estallido* include Cheril Linett's Proyecto Yeguada Latinoamericana (begun in 2017 and performed during the *estallido*), interventions by Colectivo Gata Engrifá, and light activism by Delight Lab, among others. See Vanessa M. Gubbins, "General Strike: Feminist Performance?" in *Bodies on the Front Lines: Performance, Gender and Sexuality in Latin America and the Caribbean,* ed. Brenda Werth and Katherine Zien (University of Michigan Press, 2024), 59–78; Bernadita Llanos and Milena Grass, "New Feminist Performance in the Chilean Revolt: La Yeguada Latinoamericana and LASTESIS," in *Dismantling the Nation: Contemporary Art in Chile,* ed. Florencia San Martín, Carla Macchiavello Cornejo, and Paula Solimano (Amherst College Press, 2023), 39–56; Iván Pinto Veas and María José Bello Navarro, "La revuelta performativa: Hacia una noción expandida de cuerpos e imágenes en el espacio público a partir del estallido social chileno," *Cuadernos de Música, Artes Visuales y Artes Escénicas* 17, no. 1 (2022): 192–219, https://doi.org/10.11144/javeriana.mavae17-1.rphn.

6. I begin another essay with a similar description of LASTESIS's performance and contextualization within the *estallido*. In that case it is to think through the power and legacy of feminist performance circulating in the *estallido*. I return to it here as an illustrative example of the dramaturgical acts of citizenship I consider throughout this book. See Jennifer Joan Thompson, "'An Explosion of Feminism': Dramaturgies of Excess and Revolution in Chile's New Feminist Vanguard," in Werth and Zien, *Bodies on the Front Lines*, 39–40.

7. Baz Kershaw, "Fighting in the Streets: Dramaturgies of Popular Protest, 1968–1989," *New Theatre Quarterly* 13, no. 51 (1997): 257, https://doi.org/10.1017/S0266464X0001126X. Kershaw reads protest *as* performance; here I read performance as protest.

8. Brent McDonald, "A Bullet to the Eye Is the Price of Protesting in Chile," *New York Times*, November 19, 2019, https://www.nytimes.com/2019/11/19/world/americas/chile-protests-eye-injuries.html.

9. This is similar, in some ways, to Cláudia Tatinge Nascimento's project on Brazilian post-dictatorship theater, which explores how the sociopolitical transition to democracy created the aesthetic paradigms of Brazilian contemporary theater. Cláudia Tatinge Nascimento, *After the Long Silence: The Theater of Brazil's Post-Dictatorship Generation* (Routledge, 2019), 20.

10. Nikos Papastergiadis, "Spatial Aesthetics: Rethinking the Contemporary," in *Antinomies of Art and Culture: Modernity, Postmodernity, Contemporaneity*, ed. Terry Smith, Okwui Enwezor, and Nancy Condee (Duke University Press, 2008), 375.

11. Diana Taylor, *The Archive and the Repertoire: Performing Cultural Memory in the Americas* (Duke University Press, 2003), 2–15, quote on 14.

12. Shannon Jackson, *Social Works: Performing Arts, Supporting Publics* (Routledge, 2011); Patricia Ybarra, "Fighting for a Future in a Free Trade World," in *Neoliberalism and Global Theatres: Performance Permutations*, ed. Lara D. Nielsen and Patricia Ybarra (Palgrave Macmillan, 2012): 113–127; Jen Harvie, *Fair Play: Art, Performance and Neoliberalism* (Palgrave Macmillan, 2013); Jean Graham-Jones, "Rethinking Buenos Aires Theatre in the Wake of 2001 and Emerging Structures of Resistance and Resilience," *Theatre Journal* 66, no. 1 (March 2014): 37–54, http://www.jstor.org/stable/24580242; Marcos Steuernagel, "Who Wants Money? Radical Performance and Experimental Urbanism in the Heart of São Paulo," *Journal of Global South Studies* 38, no. 1 (2021): 194–219, https://dx.doi.org/10.1353/gss.2021.0010.; Sarah Wilbur, *Funding Bodies: Five Decades of Dance Making at the National Endowment for the Arts* (Wesleyan University Press, 2021).

13. Marianne Van Kerkhoven, "On Dramaturgy," *Theaterschrift* 5–6 (1994): 8–34. Van Kerkhoven is responding to the practices that Hans-Thies Lehmann calls the "postdramatic" that emerged in Europe throughout the 1980s and '90s. Lehmann, *Postdramatic Theatre*, trans. Karen Jürs-Munby (Routledge, 2006).

14. Konstantina Georgelou, Efrosini Protopapa, and Danae Theodoridou, "Dramaturgy as Working on Actions," in *The Practice of Dramaturgy. Working on Actions in Performance*, ed. Konstantina Georgelou, Efrosini Protopapa, and Danae Theordoridou (Antennae Valiz, 2017), 79.

15. Maaike Bleeker, *Doing Dramaturgy: Thinking through Practice* (Springer Nature Switzerland, 2023), 1–2, 5–6.

16. Cathy Turner and Synne Behrndt, *Dramaturgy and Performance* (Palgrave Macmillan, 2007), 35.

17. Peter Eckersall, "Towards an Expanded Dramaturgical Practice: A Report on 'The Dramaturgy and Cultural Intervention Project,'" *Theatre Research International* 31, no. 3 (2006): 295, https://doi.org/10.1017/S0307883306002240.

18. Taylor, *The Archive and the Repertoire*, 11–15.

19. Andrea Jeftanovic identifies Soledad Lagos's dramaturgical practice, beginning in 2004, as a novelty in Chilean theater. Jeftanovic, "La 'Costura dramática' de Soledad Lagos y su trabajo pionero como dramaturgista en la escena teatral chilena de hoy," *Theatre der Zeit* (2008): 47–53.

20. Michel de Certeau, *The Practice of Everyday Life*, trans. Steven Rendall, 3rd ed. (University of California Press, 2011), 29–30.

21. Jill Dolan, *Utopia in Performance: Finding Hope at the Theater* (University of Michigan Press, 2005), 5.

22. Marcela Fuentes, *Performance Constellations: Networks of Protest and Activism in Latin America* (University of Michigan Press, 2019), 2–3.

23. Judith Butler, "Performative Acts and Gender Constitution: An Essay in Phenomenology and Feminist Theory," *Theatre Journal* 40, no. 4 (1988): 519–531, https://doi.org/10.2307/3207893.

24. May Joseph, *Nomadic Identities: The Performance of Citizenship* (University of Minnesota Press, 1999), 4.

25. Emine Fisek, *Aesthetic Citizenship: Immigration and Theater in Twenty-First-Century Paris* (Northwestern University Press, 2017).

26. T. H. Marshall, "Citizenship and Social Class," in *Inequality and Society*, ed. Jeff Manza and Michael Sauder (W. W. Norton, 2009), 149–54. Engin Isin and Bryan S. Turner offer an excellent summary of the multiple meanings and modalities of citizenship and citizenship studies in Isin and Turner, "Investigating Citizenship: An Agenda for Citizenship Studies," in *Citizenship between Past and Future*, ed. Engin F. Isin, Peter Nyers, and Bryan S. Turner (Routledge, 2008), 5–17.

27. Engin F. Isin and Greg M. Nielsen, introduction to *Acts of Citizenship*, ed. Engin F. Isin and Greg M. Nielsen (Zed Books, 2008), 4. These arguments are foundationally shaped by Bourdieu's theorization of practice. See Pierre Bourdieu, *The Logic of Practice*, trans. Richard Nice (Stanford University Press, 1980).

28. Jennifer Ponce de León, *Another Aesthetics Is Possible: Arts of Rebellion in the Fourth World War* (Duke University Press, 2021), 22.

29. Wendy Brown, *Undoing the Demos: Neoliberalism's Stealth Revolution* (Zone Books, 2015), 19.

30. Judith Butler, *Notes toward a Performative Theory of Assembly* (Harvard University Press, 2015), 2.

31. Brown, *Undoing the Demos*, 20.

32. Nelly Richard, *Cultural Residues. Chile in Transition*, trans. Alan West-Durán and Theodore Quester (University of Minnesota Press, 2004).

33. Jacques Rancière, *Dissensus: On Politics and Aesthetics*, trans. Steven Corcoran (Bloomsbury, 2010), 36.

34. Rancière, *Dissensus*, 58.

35. Nelly Richard, *The Insubordination of Signs: Political Change, Cultural Transformation, and Poetics of the Crisis*, trans. Alice A. Nelson and Silvia R. Tandeciarz (Duke University Press, 2004), 1–23.

36. Janelle Reinelt and Shirin Rai, introduction to *The Grammar of Politics and Performance*, ed. Janelle Reinelt and Shirin Rai (Routledge, 2015), 9.

37. Claire Bishop, *Artificial Hells: Participatory Art and the Politics of Spectatorship* (Verso, 2012), 284.

38. Patrick Duggan, *Trauma-Tragedy: Symptoms of Contemporary Performance* (Manchester University Press, 2015), 9.

39. See Carol Martin, *Theatre of the Real* (Palgrave Macmillan, 2013); Liz Tomlin, *Acts and Apparitions: Discourses on the Real in Performance Practice and Theory, 1990–2010* (Manchester University Press, 2013); José Antonio Sánchez, *Practicing the Real on the Contemporary Stage*, trans. Charlie Allwood (Chicago University Press, 2014); Marvin Carlson, *Shattering Hamlet's Mirror: Theatre and Reality* (University of Michigan Press, 2016); and Paola Hernández, *Staging Lives in Latin American Theater: Bodies, Objects, Archives* (Northwestern University Press, 2021).

40. Guillermo Calderón, personal interview with the author, Santiago, Chile, June 27, 2018.

41. Camila Ymay González Ortiz, "'Los dueños de Chile somos nosotros': retrato de la élite en *Los millonarios*, de Teatro La María," *Literatura y lingüística* 44 (2021): 145–46, http://dx.doi.org/10.29344/0717621x.44.3052.

42. Jennifer Joan Thompson, "Horizons of Impossibility: The Political Imperative in the Dramaturgy of Guillermo Calderón," *Theatre Journal* 73, no. 2 (June 2021): 170, https://doi.org/10.1353/tj.2021.0040.

43. See Catherine M. Boyle, *Chilean Theater, 1973–1985: Marginality, Power, Selfhood* (Fairleigh Dickinson University Press [Associated University Presses], 1992); María de la Luz Hurtado, *Teatro chileno y modernidad: identidad y crisis social* (Ediciones de Gestos, 1997); Juan Andrés Piña, *Historia del teatro en Chile, 1941–1990* (Editorial Taurus, 2014); Ana Harcha Cortés, *Prácticas de teatralidad en Chile: a partir del trabajo de Andrés Pérez Araya* (Editorial Universitaria, 2017).

44. These also included Teatro de Ensayo de la Universidad Católica in 1943, Teatro de la Universidad de Concepción in 1945, Teatro de la Universidad Técnica del Estado in 1958, and Teatro de la Universidad de Antofagasta in 1963.

45. This periodization can reinforce a bias against pre-1941 theater, casting it as sporadic and nonsystematic, and thus asserts the dominance of Chilean universities. Andrés Kalawski challenges this narrative by focusing on how the careers of actors between 1910 and 1947 demonstrate artistry and professionalism. Andrés Kalawski Isla, "Falso mutis: oficio de actores en la 'época de oro' del teatro chileno 1910–1947" (PhD diss., Pontificia Universidad Católica de Chile, 2015).

46. Harcha, *Prácticas de teatralidad*, 29.

47. See "Eduardo Frei Montalva," Memoria Chilena, accessed October 10, 2018, http://www.memoriachilena.cl. For a microhistory of the *vía chilena al socialismo*, see Peter Winn, *Weavers of the Revolution: The Yarur Workers and Chile's Road to Socialism* (Oxford University Press, 1986).

48. See María de la Luz Hurtado, Carlos Ochsensius, and Hernán Vidal, *Teatro chileno de la crisis institucional: 1973–1980* (Ceneca, 1982); Boyle, *Chilean Theater*, 33–43; Luis Pradenas, "El Teatro Popular, desde el Frente Popular a la Revolución en Libertad," in *Teatro en Chile: Huellas y trayectorias, siglos XVI–XX* (LOM Ediciones, 2006), 331–340.

49. Such as the 1972 centennial for the Communist Party, the seventh anniversary of Communist Youth, and the post-Nobel welcome of Pablo Neruda, all directed by Victor Jara at the National Stadium. Harcha, *Prácticas de teatralidad*, 41.

50. See Daniel Mansuy, *Salvador Allende: La izquierda chilena y la Unidad Popular* (Editorial Taurus, 2023), Kindle; Winn, *Weavers of the Revolution*.

51. Ramón Griffero, interview with the author, Santiago, Chile, July 7, 2018.

52. Harcha, *Prácticas de teatralidad*, 70. See also Herbert Jonkers, *Poéticas de espacio escénico: Chile 1981–1996* (Ediciones Frontera Sur, 2006); Ramón Griffero, *La dramaturgia del espacio* (Ediciones Frontera Sur, 2011).

53. Harcha, *Prácticas de teatralidad*, 261. Griffero, interview with the author; Alfredo Castro, interview with the author, Santiago, Chile, August 20, 2018.

54. Toby Miller and George Yúdice, *Cultural Policy* (Sage Publications, 2002).

55. See Néstor García Canclini, *Arte popular y sociedad en América Latina: Teorías, estéticas y ensayos de transformación* (Editorial Grijalbo, 1977); Néstor García Canclini, *Hybrid Cultures: Strategies for Entering and Leaving Modernity*, trans. Christopher Chiappari and Sylvia Lopez (University of Minnesota Press, 1995).

56. Pierre Bourdieu, *Distinction: A Social Critique of the Judgement of Taste*, trans. Richard Nice (Harvard University Press, 1984); Pierre Bourdieu, *The Field of Cultural Production: Essays on Art and Literature*, ed. Randal Johnson (Columbia University Press, 1993).

57. Arturo Navarro, *Cultura: ¿Quién paga? Gestión, infraestructura y audiencias en el modelo chileno de desarrollo cultural* (RIL editores, 2006).

58. See Catherine Boyle, "Violence in Memory: Translation, Dramatization, and Performance of the Past in Chile" in *Cultural Politics in Latin America*, ed. Anny Brooksbank Jones and Ronaldo Munck (St. Martin's Press, 2000), 93–112; and Idelber Avelar, *The Untimely Present: Postdictatorial Latin American Fiction and the Task of Mourning* (Duke University Press, 2012).

59. Quoted in Joanne Pottlitzer, "The Game of Expression under Pinochet: Four Theater Stories," *Theater* 31, no. 2 (2001): 13–14, https://muse.jhu.edu/article/34166.

60. Avelar, *Untimely Present*, 11.

61. Early governmental reports acknowledge the problem of culture's centralization in Santiago. The Consejo Nacional de Cultura y las Artes (National Council of Culture and Arts, CNCA) was created in 2003, in part with the aim of addressing this imbalance. See Comisión Asesoría Presidencial en Materias Artístico Culturales, "Chile está en deuda con la cultura," (1997). A 2005 report outlines that decentralizing culture and supporting it throughout Chile's regions should remain an ongoing priority of cultural policy. CNCA, "Chile quiere más cultura," (2005), 14–15. In 2012, the CNCA created the "Red Cultura" (Cultural Network) program with the aim of decentralizing culture. CNCA, "Memoria consejo nacional de la cultura y las artes: 2010–2014," (2014), 68.

62. Alejandra Castillo, "Feminist Political Imagination," trans. Alex Brostoff, *Critical Times* 5, no. 1 (2022): 262–264, https://doi.org/10.1215/26410478-9536615.

63. Macarena Gómez-Barris, *Beyond the Pink Tide: Art and Political Undercurrents in the Americas* (University of California Press, 2018), 1.

Chapter 1

1. Quoted in Paula Thorrington, "An Ode to Joy: Chilean Culture in the Eighties against Pinochet" (PhD diss., University of California, Los Angeles, 2011), 97.

2. Others of their actions, such as *A la hora señalada* (*High Noon*), *Residuos americanos* (*American Residues*), and *El fulgor de la huelga* (*The Splendor of the Strike*), were more akin to installations in galleries than performance, and the medium of *Viuda* (*Widow*) was print.

3. Decree Law no. 3 declared the state of siege, which was renewed every six months until it was replaced by a "state of emergency" in March 1978. Comisión Nacional de Verdad y Reconciliación, *Report of the Chilean National Commission on Truth and Reconciliation* (a.k.a. *Rettig Report*), trans. Phillip E. Berryman (University of Notre Dame Press, 1993), 1: 97.

4. Decree Law no. 27, issued on September 24, 1973, disbanded Congress. Decree Law no. 77 disbanded political parties that had supported Allende on October 13, 1973. On October 17, Decree Law no. 78 declared all other parties "in recess." In 1977, Decree Law no. 1697 banned all political organizations. See Comisión Nacional de Verdad y Reconciliación, *Report*, 1:94–95.

5. Philip D. Oxhorn, *Organizing Civil Society: The Popular Sectors and the Struggle for Democracy in Chile* (Pennsylvania State University Press, 1995), 66.

6. The curfews were issued through edicts broadcast on the radio and reprinted in the national newspaper *El Mercurio*.

7. Luis Hernán Errázuriz, "Política cultural del régimen militar chileno (1973–1976)," *Aisthesis* 40 (2006): 66, https://doi.org/10.7764/ais.40.62-78.

8. In music, the Nueva Canción (New Song) movement marshaled folkloric genres and political commitment, exemplified in the work of Victor Jara. See "La Nueva Canción chilena," *Memoria Chilena*, accessed July 6, 2018, http://www.memoriachilena.cl/602/w3-article-702.htm. In theater, university, amateur, and union theater groups performed in popular neighborhoods and to workers' groups to foment political consciousness and represent class struggle. See Pradenas, "El Teatro Popular," 331–340; Hurtado, Ochsensius, and Vidal, *Teatro Chileno*; and Boyle, *Chilean Theater*, 32–43. For visual arts and the Brigada Ramona Parra, see Eduardo Castillo Espinoza, *Puño y letra: Movimiento social y comunicación gráfica en Chile* (Ocho Libros, 2016); Camilo Trumper, *Ephemeral Histories: Public Art, Politics, and the Struggle for the Streets in Chile* (University of California Press, 2016).

9. See Anny Rivera, *Transformaciones culturales y movimiento artístico en el orden autoritario*. Chile:1973–1982 (CENECA, 1983), 54–55, 109.

10. The government encouraged the creation of private cooperatives to fund and promote the arts. These groups, which Rivera and Richard refer to as the "arte empresa" (art-company) system, organized exhibitions and funding contests. Though this system had some benefits to artists, it funded a narrow vision of culture, a "private vanguard" favoring the experimental fine arts. See Rivera, *Transformaciones culturales*, 42–53; Nelly Richard, *Márgenes e*

instituciones: Arte en Chile desde 1973, 3rd ed. (Metales Pesados, 2014), 125–126. For an example of these funding bodies' mercurial nature, see "Al que da y quita," *La Bicicleta* 7 (July–August 1980): 19.

11. Steve J. Stern, *Battling for Hearts and Minds: Memory Struggles in Pinochet's Chile: 1973–1988* (Duke University Press, 2006), 139. The full Chacarillas speech was printed in *El Mercurio* on July 10, 1977. For Stern's analysis of this speech and Pinochet's vision of democracy, which informs my own, see Stern, *Battling for Hearts and Minds*, 137–195.

12. Juan Correa-Parra, José Francisco Vergara-Perucich, and Carlos Aguirre-Nuñez, "Water Privatization and Inequality: Gini Coefficient for Water Resources in Chile," *Water* 12, no. 12 (2020): 3369, https://doi.org/10.3390/w12123369.

13. Claudia Heiss and Patricio Navia, "You Win Some, You Lose Some: Constitutional Reforms in Chile's Transition to Democracy," *Latin American Politics and Society* 49, no. 3 (2007): 163, https://doi.org/10.1111/j.1548-2456.2007.tb00386.x.

14. Stern, *Battling for Hearts and Minds*, 170–73.

15. Stern, *Battling for Hearts and Minds*, 198–230.

16. Rivera estimates that between 1975 and 1980 more than seventy cultural organizations were formed, over half of them in *poblaciones*. Additionally, José Joaquín Brunner estimates that in 1979 there were at least five hundred groups of amateur musicians and eighty theatrical groups. Rivera, *Transformaciones culturales*, 124; José Joaquín Brunner, "Políticas culturales de oposición en Chile," Material de Discusión, 78 (FLASCO, December 1985): 11.

17. Grupo Cámara Chile, "Grupo Cámara Chile: Balance de su trabajo correspondiente al año 1978," January 8, 1979, box 2943, folder 4, Fundación Documentación y Archivo de la Vicaria de la Solidaridad (hereinafter FDAVS).

18. Rivera, *Transformaciones culturales*, 114.

19. Margarita Iglesias Saldaña et al., *Centro Cultural Mapocho: Una historia por contar* (Ciebo Ediciones, 2014).

20. Interview by Rodrigo Vidal, 2010, quoted in Saldaña et al., *Centro Cultural Mapocho*, 44.

21. *La Bicicleta* 1 (September–October 1978): 53.

22. UNAC, "Informativo para las agrupaciones culturales," n.d., box 2943, folder 4, Cultura Collection, FDAVS.

23. UNAC, Llamado II, May 1979, CEDOC Artes Visuales, Centro Cultural la Moneda Digital Archive, http://centrodedocumentaciondelasartes.cl/g2/collect/cedoc/images/pdfs/3334.pdf.

24. Saldaña et al., *Centro Cultural Mapocho*, 45.

25. Grupo Cámara Chile, "Balance de su trabajo." This source does not name the two Santiago newspapers.

26. For an account of Grupo Cámara Chile's activities and financial struggles see "S.O.S.," *La Bicicleta* 2 (December 1978): 24–26; and Grupo Cámara Chile, "Balance de su Trabajo."

27. UNAC, "Llamado a la comunidad," n.d., box 2943, folder 4, Cultura Collection, FDAVS.

28. Centro por la Defensa de la Cultura Chilena, "Centro por la Defensa de la Cultura Chilena," n.d., folder 3, box 6774, FDAVS.

29. See interviews with Diamela Eltit, Lotty Rosenfeld, Juan Castillo, and Raúl Zurita in Robert Neustadt, *CADA día: La creación de un arte social* (Editorial Cuarto Propio, 2001).

30. Richard, *Márgenes e instituciones*, 28. The *escena de avanzada* refers to a heterogenous group of artists who created works in resistance to the dictatorship and who sought to break with the institutionalization of art, as well as with the politically committed artworks of the previous era. In addition to CADA, the *escena de avanzada* included Carlos Altamirano, Eugenio Dittborn, Carlos Gallardo, and Carlos Leppe, among others.

31. Willy Thayer, "El golpe como consumación de la vanguardia: Fragmentos," in *El Fragmento repetido: escritos en estado de excepción* (Metales Pesados, 2006), 15–46.

32. Nelly Richard, "Lo político y lo crítico en el arte: '¿Quién teme a la neovanguardia?' " in *Arte y política*, ed. Pablo Oyarzún, Nelly Richard, and Claudia Zaldívar (Consejo Nacional de la Cultura y las Artes, 2005), 40.

33. Miguel Valderrama, *Modernismos historiográficos: artes visuales, postdictadura, vanguardias* (Palodino, 2008), 14.

34. Diana Taylor, *Performance* (Asuntos Impresos, 2012); Eugenia Brito, "El cuerpo performático de los años 80," in *La intensidad del acontecimiento: Escrituras y relatos en torno a la performance en Chile*, ed. Mauricio Barría and Francisco Sanfuentes (Ediciones Departamento de Artes Visuales Facultad de Artes Universidad de Chile, 2011).

35. Francisco González Castro, Leonora López, and Brian Smith. *Performance art en Chile* (Ediciones Metales Pesados, 2016), 27; Diana Taylor, "Introducción: *performance*, teoría y práctica," in *Estudios avanzados de performance*, ed. Diana Taylor and Marcela Fuentes (Fondo de Cultura Económica, 2011), 7–31. CADA's work *Residuos Americanos* (*American Waste*) (1983) foregrounds the problematic of Western hegemony in Chilean history. The work consists of a pile of clothing sent from the United States to Chile for resale lying on the floor as an audiotape transmits the sound of brain tumor removal surgery. Chile has received the leftovers of American consumption, which is linked to a disease to be removed from the brain. See Nelly Richard, *Residuos y metáforas: ensayos de crítica cultural sobre el Chile de transición* (Editorial Cuarto Propio, 1998).

36. Diamela Eltit, interview with the author, Santiago, Chile, June 30, 2017.

37. See Ernesto Laclau and Chantal Mouffe, *Hegemony and Socialist Strategy: Towards a Radical Democratic Politics*, 2nd ed. (Verso, 2014); Chantal Mouffe, *The Democratic Paradox* (Verso, 2000); Chantal Mouffe, *On the Political* (Routledge, 2005); Chantal Mouffe, *Agonistics: Thinking the World Politically* (Verso, 2013).

38. Mouffe, *Agonistics*, xi.

39. Mouffe, *Agonistics*, xi.

40. Mouffe, *Agonistics*, xii. The term "agonism" derives from the Greek αγων (agōn), which refers to an athletic contest in which the struggle itself is valued more highly than victory or defeat. In addition to athletics, the notion of agōn infused political, legal, and theatrical modes of display. In ancient Greek drama the term was used to denote a scene in which the protagonists of the play confront each other center stage. See Murat Ince, "A Critique of

Agonistic Politics," *International Journal of Žižek Studies* 10, no. 1 (2016): 13; Tony Fisher, "Introduction: Performance and the Politics of the *Agōn*," in *Performing Antagonism: Theatre, Performance, and Radical Democracy*, ed. Tony Fisher and Eve Katsouraki (Palgrave Macmillan, 2017).

41. Mouffe, *Agonistics*, 7.

42. Mouffe, *Agonistics*, 7.

43. Bonnie Honig, "Toward an Agonistic Feminism: Hannah Arendt and the Politics of Identity," in *Feminist Interpretations of Hannah Arendt*, ed. Bonnie Honig (Pennsylvania State University Press, 1995), 160. See also Butler, *Notes Toward a Performative Theory of Assembly*.

44. Colectivo Acciones de Arte (CADA), October 3, 1979, box 1, folder "Documentos *Para no morir* . . . ," Colectivo Acciones de Arte Collection. The word for "blank" or "white" used throughout is *blanca*. In each instance that either of these words occurs in the English translation, the double meaning is also implied.

45. Jael Goldsmith Weil, "Milk Makes State: The Extension and Implementation of Chile's State Milk Programs, 1901–1971," *Historia (Santiago)* 50, no. 1 (2017): 79–104, http://dx.doi.org/10.4067/S0717-71942017000100003.

46. Eltit, interview by Neustadt, *CADA día*, 93.

47. Eltit, interview by Neustadt, *CADA día*, 93.

48. Colectivo Acciones de Arte, "Cronología de Actividades," n.d., box 1, folder 1, Colectivo Acciones de Arte Collection.

49. Colectivo Acciones de Arte, "It Is Not a Village," 1979, box 1, folder 2, Colectivo Acciones de Arte Collection.

50. Colectivo Acciones de Arte, "It Is Not a Village."

51. The full text of the speech can be found at "El ultimo discurso de Salvador Allende," Radio Valentín Letelier, Universidad de Valparaíso, September 11, 2020, https://rvl.uv.cl/noticias/5608-el-ultimo-discurso-de-salvador-allende-en-el-golpe-de-estado-difundido-por-radio-magallanes.

52. Mansuy, *Salvador Allende*, chap. 1, Kindle.

53. Allie Tepper charts the intersections of Vicuña's work with CADA and in particular Lotty Rosenfeld's in "Crossings: The Poetics of Public Inscription in the Works of Cecilia Vicuña and Lotty Rosenfeld," *ASAP* 7, no. 2 (2022): 409–436.

54. Writing about Argentina, Jean Graham-Jones notes that the multiple modalities in which censorship took place, as well as the multiplicity of ways that artists responded to these practices, make it difficult to track how censorship and self-censorship influence artistic production. She therefore follows Chilean scholars, such as Roberto Hozven, in considering the ways artistic productions engage in countercensorial practices. Jean Graham-Jones, *Exorcising History: Argentine Theater under Dictatorship* (Bucknell University Press, 2000), 21. See also Roberto Hozven, "Censura, autocensura, y contracensura: Reflexiones acerca de un simposio," *Chasqui* 12, no. 1 (1982): 68–73, https://doi.org/10.2307/29739790.

55. Decree Law no. 827 (1974) imposed a 20 percent book tax and a 22 percent IVA (VAT) tax on the box office income of all shows. The government granted exemption to works deemed to be of "high artistic or cultural value." This standard was intentionally broad, allowing the government to enforce these taxes at will. *La Bicicleta* 4 (August–September 1979): 24.

56. Hozven notes that the inconsistency and arbitrary nature of censorship allows it to have an even more expansive reach. Hozven, "Censura, autocensura y contracensura," 70.

57. Neustadt, *CADA día*, 25–26; Rosenfeld, interview by Neustadt, *CADA día*, 48.

58. Jackson, *Social Works*, 6.

59. Rosenfeld, interview by Neustadt, *CADA día*, 49–51.

60. Rosenfeld, interview by Neustadt, *CADA día*, 50.

61. Richard, *Insubordination of Signs*, 27.

62. Eltit, interview by Neustadt, *CADA día*, 96.

63. Lotty Rosenfeld to Dirección de Aeronáutica, June 18, 1981, box 3, folder "Documentos *¡Ay Sudamérica!*," Archivo CADA.

64. Instituto de arte contemporáneo to Dirección de Aeronáutica, June 17, 1981, box 3, folder "Documentos *¡Ay Sudamérica!*," Colectivo Acciones de Arte Collection.

65. Ana María Foxley, "Un 'maná artístico,'" *Hoy* (July 22–28, 1981): 45–46.

66. Andreas Huyssen, *Present Pasts: Urban Palimpsests and the Politics of Memory* (Stanford University Press, 2003), 7.

67. Stern, *Battling for Hearts and Minds*, 31–76.

68. Eltit, interview with the author, June 30, 2017.

69. On May 11, 1983, there was a national strike and protest led by the Copper Workers Federation. Following the May protest, large demonstrations occurred almost monthly until October 1984, and again between September 1985 and 1986. See Stern, *Battling for Hearts and Minds*, 250–261.

70. Colectivo Acciones de Arte, "AY SUDAMERICA," July 1, 1981, box 3, folder "Documentos *¡Ay Sudamérica!*," Colectivo Acciones de Arte Collection. Emphasis in English translation my own.

71. Neustadt, *CADA día*, 37.

72. Fernanda Carvajal, "Arte, política, representación. El caso del No+ del Colectivo de Acciones de Arte en el Chile dictatorial," *Revista estampa* 2, no. 4 (2013): 90–101.

73. FONDART, instituted in 1992, is a government fund that provides grants for artists and organizations through an annual application process and is one of the only public resources for arts funding in Chile today. I will engage in a more thorough discussion of the fund in chapter 3.

74. The MIR is the *Movimiento de Izquierda Revolucionaria* (Revolutionary Left Movement), a far-left group that had mounted militant resistance to the 1973 coup, and whose members the regime targeted in their political imprisonment, tortures, and disappearances.

75. Boyle writes that "the journalistic term 'apagón cultural' was coined and soon became the most common way of explaining the immediate effects of the coup on the arts." Boyle, *Chilean Theater*, 51.

76. The Museo de la Memoria y los Derechos Humanos (Museum of Memory and Human Rights) houses an exhibit documenting and preserving the memory of the coup and military regime, as well as two archives, the Centro de Documentación (CEDOC) and the Centro de Documentación Audiovisual (CEDAV), which contain a wealth of material relating to this period.

77. Antonio Kadima, interview with the author, Santiago, Chile, July 5, 2017.

78. Richard, *Márgenes e instituciones*, 11.

79. Fisher, introduction, 3.

Chapter 2

1. *La Tercera*, December 31, 2017.

2. The Concertation of Parties for the No formed in 1988 to coordinate the opposition to Pinochet during the plebiscite. It consisted of seventeen left and center parties. See Eugenio Ortega Frei, *Historia de una alianza política: el partido Socialista de Chile y el partido Demócrata Cristiano: 1973–1988* (LOM Ediciones, 1992).

3. Here I use Steve Stern's translation. The word *ya*, meaning "already," connotes immediacy and could render the slogan "Chile, happiness is already coming."

4. For this definition, see Steve Stern, *Reckoning with Pinochet: The Memory Question in Democratic Chile, 1989–2006* (Duke University Press, 2010), 16.

5. Patricio Aylwin, "En el inicio de la legislatura ordinaria del Congreso Nacional," in *La transición chilena: Discursos escogidos, marzo 1990–1992* (Andrés Bello, 1992), 33.

6. Stern, *Battling for Hearts and Minds*, 357. It is perhaps surprising that the military regime allowed the plebiscite to go forward. However, civil unrest and international pressure from foreign governments, human rights organizations, and investors, combined with a desire to establish democratic legitimacy compelled Pinochet to proceed. See Stern, *Battling for Hearts and Minds*, 353–354.

7. Stern, *Battling for Hearts and Minds*, 363; Paula T Cronovich, "'No' and *No*: The Campaign of 1988 and Pablo Larraín's Film," *Radical History Review* 124 (2016): 167–168, https://doi.org/10.1215/01636545-3160042.

8. See Juan Enrique Forch, "Talentos de la marginalidad a la legalidad" in *La campaña del NO vista por sus creadores* (Melquíades, 1989), 105; and Navarro, *Cultura: ¿Quién paga?*, 67.

9. Stern, *Reckoning with Pinochet*, 16–30.

10. See *Franja del No, capítulos 1–27* (TVN, 1988), 27 DVDs.

11. For the entire performance, see Radio Tierra, "Acto Estadio Nacional," March 12, 1990, YouTube video, 1:25:57, posted April 28, 2016, https://www.youtube.com/watch?v=ysklziDI0II.

12. Aylwin, "En el Estadio Nacional," in *La transición chilena: Discursos escogidos, marzo 1990–1992* (Andrés Bello, 1992), 17.

13. Bañados was a pioneer of Chilean television newscasting, but during the military regime he was largely marginalized as a broadcaster. See Patricio Bañados, *Confidencias de un locutor* (Editorial Cuarto Propio, 2015).

14. Osiel Vega Durán, *Himno nacional de la República de Chile* (División de Cultura del Ministerio de Educación, Sociedad Chilena del Derecho de Autor, 2000), 33.

15. Aylwin, "En el Estadio Nacional," 17.

16. Aylwin, "En el inicio," 33.

17. Patricio Aylwin, *El reencuentro de los demócratas: Del golpe al triunfo del No* (Ediciones Grupo Zeta, 1998), 10.

18. Navarro, *Cultura: ¿Quién aga?*, 67.

19. See Aylwin, "En el inicio," 55.

20. Navarro, interview with the author, Santiago, Chile, March 9, 2018.

21. Manuel Antonio Garretón, "Las políticas culturales en los gobiernos democráticos en Chile," in *Políticas culturais na Ibero-América*, ed. Antonio Albino Canelas and Rubens Bayardo (Editorial EDUFBA, 2009), 80.

22. For FONDEC's transformation into FONDART see Caterina Preda, *Art and Politics under Modern Dictatorships: A Comparison of Chile and Romania* (Palgrave, 2017).

23. Pía Gutiérrez Díaz, "Trama y archivo: condiciones de producción en la escena teatral chilena del periodo 2000–2010" (PhD diss., Pontificia Universidad Católica de Chile, 2014), 50.

24. For early biographical information relating to Pérez, see María de la Luz Hurtado, *Andrés Lorenzo Pérez Araya tiene la palabra* (Ocho Libros, 2015), 22–31.

25. Members of Teatro Itinerante included Ramón Griffero, playwright and director of the abovementioned Teatro Fin de Siglo; Alfredo Castro, actor and director and founder of *Teatro de la memoria*; and Aldo Parodi, an actor who later became a member of Gran Circo Teatro.

26. For Teatro Itinerante see María de la Luz Hurtado, *Memorias teatrales: el teatro de la Universidad Católica en su cincuentenario: 1978–1993* (Ediciones *Apuntes*, 1993); and Alfredo Castro, interview with the author, Santiago, Chile, August 20, 2018.

27. In 1980 he founded the Teatro Urbano Contemporáneo (the Urban Contemporary Theater) and in 1983 the Compañía Teatro Callejero (Street Theater Company).

28. Andrés Pérez Araya, "Lo popular me es propio por pertenencia," *Apuntes de teatro* 111 (1996): 3.

29. Hurtado, *Andrés Lorenzo Pérez*, 58–83.

30. Hurtado, *Andrés Lorenzo Pérez*, 84.

31. Harcha, *Prácticas de teatralidad*, 73; Hurtado, *Andrés Lorenzo Pérez*, 82–83.

32. Griffero, interview with the author.

33. Harcha, *Prácticas de teatralidad*, 75.

34. See Juan Villegas, "El teatro chileno de la postdictadura," 69/70 (2009): 189–206, https://www.jstor.org/stable/23288703.

35. Guillermo Semler, interview with the author, Santiago, Chile, March 2, 2018.

36. Semler, interview with the author.

37. Parra was a member of an artistically illustrious family. Born to middle-class parents, the ten Parra siblings had a profound impact on Chilean culture, particularly by popularizing Chile's folkloric musical and poetic forms. Violeta (1917–1967) was an artist, musician, and poet and one of the pioneers of the Nueva Canción movement; Nicanor (1914–2018) was a professor of mathematics and one of Chile's most important poets. Hilda (1916–1975) was also a musician; Lalo (1918–2009), Roberto (1921–1995), and José Lautaro

(1928–2013) were also folklorists and composers; and Oscar René (1930–2016) was a clown and folklorist (performing with Roberto in circuses). See Gonzalo Badal, *Roberto Parra* (Ocho Libros Editores, 1996); and Fidel Sepúlveda Llanos, "Nicanor, Violeta, Roberto Parra: Encuentro de tradición y vanguardia," *Aisthesis* 24 (1991): 29–42.

38. Hurtado, *Andrés Lorenzo Pérez*, 85. See also Carmen Romero, "Costos y sueños de la Negra Ester," *Apuntes de teatro* 98 (1989): 9.

39. Romero, "Costos y sueños," 9–10.

40. Andrés García, "La dura senda de un alquimista," *Apuntes de teatro* 122 (2002): 54.

41. As I have written elsewhere, the *travesti* figure in Chile does not neatly map onto Anglophone identity categories, as it connotes certain situated Chilean experiences and subjectivities. Terms like *trans* or *transgénero* might be used in Chile today to reference those who have access to hormonal or surgical therapies and can thus connote a kind of privilege and ability to "pass." *Travesti*, which here might translate more readily, though inadequately, to "transvestite," often refers to those who inhabit a more liminal and vulnerable space, as the character Esperanza does. Additionally, Baird Campbell notes that travesti carries connotations of calle (street)—in the sense of both working the street through prostitution and having "street smarts." It has also been marshalled—by artists such as Pedro Lemebel—as a dissident aesthetic and mode of critique. The figure of Esperanza evokes these contours of the travesti figure within the play but is also used for comic and melodramatic effect (as I will discuss later) which does contribute to a flattening and stereotyping of the character. See: Thompson, "An Explosion of Feminism," 49-50; Baird Campbell, "The Archive of the Self: Trans Self-Making and Social Media in Santiago de Chile" (PhD diss., Rice University, 2021), 191–12; Nelly Richard, *Abismos temporales: Feminismo, estéticas travestis y teoría queer* (Metales Pesados, 2018).

42. See Pedro Vicuña, "La Negra Ester," *Numero Quebrado* 2, no. 2 (1989): 40–44. Marco Antonio de la Parra, "'La negra Ester' o la redención del teatro chileno," *La Época*, January 17, 1989; María de la Luz Hurtado, "Nota Editorial," *Apuntes de teatro* 122 (2002): 3.

43. Juan Andrés Piña, "La negra Ester," *Mensaje* 377 (March–April 1989): 109–110; Juan Andrés Piña, "Espectáculos de la otra chilenidad," *Teatro al sur* 3, no. 4 (May 1996): 41–45; María de la Luz Hurtado "Escenificaciones de la tragedia popular y clásica," *Teatro Celcit* 6, no. 7 (1996): 32–35; Sergio Pereira Poza, "La Negra Ester," *La escena latinoamericana* 3 (December 1989): 19–28.

44. Marco Antonio de la Parra, "A propósito de la Negra Ester," prologue to *La Negra Ester* (Gran Circo Teatro, 1989), 7.

45. Boyle, "Violence in Memory, 93–112.

46. Juan Villegas, "Andrés Pérez: Poética teatral en tiempos de globalización y transnacionalización," *Apuntes de teatro* 119 & 120 (2001): 141–148.

47. Cristián Opazo, "Pánico a la discoteca: Teatro, transición y underground (Chile, época 1990)," *Cuadernos de literatura* 21, no. 42 (July–December 2017): 49–66, https://doi.org/10.11144/Javeriana.cl21-42.pdtt.

48. Harcha, *Prácticas de teatralidad*, 187.

49. Rosa Ramírez, interview with the author, Santiago, Chile, July 3, 2017.
50. Hurtado, *Andrés Lorenzo Pérez*, 10.
51. "Hurtado, *Andrés Lorenzo Pérez*, 86.
52. Andrés Pérez, "Andrés Pérez: Un hombre de teatro," interview by Eduardo Guerrero, *Teatrae* 5 (Summer/Fall 2022), 8.
53. García, "La dura senda," 55.
54. Fort Hidalgo, situated atop the hill, had been essential to the colonial city's defense, first from Indigenous attacks during the conquest, and later from the Spanish during the independence movement.
55. Semler, interview with the author.
56. Juan Pablo González likens the doubling of musicians in *La Negra Ester's* band to the small bands that traditionally performed with circuses, among which Roberto Parra had learned to play cuecas, foxtrots, and tangos. See Juan Pablo González R, "La música mestiza de la Negra Ester," *Apuntes de teatro* 122 (2002): 151–156.
57. Nicanor Parra invented the term "jazz *guachaca*" to describe his brother's musical style, which was an urban, *porteño* jazz inspired by Django Reinhardt. It is unclear when the term *guachaca* first emerged in Chile, though it likely derives from the Quechua term *huajcha kay*, which means "to be poor." See Mariano Muñoz-Hidalgo, "De las canciones del vino a la cultura huachaca: marginalidad e identidad," *Revista universum* 20, no. 2 (2005): 235–251, http://dx.doi.org/10.4067/S0718-23762005000200012; Pablo Huneeus, *La cultura huachaca o el aporte de la televisión* (Editora Nueva Generación, 1981).
58. Piña, "La Negra Ester," 109.
59. Vicuña, "La Negra Ester," 41.
60. Hurtado, *Andrés Lorenzo Pérez*, 91.
61. Pérez, "Lo popular me es propio por pertenencia," 3.
62. Hurtado, *Andrés Lorenzo Pérez*, 84–85.
63. Among its destinations were San Antonio, La Serena, Temuco, Viña del Mar, Copiapó, Arica, Punta Arenas, and Ovalle. Violeta Espinoza, "1988 La Negra Ester 1998," in *Memoria para un nuevo siglo: Chile, miradas a la segunda mitad del siglo XX*, ed. Mario Garcés et al. (LOM Ediciones, 2000), 369–370.
64. Quoted in "Protagonista de 'La indiada' y director de 'La negra Ester,' *El Mercurio*, September 7, 1988.
65. Harcha, *Prácticas de teatralidad*, 124.
66. The first international circus arrived in Chile in 1827, and in 1885 the Pacheco brothers created the first official Chilean circus in Valparaíso. Chilean circus blended traditions from its European antecedents with Indigenous, *criollo*, and *mestizo* culture to create a thriving popular form that traveled throughout Chile. See Pilar Ducci González, *Años de circo: historia de la actividad circense en Chile* (Latorre Literaria, 2011).
67. Hurtado categorizes the work as a "social melodrama." María de la Luz Hurtado, *Dramaturgia chilena 1890–1990: Autorías, textualidades, historicidad* (Frontera Sur, 2011), 300–305.
68. Jesús Martín-Barbero, *De los medios a las mediaciones: Comunicación, cultura y hegemonía*, 2nd ed. (Editorial Gustavo Gili, 1991), 131–132.

69. Soledad Figueroa and Javiera Larraín, *Espérame en el cielo, corazón: Melodrama en la escena chilena de los siglos XX–XXI* (Cuarto Propio, 2017), 230–231.

70. *Décimas* arrived in Chile during the conquest. *Décimas* consist of octosyllabic lines arranged in ten-line verses with the rhyme scheme *abbaaccddc*. They became one of the most popular and pervasive poetic forms in Chile. For an analysis of the history of the text see Poza, "La Negra Ester," 20–21; Maximiano Trapero, *El libro de la décima: la poesía improvisada en el mundo hispánico* (Universidad de Las Palmas de Gran Canarias, 1996).

71. His primary modifications consisted of shifting the tense from past to present and adapting the text into dialogue.

72. Roberto Parra and Andrés Pérez, "La Negra Ester," *Apuntes de teatro* 98 (Autumn–Winter 1989): 34.

73. It has been ascribed a variety of influences, including Amerindian, African, Creole Spanish, and Andalucian-Arab dances. The music alternates between a 6/8 and 3/4 meter, and it is often sung by one or two voices accompanied by a guitar, *charango* (Andean guitar), flute, and *bombo* (double-headed drum). For a history of the cueca see Gerard H. Béhague, "Music, c. 1920–c. 1980," in *A Cultural History of Latin America: Literature, Music and the Visual Arts in the 19th and 20th Centuries,* ed. Leslie Bethell (Cambridge University Press, 1998), 311–368; Samuel Claro Valdés and Carmen Peña Fuenzalida, *Chilena o cueca tradicional* (Ediciones Universidad Católica de Chile, 1994); and Rodrigo Torres, "El arte de cuequear," in *Revisitando Chile: Identidades, mitos e historia*, ed. Sonia Montecino (Presidencia de la República, Comisión Bicentenario, 2003), 149–158.

74. "Declara a la Cueca Danza Nacional de Chile," Decree no. 23, September 18, 1979.

75. Harcha, *Prácticas de teatralidad*, 143–144.

76. For the cueca's complicated status as an expression of official culture under the dictatorship as well as its function as a site of resistance see Araucaria Rojas Sotoconil, "Las cuecas como representaciones estético-políticas de chilenidad en Santiago entre 1979 y 1989," *Revista musical chilena* 212 (July–December 2009): 51–76.

77. See "La Cueca Sola," Museo de la Memoria y los Derechos Humanos, September 10, 2016, https://ww3.museodelamemoria.cl/Informate/la-cueca-sola.

78. Guillermo (Cuti) Aste, interview with the author, March 29, 2018.

79. Aste, interview with the author.

80. González, "La regia música," 156.

81. Ezequiel Adamovsky, "Ethnic Nicknaming: 'Negro' as a Term of Endearment and Vicarious Blackness in Argentina," *Latin American and Caribbean Ethnic Studies* 12, no. 3 (2017): 273–289, https://doi.org/10.1080/17442222.2017.1368895.

82. Baird Campbell, "The Archive of the Self: Trans Self-Making and Social Media in Santiago de Chile" (PhD diss., Rice University, 2021), 20.

83. Campbell, "Archive of the Self," 18.

84. Óscar Contardo, *Raro: Una historia gay de Chile* (Editorial Planeta, 2011).

85. Lemebel and Casas formed the Yeguas del Apocalipsis in 1987. They created a series of artistic-political performance interventions throughout the 90s. Their work challenged and de-sacralized official histories, institutional art, and the democratic transition, and to make queer identities and histories visible. "Yeguas del Apocalipsis," accessed May 25, 2018, http://www.yeguasdelapocalipsis.cl/inicio/.

86. See Víctor Hugo Robles, *Bandera hueca: historia del movimiento homosexual de Chile* (Editorial Cuarto Propio, 2008), 28–29; Carolina Robino, "Las últimas locas del fin del mundo," *Hoy* (1991): 42–45; "De que se ríe el presidente," Yeguas del Apocalipsis, accessed May 25, 2018, http://www.yeguasdelapocalipsis.cl/1989-de-que-se-rie-presidente/; "Mundo de la cultura proclamó candidatura del Patricio Aylwin," Fortín Mapocho, August 23, 1989; *Chile en llamas: Censura y género*, directed by Carmen Luz Parrot (ChileVisión, 2015), streaming video, http://www.chilevision.cl/chile-en-llamas.

87. Bernardo Subercaseaux, "Cultura y democracia," in *La cultura durante el período de la transición a la democracia 1990–2005*, ed. Eduardo Carrasco and Bárbara Negró (Consejo Nacional de la Cultura y las Artes, 2006), 20.

88. García, "La dura senda," 55.

89. Hurtado, *Andrés Lorenzo Pérez*, 92.

90. Vicuña, "La Negra Ester," 44.

91. Semler, "La Negra Ester por el mundo," 19.

92. Andrés Peréz quoted in *El Mercurio*, September 7, 1988.

93. Andrés Pérez, "Andrés Pérez—De la calle a la conquista del mundo," interview with Andrés Pérez *Nueva Voz*, January 19, 1990.

94. Stern, *Reckoning with Pinochet*, 204.

95. Hurtado, *Andrés Lorenzo Pérez*, 91.

96. Aylwin, "En el Estadio Nacional," 22.

97. Aste, interview with the author.

98. Cristian Soto, "¿La fiesta del amigo?," *Apuntes de teatro* 122 (2002):16.

99. Aste, interview with the author.

100. Ramírez, interview with the author.

101. Hurtado, *Andrés Lorenzo Pérez*, 82.

102. Parra and Pérez, "La Negra Ester," 51–52.

103. Parra and Pérez, "La Negra Ester," 52.

104. Eduardo Guerrero del Río, "La Negra Ester," La Época, March 8, 1996; Pedro Labra, "La Negra Ester" *Reseña 3* (April–May 1989); Anita Klesky, "La Negra Ester," *El Diario*, January 19, 1989.

105. Guerrero, "La Negra Ester."

106. See, for example, headlines such as "Protagonist of *La indiada* and Director of 'La Negra Ester' ": "Protagonista de 'La indiada' y director de 'La negra Ester,' " *El Mercurio*, September 7, 1988.

107. Klesky, "La Negra Ester."

108. Pérez, "Andrés Pérez—De la calle a la conquista del mundo."

109. " 'La negra Ester' conquista Europa," *Las Últimas Noticias*, July 3, 1989.

110. "Con los dioses del teatro y la democracia 'La Negra Ester' seguirá viviendo su fiesta," *Fortín Mapocho*, March 22, 1990.

111. Stern, *Reckoning with Pinochet*, 198.

112. Hurtado, *Andrés Lorenzo Pérez*, 136–137.

113. Pérez asserts that the show was meant to depict political people, not be itself political. Andrés Pérez, "Me fascina que haya polémica," interview by Marietta Santi, *Pluma y pincel* 132 (October 1990): 17–18.

114. Stern, *Reckoning with Pinochet*, 42.

115. Tomás Moulian, *Chile actual: Anatomía de un mito*, 3rd ed. (LOM Ediciones, 2002); María José Contreras, "A Woman Artist in the Neoliberal Chilean Jungle," in *Performance, Feminism and Affect in Neoliberal Times*, ed. Elin Diamond, Denise Varney, and Candice Amich (Palgrave Macmillan, 2017), 239–251.

116. Leonel Cornejo, interview with the author, Santiago, June 28, 2017.

117. Aste, interview with the author.

118. See, for example, Juan Antonio Muñoz, "Angustiante Estreno de 'El Gran Circo de Chile,'" *El Mercurio*, October 3, 1990; Roberto Brodsky, "Duro, filudo, raro," *Hoy* 691 (October 15, 1990): 32–33.

119. Rosario Guzmán Errázuriz, "El Circo de Chile, 'Época 70 Allende,' revivir la Unidad Popular: un . . . ¿acierto artístico?," *La Segunda*, October 9, 1990.

120. Stern, *Reckoning with Pinochet*, 54–57.

121. Aste, interview with the author.

122. Aste also recalls, though he could not be specific about the dates or circumstances, that at some point during the transition Pérez was taken by a group of men in sunglasses into a van, beaten, and thrown out on the side of the road. Aste asserts that the message was clear: Pérez should stay in line. Pérez did not want to frighten the rest of the company, so he kept this event largely to himself. Whether or not this event is true, it does speak to the vulnerability the artists felt.

123. José Esteban Muñoz, *Disidentifications: Queers of Color and the Performance of Politics* (University of Minnesota Press, 1999), 5.

124. Muñoz, *Disidentifications*, 6.

125. Daniel Palma, interview with author, Santiago, June 19, 2017.

126. Quoted in Harcha, *Prácticas de teatralidad*, 271. *Cuico* is a derogatory term for a rich or upper-class Chilean.

127. Daniel Palma, interview, *Chile en llamas: Censura y género*, directed by Carmen Luz Parrot (ChileVisión, 2015), streaming video, http://www.chilevision.cl/chile-en-llamas.

128. Palma, interview with the author.

129. Quoted in Harcha, *Prácticas de teatralidad*, 271.

130. Kemi Adeyemi, Kareem Khubchandani, and Ramón H. Rivera-Servera, introduction to *Queer Nightlife*, ed. Kemi Adeyemi, Kareem Khubchandani, and Ramón H. Rivera-Servera (University of Michigan Press, 2021), 1. While acknowledging the presence of these utopian desires, they caution against the perpetuation of "false narrative that queer nightlife or queer subject positions are inherently or necessarily utopian formations" (2).

131. Palma, interview with the author.

132. Palma, interview with the author.

133. Palma, interview with the author.

134. Palma, *Chile en llamas*.

135. Palma, interview with the author. Anthropologist Baird Cambell writes, "*Loca* is a difficult term to translate to English. Scholars often substitute queen, but *loca* is to some extent a Latin American social category without an obvious equivalent in Anglo culture. Additionally, *loca* is the feminine form of the adjective meaning 'crazy,' inscribing both femininity and mental instability on the bodies it is used to describe. Roughly, *locas* are gay identified men who walk the line between transvestism and overt female identification. They are, as in the United States, marginalized by much of the gay community for their almost total rejection of hegemonic masculine identity . . . currently, there is a tendency to use the word as a catch-all term for all markedly feminine gay men." Baird Campbell, "*MOVILH*-ization: Hegemonic Masculinity in the Queer Social Movement Industry in Santiago de Chile" (MA thesis, Tulane University, 2014), 14.

136. Palma, interview with the author.

137. Adeyemi, Khubchandani, and Rivera-Servera, introduction, 15.

138. Palma, interview with the author.

139. Concha y Toro was once one of Santiago's richest neighborhoods, but at the time of Spandex it was a more marginal, dangerous space—less central and commercial than the location of the Teatro Esmeralda.

140. Palma, interview with the author.

141. In part, the government's obstructionism toward sex education and AIDS-prevention campaigns was a result of its alliance with the Catholic Church, which had played a key role in resisting the dictatorship.

142. With the aforementioned caveats surrounding the translatability of LGBTQ identity groups, *colas* literally translates to "tail" or "butt" and is used to describe someone as a "bottom."

143. Opazo, "Pánico a la discoteca," 63.

144. Aste, interview with the author. Andrés Pérez, interview by William Haltenhoff, "Era inevitable el fin de la compañía," *La Nación*, March 11, 1994.

145. See, for example, Andrés Pérez, interview by *El Mercurio*, "Andrés Pérez '¡Pero si somos muy pobres!," *El Mercurio*, December 31, 1996; or Andrés Gomez B., "Andrés Pérez se enfrenta a la Estación Mapocho," *La Tercera*, June 21, 2000, which outlines Pérez's objection to the profit-driven decision-making that guides Estación Mapocho's programming.

146. Cornejo, interview with the author.

147. Cornejo, interview with the author. Other companies included Ramón Griffero's *Teatro fin de siglo* and *La Troppa*.

148. Opazo, "Pánico en la discoteca."

149. García, interview with the author; Aste, interview with the author.

150. Andrés Pérez, interview, *Tacos de cemento*, directed by Marcela Porta (2017; Santiago, Chile: Fondo de Creación y Cultura Artística UC, 2018), streaming video, http://tacosdecemento.cl/.

151. Ramírez, interview with the author.

152. "Andrés Pérez respondió a Ravinet," *Las Últimas Noticias*, April 18, 2001. See also "Los espacios deben ser dirigidos por los propios artistas," *La Nación*, April 15, 2001; and "Pérez dispara contra García y Ravinet," *La Tercera*, April 17, 2001.

153. Andrés Pérez, "En la Moneda les falta escuchar," interview by Rafael Grumucio, *Las Últimas Noticias*, May 22, 2001.

154. Ramírez, interview with the author.

155. Cornejo, interview with the author. Palma, interview with the author.

156. The tubes that dispensed air and pure oxygen had been mistakenly crossed. Ana María Guerra, Bernadita Méndez, and Carlos J. Concha, "El misterio de la cama 8 está penando en el Hospital San José," *La Segunda*, August 22, 2002.

157. Memoria Chilena, "Día Nacional del Teatro," accessed June 10, 2018, http://www.memoriachilena.cl/602/w3-article-92176.html.

158. Achille Mbembe, *Necropolitics* (Duke University Press, 2019).

Chapter 3

1. This narrative of the play's provenance was told to me by Héctor Morales in an interview in Santiago, Chile, on June 7, 2018.

2. Jara, an alumnus of the theater school at the University of Chile, was murdered following the military coup, and his corpse was deployed as a spectacle to intimidate political opponents. The Víctor Jara Festival carried the memories of the dictatorship's crimes as well as a reverence for politically committed art. Though the play had nothing to do with Jara, for some, its debut at the festival inscribed his memory on the play. The play was written by Manuela Infante, directed by María José Parga and Manuela Infante, designed by Fernando Briones and Claudia Yolin, and performed by Eduardo Díaz, Tomás Espinoza, José Miguel Jiménez, Eduardo Luna, Héctor Morales, Juan Pablo Peragallo, and Rodrigo Sobarzo.

3. For excellent summaries of the controversy see Fernanda Carvajal and Camila Van Diest, *Nomadismos y ensamblajes: Compañías teatrales de Chile 1990–2008* (Cuarto Propio, 2009), 46–50, 343–348; Fernanda Carvajal, "*Prat* de Teatro de Chile: Una fábula nacional prófuga atravesando las junturas entre arte y política," *Atena* 502, no. 2 (2010): 73–95; Cristián Opazo, *Pedagogías letales: ensayo sobre dramaturgias chilenas del nuevo milenio* (CELICH, 2011), 1–18, 147–174.

4. Carvajal, "*Prat* de Teatro de Chile," 74–75.

5. Since Aylwin's election in 1990, the Concertación had dominated the executive branch. Aylwin was succeeded by Eduardo Frei Ruiz-Tagle (1994–2000, also of the Christian Democratic Party). Frei was followed by Ricardo Lagos (2000–2006, of the Party for Democracy).

6. Paul Connerton, *How Societies Remember* (Cambridge University Press, 1989), 1; Huyssen, *Present Pasts*, 16; Stern, *Reckoning with Pinochet*.

7. Connerton, *How Societies Remember*, 1.

8. Elizabeth Jelin, *Los trabajos de la memoria* (Siglo XXI, 2002); Brenda Werth, *Theatre, Performance, and Memory Politics in Argentina* (Palgrave Macmillan, 2010); Avelar, *Untimely Present*; Noe Montez, *Memory, Transitional Justice, and Theatre in Postdictatorship Argentina* (Southern Illinois University Press, 2018).

9. For seminal work that explores these tensions see Pierre Nora, "Between Memory and History: Les Lieux de Mémoire," *Representations* 26 (1989): 7–24, https://doi.org/10.2307/2928520, and elaborated across the three

volumes of *Realms of Memory: The Construction of the French Past*, ed. Lawrence C. Kritzman, trans., Arthur Goldhammer (Columbia University Press, 1996–1998).

10. The body of work that considers memory politics in the Chilean transition is vast. Influential works that have posited a dichotomy between memory and forgetting include Moulian, *Chile actual*; and Elizabeth Lira and Brian Loveman, *Las ardientes cenizas del olvido: Vía chilena de reconciliación política, 1932–1994* (LOM Ediciones, 2002). Works that both invoke and trouble the binary between memory and forgetting include Mario Garcés et al., *Memoria para un nuevo siglo: Chile, miradas a la segunda mitad del Siglo XX* (LOM Ediciones, 2000); Nelly Richard, ed., *Políticas y estéticas de la memoria* (Cuarto Propio 2000); and Nelly Richard, *Crítica de la memoria: 1990–2010* (Ediciones UDP, 2010). For further reading in Chilean memory studies see Juan Armado Epple, *El arte de recordar: Ensayos sobre la memoria cultural de Chile* (Mosquito Comunicaciones, 1994); Hernán Vidal, *Política cultural de la memoria histórica: Derechos humanos y discursos cuturales en Chile* (Mosquito Comunicaciones, 1997); María Angélica Illanes, *La batalla de la memoria: Ensayos históricos de nuestro siglo, Chile, 1990–2000* (Ariel, 2002).

11. Avelar, *Untimely Present*, 14.

12. Richard, *Cultural Residues*, 17.

13. Avelar, *Untimely Present*, 2.

14. Stern, *Reckoning with Pinochet*, xxix.

15. Richard, *Cultural Residues*, 16.

16. Manuel Antonio Garretón, *Incomplete Democracy: Political Democratization in Chile and Latin America*, trans. R. Kelly Washbourne with Gregory Horvath (University of North Carolina Press, 2004), 152–153.

17. Richard, *Insubordination of Signs*, 1.

18. Alexander Wilde, "Irruptions of Memory: Expressive Politics in Chile's Transition to Democracy," *Journal of Latin American Studies* 31, no. 2 (1999): 473–500, http://www.jstor.org/stable/157911.

19. Augusto Boal highlights the politically coercive aspects of Aristotelian structures in *The Theatre of the Oppressed*, trans. Charles A. and Maria-Odilia Leal McBride and Emily Fryer (Pluto Press, 2008), 1–42.

20. Mega Oficial, "El día en que Chile celebró la democracia–Ahora Noticias," YouTube video, 14:28, April 22, 2016, https://www.youtube.com/watch?v=zTUxibiz-Ug.

21. Aylwin, "Con ocasión de los funerales del ex Presidente de Chile, don Salvador Allende G., in Aylwin, *La transición chilena*, 85.

22. Aylwin, "Con ocasión de los funerales," 86.

23. For a description of Allende's funeral see Stern, *Reckoning with Pinochet*, 39–43. For an analysis of its ritualistic performativity see Alicia del Campo, *Teatralidades de la memoria: Rituales de reconciliación en el Chile de la transición* (Mosquito Comunicaciones, 2004), 98–160.

24. Stern, *Reckoning with Pinochet*, 84–85.

25. Aylwin, "Al dar a conocer a la ciudadanía el Informe de la Comisión de Verdad y Reconciliación," in Aylwin, *La transición chilena*, 132.

26. Richard, *Insubordination of Signs*, 18.

27. Wilde, "Irruptions of Memory," 475.

28. Michael J. Lazzara, *Chile in Transition: The Poetics and Politics of Memory* (University Press of Florida, 2006), 19.

29. For one of the clearest expressions of the association of consensus with forgetting, see Moulian, *Chile actual*, in particular, 37–81.

30. Stern, *Reckoning with Pinochet*, 210–264.

31. Lessie Jo Frazier, *Salt in the Sand: Memory, Violence, and the Nation-State in Chile, 1980 to the Present* (Duke University Press, 2007), 204.

32. For analyses of the impact of Pinochet's arrest see Stern, *Reckoning with Pinochet*, 213–232; Richard, *Crítica de la memoria*, 33–40; Garretón, *Incomplete Democracy*, 159–166.

33. The text of the letter is available at "Carta a los Chilenos: las emotivas palabras que Pinochet escribió desde Londres," *Clinic*, September 3, 2013, http://www.theclinic.cl/2013/09/03/carta-a-los-chilenos-las-emotivas-palabras-que-augusto-pinochet-escribio-desde-su-prision-en-londres/.

34. Vial (1930–2009) was one of the most influential conservative intellectuals in Chile. He is infamous for his contributions to the *Libro Blanco del cambio de gobierno*, which asserted the presence of Plan Z (a conspiracy in which leftists were purported to plot government overthrow). He briefly served as Pinochet's minister of education and was critical of the human rights violations throughout the dictatorship. He continued his denouncement of human rights violations in his service on the Rettig Commission as a representative of the Right. In 1995 he wrote a biography of Arturo Prat. See "Gonzalo Vial Correa," Memoria chilena, http://www.memoriachilena.cl/602/w3-article-100642.html, accessed January 5, 2019; Gonzalo Vial Correa, *Arturo Prat* (Editorial Andres Bello, 1995).

35. Stern, *Reckoning with Pinochet*, 241; For a concise account of Vial's view on the antecedents to the coup see Gonzalo Vial, "Causas y antecedentes del 11 de septiembre de 1973," in *Análisis crítico del régimen militar*, ed. Gonzalo Vial Correa (Universidad Finis Terrae, 1998), 15–21.

36. Stern, *Reckoning with Pinochet*, 241–42.

37. Mario Garcés Duran, Sergio Grez Toso, María Eugenia Horvitz et al. "Manifiesto de Historiadores," *Punto Final*, February 5–18, 1999.

38. For Vial's response to the manifesto see Gonzalo Vial, "Reflexiones sobre un manifiesto," *La Segunda*, February 12, 1999. For an analysis of the manifesto and the subsequent debate see Stern, *Reckoning with Pinochet*, 241–243; Sergio Grez Toso, "Historiografía y memoria en Chile: Algunas consideraciones a partir del *Manifiesto de Historiadores*," *HAOL* 16 (Spring 2008): 179–183, https://doi.org/10.36132/hao.v0i16.261.

39. Stern, *Reckoning with Pinochet*, 218.

40. Stern *Reckoning with Pinochet*, 242.

41. Quoted in Stern, *Reckoning with Pinochet*, 246.

42. Eduardo Frei Ruiz-Tagle, "Mensaje Presidencial," Legislatura 340ª Sesión del Congreso Pleno, May 21, 1999, Archivo Chile, accessed January 4, 2019, http://www.archivochile.com/Gobiernos/html/gob_constitucion_edo_frei_rt.html.

43. For a consideration of Chilean *funas*, as well as their Argentinian counterparts, *escraches*, see Temma Kaplan, *Taking Back the Streets: Women, Youth, and Direct Democracy* (University of California Press), 154–175; For

a discussion of *escraches* in Argentina, see Taylor, *The Archive and the Repertoire*, 161–189.

44. Among the targets of the first *funas* were the cardiologist Alejandro Forero Álvarez and Emilio Sanjuria Alvear, an executive in the legal department at a telephone company. Kaplan, *Taking Back the Streets*, 169.

45. Kaplan, *Taking Back the Streets*, 159.

46. Taylor, *The Archive and the Repertoire*, 168.

47. Marianne Hirsch, "The Generation of Postmemory," *Poetics Today* 29, no. 1 (2008): 106, https://doi.org/10.1215/03335372-2007-019.

48. Cristián Opazo notes that between 2000 and 2010 there were more than a dozen published accounts of Prat's life. Opazo, *Pedagogías letales*, 148.

49. For a historical analysis of the cultural significance and iconic status of Prat, see William F. Sater, *The Heroic Image in Chile: Arturo Prat, Secular Saint* (University of California Press, 1973).

50. Sarah Misemer, *Secular Saints: Performing Frida Kahlo, Carlos Gardel, Eva Perón and Selena* (Tamesis, 2008), 1.

51. Jean Graham-Jones, *Evita Inevitably: Performing Argentina's Female Icons before and after Eva Perón* (University of Michigan Press, 2014), 5.

52. Sater, *Heroic Image in Chile*, 16–34; "Arturo Prat Chacón," Memoria chilena, accessed January 4, 2019, http://www.memoriachilena.cl/602/w3-article-3308.html.

53. Carvajal, "*Prat* de Teatro de Chile," 79.

54. Sater, *Heroic Image in Chile*, 56.

55. Morales, interview with the author.

56. Jacques Rancière, "The Concept of Anachronism and the Historian's Truth," trans. Noel Fitzpatrick and Tim Stot, *In/Print* 3, no. 1 (2015): 22, https://doi.org/10.21427/d7vm6f.

57. Rancière, "Concept of Anachronism," 47.

58. Richard, *Insubordination of Signs*, 2.

59. Avelar, *Untimely Present*, 11.

60. Manuela Infante, "Hay curas que nos han felicitado," interview by Catalina May, *Clinic*, February 8, 2009.

61. Preda, *Art and Politics*, 108; Garretón, "Las políticas culturales," 110.

62. Marisol Saborido, Rodrigo Vega, and Humberto Zamorano, *Informe final de evaluación, Fondo Nacional de Desarrollo Cultural y Las Artes*" (Consejo Nacional de la Cultura y Las Artes, 2008), 4.

63. Garretón, "Las políticas culturales," 111.

64. Felipe Montero Morales, ed., *Legislación cultural chilena* (Consejo Nacional de Cultura y las Artes, 2014), 118.

65. Carvajal and Van Diest, *Nomadismos y ensamblajes*, 35.

66. Universidad Diego Portales, Facultad de Derecho, *Informe anual sobre derechos humanos en Chile 2003: Hechos de 2002* (La Facultad, 2003), 207–209; Human Rights Watch, *Los límites de tolerancia* (LOM Ediciones, 1998), 49.

67. Film censorship was exercised via the Consejo de Calificación Cinematográfica (Film Rating Council) formed in October 1974.

68. González was later the director of the Teatro Nacional (National Theater). "Fernando González: Un maestro del teatro gana el Premio Nacional," *El Mercurio*, August 27, 2005.

69. *Chile en llamas*, episode 3, "Censura y patria," directed by Carmen Luz Parrot (ChileVisión, 2015), streaming video, http://www.chilevision.cl/chile-en-llamas.

70. "Libro 'Gay' con platas fiscales," *La Segunda*, August 22, 1994. Sutherland was the director of one of Chile's most important LGBT advocacy groups, Movilh (Movimiento de Integración y Liberación Homosexual, Movement for Homosexual Integration and Liberation).

71. "Casa de Vidrio: Sociedad chilena al desnudo," *El Aguijon*, March 30, 2000.

72. "Casa de Vidrio: Tramitan querella por ultrajes," *El Mercurio*, February 1, 2000.

73. *Chile en llamas*, episode 1 "Censura al desnudo," directed by Carmen Luz Parrot (ChileVisión, 2015), streaming video, http://www.chilevision.cl/chile-en-llamas.

74. Palma, quoted in Robles, *Bandera hueca*, 71.

75. *Chile en llamas*, "Censura y patria."

76. Luis H. Bastías Sandoval, letter to the editor, *La Segunda*, August 29, 2002.

77. In a statement published on August 3, 2002, in *Las Últimas Noticias*, he maintained, "This has a political undertone. The Gramscian doctrine is to destroy all the values to take power."

78. Compañía Teatro de Chile, introduction to *Prat seguida de Juana*, by Manuela Infante (Cierto Pez, 2005), 10–11.

79. Morales, interview with the author.

80. The note read, "The original spelling of the approved text has been respected." *La Segunda*, September 17, 2002.

81. Morales, interview with the author.

82. Manuela Infante, *Prat seguida de Juana* (Cierto Pez, 2005).

83. Infante, *Prat*, 16. For ease of citation I am citing the text published by Infante and the company; in each instance I have cross-referenced them to be sure they were reproduced in the version published in *La Segunda*.

84. Mouffe, *Agonistics*, 18.

86. Infante, *Prat*, 22.

84. Infante, *Prat*, 27.

87. Infante, *Prat*, 28.

88. Infante, *Prat*, 28–29.

89. Infante, *Prat*, 41. *Explotar* here has a double meaning—"explode" and "exploit"—suggesting that Chile exploits boys and then kills them.

90. Morales's delivery emphasizes the irony of the universalizing lines. At this point he plays Prat drunk and emotionally spent.

91. Infante, *Prat*, 44–45.

92. Infante, *Prat*, 45–49.

93. Gonzalo Vial Correa, "Prat en el teatro," *La Segunda*, September 17, 2002.

94. Vial, "Prat en el teatro." Orlando Letelier was an economist, politician, and diplomat during Allende's presidency. He was assassinated in Washington, DC, by a car bomb in 1976 (orchestrated by DINA). Tucapel Jiménez was a Socialist labor leader, also assassinated by the military government in 1982.

95. *La Segunda*, September 20, 2002.

96. "Fondart y teatristas insisten en polémica obra Prat," *La Segunda*, September 26, 2002.

97. Letter printed in *La Segunda*, September 30, 2002.

98. "Indignación PS por caso Fondart: Piden reunión con Lagos," *La Segunda*, October 1, 2002.

99. "Los *otros* incidentes: Toma pro Prat," *La Segunda*, October 3, 2002.

100. Senate protocol dictated that following official business each party was given time to bring up matters of further concern. By the time Arancibia's turn came, many of the moderate senators had spoken and left so as not to get embroiled in the controversy—thus the transcript of the debate is far more one-sided than the general sentiment of the Senate might have been.

101. *Diario de Sesiones del Senado*, Legislatura 348ª, Extraordinaria, Sesión 2ª (October 2, 2002).

102. "Presidente Lagos deplora informe FACh," *El Mercurio*, September 30, 2002. The air force had attempted to destroy evidence that the disappearances were political murders by exhuming mass graves. In a report mandated by the Dialogue Table, the air force tried to cover up the cover-up, for which the air force commander in chief, Patricio Ríos, was forced to retire. Stern, *Reckoning with Pinochet*, 276.

103. *Diario de Sesiones del Senado*.

104. *Diario de Sesiones del Senado*.

105. "Querellante contra la polémica obra de Prat lucha por detener el estreno de 17 de octubre," *El Mostrador*, September 23, 2002.

106. See Universidad Diego Portales, Facultad de Derecho, *Informe*, 215.

107. "Nuevo recurso por obra Prat," *El Mostrador*, October 9, 2002. Nuevo recurso por obra Prat

108. "Diputados proponen suspensión temporal de Fondart y de obra 'Prat,' " *La Segunda* October 11, 2002. Diputados proponen suspensión temporal de Fondart y de obra

109. Claudio Undurraga Abbot y Otros Contra Manuela Infante y Otros, Recurso de protección 5681–2002 (Corte de Apelaciones de Santiago, October 24, 2002).

110. Jorge Contesse Singh, "Comentario: Comentario sobre jurisprudencia: Caso Prat," *Jurisprudencia comentada* 278 (August 2002): 50–56.

111. *Chile en llamas*, "Censura y patria"; Morales, interview with the author.

112. *Chile en llamas*, "Censura y patria."

113. Manuela Infante, anonymous interview, "Después de 'Prat' llega 'Juana,'" 41.

114. *Chile en llamas*, "Censura y patria."

115. *Chile en llamas*, "Censura y patria."

116. María José Parga, notebook for *Prat*, July–November 2001, Teatro de Chile online archive, http://archivo.teatrodechile.cl/obras/prat/cuaderno-apuntes-prat-3/.

117. Alexandra Ripp, "RePresenting the Past: Chilean Theater and Memory Politics, 1998–2010" (PhD diss., Yale University, 2017), 134.

118. Morales, interview with the author.

119. Morales, interview with the author.

120. Carvajal and Van Diest, *Nomadismos y ensamblajes*, 42–44.

121. Morales, interview with the author.

122. Manuela Infante, interview by Carvajal and Van Diest, quoted in *Nomadismos y ensamblajes*, 346.

123. Carvajal and Van Diest, *Nomadismos y ensamblajes*, 47.

124. Carlos Labbé and Mónica Ríos, "Entre el texto, la puesta en escena y la performance del registro en la escritura de Manuela Infante y el Teatro de Chile," *INTI* 69/70 (2009): 213–214.

125. Carvajal and Van Diest in *Nomadismos y ensamblajes*. Quoted, 347.

126. Carvajal and Van Diest, *Nomadismos y ensamblajes*, 344.

127. "Historia," Teatro de Chile, http://www.teatrodechile.cl/en/historia/resena/, accessed January 8, 2019. The company received FONDART grants in 2003 (*Juana*), 2005 (*Narciso*), 2007 (*Cristo*), 2009 (*Multicancha*), and 2011 (*Multicancha*).

Chapter 4

1. Guillermo Calderón, *Escuela*, unpublished manuscript, August 24, 2013, New York, 62.

2. Fundación Santiago a Mil, "*Escuela* de Guillermo Calderón: 'La obra es importante, siempre va a ser contingente,'" press release, April 2, 2017, http://fundacionteatroamil.cl/noticia/escuela-guillermo-calderon-la-obra-importante-siempre-va-contingente/.

3. Carvajal and Diest, *Nomadismos y ensamblajes*, 126 (emphasis in the original).

4. Carvajal and Van Diest, *Nomadismos y ensamblajes*, 272.

5. Guillermo Calderón, "When a 'Kiss' Is Not Just a Kiss," interview by Elyse Dodgson, *American Theatre*, September 25, 2017, accessed February 13, 2019, https://www.americantheatre.org/2017/09/25/when-a-kiss-is-not-just-a-kiss/.

6. Calderón, *Neva*, trans. Andrea Thome (Theatre Communications Group, 2016), 58.

7. The term "Chilean paradox" is used in a United Nations Development Programme report from 1998 to explain the tension between Chile's achievement of traditional markers of success (as defined by the UNDP)—democracy, political stability, economic prosperity—and dissatisfaction with democracy, declining political participation, and vast income inequality. United Nations Development Programme, *The Paradox of Modernization: Human Development Report in Chile* (United Nations Development Programme, 1998); United Nations Development Programme, *Democracy in Latin America: Towards a Citizens' Democracy* (United Nations Development Programme, 2004).

8. In recent years a robust body of literature has emerged around the concepts of postpolitics and post-democracy. Its theoretical foundations are usually traced to the work of Rancière, Mouffe, Jean-Luc Nancy, and Slavoj Žižek. See, for example, Colin Crouch, *Post-democracy* (Polity, 2004); Bülent Diken, "Radical Critique as the Paradox of Post-political Society," *Third Text* 23, no. 5 (2009): 579–586, https://doi.org/10.1080/09528820903184815; Philippe Lacoue-Labarte and Jean-Luc Nancy, *Retreating the Political*, ed.

Simon Sparks (Routledge, 1997); Mouffe, *On the Political*; Jacques Rancière, *Chronicles of Consensual Times*, trans. Steven Corcoran (Continuum, 2010); and Slavoj Žižek, *The Ticklish Subject: The Absent Center of Political Ontology* (Verso,1999).

9. Japhy Wilson and Erik Swyngedouw, "Seeds of Dystopia: Post-politics and the Return of the Political," in *The Post-political and Its Disconontents: Spaces of Depoliticisation, Spectres of Radical Politics*, ed. Japhy Wilson and Erik Swyngedouw (Edinburgh University Press, 2014), 6.

10. Francis Fukuyama, *The End of History and the Last Man* (Free Press, 1992).

11. Fredric Jameson, "Future City," *New Left Review* 21 (2004): 76.

12. Florian Malzacher, "No Organum to Follow: Possibilities of Political Theatre Today," in *Not Just a Mirror: Looking for the Political Theatre Today*, ed. Florian Malzacher (House on Fire / Alexander Verlang, 2015), 16–30.

13. Guillermo Calderón, "Guillermo Calderón en conversación: Chile como nación puede acabarse," interview by Catalina Forttes, *Mester* 39, no. 1 (2010): 59.

14. Calderón, interview with the author, Santiago, Chile, June 27, 2018. *La manzana de Adán* (1990) was the first installment of Alfredo Castro's testimonial trilogy with Teatro La Memoria. The play drew from interviews and research conducted by Claudia Donoso and photographer Paz Errázuriz interrogating the relationship between travesti sex workers (see note 41, ch. 2).

15. Calderón, "Guillermo Calderón en conversación," 59.

16. Calderón, "Guillermo Calderón en conversación," 65–66.

17. Calderón, "Guillermo Calderón en conversación," 59.

18. Guillermo Calderón, interview with the author, Santiago, Chile, July 3, 2018.

19. Ripp, "RePresenting the Past, 189.

20. Calderón, "Tres actores en escena, una estufa, algunas sillas. Diálogo entre Guillermo Calderón y Soledad Lagos a propósito de *Neva*," interview by Soledad Lagos, *Telondefondo* 6 (2007): 1.

21. Calderón, "Tres actores en escena, una estufa, algunas sillas," 2; Carola Oyarzún, "Entre el teatro y la vida," in *Antología: un siglo de dramaturgia chilena, 1910–2010*, ed. María de la Luz Hurtado and Mauricio Barría (Publicaciones Comisión Bicentenario Chile, 2010), 4:304–305.

22. Calderón, *Neva*, 23–24.

23. Calderón, "Tres actores en escena, una estufa, algunas sillas," 5.

24. Calderón, *Neva*, 66.

25. Calderón, "Guillermo Calderón en conversación," 61.

26. Quoted in Larry Rohter, "Rehearsals for the Revolution," *New York Times*, March 6, 2013.

27. See, for example, Marietta Santi, "*Neva*: Una joyita en la cartelera capitalina," *La Hora*, November 13, 2006; Pedro Labra Herrera, "Actitud ambivalente," *El Mercurio*, January 1, 2007; Javier Ibacache, "Sin temor a las palabras," *Ciertopez* 4 (2007): 49–50.

28. The Art Critics' Circle Award is given by a society of art critics. The Altazor Award is one of Chile's highest artistic honors, given by a national jury of creators and performers.

29. Carmen Romero, , "Where Art Leads the Way: Carmen Romero's Journey with Santiago a Mil," interview by Olga Garay-English, *American Theatre* (May/June 2015), https://www.americantheatre.org/2015/04/23/where-art-leads-the-way-carmen-romeros-journey-with-santiago-a-mil/.

30. See *La Tercera*, January 7, 1997.

31. Jean Graham-Jones, "International Festivals in Latin America: Festival Santiago a Mil and Festival Internacional de Buenos Aires," in *The Cambridge Companion to International Theatre Festivals*, ed. Ric Knowles (Cambridge University Press, 2020), 231.

32. Calderón, interview with the author.

33. Calderón, interview with the author.

34. "The Royal Court Theatre Announces New Season of Work for Winter 2017/18," *Royal Court Theatre*, July 10, 2017, https://royalcourttheatre.com/royal-court-theatre-announces-new-season-work-autumnwinter-201718.

35. Quoted in Isabel Baboun Garib, "Guillermo Calderón: Tres motivos para una poética casi trágica," *Apuntes de teatro* no. 131 (2009): 23, https://doi.org/10.7764/apuntesdeteatro.131.56647.2009.

36. See Garib, "Guillermo Calderón," 20–28; and Alicia del Campo, "Nuevos realismos para viejos discursos: las guerras prometidas y el fin del Chile neoliberal en *Diciembre* de Guillermo Calderón," *FIT 2008: El teatro iberoamericano en el siglo XXI* (Gestos, 2009), 121–131.

37. Cristián Bellei, *El gran experimento: Mercado y privatización de la educación chilena* (Santiago, Chile: LOM ediciones, 2015); Paulo Hidalgo, *El ciclo político de la Concertación (1990–2010)* (Uqbar, 2011), 218–221; Manuel Larrabure and Carlos Torchia, "The 2011 Chilean Student Movement and the Struggle for a New Left," *Latin American Perspectives* 42, no. 5 (September 2015): 248–268, http://www.jstor.org/stable/24574880.

38. Calderón, interview with the author.

39. Jacques Rancière, *Disagreement*, trans. Julie Rose (University of Minnesota Press, 1999), x.

40. Rancière, *Disagreement*, 11.

41. Rancière, *Dissensus*, 36.

42. Rancière, *Dissensus*, 16–17.

43. Rancière, *Dissensus*, 37.

44. Michel Foucault, "Of Other Spaces: Utopias and Heterotopias," trans. Jay Miskowiec, *Architecture/Mouvement/Continuité* (October 1984): 48–49.

45. Garib, "Guillermo Calderón," 23.

46. Calderón, "Guillermo Calderón en conversación," 63.

47. Guillermo Calderón, *Clase*, in *Teatro I: Neva, Diciembre, Clase* (LOM Ediciones, 2012), 163. The *siete coma uno* that I have translated as "A+" is not a real grade in Chile. Thus, he is not only making fun of their struggle but also underlining how unreal it is.

48. Guillermo Calderón, *Diciembre*, in *Teatro I: Neva, Diciembre, Clase* (LOM Ediciones, 2012), 66.

49. Calderón, *Diciembre*, 60.

50. Opazo. *Pedagogías letales*, 117.

51. Calderón, *Clase*, 131.

52. Sofía Castaño, "Ilusión y teatralización en *Diciembre* de Guillermo Calderón y *Lote 77* de Marcelo Mininno," *Telondefondo* 11 (July 2010): 5.

53. Calderón, *Diciembre*, 109.

54. In a conversation with Jean Graham-Jones he explains this symbolism, using the phrase "nothing is more Chilean than beans." See Guillermo Calderón, interview by Jean Graham-Jones, Performance and Justice Symposium, John Jay College of Criminal Justice, May 16, 20013, YouTube video, 40:43, https://www.youtube.com/watch?v=W9UVIujeT54.

55. Calderón, "Guillermo Calderón en conversación," 64.

56. Calderón, "*Clase*, 166.

57. Ripp, "RePresenting the Past," 216.

58. *Discurso* was developed through an exchange facilitated by Santiago a Mil, the CNCA, and the British Arts Council, with the Royal Court Theatre in London.

59. Hidalgo, *El ciclo político de la Concertación*, 149.

60. Calderón, interview with the author.

61. Quoted in Joanne Pottlitzer, "Forgetting Filled with Memory," *Theater* 43, no. 2 (2013): 58, https://doi.org/10.1215/01610775-1966580.

62. "'Villa + Discurso' de Guillermo Calderón en la Sala UPLA," *El Martutino*, April 18, 2011. See "Historia," Villa Grimaldi: Corporación Parque por la Paz, accessed January 22, 2018, http://villagrimaldi.cl/; Diana Taylor, *Villa Grimaldi*, accessed February 15, 2019, http://villagrimaldi.typefold.com/. For a historical examination of and critical commentary on the development of Villa Grimaldi into the peace park, see Milena Grass Kleiner, "Memoria intermedial: Villa Grimaldi en el cine, la novela y el teatro chileno" (PhD diss., Pontificia Universidad Católica de Chile, 2015), 69–137.

63. To reduce confusion in the script, the roles are delineated by the names of the actors, which I will reference throughout my analysis.

64. Ethan Madarieta, "'Marichiweu': Performances of Memory and Mapuche Presence in Guillermo Calderón's Villa," *Latin American Theatre Review* 53, no. 2 (2020): 91, https://journals.ku.edu/latr/article/view/13764.

65. Guillermo Calderón, *Villa*, in *Teatro II: Villa, Discurso, Beben* (LOM Ediciones, 2012), 68.

66. Calderón, *Villa*, 72.

67. The site was constructed as a residence in 1925. In 1970 it was acquired as a seat of the Socialist Party. See "Historia," Londres 38, accessed March 18, 2019, http://www.londres38.cl/1937/w3-propertyname-3006.html.

68. Milena Grass notes that each site elicited a different response from the audience. Milena Grass Kleiner, "El teatro político de Guillermo Calderón: realidadficción y espacio público," in *Perspectivas políticas de la escena latinoamericana: Diálogos en tiempos presente*, ed. Lola Proaño-Gómez and Lorena Verzero (Argus-*a*, 2017), 124–125.

69. Calderón, *Villa*, 79.

70. Calderón, *Villa*, 83.

71. Calderón, *Villa*, 76.

72. See Antonio Traverso, "*La Flaca Alejandra*: Post-dictatorship Documentary and (No) Reconciliation in Chile," *Critical Arts* 31, no. 5 (2017): 91–106, https://doi.org/10.1080/02560046.2017.1345970.

73. Calderón, *Villa*, 95–96.

74. Madarieta maintains that the officer's Germanness suggests an officer perhaps of the Third Reich, "many of whom escaped to South America and took part in the dictatorial regime's ongoing crimes against humanity. . . . It is also suggestive of earlier forced integration through rape of Mapuche house servants of German colonists of this region of Chile in the latter half of the nineteenth and early twentieth centuries." Madarieta, "'Maricheweu,'" 95.

75. Grass, "Memoria intermedial," 293.

76. Madarieta, "'Marichiweu,'" 95.

77. Calderón, *Villa*, 97.

78. Calderón, *Villa*, 97.

79. Pottlitzer, "Forgetting Filled with Memory," 57.

80. At the Royal Court it was performed as a stand-alone piece by one woman.

81. Calderón, interview with the author.

82. Guillermo Calderón, *Discurso*, in *Teatro II: Villa, Discurso, Beben* (LOM Ediciones, 2012), 100.

83. Quoted in Pottlitzer, "Forgetting Filled with Memory," 57.

84. Calderón, *Discurso*, 100–101.

85. Calderón, *Discurso*, 108.

86. Calderón, *Discurso*, 102.

87. Calderón, *Discurso*, 109.

88. Calderón, *Discurso*, 111.

89. Calderón, *Discurso*, 117.

90. Calderón, *Discurso*, 114–115.

91. Calderón, *Discurso*, 115.

92. Calderón, *Discurso*, 118.

93. Calderón, *Discurso*, 118.

94. Calderón, *Discurso*, 119.

95. The glasses were placed on the table by the women in *Villa*, as they would repeatedly go to get water.

96. Paola Hernández, "Remapping Memory Discourses: *Villa + Discurso* by Guillermo Calderón," *South Central Review* 30, no. 3 (Fall 2013): 66, https://dx.doi.org/10.1353/scr.2013.0029.

97. Larrabure and Torchia, "2011 Chilean Student Movement," 248–268; Stern, *Reckoning with Pinochet*, 337.

98. William Moss Willson, "Just Don't Call Her Che," *New York Times*, January 28, 2012.

99. Quoted in Benjamin Witte-Lebhar, "After Long Lull, Chile's Student Movement Rumbles Back to Life," *Notisur* (2012): 3.

100. Gabriel Boric, "Mi Manifiesto: Gabriel Boric, presidente de la FECH," *La Tercera*, May 5, 2012, https://www.latercera.com/diario-impreso/mi-manifiesto-gabriel-boric-presidente-de-la-fech/.

101. Ernesto Muñoz-Lamartine, "Student Leaders Reinvent the Protest," *Berkeley Review of Latin American Studies* (Fall–Winter 2011): 29. This was in line with Chilean public opinion: at the peak of the protests, 77 percent of Chileans expressed a positive view of the student leaders, and 82 percent agreed with their demands. Meanwhile Piñera garnered a 26 percent approval rating and the Concertación, 17 percent.

102. Calderón, interview with the author.

103. Calderón, interview with the author.

104. Though he was not credited as part of the official cast, Calderón performed in a limited number of performances in Santiago, an act that would have doubly underscored the personal nature of this play.

105. Jorge Mateluna was a member of the Frente Patriótico Manuel Rodríguez (Manuel Rodriguez Patriotic Front, FPMR), a Marxist-Leninist paramilitary organization founded in 1983 with the goal to overthrow Augusto Pinochet. See "Frente Patriótico Manuel Rodríguez," *Frente Patriótico Manuel Rodríguez*, accessed February 15, 2019, http://www.fpmr.cl/.

106. Guillermo Calderón, "Guillermo Calderón: 'Cada vez queda más claro que la dictadura nunca fue derrotada," interview by Melissa Gutierrez, *Clinic*, April 18, 2013.

107. Calderón, "Guillermo Calderón."

108. Quoted in Javiera Larraín, "Hacia una poética directoral de Guillermo Calderón: Una cartografía de la palabra escénica," (master's thesis, University of Chile, 2017), 157–158.

109. Calderón, *Escuela*, 54.

110. Calderón, *Escuela*, 56.

111. Calderón, *Escuela*, 61.

112. Calderón, *Escuela*, 66.

113. Calderón, *Escuela*, 66.

114. Calderón, interview with the author.

115. Calderón, *Mateluna*, unpublished manuscript, February 7, 2019, PDF file, 20.

116. Calderón, *Mateuluna*, 13.

117. Cristián Opazo and Carlos Benítez, "'A Little Respect': Mateluna, de Guillermo Calderón," *Revista conjunto*, no. 185 (2017): 14.

118. See Marietta Santi, "Santiago a Mil: Un 'Mateluna' valiente pero confuso," *Santi Teatro y Danza*, January 27, 2018, http://www.santi.cl/index.php/criticas-de-teatro/1430-stgoa-mil. In *La Tercera* Pedro Bahamondes summarizes the range of opinions around Mateluna: "Some consider it revelatory and urgent, and others on the border of the *panfletario*." Pedro Bahamondes, "Mateluna: ¿provocación o transgresión?," *La Tercera*, April 25, 2017.

119. Guillermo Calderón, email exchange with the author, August 27, 2020.

120. Leslie Ayala and Sebastián Rivas, "El indulto a Jorge Mateluna," *La Tercera*, March 12, 2018, https://www.latercera.com/nacional/noticia/indulto-jorge-mateluna-la-otra-decision-michelle-bachelet-ex-ministro-justicia-no-curso/96725/.

121. Later, Calderón explained that the condition of the pardon was that Mateluna accept the guilty verdict, which his lawyers opted to do in the interests of obtaining his freedom; the premise of the Mateluna Inocente campaign, however, was that Mateluna was innocent. Calderón feared that by maintaining this position in the play they might cause issues for Mateluna's legal standing. Calderón, interview by Pedro Bahamondes Chaud, "Guillermo Calderón vuelve al caso Mateluna en su neuva obra," March 26, 2023, https://www.theclinic.cl/2023/03/26/guillermo-calderon-vuelve-al-caso-mateluna-en-su-nueva-obra-el-intento-por-anular-los-indultos-es-totalmente-inmoral/.

Chapter 5

1. Macarena Segovia, "La pizza más cara de Piñera: la cadena de errores del Presidente en el manejo de crisis y que ha terminado con tanques en las calles," *El Mostrador*, October 19, 2019.

2. The phrase "Chile despertó" served as a chant and hashtag widely circulating throughout the movement.

3. See Pascale Bonnefoy, "Mounting Evidence of Abuse by Chile's Police Force Leads to Calls for Reform," *New York Times*, December 13, 2019, https://www.nytimes.com/2019/12/13/world/americas/chile-police-protests.html.

4. César Jiménez-Yañez, "#Chiledespertó: Causas del estallido social en Chile," *Revista mexicana de sociología* 82, no. 4 (2020): 949–957, https://doi.org/10.22201/iis.01882503p.2020.4.59213.

5. Lisa Hilbink and Valentina Salas, "The Path to a New Constitution in Chile: How the Unthinkable Became the Inescapable," ConstitutionNet, International Idea, November 27, 2019, https://constitutionnet.org/news/path-new-constitution-chile-how-unthinkable-became-inescapable. The full agreement is included in an annex to Pablo Ruiz-Tagle, *Five Republics and One Tradition: A History of Constitutionalism in Chile 1810–2020*, Cambridge Studies in Law and Society (Cambridge University Press, 2021), 282–284.

6. One of the campaigns was the Marca AC, supported by many in the intellectual and political elite, including Javiera Parada, Gabriel Boric, Fernando Atria, and Pedro Lemebel. See Javier Sajuria, "El largo camino hacia una Constitución en democracia," *La Tercera*, October 13, 2020, https://www.latercera.com/opinion/noticia/el-largo-camino-hacia-una-constitucion-en-democracia/LMMPLNLRZNG3PEN6H6UVWKY5RE/.

7. Garretón, *Incomplete Democracy*, 151.

8. Ruiz-Tagle, *Five Republics and One Tradition*, 263.

9. For this reason, the Communist Party did not sign the agreement.

10. The tensions at the heart of this question were described by Brunner as marking the distinction between Octubrismo/Noviembrismo, a tension that has run throughout Chile's history (and the history of socialism) and was taken up in the political discourse at the time. Juan Andrés Quezada, "Octubristas v/s noviembristas: las dos miradas que se enfrentan dentro y fuera de la Convención," *La Tercera*, October 17, 2021, https://www.latercera.com/la-tercera-domingo/noticia/octubristas-vs-noviembristas-las-dos-miradas-que-se-enfrentan-dentro-y-fuera-de-la-convencion/TEY5ZYY7SVENRLVC6MWB655SW4/.

11. Law nos. 21.216 and 21.298. See "Publicación de la Ley N° 21.216: Paridad de género para el proceso constituyente," *Biblioteca del Congreso Nacional de Chile*, December 21, 2020, https://www.bcn.cl/procesoconstituyente/detalle_cronograma?id=f_publicacion-de-la-ley-21–216-paridad-de-genero-para-el-proceso-constituyente; "Modifica la carta fundamental de los pueblos indígenas en la convención constitucional," *Biblioteca del Congreso Nacional de Chile*, December 23, 2020, https://www.bcn.cl/leychile/navegar?idNorma=1153843.

12. See Marcia Carmo, "'Chile despertó': Susana Hidalgo, la famosa actriz que tomó la imagen más icónica de las protestas," *BBC News*, October 30, 2019, https://www.bbc.com/mundo/noticias-america-latina-50239591; Llanos and Grass Kleiner, "New Feminist Performance."

13. Milena Grass Kleiner, "*TREWA: Estado-nación o el espectro de la traición*: El ensayo de un teatro plurinacional," *Talia: Revista de estudios teatrales* 4 (2022): 58, https://doi.org/10.5209/tret.80830.

14. See, for example, Alejandro Corvalán, "Crisis de representación en Chile," *Mensaje* 61, no. 607 (2012): 6–9; Vicente Espinoza, "De la política social a la participación en un nuevo contrato de ciudadanía," *Política*, no. 43 (2004): 149–183; Julia Paley, *Marketing Democracy: Power and Social Movements in Post-dictatorship Chile* (University of California Press, 2001).

15. Sebastián Ureta et al., "Constituting Chileans: The *Cabildos* of October 2019 and the Trouble of Instrumental Participation," *Social Identities* 27, no. 5 (2021): 522, https://doi.org/10.1080/13504630.2021.1931087.

16. Despite the inclusion of nonpoliticians, most of the constituents had school degrees and the majority were lawyers (59 out of 155). Emilio Contreras, "Las profesiones y ocupaciones de los 155 constituyentes," *Bío Bío Chile*, May 20, 2021.

17. Claudia Heiss, "Chile: la Constitución que viene," *Nueva Sociedad*, May 2021, https://www.nuso.org/articulo/chile-la-constitucion-que-viene/. Loncón's academic work and advocacy largely revolves around the teaching and recognition of Mapudungun. "Quién es Elisa Loncón, la profesora mapuche elegida presidenta de la Convención Constituyente de Chile," *El Mostrador*, July 4, 2021, https://www.elmostrador.cl/nueva-constitucion/2021/07/04/quien-es-elisa-loncon-la-profesora-mapuche-elegida-presidenta-de-la-convencion-constituyente-de-chile/.

18. Jack Nicas, "Chile Votes on Constitution That Would Enshrine Record Number of Rights," *New York Times*, September 3, 2022. Unlike the US Constitution, the Chilean Constitution is not based on common law, which explains the necessity of enshrining rights at length.

19. Here I am translating the document as it is currently in effect. This document incorporates multiple changes and amendments through 2021.

20. Constitutional Reform Law 19.611.

21. In contrast, the 2022 document recognizes diverse forms of sexuality and gender identity (article 6) and protects diverse familial forms and ways of life (article 10).

22. See Benjamin Alemparte, "Towards a Theory of Neoliberal Constitutionalism: Addressing Chile's First Constitution-Making Laboratory," *Global Constitutionalism* 11, no. 1 (2022): 82–109.

23. Fernando Atria, Constanza Salgado, and Javier Wilenmann, *El proceso constituyente en 138 preguntas y respuestas* (LOM Ediciones, 2020), 187–188.

24. Heiss and Navia, "You Win Some, You Lose Some," 163.

25. Atria, Salgado, and Wilenmann, *El proceso constituyente*, 192.

26. María José Oyarzún, Giovanna Roa, and Beatriz Sánchez, "Chile, una república solidaria," *Nuevo Poder*, February 2, 2022.

27. Arto Laitinen and Anne Brigitta Pessi, introduction to *Solidarity: Theory and Practice*, ed. Arto Latinen and Anne Brigitta Pessi (Lexington Books 2014), 1–2.

28. Sally J. Scholz, *Political Solidarity* (Pennsylvania State University Press, 2008), 5.

29. Jacques Rancière, *On the Shores of Politics*, trans. Liz Heron (Verso, 2007), 32.

30. Rancière, *On the Shores of Politics*, 32.

31. Todd May, "Humanism and Solidarity," *Parrhesia* 18 (2013): 16.

32. Rancière, *On the Shores of Politics*, 32–33.

33. Jodi Dean, *Solidarity of Strangers: Feminism after Identity Politics* (University of California Press, 1996), 7. Kathleen B. Jones, *Compassionate Authority: Democracy and the Representation of Women* (Routledge, 1993), 228–229.

34. bell hooks, "Sisterhood: Political Solidarity between Women," *Feminist Review* 23 (1986): 126, https://doi.org/10.2307/1394725.

35. Chandra Talpade Mohanty, *Feminism without Borders: Decolonizing Theory, Practicing Solidarity* (Duke University Press, 2003), 242.

36. Mohanty, *Feminism without Borders*, 231.

37. Nira Yuval-Davis, "What Is 'Transversal Politics'?," *soundings* 12 (1999): 94–95.

38. In the final chapter of the Spanish edition of *Performance Constellations*, Fuentes turns to transnational feminist movements and elucidates the workings of this image in this case. See Marcela Fuentes, "Decir y hacer ni una menos: Constelaciones feministas contra la crueldad neoconservadora," in *Activismos tecnopolíticos. Constelaciones de performance* (Eterna Cadencia, 2020), 199–252.

39. Drawing from the work of Anibal Quijano, Walter Mignolo posits the coloniality of power as a means by which epistemologies have been subjugated and argues for "border thinking" or "gnosis" to reinstate situated knowledges. See Walter D. Mignolo, *Local Histories/Global Designs: Coloniality, Subaltern Knowledges and Border Thinking* (Princeton University Press, 2012), 17–18; Anibal Quijano, "Colonialidad del poder, cultura y conocimiento en América Latina," *Anuario Mariateguiano* 9, no. 9 (1997): 113–121, http://www.jstor.org/stable/41491587.

40. Pascal Lupien, "The Incorporation of Indigenous Concepts of Plurinationality into the New Constitutions of Ecuador and Bolivia," *Democratization* 18, no. 3 (2011): 774–796, https://doi.org/10.1080/13510347.2011.563116

41. Boaventura de Sousa Santos, *The End of the Cognitive Empire* (Duke University Press, 2018); and *Epistemologies of the South: Justice against Epistemicide* (Routledge, 2014). I cite Santos with reservation, especially in a chapter about feminist and Indigenous solidarity. His thinking, developed with researchers at the Center for Social Studies at the University of Coimbra, makes clear links between feminist and Indigenous epistemologies and the solidarity advanced by the Chilean Constitution and therefore informs my thinking. However, several women have made public accusations of sexual misconduct and abuse of power against Santos. I therefore think it is important to acknowledge this, as well as the intellectual debt he owes to those

he has worked with at the Center and elsewhere. Alexandra Inácio and Rita Neves Costa, "Relatório confirma indícios de assédio no CES em Coimbra," *Jornal de Noticias*, March 13, 2024, https://www.jn.pt/4775175593/relatorio-confirma-indicios-de-assedio-no-ces-em-coimbra/.

42. Santos, *End of the Cognitive Empire*, 10.

43. *Suma qamaña* and *sumac kawsay*, often translated as "buen vivir" or "living well," is a philosophical and ethical orientation around living harmoniously with community and the natural world. Javier Medina, ed. *Suma Quamaña: La comprensión indígena de la Vida Buena* (Federación de Asociaciones Municipales de Bolivia, 2001).

44. José Quidel Lincoleo, "Pu Mapuche ka pu Wigka, chumgechi ñi xokituwün: Las relaciones interétnicas a través de la religión: El caso de los mapuche y no mapuche en Chile," *Anthropos* 207 (2005): 153–166, citation on 158. See also Patricia Viera-Bravo, "Principios del mapuche mongen para la resignificación de la economía en tiempos de crisis del capitalismo neoliberal, desde el sur de Chile," *Revista Iberoamericana de Estudios de Desarrollo* 10, no. 2 (2021): 84–107, https://doi.org/10.26754/ojs_ried/ijds.587.

45. Santos, *End of the Cognitive Empire*, 236.

46. Nino Pagliccia, "Solidaridad: el renacimiento de un viejo concept socialista," in *Vivir bien: ¿Paradigma no capitalista?*, ed. Ivonne Farah H. and Luciano Vasapollo (Plural Editores, 2011), 145–158.

47. Javier García Bustos, "Cultura y procesos constituyente: un debate de primera necesidad," *Palabra pública*, Universidad de Chile, November 3, 2020, https://palabrapublica.uchile.cl/2020/11/03/cultura-y-proceso-constituyente-un-debate-de-primera-necesidad/.

48. Manuel de J. Jiménez, "Los derechos culturales en la futura Constitución chilena," *Revista Común*, January 12, 2021, https://revistacomun.com/blog/los-derechos-culturales-en-la-futura-constitucion-chilena/.

49. Article 96, section 2.

50. KIMVN Teatro, "Retrospectiva KIMVN Teatro Documental 2008–2018," Museo de Memoria, PDF File, https://web.museodelamemoria.cl/wp-content/uploads/2017/12/RESTROSPECTIVA-KIMVN-TEATRO-21-AGOSTO.pdf.

51. This, and subsequent autobiographical information, was related to me in Paula González Seguel, interview with the author, Santiago, September 2, 2022. She also recounts elements of this story in Paula González Seguel, "Teatro documental, memoria y vida," in *Dramaturgias de la resistencia: KIMVN teatro documental marry xipantv* (Pehuén, 2018), 34–35.

52. González, interview with the author.

53. González, interview with the author.

54. Cristián Opazo, "El cuento del tío. El trabajo del parentesco en *Galvarino* (2012) de Paula González," *Literatura y lingüística*, no. 44 (2021): 191, https://hdl.handle.net/11299/253512.

55. Macarena Gómez-Barris, *The Extractive Zone: Social Ecologies and Decolonial Perspectives* (Duke University Press, 2017), 67.

56. Amie Campos, "Territorial Conflicts, Bureaucracy, and State Formation in Chile's Southern Frontera 1866–1912" (PhD diss., University of California San Diego, 2022), 6.

57. Patricia Richards, *Race and the Chilean Miracle: Neoliberalism, Democracy, and Indigenous Rights* (University of Pittsburgh Press, 2013), 2.

58. Richards, *Race and the Chilean Miracle*, 2.

59. See Martín Correa, Raúl Molina, and Nancy Yáñez, *La reforma agraria y las tierras Mapuches: Chile 1962–1975* (LOM Ediciones, 2005); Andrés Carvajal, José Peralta, and Carlos Ribera, eds. *A desalambrar: Historias de mapuches y chilenos en la lucha por la tierra* (Santiago, Chile: Editorial Ayun, 2006); Antonio Bellisario, "The Chilean Agrarian Transformation: Agrarian Reform and Capitalist 'Partial' Counter-Agrarian Reform, 1964–1980," *Journal of Agrarian Change* 7, no. 2 (April 2007): 145–182, https://doi.org/10.1111/j.1471-0366.2007.00138.x.

60. Robinson Torres et al., "Water Extractivism and Decolonial Struggles in Mapuche Territory, Chile," *Water Alternatives* 15, no. 1 (2022): 150–174.

61. Richards, *Race and the Chilean Miracle*, 2.

62. Gómez-Barris, *The Extractive Zone*, 71.

63. Helene Risør and Daniela Jacob, "'Interculturalism as Treason': Policing, Securitization, and Neoliberal State Formation in Southern Chile," *Latin American and Caribbean Ethnic Studies* 13, no. 3 (2018): 247, https://doi.org/10.1080/17442222.2018.1510165.

64. See also Kelly Bauer, *Negotiating Autonomy: Mapuche Territorial Demands and Chilean Land Policy* (University of Pittsburgh Press, 2021).

65. Ignacia Cortés Rojas and Ignacio Pastén assert as much in "La escenificación de la violencia estatal en dos obras mapuche recientes: *Malen* de Ricardo Curaqueo y *Trewa: Estado-nación o espectro de la traición* de Paula González," *Latin American Theatre Review* 54, no. 2 (Spring 2021): 71–95. They contend that this has been shifting in recent years with more works by and about Mapuche people featured in the seasons of official cultural circuits.

66. Pía Gutiérrez Díaz "Revelaciones de archivo: representación y autorrepresentación del pueblo Mapuche en algunas manifestaciones teatrales chilenas a partir de 1940," *Palimpsesto* 8, no. 11 (January–June 2017): 191–205. Gutiérrez traces the activities of the Conjunto Artístico Araucano Llefquehuenu as an example of Mapuche autorepresentation outside of official circuits. She cites both the original production and a revival (directed by Guillermo Calderón) of Aguirre's *Los que van quedando en el camino* as an example of the ways the Mapuche are present in the theater, but this presence is de-emphasized or its political stakes are neutralized in its production and reception.

67. Grass Kleiner, "*TREWA: Estado-nación o el espectro de la traición*," 58.

68. This encouragement was recounted in González, "Teatro documental, memoria y yida," 35.

69. Evelyn González Seguel, "Biografía KIMVN Teatro," in *Dramaturgias de la resistencia*, 18.

70. Paula González, interview with the author, Santiago, Chile, September 3, 2022.

71. Patricia Henríquez Puentes and Mauricio Ostria González, "*Ñi pu tremen: Mis antepasados* de Paula González Seguel," *Literatura y Lingüistica* 43 (2021): 143, http://dx.doi.org/10.29344/0717621x.43.2670.

72. Paula González Seguel, "Ñi pu tremen: Mis antepasados," in *Dramaturgias de la Resistencia*, 52.

73. Gonzalez, "Ñi pu tremen," 53.
74. González, interview with the author.
75. Evelyn González, "Biografía KIMVN," 17.
76. The Raguileo alphabet is one of the accepted Mapudungun alphabets, devised by the Mapuche linguist Anselmo Raguileo. In contrast with the Unified Mapuche alphabet, it offers a greater distinction from the Spanish alphabet and is favored by those seeking more linguistic and cultural differentiation and autonomy. Francesco Chiodi and Elisa Loncón, *Crear nuevas palabras. Innovación y expansión de los recursos lexicales del Mapudungun* (Instituto de Estudios Indígenas, 1999), 10.
77. Evelyn González, "Biografía KIMVN," 21.
78. Evelyn González, "Biografía KIMVN," 21.
79. Marcela Fuentes traces the interplay of street demonstrations, symbolic performance, and social media activism in the growth of Ni Una Menos from its inception as a singular mobilization to its continued life as an ongoing, transnational movement in Fuentes, "#NiUnaMenos (#NotOneWomanLess): Hashtag Performativity, Memory, and Direct Action against Gender Violence in Argentina," in *Women Mobilizing Memory*, ed. Ayşe Gül Altýnay et al. (Columbia University Press, 2019), 172–191.
80. Débora de Fina Gonzalez and Francisca Figueroa Vidal, "Nuevos 'campos de acción política' feminista: Una mirada a las recientes movilizaciones en Chile," *Revista punto género*, no. 11 (2019): 51–72, reference on 65, https://doi.org/10.5354/2735-7473.2019.53880.
81. Nelly Richard, "La insurgencia feminista de mayo 2018," in *Mayo feminista: La rebelión contra el patriarcado, ed.* Faride Zerán Cherich (LOM Ediciones, 2018), 118.
82. Thompson, "'An Explosion of Feminism,'" 45.
83. Silvia Federici, *Caliban and the Witch: Women, the Body, and Primitive Accumulation*, rev. ed. (Autonomedia, 2014).
84. Excerpted in LASTESIS, *Set Fear on Fire: The Feminist Call That Set the Americas Ablaze*, trans. Camila Valle (London: Verso 2021), 21.
85. Sibila Sotomayor and Dafne Valdés, "LASTESIS: 'La nueva sociedad no patriarcal la tenemos que construir entre todas, todes, y todos también," interview by Marta Borraz, *El Diario*, March 16, 2022. https://www.eldiario.es/sociedad/lastesis-nueva-sociedad-no-patriarcal-construir-todes_128_8836387.html.
86. LASTESIS, *Set Fear on Fire*, 9.
87. Llanos and Grass, "New Feminist Performance, 48.
88. Sotomayor and Valdés, "LASTESIS."
89. Andrea Bustos C., "Cuatro años sin justicia para Macarena Valdés: familia y organizaciones continúan sosteniendo un 'femicido empresarial,'" *Diario U Chile*, August 21, 2020, https://radio.uchile.cl/2020/08/21/cuatro-anos-sin-justicia-para-macarena-valdes-familia-y-organizaciones-continuan-sosteniendo-un-femicidio-empresarial/.
90. "Nuevo Servicio integral, social, y de seguridad para pueblos originarios," *Revista Carabineros de Chile*, no. 698 (June 2013): 23. Currently there are ten PACI patrols throughout Chile, embedded in Mapuche, Aymara, Pehuenche, and Lafkenche communities. Paula Huenchumil, "El fracaso de las

Paci, el proyecto social de Carabineros en comunidades indígenas," *Interferencia*, December 16, 2020, https://interferencia.cl/articulos/el-fracaso-de-las-paci-el-proyecto-social-de-carabineros-en-comunidades-indigenas.

91. Helene Risør and Daniela Jacob, "'Interculturalism as treason,'" 239.

92. Quoted in Huenchumil, "El fracaso de las Paci."

93. Pedro Cayuqueo, Verónica Figueroa Huancho, Salvador Millaleo, and Antonia Rivas, "De qué hablamos de un Estado plurinacional: expertos en pueblos originarios y DD.HH. responden," interview by Andrés Muñoz, *La Tercera*, July 15, 2020, https://www.latercera.com/la-tercera-pm/noticia/de-que-hablamos-cuando-hablamos-de-un-estado-plurinacional-expertos-en-pueblos-originarios-y-ddhh-responden/DZYYZU6MDREQBNMDG4QCGJSKDM/.

94. Catrileo, Carrión, and Garzo replace the C in "Chile" with a $ sign to render the concept of Chile contingent and link it with capitalist logic. Antonio Catrileo Araya, Manuel Carrión Lira, and Marcelo Garzo Montalvo, "$hileyem (Chile se acabó, The End of Chile): Indigenous Media and Decolonial Futurities beyond the Settler State," in *Dismantling the Nation: Contemporary Art in Chile*, ed. Florencia San Martín, Carla Macchiavello Cornejo, and Paula Solimano (Amherst College Press, 2023), 207.

95. The group was especially influenced by Rita Laura Segato, *La guerra contra las mujeres* (Traficantes de Sueños, 2016).

96. Rita Laura Segato, "Patriarchy from Margin to Center: Discipline, Territoriality, and Cruelty in the Apocalyptic Phase of Capital," *South Atlantic Quarterly* 115, no. 3 (2016): 615–624, https://doi.org/10.1215/00382876-3608675.

97. Verónica Gago and Liz Mason-Deese, "Rethinking Situated Knowledge from the Perspective of Argentina's Feminist Strike," *Journal of Latin American Geography* 18, no. 3 (2019): 205, https://dx.doi.org/10.1353/lag.2019.0047.

98. Werth and Zien, *Bodies on the Front Lines*, 2.

99. My analysis here builds on an interpretation of this work in Thompson, "'An Explosion of Feminism,'" 53.

100. Campbell, "Archive of the Self," 10.

101. Quoted in Paula González Seguel, *Trewa: Estado—nación o el espectro de la traición*, unpublished manuscript, September 2022, PDF file, 2. Ileana Caballero Diéguez, *Cuerpos sin duelo: Iconografías y teatralidades del dolor* (Publicaciones Universidad Autónoma de Nuevo León, 2016), 82.

102. Diéguez, *Cuerpos sin duelo*, 32. Quoted in Cortés and Pastén, "La escenificación de la violencia," 74.

103. Tomás González F., "Sangre de plomo: La vida de Brandon con 90 perdigones," *Diario U Chile*, February 3, 2019, https://radio.uchile.cl/2019/02/03/sangre-de-plomo-la-vida-de-brandon-con-90-perdigones/.

104. González, *Trewa*, 13. *Lamngen* is a Mapudungun word meaning "brother" or "sister" and is used as a cordial address to the Mapuche community.

105. González, *Trewa*, 16.

106. González, *Trewa*, 30.

107. Javier Arroyo Olea and Valeria Torreblanca López, "Casos de montajes policiales: Una aproximación desde las prácticas de Carabineros de Chile

y la Policía de Investigaciones entre 1993 y 2018," *Revista némesis*, 16 (2020): 99–104.

108. González, *Trewa*, 31–32.

109. Brenda Werth, "Reinventing Feminist Activism through Pandemic Performance in Argentina" (paper presented at the American Society of Theatre Research Conference, New Orleans, LA, November 4, 2022), 3.

110. Gago and Mason-Deese, "Rethinking Situated Knowledge," 206.

111. Fuentes, "#NiUnaMenos (#NotOneWomanLess)," 177.

112. Segato, "Patriarchy from Margin to Center," 622.

113. Segato, "Patriarchy from Margin to Center," 617.

114. Segato, "Patriarchy from Margin to Center," 618.

115. Juan Manuel Aldape Muñoz theorizes how forensic performances configure claims to social justice in Aldape Muñoz, "Forensic Performances: Searching for Justice in NAKA Dance Theater's *BUSCARTE: Duet*," *Theatre Research International* 47, no. 1 (2022): 47, https://doi.org/10.1017/S0307883321000493.

116. María José Lucero Díaz, *Ausencia del cuerpo y cosmología de la muerte en el mundo mapuche: Memorias en torno a la condición del detenido desaparecido* (Museo de la Memoria y los Derechos Humanos, 2017), 65–67.

117. María Pia López, *Not One Less: Mourning, Disobedience and Desire*, trans. Frances Riddle (Polity Press, 2020), 2.

118. LASTESIS, "El cuerpo como espacio político," interview by Cataloga Revista, *Cataloga Revista* 1 (2022): 21.

119. Gago and Mason-Deese, "Rethinking Situated Knowledge," 202.

120. See Hernández, *Staging Lives*; Martin, *Theatre of the Real*; Sánchez, *Practicing the Real on the Contemporary Stage*.

121. Hernández, *Staging Lives*, 10.

122. González, *Trewa*, 4.

123. *Kalfü* is the concept of a spiritual dimension that is symbolically situated in the sky and is associated with the color blue. *Chachai* and *papay* are both terms of respect, particularly for elders (men and women respectively). Patricio Cayupil Vásquez, *Kalfü y Likan: Un viaje mágico por los ríos* (Programa de Educación Intercultural Bilingüe, 2019), 44.

124. González, *Trewa*, 11.

125. Lucero Díaz, *Ausuncio del cuerpo*, 63.

126. Cortés and Pastén, "La escenificación de la violencia," 87.

127. Grass, "*Trewa*," 59–61.

128. González, *Trewa*, 21. It bears noting that here the term of endearment, "la Negra," has more overt racial and political overtones, in contrast with its usage in Andrés Pérez's *La Negra Ester*.

129. J. L. Austin, *How to Do Things With Words*, 2nd ed. (Harvard University Press, 1975); Judith Butler, *Gender Trouble: Feminism and the Subversion of Identity*, 2nd ed. (Routledge, 1999).

130. Andrew Goldberg, "Political Theatre After Occupy: Participation, Interpellation, and the Search for New Subjectivities in the Theatre" (PhD diss., CUNY Graduate Center, 2023), 14. Louis Althusser, "Ideology and Ideological State Apparatuses," in *Lenin and Philosophy and Other Essays*, ed. Louis Althusser, trans. Ben Brewster (Monthly Review Press, 2001).

131. Dean, *Solidarity of Strangers*, 3; Mohanty, *Feminism without Borders*, 7.

132. Fuentes, *Performance Constellations*, 2–3.

133. Thompson, "'An Explosion of Feminism,'" 54.

134. The lyrics for the hymn were written in 1910 by Francisco Flores Ruiz and set to music by Arturo Arancibia Uribe in 1928. This section was omitted from the English translation circulated by the collective. For the Spanish lyrics see LASTESIS's Instagram on November 23, 2019 (@lastesis), https://www.instagram.com/p/B5Nl542FjmR/.

135. Nelly Richard, *Masculine/Feminine: Practices of Difference(s)*, trans. Alice A. Nelson and Silvia R. Tandeciarz (Duke University Press, 2004), 29.

136. Deborah Martin and Deborah Shaw, "Chilean and Transnational Performances of Disobedience: LasTesis and the Phenomenon of *Un violador en tu camino*," *Bulletin of Latin American Research* 40, no. 5 (2021): 717, https://doi.org/10.1111/blar.13215.

137. "Mujeres mapuche entonan 'Un violador en tu camino en mapudungun,'" *El Mostrador*, December 6, 2019, https://www.elmostrador.cl/noticias/multimedia/2019/12/06/mujeres-mapuche-entonan-un-violador-en-tu-camino-en-mapudungun/; Cuffe, "Chile's 'A Rapist in your Path' Chant Hits 200 Cities: Map." Geochicas, a feminist mapping collective, has mapped the global performances. "Mapa Un violador en tu camino," Geochicas, updated May 2022, https://geochicas.org/index.php/que-hacemos/proyectos/mapa-un-violador-en-tu-camino/. Mia Liinason traces how the lyrics were adapted to respond to various local contexts in Mia Liinason, "The Performance of Protest. Las Tesis and the New Feminist Radicality at the Conjunction of Digital Spaces and the Streets," *Feminist Media Studies* (April 2023): 12, https://doi.org/10.1080/14680777.2023.2200472.

138. Javiera Manzi and Fernanda Carvajal, "La violencia que no ves. Interrupciones feministas y cuerpos fuera de lugar en la performance de LasTesis," *Mora* 26, no. 1 (2020): 306.

139. Paula Cometa, "Las Tesis sobre 'Un violador en tu camino': 'Se nos escapó de las manos y lo hermoso es que fue apropiado por otras,'" interview by Ana Pais, *BBC News Mundo*, December 6, 2019.Throughout this section I draw from arguments made in Thompson, "'An Explosion of Feminism,'" 53–54.

140. González, *Trewa*, 33.

141. González, *Trewa* 34.

Epilogue

1. González, interview with the author.

2. Quoted in Jimmy A. Noriega, "KIMVN Teatro and Paula González Seguel," in *Fifty Key Figures in Latinx and Latin American Theatre*, ed. Paola Hernández and Analola Santana (Routledge, 2022), 94.

3. Dolan, *Utopia in Performance*.

4. Sara Ahmed, *The Cultural Politics of Emotion* (Routledge, 2004), 184.

BIBLIOGRAPHY

Archives Consulted

Archivo de la Escena Teatral, Pontificia Universidad Católica, Santiago.
Archivo de Referencias Críticas, Biblioteca Nacional, Santiago.
Colectivo Acciones de Arte Collection, CEDOC, Museo de la Memoria, Santiago.
Cultura Collection, Fundación Documentación y Archivo de la Vicaría de la Solidaridad, Santiago.
Plebiscito 1988 Collection, CEDAV, Museo de la Memoria, Santiago.
Prat Collection, Archivo Teatro de Chile, http://archivo.teatrodechile.cl/, online.
UNAC, UNAC Collection, CEDOC Artes Visuales, Centro Cultural la Moneda Digital Archive. http://centrodedocumentaciondelasartes.cl/g2/collect/cedoc/images/pdfs/5554.pdf, online.
Las Yeguas del Apocalipsis, Género Collection, Archivo Nacional, Santiago.

Interviews

Aste, Guillermo (Cuti). Personal interview, Santiago, March 29, 2018.
Bañados, Patricio. Personal interview, Santiago, June 26, 2018.
Calderón, Guillermo. Personal interview, Santiago, July 3, 2018.
Castro, Afredo. Personal interview. Santiago, August 20, 2018.
Cornejo, Leonel. Personal interview, Santiago, June 28, 2017.
Eltit, Diamela. Personal interview, Santiago, June 30, 2017.
García, Andrés. Personal interview, Santiago, June 13, 2017.
González Seguel, Paula. Personal interview, Santiago, September 3, 2022.
Griffero, Ramón. Personal interview, Santiago, August 3, 2018.
Kadima, Antonio. Personal interview, Santiago, July 5, 2017.
Letelier, Jorge. Personal interview, Santiago, April 25, 2018.
Morales, Héctor. Personal interview, Santiago, June 7, 2018.
Navarro, Arturo. Personal interview, Santiago, March 9, 2018.
Palma, Daniel. Personal interview, Santiago, June 19, 2017.
Ramírez, Rosa. Personal interview, Santiago, July 3, 2017.
Semler, Guillermo (Willy). Personal interview, Santiago, March 2, 2018.

Books and Articles

Adamovsky, Ezequiel "Ethnic Nicknaming: 'Negro' as a Term of Endearment and Vicarious Blackness in Argentina," *Latin American and Caribbean Ethnic Studies* 12, no. 3 (2017): 273–289. https://doi.org/10.1080/17442222.2017.1368895.

Adeyemi, Kemi, Kareem Khubchandani, and Ramón H. Rivera-Servera. Introduction to *Queer Nightlife*, edited by Kemi Adeyemi, Kareem Khubchandani, and Ramón H. Rivera-Servera, 1–16. University of Michigan Press, 2021.

Ahmed, Sara. *The Cultural Politics of Emotion*. Routledge, 2004.

Aldape Muñoz, Juan Manuel. "Forensic Performances: Searching for Justice in NAKA Dance Theater's *BUSCARTE: Duet*." *Theatre Research International* 47, no. 1 (2022): 46–62. https://doi.org/10.1017/S0307883321000493.

Althusser, Louis. "Ideology and Ideological State Apparatuses." *Lenin and Philosophy and Other Essays*. Edited by Louis Althusser. Translated by Ben Brewster. Monthly Review Press, 2001.

Arroyo Olea, Javier, and Valeria Torreblanca López. "Casos de montajes policiales: Una aproximación desde las prácticas de Carabineros de Chile y la Policía de Investigaciones entre 1993 y 2018." *Revista Némesis* 16 (2020): 99–104.

Atria, Fernando, Constanza Salgado, and Javier Wilenmann. *El proceso constituyente en 138 preguntas y respuestas*. LOM Ediciones, 2020.

Austin, J. L. *How to Do Things with Words*. 2nd ed. Harvard University Press, 1975.

Avelar, Idelber. *The Untimely Present: Postdictatorial Latin American Fiction and the Task of Mourning*. Duke University Press, 2012.

Aylwin Azócar, Patricio. *El reencuentro de los demócratas: Del golpe al triunfo del No*. Ediciones Grupo Zeta, 1998.

Aylwin Azócar, Patricio. *La transición chilena: Discursos escogidos, marzo 1990–1992*. Andrés Bello, 1992.

Baboun Garib, Isabel. "Guillermo Calderón: Tres motivos para una poética casi trágica." *Apuntes de teatro* 131 (2009): 20–28. https://doi.org/10.7764/apuntesdeteatro.131.56647.2009.

Badal, Gonzalo. *Roberto Parra*. Ocho Libros Editores, 1996.

Bañados, Patricio. *Confidencias de un locutor*. Editorial Cuarto Propio, 2015.

Barría Jara, Mauricio. "Desmantelar aparatos con otros aparatos: *Mateluna* de Guillermo Calderón. Teatro político en la época de la pospolítica." *Revista Artescena*, no. 5 (2018): 1–19.

Bauer, Kelly. *Negotiating Autonomy: Mapuche Territorial Demands and Chilean Land Policy*. University of Pittsburgh Press, 2021.

Béhague, Gerard H. "Music, c. 1920–c. 1980." In *A Cultural History of Latin America: Literature, Music and the Visual Arts in the 19th and 20th Centuries*, edited by Leslie Bethell, 311–368. Cambridge University Press, 1998.

Bellei, Cristián. *El gran experimento: Mercado y privatización de la educación chilena*. LOM Ediciones, 2015.

Bellisario, Antonio. "The Chilean Agrarian Transformation: Agrarian Reform and Capitalist 'Partial' Counter-Agrarian Reform, 1964–1980." *Journal of Agrarian Change* 7, no. 2 (April 2007): 145–182. https://doi.org/10.1111/j.1471-0366.2007.00138.x.

Bianchi, Soledad. "La política cultural oficialista y el movimiento artístico." *Araucaria de Chile* 17 (1982): 135–141.

Bishop, Claire. *Artificial Hells: Participatory Art and the Politics of Spectatorship*. Verso, 2012.

Bleeker, Maaike. *Doing Dramaturgy: Thinking through Practice*. Springer Nature Switzerland, 2023.

Boal, Augusto. *The Theatre of the Oppressed*. Translated by Charles A. and Maria-Odilia Leal McBride and Emily Fryer. Pluto Press, 2008.

Boeninger, Edgardo. *Democracia en Chile: Lecciones para la gobernabilidad*. Andrés Bello, 1997.

Bourdieu, Pierre. *Distinction: A Social Critique of the Judgement of Taste*. Translated by Richard Nice. Harvard University Press, 1984.

Bourdieu, Pierre. *The Field of Cultural Production: Essays on Art and Literature*. Edited by Randal Johnson. Columbia University Press, 1993.

Bourdieu, Pierre. *The Logic of Practice*. Translated by Richard Nice. Stanford University Press, 1980.

Boyle, Catherine. *Chilean Theater, 1973–1985: Marginality, Power, Selfhood*. Fairleigh Dickinson University Press (Associated University Presses), 1992.

Boyle, Catherine. "Violence in Memory: Translation, Dramatization, and Performance of the Past in Chile." In *Cultural Politics in Latin America*, edited by Anny Brooksbank Jones and Ronaldo Munck, 93–113. St. Martin's Press, 2000.

Brito, Eugenia. "El cuerpo performático de los años 80." In *La intensidad del acontecimiento: Escrituras y relatos en torno a la performance en Chile*, edited by Mauricio Barría and Francisco Sanfuentes. Ediciones Departamento de Artes Visuales Facultad de Artes Universidad de Chile, 2011.

Brown, Wendy. *Undoing the Demos: Neoliberalism's Stealth Revolution*. Zone Books, 2015.

Brunner, José Joaquín. "Lucha cultural y política." In *Ruptura: Documento de arte*. Ediciones CADA, 1982.

Brunner, José Joaquín. "Políticas culturales de oposición en Chile." Material de Discusión, 78. FLASCO, December 1985.

Butler, Judith. *Gender Trouble: Feminism and the Subversion of Identity*. 2nd ed. Routledge, 1999.

Butler, Judith. *Notes toward a Performative Theory of Assembly*. Harvard University Press, 2015.

Butler, Judith. "Performative Acts and Gender Constitution: An Essay in Phenomenology and Feminist Theory." *Theatre Journal* 40, no. 4 (1988): 519–531. https://doi.org/10.2307/3207893.

Calderón, Guillermo. *B*. Translated by William Gregory. Oberon Books, 2017.

Calderón, Guillermo. *Escuela*. August 24, 2013. Manuscript shared by the author. New York.

Calderón, Guillermo. "Guillermo Calderón en conversación: 'Chile como nación puede acabarse.' " Interview by Catalina Forttes. *Mester* 39, no. 1 (2010): 57–66.

Calderón, Guillermo. Interview by Jean Graham-Jones. Performance and Justice Symposium, John Jay College of Criminal Justice, May 16, 2013.

Calderón, Guillermo. *Mateluna*. February 7, 2019. Manuscript shared by the author. New York.

Calderón, Guillermo. *Neva*. Translated by Andrea Thome. Theatre Communications Group, 2016.

Calderón, Guillermo. *Teatro I: Neva, Diciembre, Clase*. LOM Ediciones, 2012.

Calderón, Guillermo. *Teatro II: Villa, Discurso, Beben*. LOM Ediciones, 2012.

Calderón, Guillermo. "Tres actores en escena, una estufa, algunas sillas. Diálogo entre Guillermo Calderón y Soledad Lagos a propósito de *Neva*." Interview by Soledad Lagos. *Telondefondo* 6 (December 2007): 1–9.

Calderón, Guillermo. "*Villa*." Translated by William Gregory. *Theater* 43, no. 2 (2013): 99–119.

Calderón, Guillermo. "When a 'Kiss' Is Not Just a Kiss." Interview by Elyse Dodgson. *American Theatre*, September 25, 2017. https://www.americantheatre.org/2017/09/25/when-a-kiss-is-not-just-a-kiss/.

Campbell, Baird. "The Archive of the Self: Trans Self-Making and Social Media in Santiago de Chile." PhD diss., Rice University, 2021.

Campbell, Baird. "*MOVILH*-ization: Hegemonic Masculinity in the Queer Social Movement Industry in Santiago de Chile." MA thesis, Tulane University, 2014.

del Campo, Alicia. "Nuevos realismos para viejos discursos: Las guerras prometidas y el fin del Chile neoliberal en *Diciembre* de Guillermo Calderon." *FIT 2008: El teatro iberoamericano en el siglo XXI*. Gestos, 2009.

del Campo, Alicia. *Teatralidades de la memoria: Rituales de reconciliación en el Chile de la transición*. Mosquito Comunicaciones, 2004.

Campos, Aime. "Territorial Conflicts, Bureaucracy, and State Formation in Chile's Southern Frontera 1866–1912." PhD diss., University of California San Diego, 2022.

Cánovas, Raúl. *El arte de la palabra*. Pomaire, 1980.

Cánovas, Rodrigo. *Lihn, Zurita, Ictus, Radrigán: Literatura chilena y experiencia autoritaria*. Flasco, 1986.

Carlson, Marvin. *Shattering Hamlet's Mirror: Theatre and Reality*. University of Michigan Press, 2016.

Carvajal, Andrés, José Peralta, and Carlos Ribera, eds. *A desalambrar: Historias de mapuches y chilenos en la lucha por la tierra*. Editorial Ayun, 2006.

Carvajal, Fernanda. "Arte, política, representación. El caso del No+ del Colectivo de Acciones de Arte en el Chile dictatorial." *Revista estampa* 2, no. 4 (2013): 90–101.

Carvajal, Fernanda. "*Prat* de Teatro de Chile: Una fábula nacional prófuga atravesando las junturas entre arte y política." *Atena* 502, no. 2 (2010): 73–95.

Castaño, Sofía. "Ilusión y teatralización en *Diciembre* de Guillermo Calderón y *Lote 77* de Marcelo Mininno." *Telondefondo* 11 (July 2010): 1–8.

Castillo, Alejandra. "Feminist Political Imagination." Translated by Alex Brostoff. *Critical Times* 5, no. 1 (2022): 262–264. https://doi.org/10.1215/26410478-9536615.

Castillo Espinoza, Eduardo. *Puño y letra: Movimiento social y comunicación gráfica en Chile*. Ocho Libros, 2016.

Catrileo Araya Antonio, Manuel Carrión Lira, and Marcelo Garzo Montalvo. "$hileyem (Chile se acabó, The End of Chile): Indigenous Media and Decolonial Futurities beyond the Settler State." In *Dismantling the Nation: Contemporary Art in Chile*, ed. Florencia San Martín, Carla Macchiavello Cornejo, and Paula Solimano. Amherst College Press, 2023.

Castro, Oscar. "El teatro en los campos de concentración." Interview by Ariel Dorfman. *Arucaria de Chile* 6 (1979): 3–34.

Certeau, Michel de. *The Practice of Everyday Life*. 3rd ed. Translated by Steven Rendall. University of California Press, 2011.

Chiodi, Francesco, and Elisa Loncón. *Crear nuevas palabras. Innovación y expansión de los recursos lexicales del Mapudungun*. Instituto de Estudios Indígenas, 1999.

Clark, Paul Berry. *Deep Citizenship*. Pluto Press, 1996.

Claro Valdés, Samuel, and Carmen Peña Fuenzalida. *Chilena o cueca tradicional*. Ediciones Universidad Católica de Chile, 1994.

Cobos, Carla Pinochet. "Disrupting Normalcy: Artistic interventions and political mobilisation against the neoliberal city (Santiago, Chile, 2019)." *Social Identities* 27, no. 5 (2021): 538–554. https://doi.org/10.1080/13504630.2021.1931091.

Collier, Simon, and William F. Sater. *A History of Chile, 1808–2002*. Cambridge University Press, 2004.

Comisión Asesoría Presidencial en Materias Artístico Culturales. "Chile está en deuda con la cultura." Valparaíso, Chile: 1997.

Comisión Nacional de Verdad y Reconciliación. *Report of the Chilean National Commission on Truth and Reconciliation* (a.k.a. *Rettig Report*). Translated by Phillip E. Berryman. University of Notre Dame Press, 1993.

Connerton, Paul. *How Societies Remember*. Cambridge University Press, 1989.

Connolly, William. *Identity/Difference: Democratic Negotiations of Political Paradox*. University of Minnesota Press, 1991.

Consejo Nacional de las Culturas y las Artes. "Chile quiere más cultura." Valparaíso, Chile: 2005.

Consejo Nacional de las Culturas y las Artes. "Memoria consejo nacional de la cultura y las artes: 2010–2014." Valparaíso, Chile: 2014.

Contardo, Óscar. *Raro: Una historia gay de Chile*. Editorial Planeta, 2011.

Contesse Singh, Jorge. "Comentario: Comentario sobre jurisprudencia: Caso Prat." *Jurisprudencia comentada* 278 (August 2002): 50–56.

Contreras, María Jose. "A Woman Artist in the Neoliberal Chilean Jungle." In *Performance, Feminism and Affect in Neoliberal Times*, edited by Elin Diamond, Denise Varney, and Candice Amich, 239–51. Palgrave Macmillan, 2017.

Correa, Martín, Raúl Molina, and Nancy Yáñez. *La reforma agraria y las tierras Mapuches: Chile 1962–1975*. LOM Ediciones, 2005.

Correa-Parra, Juan, José Francisco Vergara-Perucich, and Carlos Aguirre Nuñez, "Water Privatization and Inequality: Gini Coefficient for Water Resources in Chile." *Water* 12, no. 12 (2020): 3369. https://doi.org/10.3390/w12123369.

Cortés Rojas, Ignacia, and Ignacio Pastén. "La escenificación de la violencia estatal en dos obras mapuche recientes: *Mulen* de Ricardo Curaqueo y *Trewa: Estado-nación o espectro de la traición* de Paula González." *Latin American Theatre Review* 54, no. 2 (Spring 2021): 71–95.

Corvalán, "Crisis de representación en Chile." *Mensaje* 61, no. 607 (2012): 6–9.

Cronovich, Paula. "'No' and *No*: The Campaign of 1988 and Pablo Larraín's Film." *Radical History Review* 124 (2016): 165–176. https://doi.org/10.1215/01636545-3160042.

Crouch, Colin. *Post-democracy*. Polity, 2004.

Danneman, Manuel. "Situación actual de la música folklórica chilena según el 'Atlas del Folklore de Chile.'" *Revista musical chilena* 29, no. 131 (April–June 1978): 5–21.

Dávila, Juan Diego. *El sacrificio de Arturo Prat*. Ediciones AESIR, 2005.

Dean, Jodi. *Solidarity of Strangers: Feminism after Identity Politics*. University of California Press, 1996.

Delamaza, Gonzalo. *Enhancing Democracy*. Berghahn Books, 2014.

de la Parra, Marco Antonio. "A propósito de la Negra Ester," Prologue to *La Negra Ester*. Gran Circo Teatro, 1989.

Diéguez Caballero, Ileana. *Cuerpos sin duelo: Iconografías y teatralidades del dolor*. Publicaciones Universidad Autónoma de Nuevo León, 2016.

Diéguez Caballero, Ileana. *Escenarios liminales: Teatralidades, performances y política*. Actuel, 2007.

Diken, Bülent. "Radical Critique as the Paradox of Post-political Society." *Third Text* 23, no. 5 (2009): 579–586. https://doi.org/10.1080/09528820903184815.

Dolan, Jill. *Utopia in Performance: Finding Hope at the Theater*. University of Michigan Press, 2005.

Dubatti, Jorge. *Filosofía del teatro I: Convivio, experiencia, subjetividad*. Actuel, 2007.

Ducci González, Pilar. *Años de circo: Historia de la actividad circense en Chile*. Latorre Literaria, 2011.

Duggan, Patrick. *Trauma-Tragedy: Symptoms of Contemporary Performance*. Manchester University Press, 2015.

Eckersall, Peter. "Towards an Expanded Dramaturgical Practice: A Report on 'The Dramaturgy and Cultural Intervention Project.'" *Theatre Research International* 31, no. 3 (2006): 283–297. https://doi.org/10.1017/S0307883306002240.

Epple, Juan Armando. *El arte de recordar: Ensayos sobre la memoria cultural de Chile*. Mosquito Comunicaciones, 1994.

Errázuriz, Luis Hernán. "Política cultural del régimen militar chileno (1973–1976)." *Aisthesis* 40 (2006): 62–78. https://doi.org/10.7764/ais.40.62-78.

Espinoza, Vicente. "De la política social a la participación en un nuevo contrato de ciudadanía." *Política*, no. 43 (2004): 149–183.

Espinoza, Violeta. "1988 La Negra Ester 1998." In *Memoria para un nuevo siglo: Chile miradas a la segunda mitad del siglo XX*, edited by Mario Garcés, et al., 369–77. LOM Ediciones, 2000.

Federici, Silvia. *Caliban and the Witch: Women, the Body, and Primitive Accumulation*. Rev. ed. Autonomedia, 2014.

Figueroa, Soledad, and Javiera Larraín. *Espérame en el cielo, corazón: Melodrama en la escena chilena de los siglos XX–XXI*. Cuarto Propio, 2017.

de Fina Gonzalez, Débora, and Francisca Figueroa Vidal. "Nuevos 'campos de acción política' feminista: Una mirada a las recientes movilizaciones en Chile." *Revista punto género*, no. 11 (2019): 51–72. https://doi.org/10.5354/2735-7473.2019.53880.

Fischer Lichte, Erika. *The Transformative Power of Performance: A New Aesthetics*. Translated by Saskya Iris Jain. Routledge, 2008.

Fisek, Emine. *Aesthetic Citizenship: Immigration and Theater in Twenty-First-Century Paris*. Northwestern University Press, 2017.

Fisher, Tony. "Introduction: Performance and the Politics of the *Agōn*." In *Antagonism: Theatre, Performance, and Radical Democracy*, edited by Tony Fisher and Eve Katsouraki, 1–23. Palgrave Macmillan, 2017.

Forch, Juan Enrique. "Talentos de la marginalidad a la legalidad." In *La campaña del NO vista por sus creadores*, 105–8. Melquíades, 1989.

Foucault, Michel. "Of Other Spaces: Utopias and Heterotopias." Translated by Jay Miskowiec, *Architecture/Mouvement/Continuité* (October 1984): 46–49.

Frazier, Lessie Jo. *Salt in the Sand: Memory, Violence, and the Nation-State in Chile, 1980 to the Present*. Duke University Press, 2007.

Fuentes, Marcela. *Activismos tecnopolíticos. Constelaciones de performance*. Eterna Cadencia, 2020.

Fuentes, Marcela. "#NiUnaMenos (#NotOneWomanLess): Hashtag Performativity, Memory, and Direct Action against Gender Violence in Argentina." In *Women Mobilizing Memory*, edited by Ayşe Gül Altýnay et al., 172–91. Columbia University Press, 2019.

Fuentes, Marcela. *Performance Constellations: Networks of Protest and Activism in Latin America*. University of Michigan Press, 2019.

Fukuyama, Francis. *The End of History and the Last Man*. Free Press, 1992.

Gago, Verónica, and Liz Mason-Deese. "Rethinking Situated Knowledge from the Perspective of Argentina's Feminist Strike." *Journal of Latin American Geography* 18, no. 3 (2019): 202–209. https://dx.doi.org/10.1353/lag.2019.0047.

Garcés, Mario, Pedro Milos, Myriam Olguín, Julio Pinto, María Teresa Rojas, and Miguel Urrutia, comps. *Memoria para un nuevo siglo: Chile, miradas a la segunda mitad del Siglo XX*. LOM Ediciones, 2000.

García, Andrés. "La dura senda de un alquimista." *Apuntes de teatro* 122 (2002): 54–57.

García Canclini, Néstor. *Arte popular y sociedad en América Latina*. Editorial Grijalbo, 1977.

García Canclini, Néstor. *Hybrid Cultures: Strategies for Entering and Leaving Modernity*. Translated by Christopher Chiappari and Sylvia Lopez. University of Minnesota Press, 1995.

García Canclini, Néstor. *Imaginarios urbanos*. 4th ed. Eudeba, 2010.

García Canclini, Néstor, ed. *Políticas culturales en América Latina*. Editorial Grijalbo, 1987.

Garretón, Manuel Antonio. *Incomplete Democracy: Political Democratization in Chile and Latin America*. Translated by R. Kelly Washbourne with Gregory Horvath. University of North Carolina Press, 2004.

Garretón, Manuel Antonio. "Las políticas culturales en los gobiernos democráticos en Chile." In *Políticas culturais na Ibero-América*, edited by Antonio Albino Canelas and Rubens Bayardo. Editorial EDUFBA, 2009.

Garretón, Manuel Antonio. "Movilizaciones y movimiento social en la democratización política chilena." In *La sociedad española en la Transición: Los movimientos sociales en el proceso democratizador*, edited by Rafael Quirosa-Cheyrouze y Muñoz, 75–118. Biblioteca Nueva, 2011.

Georgelou, Konstantina, Efrosini Protopapa, and Danae Theodoridou. "Dramaturgy as Working on Actions." In *The Practice of Dramaturgy. Working on Actions in Performance*, edited by Konstantina Georgelou, Efrosini Protopapa, and Danae Theordoridou, 107–19. Antennae Valiz, 2017.

Goldberg, Andrew. "Political Theatre After Occupy: Participation, Interpellation, and the Search for New Subjectivities in the Theatre." PhD diss., CUNY Graduate Center, 2023.

Gómez-Barris, Macarena. *Beyond the Pink Tide: Art and Political Undercurrents in the Americas*. University of California Press, 2018.

Gómez-Barris, Macarena. *The Extractive Zone: Social Ecologies and Decolonial Perspectives*. Duke University Press, 2017.

González Castro, Francisco, Leonora López, and Brian Smith. *Performance art en Chile*. Ediciones Metales Pesados, 2016.

González, Daniela. "Guillermo Calderón: El dramaturgo." *Revista PAT* 56 (Winter 2013): 10–13.

González Ortiz, Camila Ymay. "'Los dueños de Chile somos nosotros': Retrato de la élite en *Los millonarios*, de Teatro La María." *Literatura y lingüística* 44 (2021): 141–167. http://dx.doi.org/10.29344/0717621x.44.3052.

González R., Juan Pablo. "La regia música mestiza de la Negra Ester." *Apuntes de teatro* 122 2002): 151–156.

González Seguel, Evelyn. "Biografía KIMVN Teatro," In *Dramaturgias de la resistencia: KIMVN teatro documental marry xipantv*. Edited by Paula González Seguel. Pehuén, 2018.

González Seguel, Paula. "Ñi pu tremen: Mis antepasados." In *Dramaturgias de la Resistencia: KIMVN teatro documental marry xipantv*. Edited by Paula González Seguel. Pehuén, 2018.

González Seguel, Paula. "Teatro documental, memoria y vida." In *Dramaturgias de la resistencia: KIMVN teatro documental marry xipantv*. Edited by Paula González Seguel. Pehuén, 2018.

Graham-Jones, Jean. *Evita Inevitably: Performing Argentina's Female Icons before and after Eva Perón*. University of Michigan Press, 2014.

Graham-Jones, Jean. *Exorcising History: Argentine Theater under Dictatorship*. Bucknell University Press (Associated University Presses), 2000.

Graham-Jones, Jean. "International Festivals in Latin America: Festival Santiago a Mil and Festival Internacional de Buenos Aires." In *The Cambridge Companion to International Theatre Festivals*, edited by Ric Knowles. Cambridge University Press, 2020.

Graham-Jones, Jean. "Rethinking Buenos Aires Theatre in the Wake of 2001 and Emerging Structures of Resistance and Resilience." *Theatre Journal* 66, no. 1 (March 2014): 37–54. http://www.jstor.org/stable/24580242.

Grass Kleiner, Milena. "El teatro político de Guillermo Calderón: Realidadficción y espacio público." In *Perspectivas políticas de la escena latinoamericana: Diálogos en tiempos presente*, edited by Lola Proaño-Gómez and Lorena Verzero, 113–32. Argus-*a*, 2017.

Grass Kleiner, Milena. "Memoria intermedial: Villa Grimaldi en el cine, la novela y el Teatro chileno." PhD diss., Pontificia Universidad Católica de Chile, 2015.

Grass Kleiner, Milena. "*TREWA: Estado-nación o el espectro de la traición*: El ensayo de un teatro plurinacional." *Talia: Revista de estudios teatrales* 4 (2022): 57–65. https://doi.org/10.5209/tret.80830.

Grez Toso, Sergio. "Historiografía y memoria en Chile: Algunas consideraciones a partir del *Manifiesto de Historiadores*." *HAOL* 16 (Spring 2008): 179–183. https://doi.org/10.36132/hao.v0i16.261.

Griffero, Ramón. *La dramaturgia del espacio*. Ediciones Frontera Sur, 2011.

Gubbins, Vanessa M. "General Strike: Feminist Performance?" In *Bodies on the Front Lines: Performance, Gender and Sexuality in Latin America and the Caribbean*, edited by Brenda Werth and Katherine Zien. University of Michigan Press, 2024.

Gutiérrez Díaz, Pía. "Revelaciones de archivo: Representación y autorrepresentación del pueblo Mapuche en algunas manifestaciones teatrales chilenas a partir de 1940." *Palimpsesto* 8, no. 11 (January–June 2017): 191–205.

Gutiérrez Díaz, Pía. "Revelaciones de archivo: "Trama y archivo: Condiciones de producción en la escena teatral chilena del periodo 2000–2010." PhD diss., Pontificia Universidad Católica de Chile, 2014.

Harcha Cortés, Ana. *Prácticas de teatralidad en Chile: A partir del trabajo de Andrés Pérez Araya*. Editorial Universitaria, 2017.

Harvie, Jen. *Fair Play: Art, Performance and Neoliberalism*. Palgrave Macmillan, 2013.

Heiss, Claudia, and Patricio Navia. "You Win Some, You Lose Some: Constitutional Reforms in Chile's Transition to Democracy." *Latin American Politics and Society* 49, no. 3 (2007): 163–190. https://doi.org/10.1111/j.1548-2456.2007.tb00386.x.

Henríquez Puentes, Patricia, and Mauricio Ostria González. "*Ñi pu tremen: Mis antepasados* de Paula González Seguel." *Literatura y lingüistica* 43 (2021): 129–147. http://dx.doi.org/10.29344/0717621x.43.2670.

Hernández, Paola S. *El teatro de Argentina y Chile: Globalización, resistencia y desencanto*. Corregidor, 2009.

Hernández, Paola S. "Remapping Memory Discourses: *Villa + Discurso* by Guillermo Calderón." *South Central Review* 30, no. 3 (Fall 2013): 61–82. https://dx.doi.org/10.1353/scr.2013.0029.

Hernández, Paola S. *Staging Lives in Latin American Theater: Bodies, Objects, Archives*. Northwestern University Press, 2021.

Hidalgo, Paulo. *El ciclo político de la Concertación (1990–2010)*. Uqbar, 2011.

Hirsch, Marianne. "The Generation of Postmemory." *Poetics Today* 29, no. 1 (2008): 103–128. https://doi.org/10.1215/03335372-2007-019.

Honig, Bonnie. "Toward an Agonistic Feminism: Hannah Arendt and the Politics of Identity." In *Feminist Interpretations of Hannah Arendt*, edited by Bonnie Honig, 135–66. Pennsylvania State University Press, 1995.

hooks, bell. "Sisterhood: Political Solidarity between Women." *Feminist Review* 23 (1986): 125–138. https://doi.org/10.2307/1394725.

Hozven, Roberto. "Censura, autocensura y contracensura: Reflexiones acerca de un simposio." *Chasqui* 12, no. 1 (November 1982): 68–73, https://doi.org/10.2307/29739790.

Human Rights Watch. *Los límites de tolerancia: Libertad de expresión y debate público en Chile*. LOM Ediciones, 1998.

Huneeus, Pablo. *La cultura huachaca o el aporte de la televisión*. Editora Nueva Generación, 1981.

Hurtado, María de la Luz. *Andrés Lorenzo Pérez Araya tiene la palabra*. Ocho Libros, 2015.

Hurtado, María de la Luz. *Dramaturgia chilena 1890–1990: Autorías, textualidades, historicidad*. Frontera Sur, 2011.

Hurtado, María de la Luz. "Escenificaciones de la tragedia popular y clásica." *Teatro Celcit* 6, no. 7 (1996): 32–35.

Hurtado, María de la Luz. "La Negra Ester, El desquite y Nemesio Pelao, teatralidad transculturada en la trilogía de melodramas dirigidos por Andrés Pérez." *Apuntes de teatro* 119–120 (2001): 149–169.

Hurtado, María de la Luz. *Memorias teatrales: el teatro de la Universidad Católica en su cincuentenario: 1978–1993*. Ediciones *Apuntes*, 1993.

Hurtado, María de la Luz. "Nota Editorial." *Apuntes de teatro* 122 (2002): 2–3.

Hurtado, María de la Luz. *Teatro chileno y modernidad: Identidad y crisis social*. Ediciones de Gestos, 1997.

Hurtado, María de la Luz, Carlos Ochsenius, and Hernán Vidal. *Teatro chileno de la crisis institucional: 1973–1980*. Ceneca, 1982.

Hurtado, María de la Luz, Carlos Ochsenius, and Hernán Vidal. *Teatro Ictus*. Ceneca, 1980.

Huyssen, Andreas. *Present Pasts: Urban Palimpsests and the Politics of Memory*. Stanford University Press, 2003.

Iglesias Saldaña, Margarita, Lieta Vivaldi Macho, Valentina Álvarez López, and Carla Núñez Matus. *Centro Cultural Mapocho: Una historia por contar*. Ciebo Ediciones, 2014.

Illanes, María Angélica. *La batalla de la memoria: Ensayos históricos de nuestro siglo, Chile, 1990–2000*. Ariel, 2002.

Ince, Murat. "A Critique of Agonistic Politics." *International Journal of Žižek Studies* 10, no. 1 (2016): 1–17.

Infante, Manuela. *Prat seguida de Juana*. Cierto Pez, 2005.

Isin, Engin F., and Greg M. Nielsen. Introduction to *Acts of Citizenship*, edited by Engin F. Isin and Greg M. Nielsen, 1–12. Zed Books, 2008.

Isin, Engin F., and Bryan S. Turner. "Investigating Citizenship: An Agenda for Citizenship Studies." In *Citizenship Between Past and Future*, edited by Engin F. Isin, Peter Nyers, and Bryan S. Turner, 5–17. Routledge, 2008.

Ivelic, Milan, and Gaspar Galaz. *Chile: Arte actual*. Ediciones Universitarias de Valparaíso, 1988.

Jackson, Shannon. *Social Works: Performing Arts, Supporting Publics*. Routledge, 2011.

Jameson, Fredric. "Future City." *New Left Review* 21 (2004): 65–79.

Jeftanovic, Andrea. "La 'Costura dramática' de Soledad Lagos y su trabajo pionero como dramaturgista en la escena teatral chilena de hoy." *Theatre der Zeit* (2008): 47–53.

Jelin, Elizabeth. *Los trabajos de la memoria*. Siglo XXI, 2002.

Jelin, Elizabeth, and Susana G. Kaufman. "Layers of Memories: Twenty Years after in Argentina." In *The Politics of War Memory and Commemoration*, edited by T. G. Ashplant, Graham Dawson, and Margaret Roper, 80–110. Routledge, 2000.

Jiménez-Yañez, César. "#Chiledespertó: Causas del estallido social en Chile." *Revista mexicana de sociología* 82, no. 4 (2020): 949–957. https://doi.org/10.22201/iis.01882503p.2020.4.59213.

Jones, Kathleen B. *Compassionate Authority: Democracy and the Representation of Women*. Routledge, 1993.

Jonkers, Herbert. *Poéticas de espacio escénico: Chile 1981–1996*. Ediciones Frontera Sur, 2006.

Joseph, May. *Nomadic Identities: The Performance of Citizenship*. University of Minnesota Press, 1999.

Junta Militar de Gobierno. *Política cultural del gobierno de Chile*. Asesoría Cultural de la Junta de Gobierno y Departamento Cultural de la Secretaría General de Gobierno, 1975.

Kalawski Isla, Andrés. "Falso mutis: Oficio de actores en la 'época de oro' del teatro chileno 1910–1947." PhD diss., Pontificia Universidad Católica de Chile, 2015.

Kaplan, Temma. *Taking Back the Streets: Women, Youth, and Direct Democracy*. University of California Press, 2004.

Kershaw, Baz. "Fighting in the Streets: Dramaturgies of Popular Protest, 1968–1989." *New Theatre Quarterly* 13, no. 51 (1997): 255–276. https://doi.org/10.1017/S0266464X0001126X.

Klein, Naomi. *The Shock Doctrine: The Rise of Disaster Capitalism*. 2nd ed. Picador, 2009.

Labbé, Carlos, and Mónica Ríos. "Entre el texto, la puesta en escena y la performance del registro en la escritura de Manuela Infante y el Teatro de Chile." *INTI* 69/70 (2009): 207–219.

Laclau, Ernesto, and Chantal Mouffe. *Hegemony and Socialist Strategy: Towards a Radical Democratic Politics*. 2nd ed. Verso, 2014.

Lacoue-Labarte, Philippe, and Jean-Luc Nancy. *Retreating the Political*. Routledge, 1997.

Lagos, M. Soledad. *Creación colectiva: Teatro chileno a fines de la década de los 80*. Lang, 1994.

Lagos, M. Soledad. "*Diciembre*, de Guillermo Calderón: Las complejas territorialidades de las celebraciones familiares." *Apuntes de teatro* 131 (2009): 12–19.

Laitinen, Arto and Anne Brigitta Pessi, Introduction to *Solidarity: Theory and Practice*. Edited by Arto Laitinen and Anne Brigitta Pessi. Lexington Books, 2014.

Larrabure, Manuel, and Carlos Torchia. "The 2011 Chilean Student Movement and the Struggle for a New Left." *Latin American Perspectives* 42, no. 5 (September 2015): 248–268. http://www.jstor.org/stable/24574080.

Larraín, Javiera. "Hacia una poética directoral de Guillermo Calderón: Una cartografía de la palabra escénica." Master's thesis, University of Chile, 2017.

LASTESIS Colectivo. "El cuerpo como espacio político." Interview by Cataloga Revista. *Cataloga Revista* 1 (2022): 21–23.

LASTESIS Colectivo. *Set Fear on Fire: The Feminist Call That Set the Americas Ablaze*. Translated by Camila Valle. Verso, 2021

LASTESIS Colectivo. *Quemar el miedo: Un manifiesto*. Editorial Planeta, 2021.

Lazzara, Michael J. *Chile in Transition: The Poetics and Politics of Memory*. University Press of Florida, 2006.

Lehmann, Hans-Thies. *Postdramatic Theatre*. Translated by Karen Jürs-Munby. Routledge, 2006.

Liinason, Mia. "The Performance of Protest: Las Tesis and the New Feminist Radicality at the Conjunction of Digital Spaces and the Streets." *Feminist Media Studies* (April 2023): 1–18. https://doi.org/10.1080/14680777.2023.2200472.

Lira, Elizabeth, and Brian Loveman. *Las ardientes cenizas del olvido: Vía chilena de reconciliación política, 1932–1994*. LOM Ediciones, 2002.

López, María Pia. *Not One Less: Mourning, Disobedience and Desire*. Translated by Frances Riddle. Polity Press, 2020.

López, Pamela R., Isabel Sierralta R., and Pablo Cisternas A., "Públicos y consumidores: Desafíos para las compañías de teatro en Chile." *Apuntes de teatro* 137 (2013): 19–32.

Loveman, Brian. *Chile: The Legacy of Hispanic Capitalism*. Oxford University Press, 1979.

Lucero Días, María José. *Ausencia del cuerpo y cosmología de la muerte en el mundo mapuche: Memorias en torno a la condición del detenido desaparecido*. Museo de la Memoria y los Derechos Humanos, 2017.

Lupien, Pascal. "The Incorporation of Indigenous Concepts of Plurinationality into the New Constitutions of Ecuador and Bolivia." *Democratization* 18, no. 3 (2011): 774–796. https://doi.org/10.1080/13510347.2011.563116.

Llanos Bernadita and Milena Grass. "New Feminist Performance in the Chilean Revolt: La Yeguada Latinoamericana and LASTESIS." In *Dismantling the Nation: Contemporary Art in Chile*, ed. Florencia San Martín, Carla Macchiavello Cornejo, and Paula Solimano. Amherst College Press, 2023.

Madarieta, Ethan. "'Marichiweu': Performances of Memory and Mapuche Presence in Guillermo Calderón's Villa," *Latin American Theatre Review* 53, no. 2 (2020): 81–103. https://journals.ku.edu/latr/article/view/13764.

Malzacher, Florian. "No Organum to Follow: Possibilities of Political Theatre Today." In *Not Just a Mirror: Looking for the Political Theatre Today*, edited by Florian Malzacher, 16–30. House on Fire / Alexander Verlang, 2015.

Mansuy, Daniel. *Salvador Allende: La izquierda chilena y la Unidad Popular*. Editorial Taurus, 2023.

Manzi, Javiera, and Fernanda Carvajal. "La violencia que no ves. Interrupciones feministas y cuerpos fuera de lugar en la *performance* de LasTesis." *Mora* 26, no. 1 (2020): 303–310.

Marshall, T. H. "Citizenship and Social Class." In *Inequality and Society*, edited by Jeff Manza and Michael Sauder, 149–54. W. W. Norton, 2009.

Martin, Carol. *Theatre of the Real*. Palgrave Macmillan, 2013.

Martin, Deborah, and Deborah Shaw. "Chilean and Transnational Performances of Disobedience: LasTesis and the Phenomenon of *Un violador en tu camino.*" *Bulletin of Latin American Research* 40, no. 5 (2021): 712–729. https://doi.org/10.1111/blar.13215.

Martín-Barbero, Jesús. *De los medios a las mediaciones: Comunicación, cultura y hegemonía*. Editorial Gustavo Gili, 1991.

May, Todd. "Humanism and Solidarity." *Parrhesia* 18 (2013): 11–21.

Mbembe, Achille. *Necropolitics*. Duke University Press, 2019.

Medina, Javier, ed. *Suma Quamaña: La comprensión indígena de la Vida Buena*. Federación de Asociaciones Municipales de Bolivia, 2001.

Mignolo, Walter D. *Local Histories / Global Designs: Coloniality, Subaltern Knowledges and Border Thinking*. Princeton University Press, 2012.

Miller, Toby, and George Yúdice. *Cultural Policy*. Sage Publications, 2002.

Misemer, Sarah M. *Secular Saints: Performing Frida Kahlo, Carlos Gardel, Eva Perón and Selena*. Tamesis, 2008.

Mohanty, Chandra Talpade. *Feminism without Borders: Decolonizing Theory, Practicing Solidarity*. Duke University Press, 2003.

Montez, Noe. *Memory, Transitional Justice, and Theatre in Postdictatorship Argentina*. Southern Illinois University Press, 2018.

Morales, Felipe Montero, ed. *Legislación cultural chilena*. Santiago: Consejo Nacional de Cultura y las Artes, 2014.

Mouffe, Chantal. *Agonistics: Thinking the World Politically*. Verso, 2013.

Mouffe, Chantal. *The Democratic Paradox*. Verso, 2000.

Mouffe, Chantal. *On the Political*. Routledge, 2005.

Moulian, Tómas. *Chile actual: Anatomía de un mito*. 3rd ed. LOM Ediciones, 2002.

Muñoz, José Esteban. *Disidentifications: Queers of Color and the Performance of Politics*. University of Minnesota Press, 1999.

Muñoz-Hidalgo, Mariano. "De las canciones del vino a la cultura huachaca: Marginalidad e identidad." *Revista universum* 20, no. 2 (2005): 235–251. http://dx.doi.org/10.4067/S0718-23762005000200012.

Muñoz-Lamartine, Ernesto. "Student Leaders Reinvent the Protest." *Berkeley Review of Latin American Studies* (Fall–Winter 2011): 25–30.

Navarro, Arturo. *Cultura: ¿Quién paga? Gestión, infraestructura y audiencias en el modelo chileno de desarrollo cultural*. RIL editores, 2006.

Neustadt, Robert. *CADA día: La creación de un arte social*. Editorial Cuarto Propio, 2001.

Nora, Pierre. "Between Memory and History: Les Lieux de Mémoire." *Representations* 26 (1989): 7–24. https://doi.org/10.2307/2928520.

Nora, Pierre. *Realms of Memory. The Construction of the French Past*. Edited by Lawrence C. Kritzman. Translated by Arthur Goldhammer. 3 vols. Columbia University Press, 1996–1998.

Noriega, Jimmy A. "KIMVN Teatro and Paula González Seguel." In *Fifty Key Figures in Latinx and Latin American Theatre*. Edited by Paula Hernández and Analola Santana. Routledge, 2022.

Opazo, Cristián. "El cuento del tío. El trabajo del parentesco en *Galvarino* (2012) de Paula González." *Literatura y Linguística*, no. 44 (2021): 185–202. https://hdl.handle.net/11299/253512.

Opazo, Cristián. "Pánico a la discoteca: Teatro, transición y underground (Chile, época 1990)." *Cuadernos de literatura* 21, no. 42 (July–December 2017): 49–66. https://doi.org/10.11144/Javeriana.cl21-42.pdtt.

Opazo, Cristián. *Pedagogías letales: Ensayos sobre dramaturgias chilenas del nuevo milenio*. CELICH, 2011.

Opazo, Cristián, and Carlos Benítez, "'A Little Respect': Mateluna, de Guillermo Calderón." *Revista conjunto*, no. 185 (2017): 8–15.

Ortega, Eugenio and Carolina Morena, eds. *¿La concertación desconcertada? Reflexiones sobre su historia y su futuro*. LOM Ediciones, 2002.

Ortega Frei, Eduardo. *Historia de una alianza política: El partido Socialista de Chile y el partido Demócrata Cristiano: 1973–1988*. LOM Ediciones, 1992.

Otano, Rafael. *Crónica de la transición*. Antárctica, 1995.

Oxhorn, Philip D. *Organizing Civil Society: The Popular Sectors and the Struggle for Democracy in Chile*. Pennsylvania State University Press, 1995.

Oyarzún, Carola. "Entre el teatro y la vida." In *Antología: Un siglo de dramaturgia chilena, 1910–2010*. Vol. 4, edited by María de la Luz Hurtado and Mauricio Barría, 303–6. Publicaciones Comisión Bicentenario Chile, 2010.

Pagliccia, Nino. "Solidaridad: El renacimiento de un viejo concept socialista." In *Vivir bien: ¿Paradigma no capitalista?*, ed. Ivonne Farah H. and Luciano Vasapollo, 145–58. Plural Editores, 2011.

Paley, Julia. *Marketing Democracy: Power and Social Movements in Post-dictatorship Chile*. University of California Press, 2001.

Papastergiadis, Nikos. "Spatial Aesthetics: Rethinking the Contemporary." In *Antinomies of Art and Culture: Modernity, Postmodernity, Contemporaneity*, edited by Terry Smith, Okwui Enwezor, and Nancy Condee, 363–83. Duke University Press, 2008.

Parra, Roberto and Andrés Pérez, "La Negra Ester," *Apuntes de teatro* 98 (Autumn–Winter 1989): 33–54.

Pérez Araya, Andrés. "Andrés Pérez: Un hombre de teatro." Interview by Eduardo Guerrero. *Teatrae* 5 (Summer/Fall 2002).

Pérez Araya, Andrés. "Lo popular me es propio por pertenencia." *Apuntes de teatro* 111 (1996): 3–5.

Pérez Araya, Andrés. "Lo que me pasó con *Nemesio Pelao, ¿qué es lo que te ha pasao?* de Cristián Soto." *Apuntes de teatro* 119–120 (2001): 134–137.

Pereira Poza, Sergio. "La Negra Ester." *La escena latinoamericana* 3 (December 1989): 19–28.

Piña, Juan Andrés. "Espectáculos de la otra chilenidad." *Teatro al sur* 3, no. 4 (May 1996): 41–45.

Piña, Juan Andrés. *Historia del teatro en Chile, 1941–1990*. Editorial Taurus, 2014.

Piña, Juan Andrés. "La negra Ester." *Mensaje* 377 (March–April 1989): 109–110.

Pinto Veas, Iván, and María José Bello Navarro. "La revuelta performativa: Hacia una noción expandida de cuerpos e imágenes en el espacio público a partir del estallido social chileno." *Cuadernos de Música, Artes Visuales y Artes Escénicas* 17, no. 1 (2022): 192–219. https://doi.org/10.11144/javeriana.mavae17-1.rphn.

Policzer, Pablo. *The Rise and Fall of Repression in Chile*. Notre Dame University Press, 2009.

Ponce de León, Jennifer. *Another Aesthetics Is Possible: Arts of Rebellion in the Fourth World War*. Duke University Press, 2021.

Pottlitzer, Joanne. "Forgetting Filled with Memory." *Theater* 43, no. 2 (2013): 57–63. https://doi.org/10.1215/01610775-1966580.

Pottlitzer, Joanne. "The Game of Expression under Pinochet: Four Theater Stories." *Theater* 31, no. 2 (2001): 3–33. https://muse.jhu.edu/article/34166.

Pradenas, Luis. *Teatro en Chile: Huellas y trayectorias, siglos XVI–XX*. LOM Ediciones, 2006.

Preda, Caterina. *Art and Politics under Modern Dictatorships: A Comparison of Chile and Romania*. Palgrave, 2017.

Puga, Ana Elena. *Memory, Allegory, and Testimony in South American Theater: Upstaging Dictatorship*. Routledge, 2008.

Quidel Lincoleo, José. "Pu Mapuche ka pu Wigka, chumgechi ñi xokituwün: Las relaciones interétnicas a través de la religión: El caso de los mapuche y no mapuche en Chile." *Anthropos* 207 (2005): 153–166.

Quijano, Anibal. "Colonialidad del poder, cultura, y conocimiento en América Latina," *Anuario Mariateguiano* 9, no. 9 (997): 113–121. http://www.jstor.org/stable/41491587.

Rancière, Jacques. *Chronicles of Consensual Times*. Translated by Steve Corcoran. Continuum, 2010.

Rancière, Jacques. "The Concept of Anachronism and the Historian's Truth." Translated by Noel Fitzpatrick and Tim Stot. *In/Print* 3, no. 1 (2015): 21–52. https://doi.org/10.21427/d7vm6f.

Rancière, Jacques. *Disagreement*. Translated by Julie Rose. University of Minnesota Press, 1999.

Rancière, Jacques. *Dissensus: On Politics and Aesthetics*. Translated by Steven Corcoran. Bloomsbury, 2010.

Rancière, Jacques. *The Emancipated Spectator*. Translated by Gregory Elliott. Verso, 2009.

Rancière, Jacques. *On the Shores of Politics*. Translated by Liz Heron. Verso, 2007.

Reinelt, Janelle, and Shirin M. Rai, "Introduction." In *The Grammar of Politics and Performance*, edited by Janelle Reinelt and Shirin M. Rai. Routledge, 2015.

Richard, Nelly. *Abismos Temporales: feminismo, estéticas travestis y teoría queer*. Metales Pesados, 2018.

Richard, Nelly. "City, Art, Politics." In *City/Art: The Urban Scene in Latin America*, edited by Rebecca E. Biron, 115–27. Duke University Press, 2009.

Richard, Nelly. *Crítica de la memoria: 1990–2010*. Ediciones UDP, 2010.

Richard, Nelly. *Cultural Residues: Chile in Transition*. Translated by Alan West-Durán and Theodore Quester. University of Minnesota Press, 2004.

Richard, Nelly. *The Insubordination of Signs: Political Change, Cultural Transformation, and Poetics of the Crisis*. Translated by Alice A. Nelson and Silvia R. Tandeciarz. Duke University Press, 2004.

Richard, Nelly. "La insurgencia feminista de mayo 2018." In *Mayo feminista: La rebelión contra el patriarcado*, edited by Faride Zerán Cherich, 115–35. LOM Ediciones, 2018.

Richard, Nelly. "Lo político y lo crítico en el arte: '¿Quién teme a la nevanguardia?' " In *Arte y política*, edited by Pablo Oyarzún, Nelly Richard, and Claudia Zaldívar, 22–46. Consejo Nacional de Cultura y las Artes, 2005.

Richard, Nelly. *Márgenes e instituciones: Arte en Chile desde 1973*. Metales Pesados, 2014.

Richard, Nelly. *Masculine/Feminine: Practices of Difference(s)*. Translated by Alice A. Nelson and Silvia R. Tandeciarz. Duke University Press, 2004.

Richard, Nelly, ed. *Políticas y estéticas de la memoria*. Cuarto Propio, 2000.

Richard, Nelly. *Residuos y metáforas: Ensayos de crítica cultural en el Chile de la transición*. Editorial Cuarto Propio, 1998.

Richards, Patricia. *Race and the Chilean Miracle: Neoliberalism, Democracy, and Indigenous Rights*. University of Pittsburgh Press, 2013.

Ripp, Alexandra. "RePresenting the Past: Chilean Theater and Memory Politics, 1998–2010." PhD diss., Yale University, 2017.

Risør, Helene, and Daniela Jacob. " 'Interculturalism as Treason': Policing, Securitization, and Neoliberal State Formation in Southern Chile." *Latin American and Caribbean Ethnic Studies* 13, no. 3 (2018): 237–258, https://doi.org/10.1080/17442222.2018.1510165.

Rivera, Anny. *Transformaciones culturales y movimiento artístico en el orden autoritario. Chile: 1973–1982*. CENECA, 1983.

Rivera Cusicanqui, Silvia. "The Notion of 'Rights' and the Paradoxes of Postcolonial Modernity: Indigenous Peoples and Women in Bolivia." Translated by Molly Geidel, *Qui Parle: Critical Humanities and Social Sciences* 18, no. 2 (2010): 29–54. https://doi.org/10.5250/quiparle.18.2.29.

Robles, Víctor Hugo. *Bandera hueca: Historia del movimiento homosexual de Chile*. Editorial Cuarto Propio, 2008.

Rojas Sotoconil, Araucaria. "Las cuecas como representaciones estético-políticas de chilenidad en Santiago entre 1979 y 1989." *Revista musical chilena* 212 (July–December 2009): 51–76.

Romero, Carmen. "Costos y sueños de la Negra Ester." *Apuntes de teatro* 98 (Autumn–Winter 1989): 9–11.

Ruiz-Tagle, Pablo. *Five Republics and One Tradition: A History of Constitutionalism in Chile 1810–2020*. Cambridge Studies in Law and Society. Cambridge University Press, 2021.

Saborido, Marisol, Rodrigo Vega, and Humberto Zamorano. *Informe final de evaluación, Fondo Nacional de Desarrollo Cultural y Las Artes*. Consejo Nacional de la Cultura y Las Artes, 2008.

Sánchez, José Antonio. *Practicing the Real on the Contemporary Stage*. Translated by Charlie Allwood. University of Chicago Press, 2014.

Sandoval Ambiado, Carlos. *MIR (una historia)*. Sociedad Editorial Trabajadores, 1990.

Santa Cruz A., Eduardo. "Cultura popular." In *Pensamiento crítico latinoamericano*, edited by Ricardo Salas Astrain, 101–13. Ediciones Universidad Católica Silva Henríquez, 2005.

Santos, Boaventura de Sousa. *The End of the Cognitive Empire*. Duke University Press, 2018.

Santos, Boaventura de Sousa. *Epistemologies of the South: Justice against Epistemicide*. Routledge, 2014.

Sater, William F. *The Heroic Image in Chile: Arturo Prat, Secular Saint*. University of California Press, 1973.

Scholz, Sally J. *Political Solidarity*. Pennsylvania State University Press, 2008.

Segato, Rita Laura. *La guerra contra las mujeres*. Traficantes de Sueños, 2016.

Segato, Rita Laura. "Patriarchy from Margin to Center: Discipline, Territoriality, and Cruelty in the Apocalyptic Phase of Capital." *South Atlantic Quarterly* 115, no. 3 (2016): 615–624, https://doi.org/10.1215/00382876-3608675.

Semler, Willy. "La Negra Ester." *Apuntes de teatro* 98 (Autumn–Winter 1989): 6–7.

Semler, Willy. "La Negra Ester por el mundo." *Apuntes de teatro* 98 (Autumn–Winter 1989): 12–26.

Sepúlveda Ll., Fidel. "Nicanor, Violeta, Roberto Parra: Encuentro de tradición y vanguardia." *Aisthesis* 24 (1991): 29–42.

Soto, Cristián. "¿La fiesta del amigo?" *Apuntes de teatro* 122 (2002): 16–19.

Spencer, Catherine. "Entrap, Engulf, Overwhelm: From Existentialism to Counterculture in the Work of Marta Minujín." In *Sabotage Art: Politics and Iconoclasm in Contemporary Latin America*, edited by Sophie Halart and Mara Polgovsky Ezcurra. I. B. Tauris, 2016.

Stern, Steve J. *Battling for Hearts and Minds: Memory Struggles in Pinochet's Chile: 1973–1988*. Duke University Press, 2006.

Stern, Steve J. *Reckoning with Pinochet: The Memory Question in Democratic Chile, 1989–2006*. Duke University Press, 2010.

Stern, Steve J. *Remembering Pinochet's Chile: On the Eve of London 1988*. Duke University Press, 2006.

Steuernagel, Marcos. "Who Wants Money? Radical Performance and Experimental Urbanism in the Heart of São Paulo." *Journal of Global South Studies* 38, no. 1 (2021): 194–219. https://dx.doi.org/10.1353/gss.2021.0010.

Subercaseaux, Bernardo. "Cultura y democracia." In *La cultura durante el período de la transición a la democracia 1990–2005*, edited by Eduardo Carrasco and Bárbara Negró. Consejo Nacional de Cultura y la Artes, 2006.

Sznajder, Mario. "Citizenship and the Contradictions of Free Market Policies in Chile and Latin America." In *Shifting Frontiers of Citizenship: The Latin American Experience*, edited by Luis Roninger, Mario Sznajder, and Carlos A. Forment. Brill Academic Publishers, 2013.

Tatinge Nascimento, Cláudia. *After the Long Silence: The Theater of Brazil's Post-Dictatorship Generation*. Routledge, 2019.

Taylor, Diana. *The Archive and the Repertoire: Performing Cultural Memory in the Americas*. Duke University Press, 2003.

Taylor, Diana. *Disappearing Acts: Spectacles of Gender and Nationalism in Argentina's Dirty War*. Duke University Press, 1997.

Taylor, Diana. *Performance*. Asuntos Impresos, 2012.

Taylor, Diana, and Marcela Fuentes, eds. *Estudios avanzados de performance*. Mexico City: Fondo de Cultura Económica, 2011.

Tepper, Allie. "Crossings: The Poetics of Public Inscription in the Works of Cecilia Vicuña and Lotty Rosenfeld." *ASAP* 7, no. 2 (2022): 409–436. https://dx.doi.org/10.1353/asa.2022.0022.

Thayer, Willy. "El golpe como consumación de la vanguardia. Fragmentos." In *El Fragmento repetido: Escritos en estado de excepción*, 15–46. Metales Pesados, 2006.

Thompson, Jennifer Joan. "Horizons of Impossibility: The Political Imperative in the Dramaturgy of Guillermo Calderón." *Theatre Journal* 73, no. 2 (June 2021): 169–187, https://doi.org/10.1353/tj.2021.0040.

Thompson, Jennifer Joan. "'An Explosion of Feminism: Dramaturgies of Excess and Revolution in Chile's New Feminist Vanguard." In *Bodies on the Front Lines: Performance, Gender, and Sexuality in Latin America and the Caribbean*, edited by Brenda Werth and Katherine Zien, 39–58. University of Michigan Press, 2024.

Thorrington, Paula. "*An Ode to Joy: Chilean Culture in the Eighties against Pinochet*." PhD diss., University of California, Los Angeles, 2011.

Tomlin, Liz. *Acts and Apparitions: Discourses on the Real in Performance Practice and Theory, 1990–2010*. Manchester University Press, 2013.

Torres, Osvaldo. *Democracia y lucha armada. MIR y MLN–Tupamaros*. Pehuén Editores, 2012.

Torres, Robinson, Gerardo Azócar, Roberto Gallardo, and Julio Mendoza, "Water Extractivism and Decolonial Struggles in Mapuche Territory, Chile." *Water Alternatives* 15, no. 1 (2022): 150–174.

Torres, Rodrigo. "El arte de cuequear." In *Revisitando Chile: Identidades, mitos e historias*, edited by Sonia Montecino, 149–58. Presidencia de la Republica, Comisión Bicentenario, 2003.

Trapero, Maximiano. *El libro de la décima: La poesía improvisada en el mundo hispánico*. Universidad de las Palmas de Gran Canarias, 1996.

Traverso, Antonio. "*La Flaca Alejandra*: Post-dictatorship Documentary and (No) Reconciliation in Chile." *Critical Arts* 31, no. 5 (2017): 91–106. https://doi.org/10.1080/02560046.2017.1345970.

Trencsényi, Katalin, and Bernadette Cochrane, eds. *New Dramaturgy: International Perspectives on Theory and Practice*. Bloomsbury, 2014.

Trumper, Camilo. *Ephemeral Histories: Public Art, Politics, and the Struggle for the Streets in Chile*. University of California Press, 2016.

Turner, Cathy, and Synne Behrndt. *Dramaturgy and Performance*. Palgrave Macmillan, 2007.

United Nations Development Programme. *Democracy in Latin America: Towards a Citizens' Democracy*. United Nations Development Programme, 2004.

United Nations Development Programme. *The Paradox of Modernization: Human Development Report in Chile*. United Nations Development Programme, 1998.

Universidad Diego Portales, Facultad de Derecho. *Informe anual sobre derechos humanos en Chile 2003: Hechos de 2002*. La Facultad, 2003.

Ureta, Sebastián et al. "Constituting Chileans: The *Cabildos* of October 2019 and the Trouble of Instrumental Participation." *Social Identities* 27, no. 5 (2021): 521–537. https://doi.org/10.1080/13504630.2021.1931087.

Valderrama, Miguel. *Modernismos historiográficos: artes visuales, postdictadura, vanguardias*. Palodino, 2008.

Van Diest, Camila, and Fernanda Carvajal. *Nomadismos y ensamblajes: Compañías teatrales de Chile 1990–2008*. Cuarto Propio, 2009.

Van Kerkhoven, Marianne. "On Dramaturgy." *Theaterschrift* 5–6 (1994): 8–34.

Vega Durán, Osiel. *Himno nacional de la República de Chile*. División de Cultura del Ministerio de Educación, Sociedad Chilena del Derecho de Autor, 2000.

Vial Correa, Gonzalo. *Arturo Prat*. Editorial Andres Bello, 1995.

Vial Correa, Gonzalo. "Causas y antecedentes del 11 de septiembre de 1973." In *Análisis crítico del régimen militar*, edited by Gonzalo Vial Correa, 15–21. Universidad Finis Terrae, 1998.

Vicuña, Pedro. "La Negra Ester." *Numero quebrado* 2, no. 2 (December 1989): 40–44.

Vidal, Hernán. *Política cultural de la memoria histórica: Derechos humanos y discursos culturales en Chile*. Mosquito Comunicaciones, 1997.

Vidal, Hernán. *Presencia del MIR. 14 claves existenciales*. Mosquito Editores, 1999.

Viera-Bravo, Patricia. "Principios del mapuche mongen para la resignificación de la economía en tiempos de crisis del capitalismo neoliberal, desde el sur de Chile." *Revista iberoamericana de estudios de desarrollo* 10, no. 2 (2021): 84–107, https://doi.org/10.26754/ojs_ried/ijds.587.

Villegas, Juan. "Andrés Pérez: Poética teatral en tiempos de globalización y transnacionalización." *Apuntes de teatro* 119 & 120 (2001): 141–148.

Villegas, Juan. "Discursos teatrales en Chile en la segunda mitad del siglo XX." In *Resistencia y poder: Teatro en Chile*, edited by Heidrun Adler and George Woodyard. Verveurt Verlag and Iberoamericana, 2000.

Villegas, Juan. "El teatro chileno de la postdictadura." *INTI* 69/70 (2009): 189–195. https://www.jstor.org/stable/23288703.

Villegas, Juan. *Historia del teatro y teatralidades en América Latina*. Ediciones de Gestos, 2011.

Villegas, Juan. "La internacionalización del teatro latinoamericano en tiempos de globalización, neoliberalismo y posmodernidad." In *Aspectos actuales del hispanismo mundial: Literatura—cultura—lengua*, edited by Christoph Strosetzki, 105–28. De Gruyter, 2018.

Weil, Jael Goldsmith. "Milk Makes State: The Extension and Implementation of Chile's State Milk Programs, 1901–1971." *Historia* (Santiago) 50, no. 1 (June 2017): 79–104. http://dx.doi.org/10.4067/S0717-71942017000100003.

Werth, Brenda. *Theatre, Performance, and Memory Politics in Argentina*. Palgrave Macmillan, 2010.

Werth, Brenda, and Katherine Zien. *Bodies on the Front Lines: Performance, Gender and Sexuality in Latin America and the Caribbean*. University of Michigan Press, 2024.

Wilbur, Sarah. *Funding Bodies: Five Decades of Dance Making at the National Endowment for the Arts*. Wesleyan University Press, 2021.

Wilde, Alexander. "Irruptions of Memory: Expressive Politics in Chile's Transition to Democracy." *Journal of Latin American Studies* 31, no. 2 (1999): 473–500. http://www.jstor.org/stable/157911.

Wilson, Japhy, and Erik Swyngedouw. "Seeds of Dystopia: Post-politics and the Return of the Political." In *The Post-political and Its Disconontents: Spaces of Depoliticisation, Spectres of Radical Politics*, edited by Japhy Wilson and Erik Swyngedouw, 1–24. Edinburgh University Press, 2014.

Winn, Peter. *Weavers of the Revolution: The Yarur Workers and Chile's Road to Socialism*. Oxford University Press, 1986.

Ybarra, Patricia. "Fighting for a Future in a Free Trade World." In *Neoliberalism and Global Theatres: Performance Permutations*, edited by Lara D. Nielsen and Patricia Ybarra, 113–28. Palgrave Macmillan, 2012.

Yuval-Davis, Nira. "What Is 'Transversal Politics'?" *soundings* 12 (1999): 94–98.

Žižek, Slavoj. *The Ticklish Subject: The Absent Center of Political Ontology*. Verso, 1999.

INDEX

Page numbers for illustrations appear in italics.